# ZATCH BELL!™

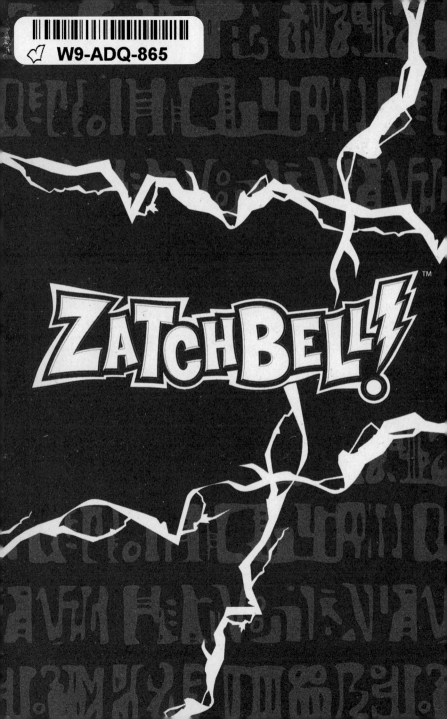

# ZATCH BELL!

## Vol. 3

STORY AND ART BY
**MAKOTO RAIKU**

English Adaptation/Fred Burke
Translation/David Ury
Touch-up Art & Lettering/Melanie Lewis
Design/Izumi Hirayama
Special Thanks/Jessica Villat, Miki Macaluso, Mitsuko Kitajima, and Akane Matsuo
Editor/Frances E. Wall

Managing Editor/Annette Roman
Director of Production/Noboru Watanabe
Vice President of Publishing/Alvin Lu
Sr. Director of Acquisitions/Rika Inouye
Vice President of Sales & Marketing/Liza Coppola
Publisher/Hyoe Narita



Printed in the U.S.A.

Published by VIZ Media, LLC
P.O. Box 77010
San Francisco, CA 94107

10 9 8 7 6 5 4 3 2 1
First printing, September 2005

RATED T FOR TEEN

**PARENTAL ADVISORY**
ZATCH BELL! is rated T for Teen and is recommended for ages 13 and up. This volume contains realistic and fantasy violence.

www.viz.com
store.viz.com

# ZATCH BELL!™

3

### STORY AND ART BY

## MAKOTO RAIKU

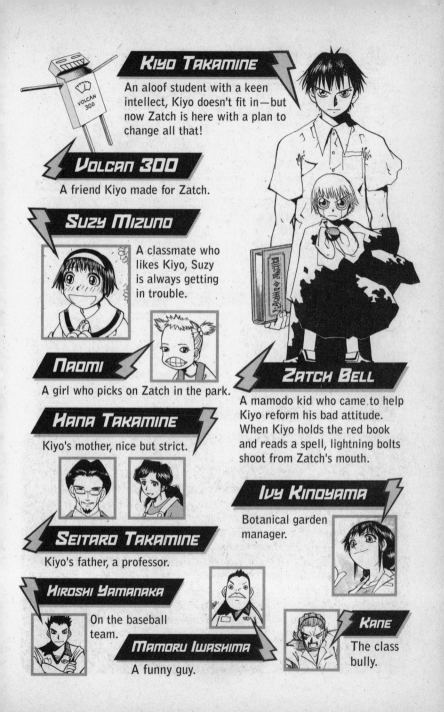

## Kiyo Takamine

An aloof student with a keen intellect, Kiyo doesn't fit in—but now Zatch is here with a plan to change all that!

VOLCAN 300

## Volcan 300

A friend Kiyo made for Zatch.

## Suzy Mizuno

A classmate who likes Kiyo, Suzy is always getting in trouble.

## Naomi

A girl who picks on Zatch in the park.

## Zatch Bell

A mamodo kid who came to help Kiyo reform his bad attitude. When Kiyo holds the red book and reads a spell, lightning bolts shoot from Zatch's mouth.

## Hana Takamine

Kiyo's mother, nice but strict.

## Seitaro Takamine

Kiyo's father, a professor.

## Ivy Kinoyama

Botanical garden manager.

## Hiroshi Yamanaka

On the baseball team.

## Mamoru Iwashima

A funny guy.

## Kane

The class bully.

# ZATCH'S PAST OPPONENTS

**KOLULU**    **SUGINO**    **GOFURE**    **BRAGO**    **REYCOM**

# THE STORY THUS FAR

Kiyo is a junior high student who's so intelligent that he's bored by life and doesn't even go to school. But Kiyo's life changes when his father sends him an amazing child named Zatch as a birthday present. When Kiyo holds Zatch's red book (which only Kiyo can read) and utters a spell, Zatch displays awesome powers.

Soon the duo finds out that Zatch is one of many mamodo children chosen to fight in a battle which will determine who is king of the mamodo world for the next 1,000 years. Zatch is saddened to learn the truth about his situation, but the bond between Zatch and Kiyo deepens as they're forced to fight for their own survival.

After battling with a sweet mamodo girl named Kolulu, Zatch makes up his mind to fulfill her wish that he become a "kind king"....

# ZATCH BELL! 3

# CONTENTS

# LEVEL 19: The Third Spell

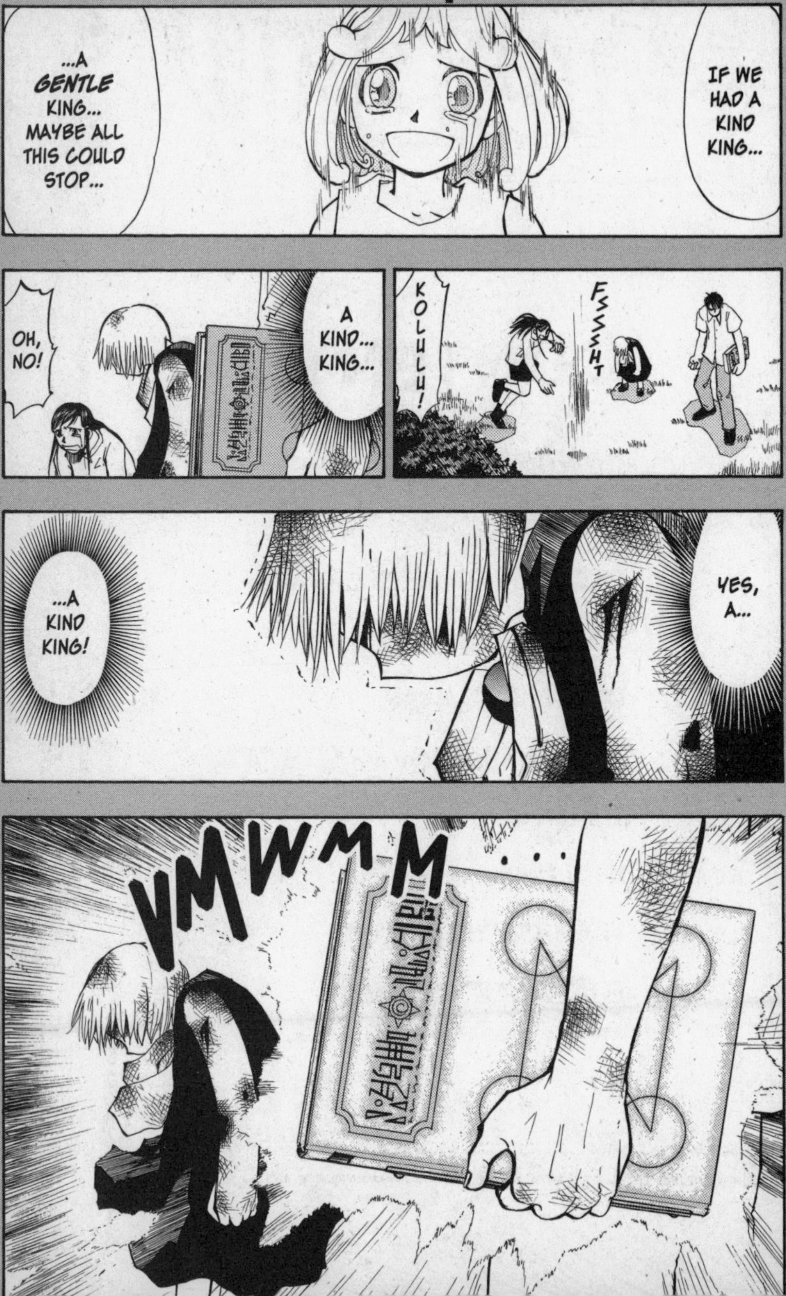
IF WE HAD A KIND KING...
...A GENTLE KING... MAYBE ALL THIS COULD STOP...
FSSSHT
KOLULU!
A KIND... KING...
OH, NO!
YES, A...
...A KIND KING!
VMWMM
...

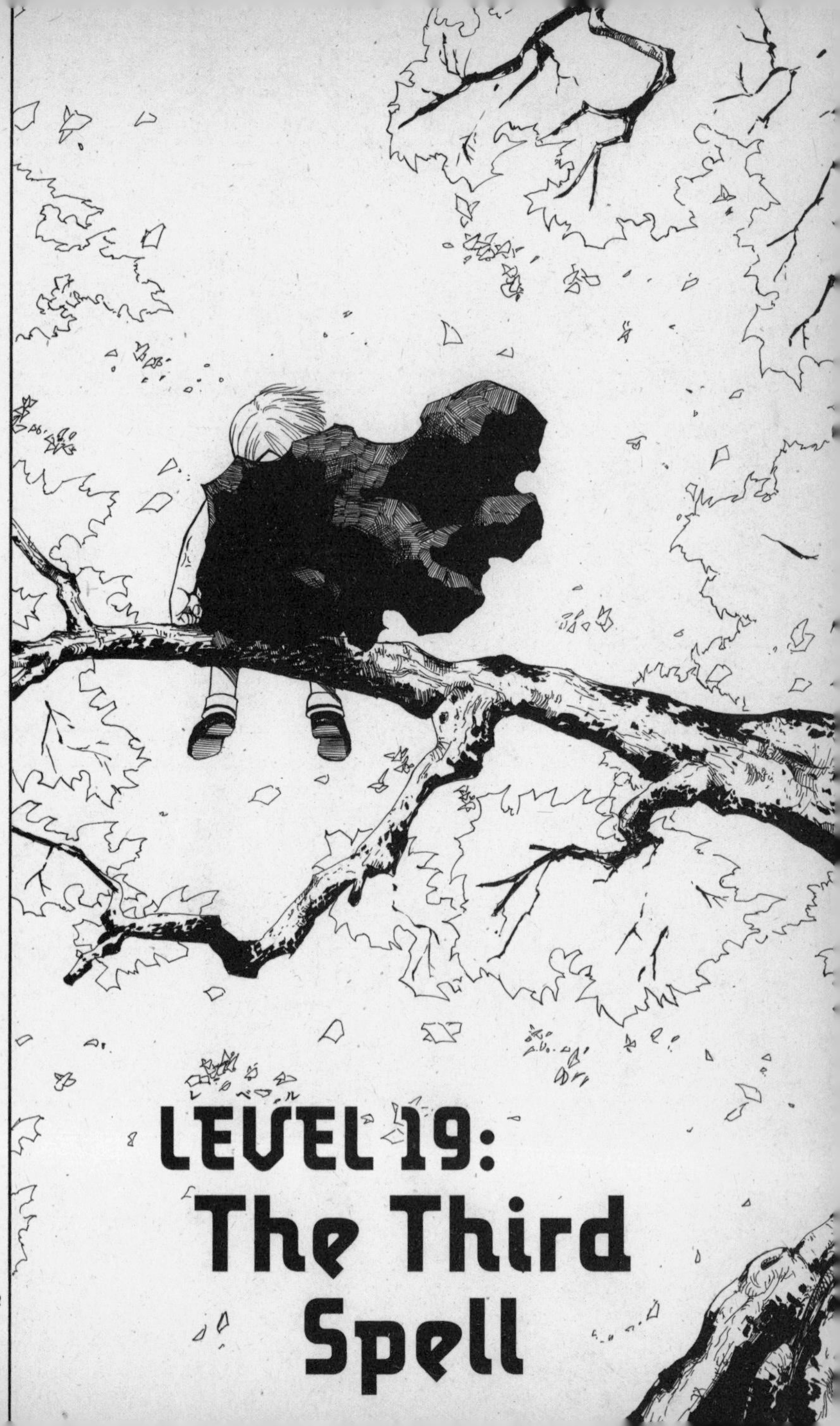
LEVEL 19:
The Third Spell

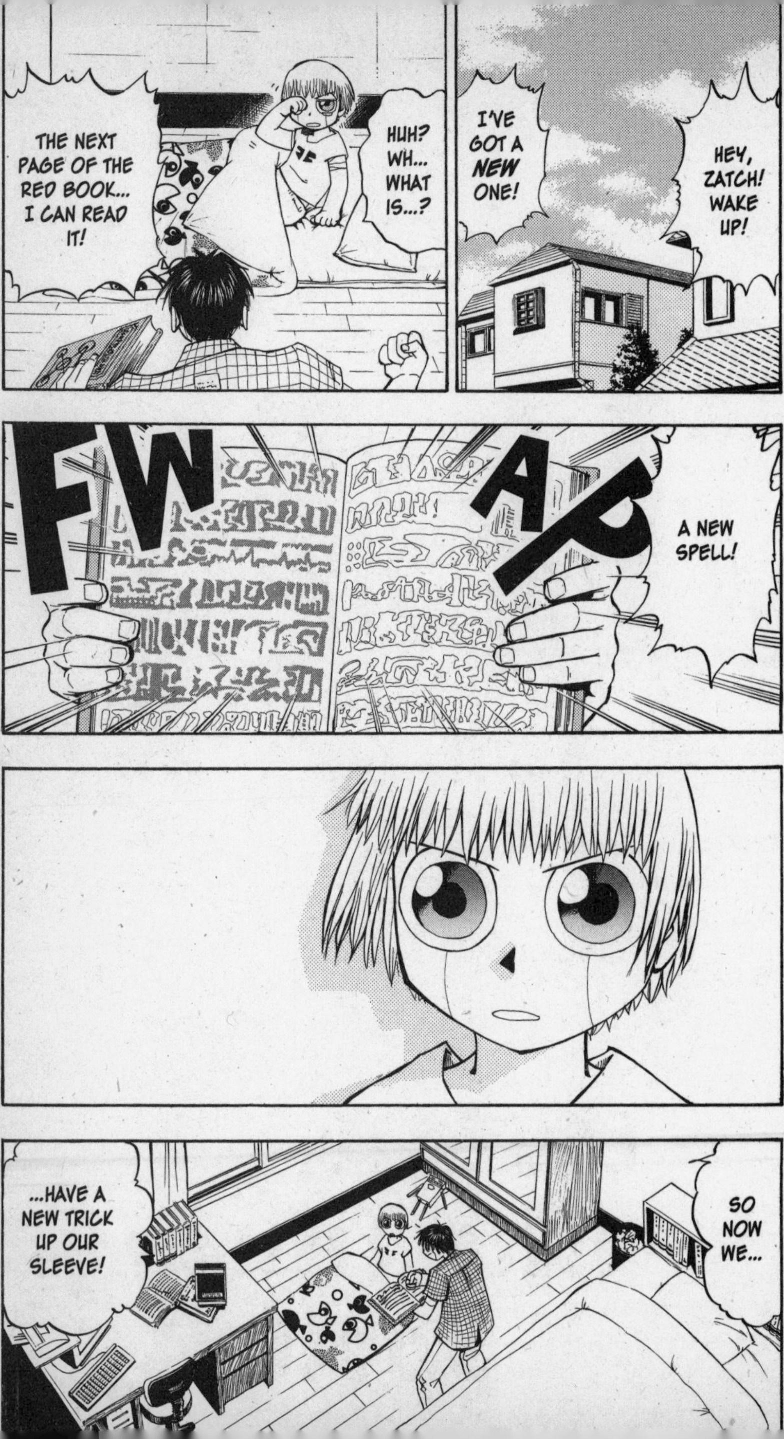
HEY, ZATCH! WAKE UP!
I'VE GOT A *NEW* ONE!
HUH? WH... WHAT IS...?
THE NEXT PAGE OF THE RED BOOK... I CAN READ IT!
FWAP
A NEW SPELL!
SO NOW WE...
...HAVE A NEW TRICK UP OUR SLEEVE!

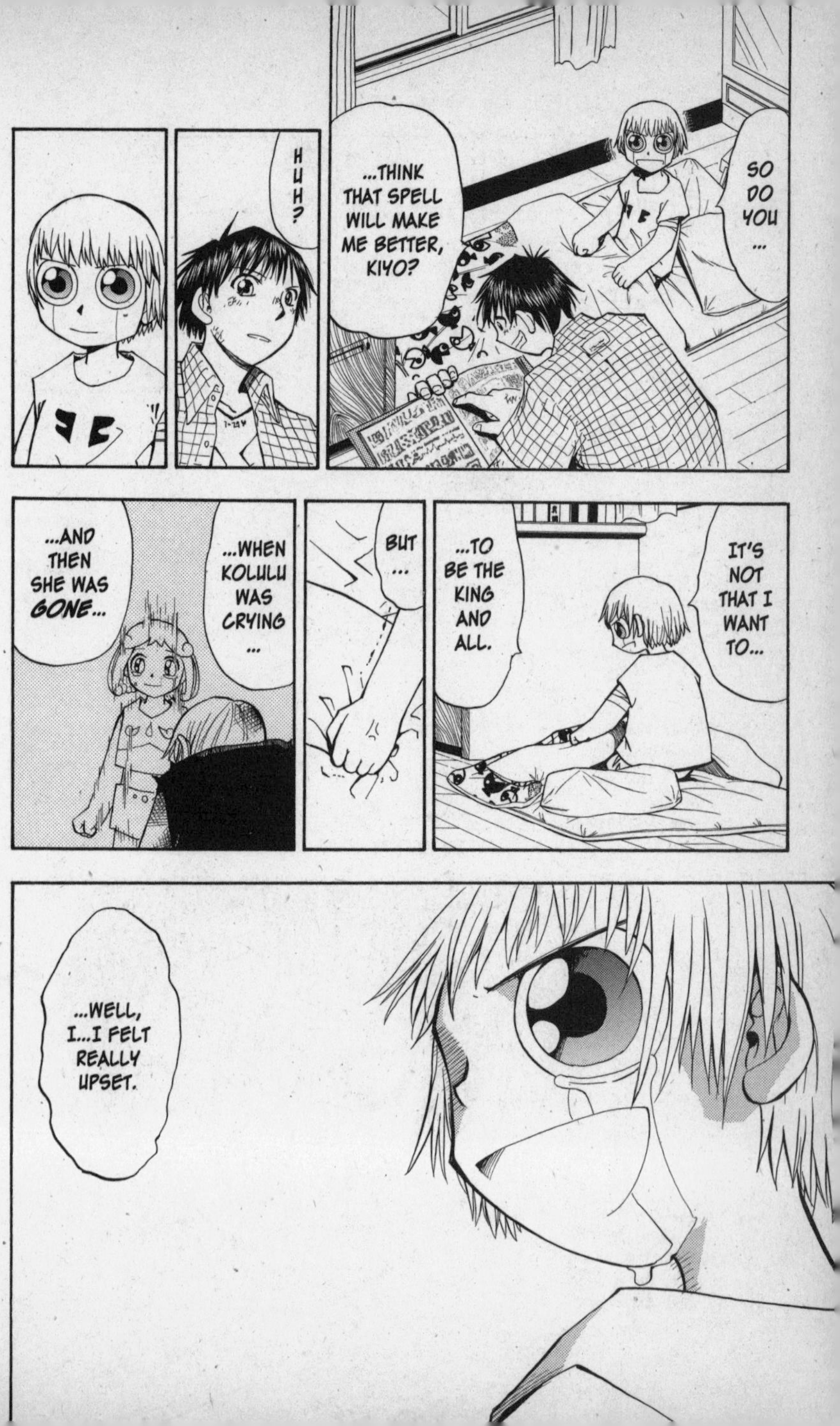
SO DO YOU...
...THINK THAT SPELL WILL MAKE ME BETTER, KIYO?
HUH?
IT'S NOT THAT I WANT TO...
...TO BE THE KING AND ALL.
BUT...
...WHEN KOLULU WAS CRYING...
...AND THEN SHE WAS *GONE*...
...WELL, I...I FELT REALLY UPSET.

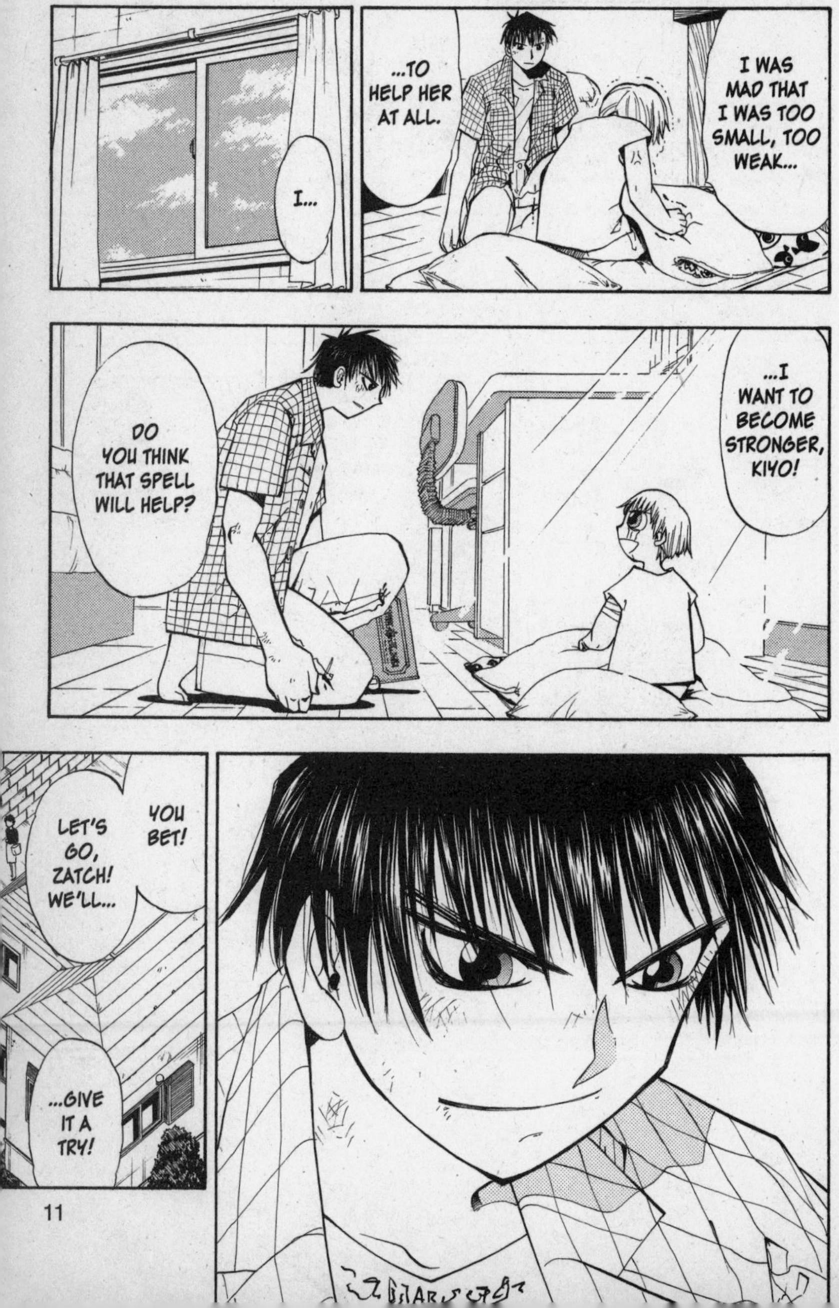
I WAS MAD THAT I WAS TOO SMALL, TOO WEAK...
...TO HELP HER AT ALL.
I...
...I WANT TO BECOME STRONGER, KIYO!
DO YOU THINK THAT SPELL WILL HELP?
YOU BET!
LET'S GO, ZATCH! WE'LL...
...GIVE IT A TRY!

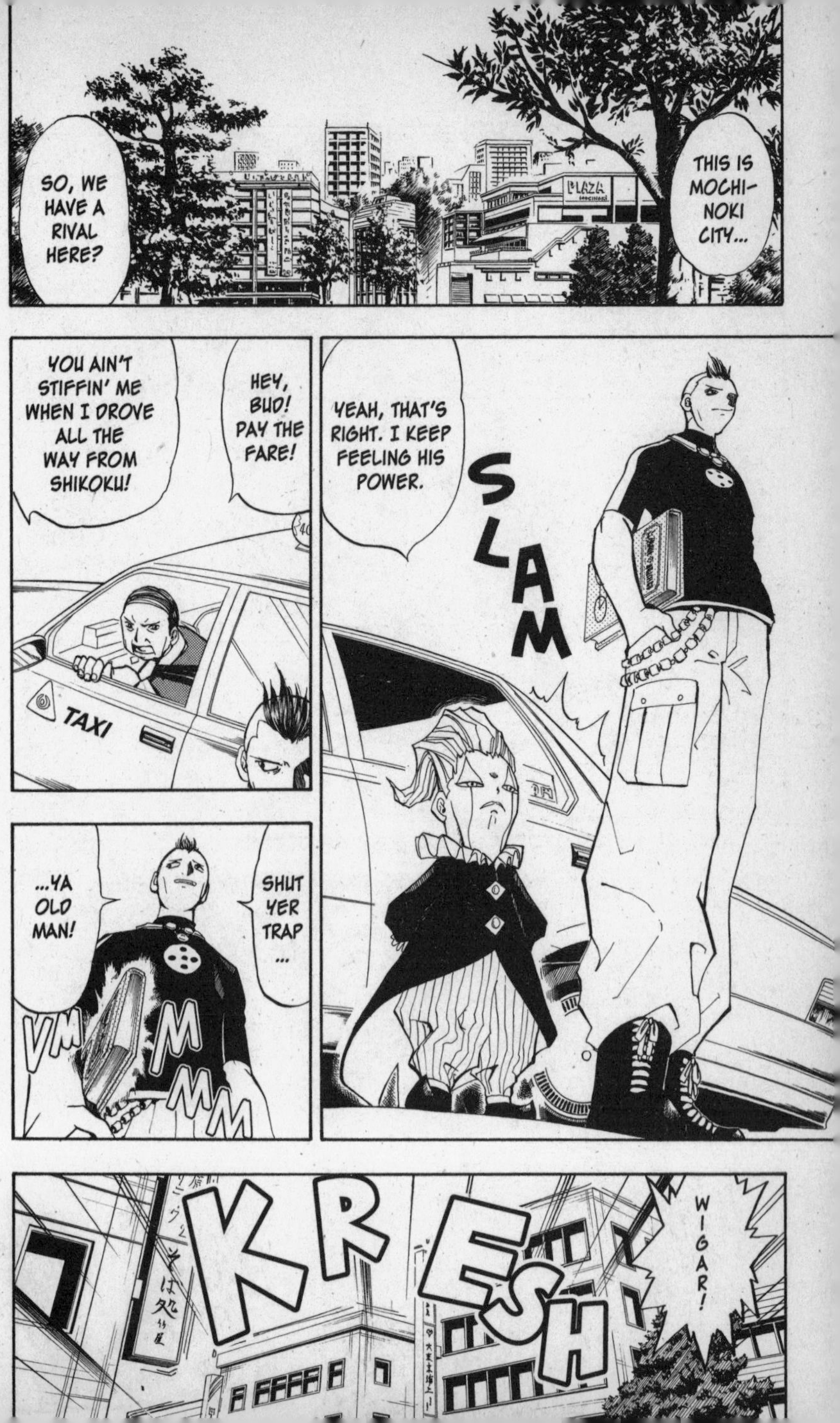
THIS IS MOCHI-NOKI CITY...
SO, WE HAVE A RIVAL HERE?
PLAZA
YEAH, THAT'S RIGHT. I KEEP FEELING HIS POWER.
SLAM
HEY, BUD! PAY THE FARE!
YOU AIN'T STIFFIN' ME WHEN I DROVE ALL THE WAY FROM SHIKOKU!
TAXI
SHUT YER TRAP...
...YA OLD MAN!
VMMMMM
WIGAR!
KRESH

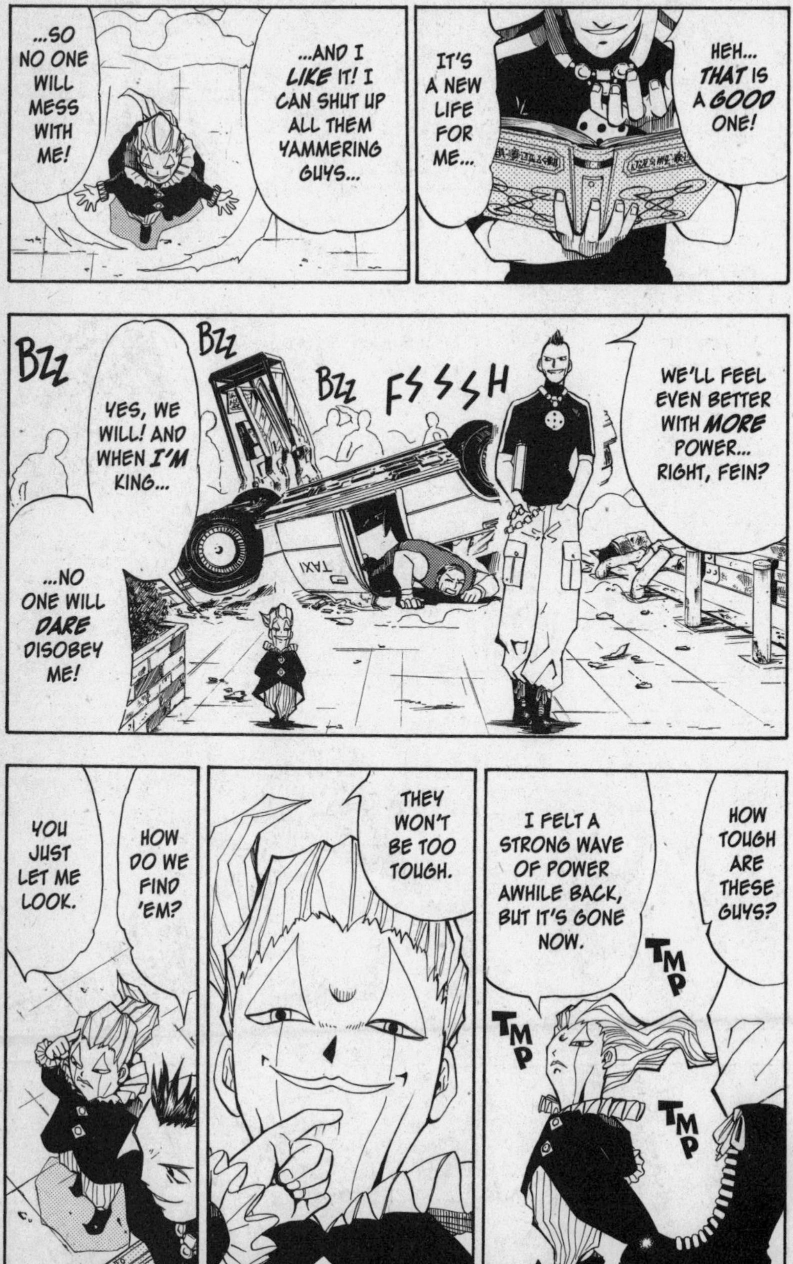
HEH... THAT IS A GOOD ONE!
IT'S A NEW LIFE FOR ME...
...AND I LIKE IT! I CAN SHUT UP ALL THEM YAMMERING GUYS...
...SO NO ONE WILL MESS WITH ME!
WE'LL FEEL EVEN BETTER WITH MORE POWER... RIGHT, FEIN?
FSSSH
BZZ
BZZ
YES, WE WILL! AND WHEN I'M KING...
...NO ONE WILL DARE DISOBEY ME!
BZZ
HOW TOUGH ARE THESE GUYS?
I FELT A STRONG WAVE OF POWER AWHILE BACK, BUT IT'S GONE NOW.
TMP
TMP
TMP
THEY WON'T BE TOO TOUGH.
HOW DO WE FIND 'EM?
YOU JUST LET ME LOOK.

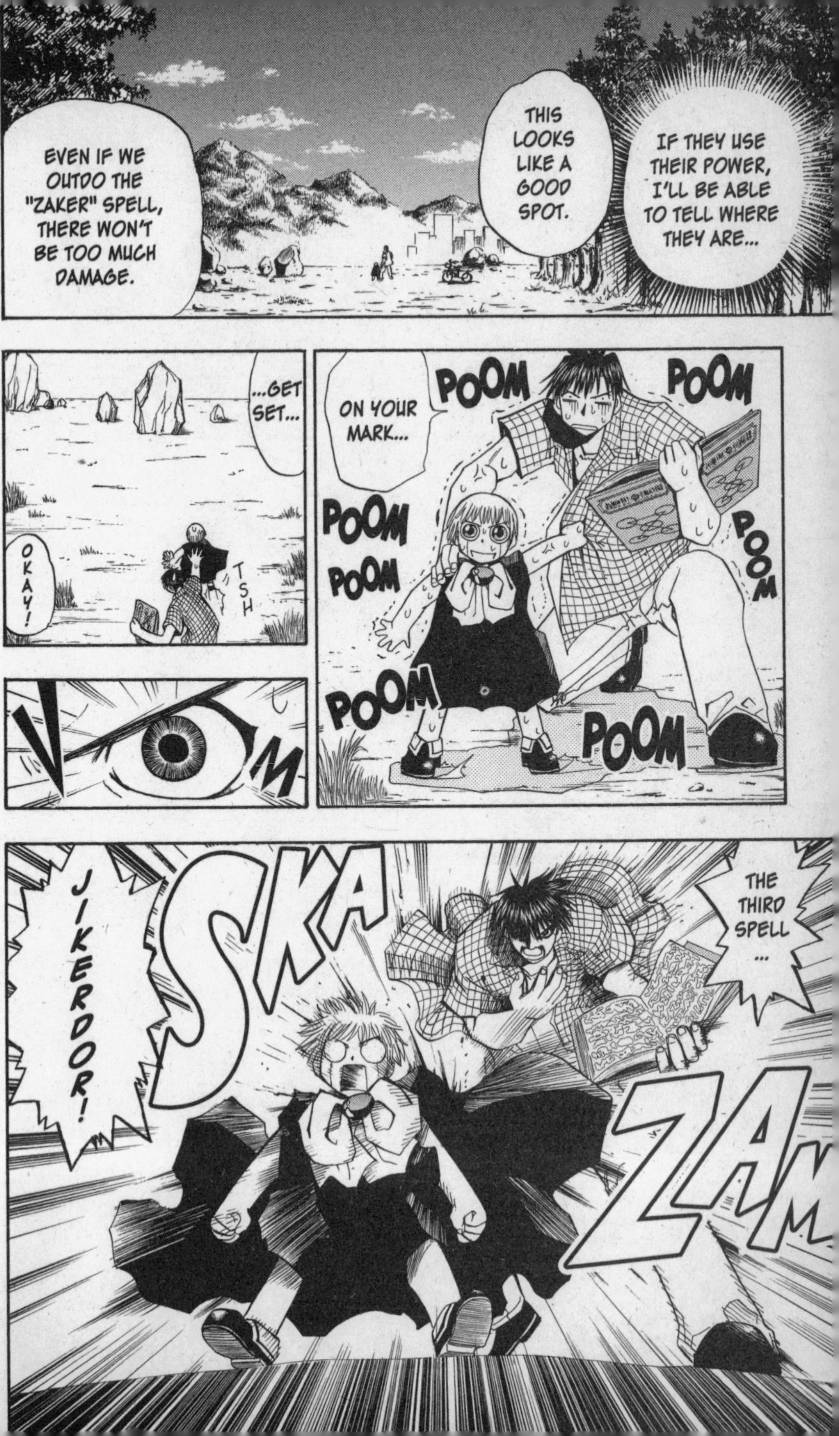
IF THEY USE THEIR POWER, I'LL BE ABLE TO TELL WHERE THEY ARE...
THIS LOOKS LIKE A GOOD SPOT.
EVEN IF WE OUTDO THE "ZAKER" SPELL, THERE WON'T BE TOO MUCH DAMAGE.
POOM
POOM
ON YOUR MARK...
POOM
POOM
POOM
POOM
POOM
...GET SET...
OKAY!
TSH
THE THIRD SPELL ...
JIKERDOOR!
SKA
ZAM

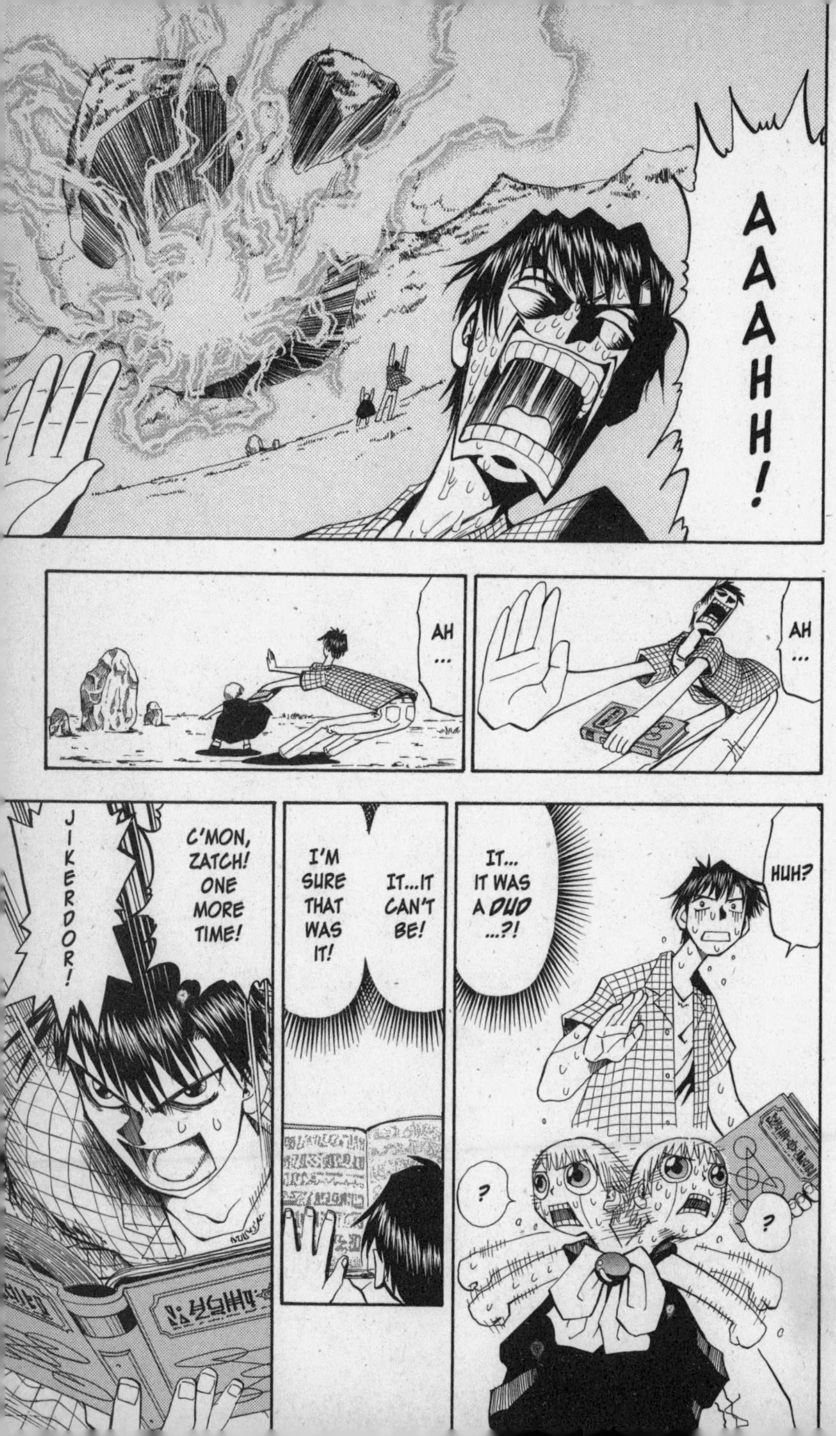
AAAAHH!
AH ...
AH ...
HUH?
IT... IT WAS A *DUD* ...?!
?
?
IT...IT CAN'T BE!
I'M SURE THAT WAS IT!
C'MON, ZATCH! ONE MORE TIME!
JIKERDOR!

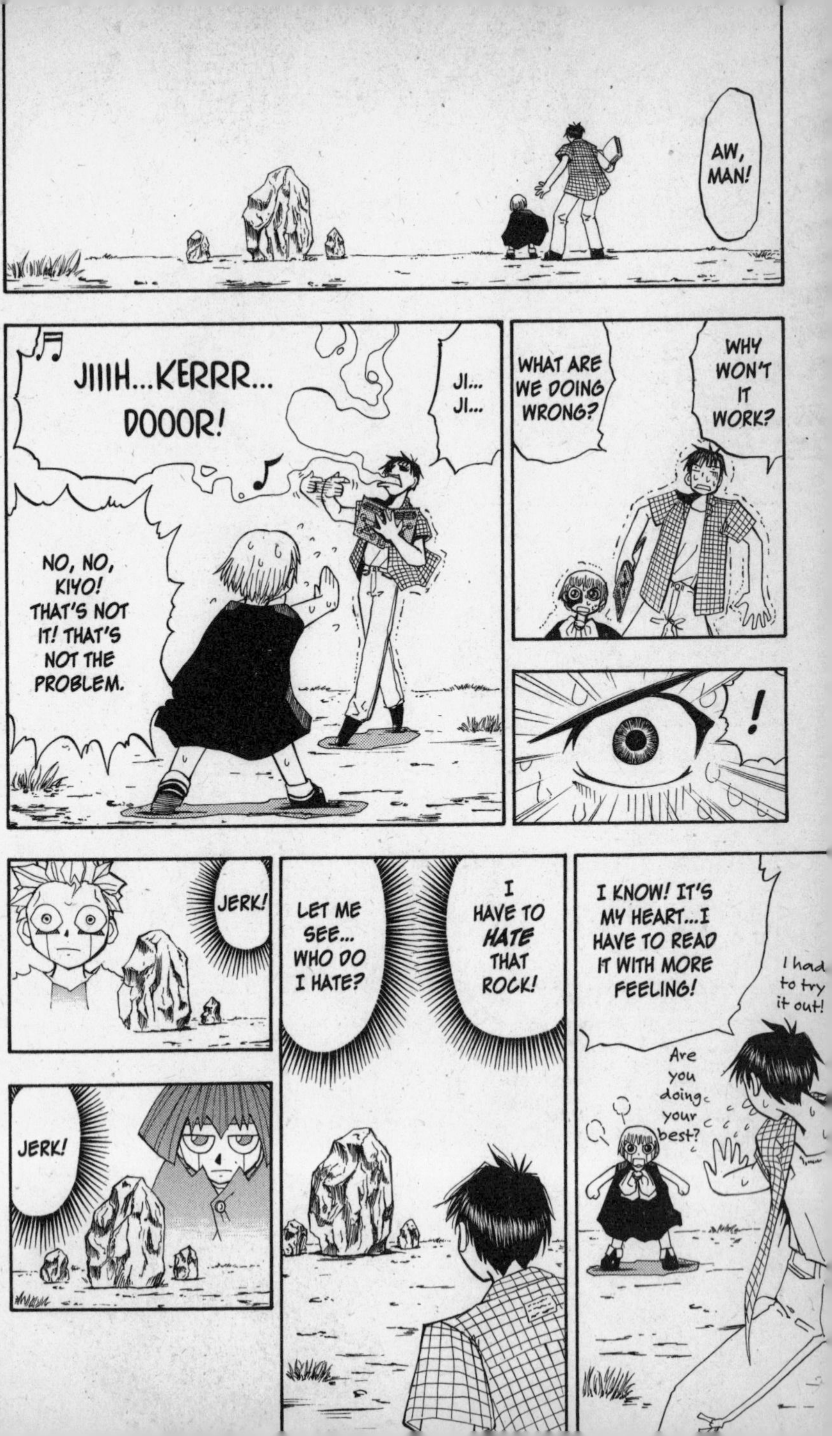
AW, MAN!
WHY WON'T IT WORK?
WHAT ARE WE DOING WRONG?
!
JI... JI...
JIIIH...KERRR... DOOOR!
NO, NO, KIYO! THAT'S NOT IT! THAT'S NOT THE PROBLEM.
I KNOW! IT'S MY HEART...I HAVE TO READ IT WITH MORE FEELING!
I had to try it out!
Are you doing your best?
I HAVE TO HATE THAT ROCK!
LET ME SEE... WHO DO I HATE?
JERK!
JERK!

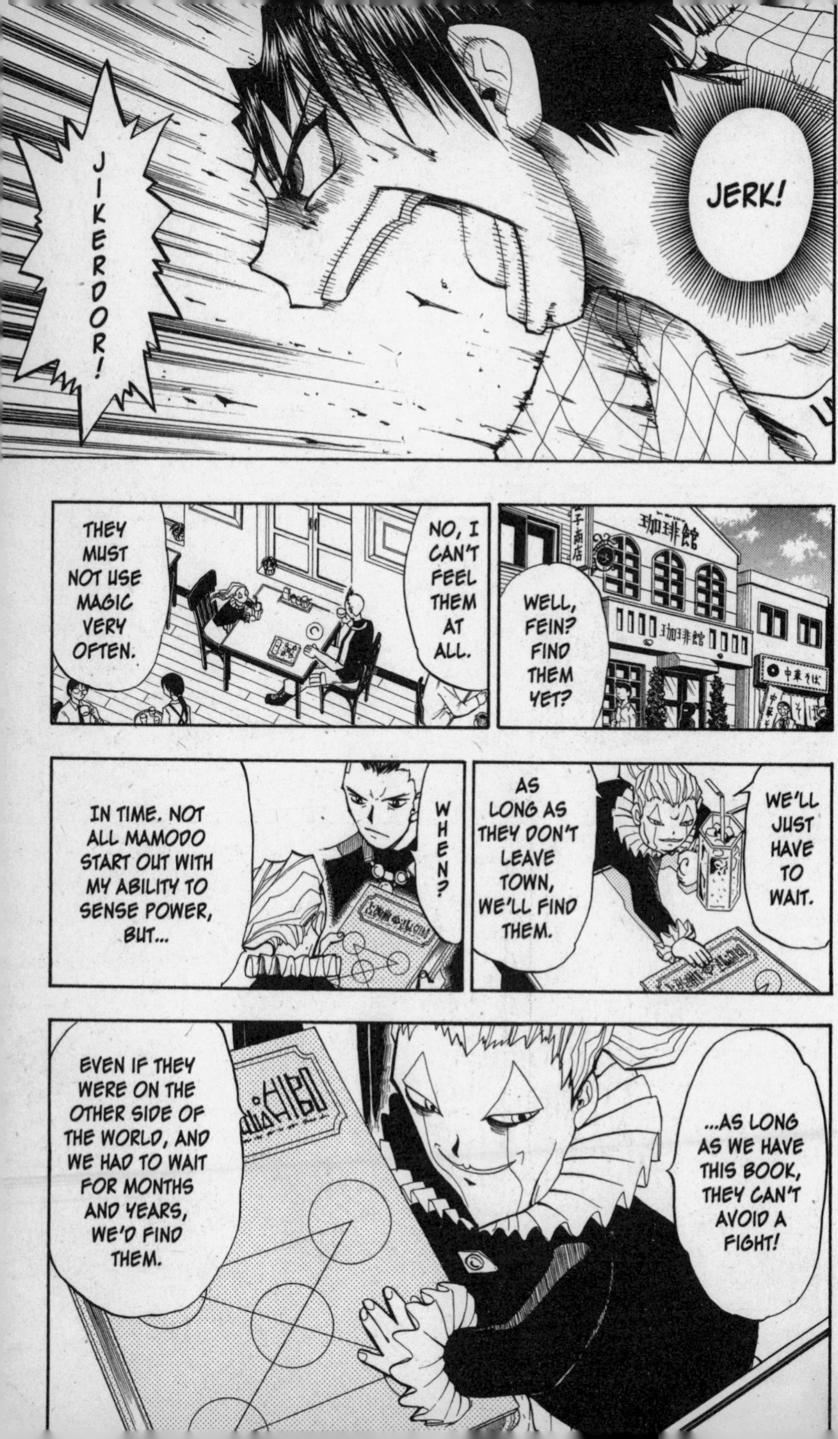
JERK!
JIKERDOR!
WELL, FEIN? FIND THEM YET?
NO, I CAN'T FEEL THEM AT ALL.
THEY MUST NOT USE MAGIC VERY OFTEN.
WE'LL JUST HAVE TO WAIT.
AS LONG AS THEY DON'T LEAVE TOWN, WE'LL FIND THEM.
WHEN?
IN TIME. NOT ALL MAMODO START OUT WITH MY ABILITY TO SENSE POWER, BUT...
EVEN IF THEY WERE ON THE OTHER SIDE OF THE WORLD, AND WE HAD TO WAIT FOR MONTHS AND YEARS, WE'D FIND THEM.
...AS LONG AS WE HAVE THIS BOOK, THEY CAN'T AVOID A FIGHT!

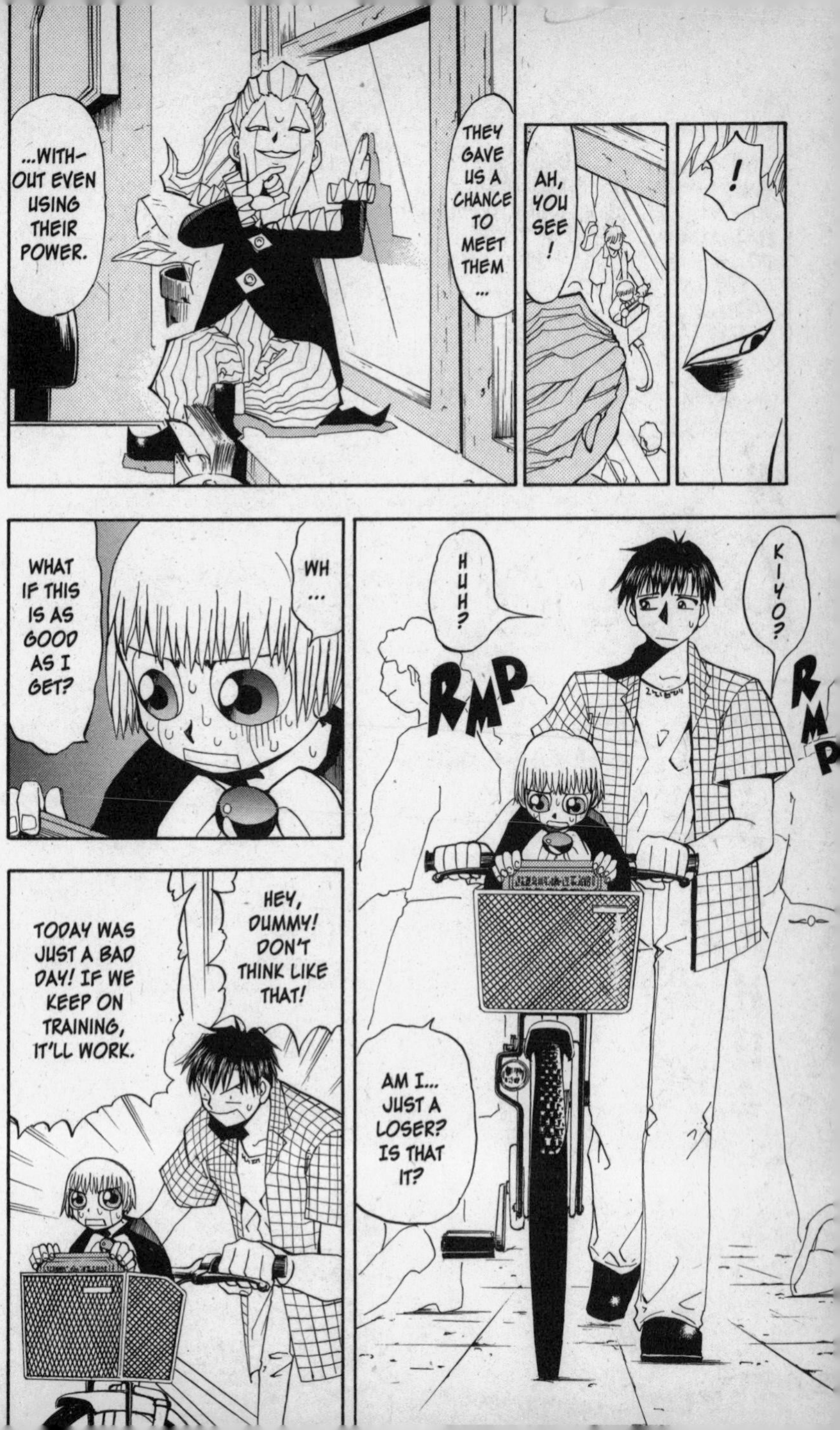
!
AH, YOU SEE!
THEY GAVE US A CHANCE TO MEET THEM...
...WITH-OUT EVEN USING THEIR POWER.
KIYO?
RMP
HUH?
RMP
AM I... JUST A LOSER? IS THAT IT?
WH...
WHAT IF THIS IS AS GOOD AS I GET?
HEY, DUMMY! DON'T THINK LIKE THAT!
TODAY WAS JUST A BAD DAY! IF WE KEEP ON TRAINING, IT'LL WORK.

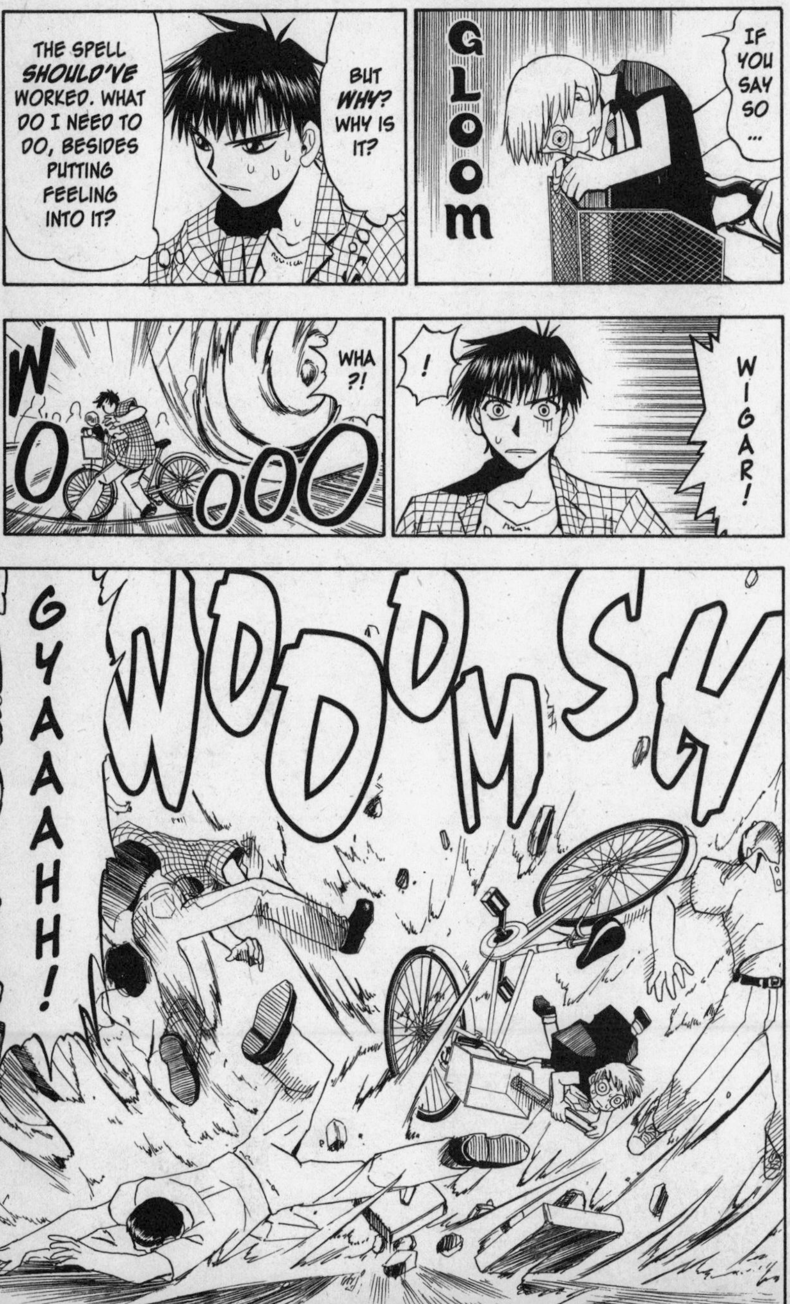

IF YOU SAY SO ...
GLOOM
BUT WHY? WHY IS IT?
THE SPELL SHOULD'VE WORKED. WHAT DO I NEED TO DO, BESIDES PUTTING FEELING INTO IT?
WIGAR!
!
WHA ?!
WOOOOO
WOOMSH
GYAAAHH!

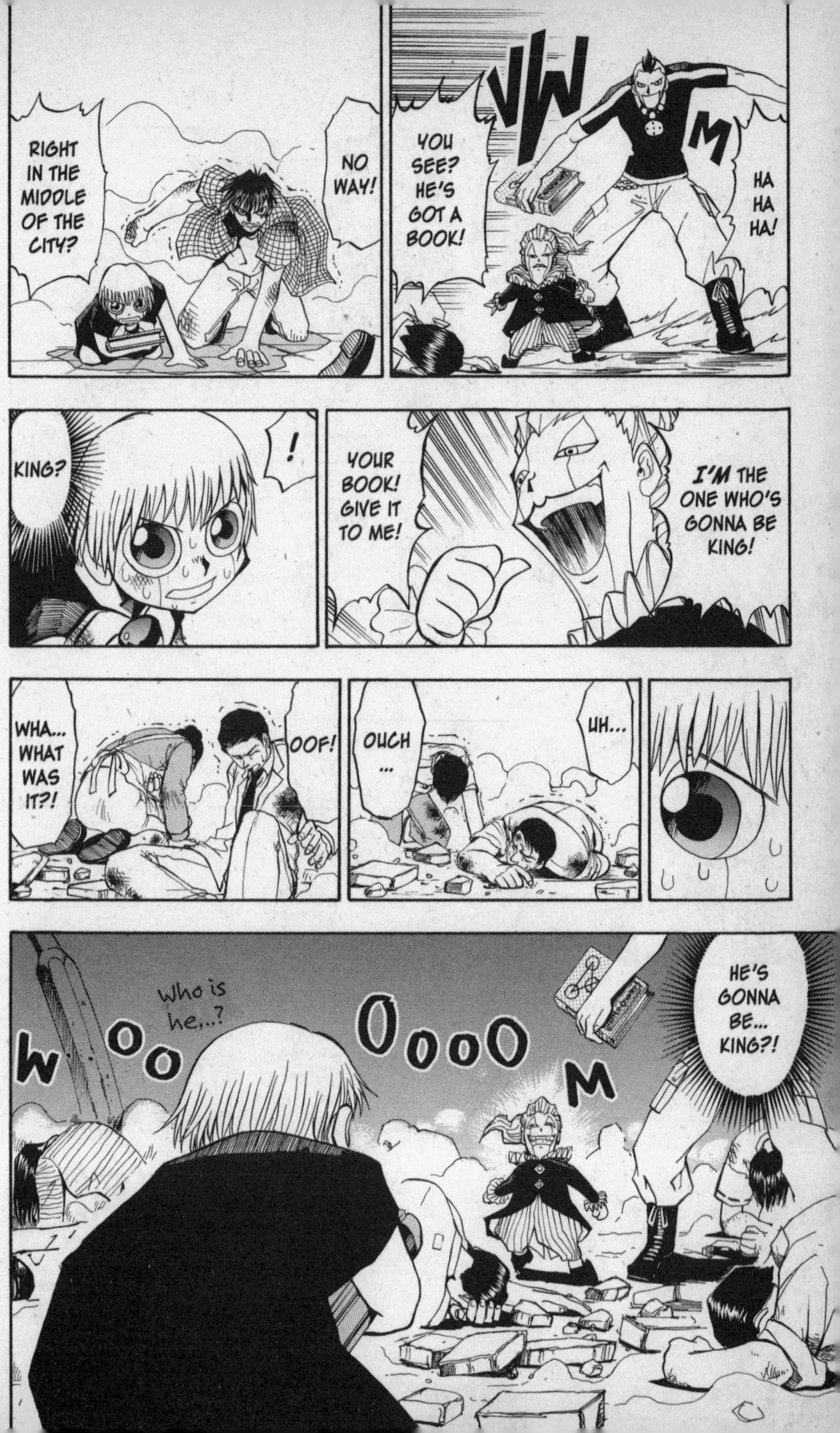
VWM
HA HA HA!
YOU SEE? HE'S GOT A BOOK!
NO WAY!
RIGHT IN THE MIDDLE OF THE CITY?
I'M THE ONE WHO'S GONNA BE KING!
YOUR BOOK! GIVE IT TO ME!
!
KING?
UH...
OUCH ...
OOF!
WHA... WHAT WAS IT?!
HE'S GONNA BE... KING?!
WOOOOOOM
Who is he...?

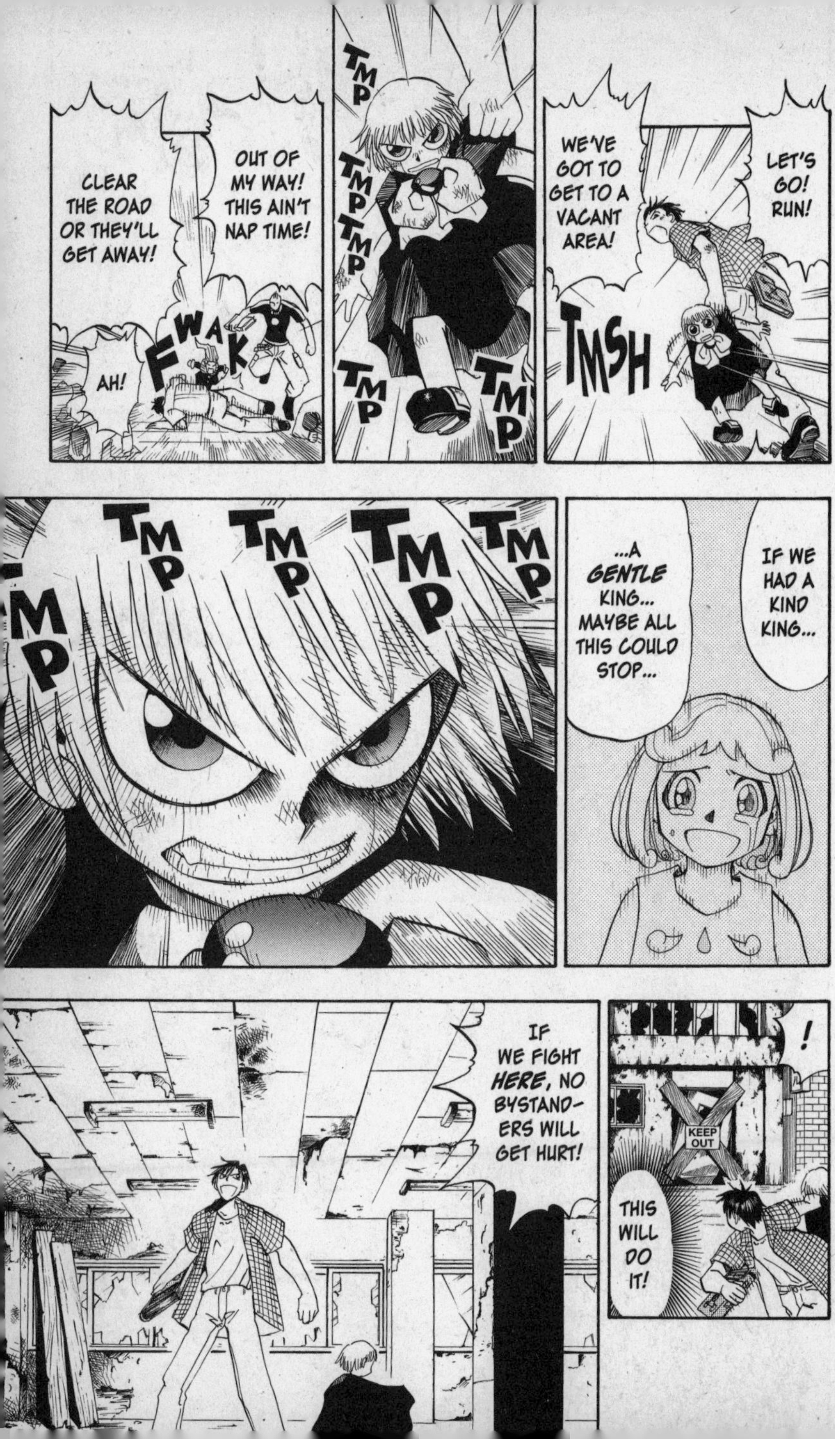

LET'S GO! RUN!
WE'VE GOT TO GET TO A VACANT AREA!
TMSH
TMP
TMP
TMP
TMP
TMP
OUT OF MY WAY! THIS AIN'T NAP TIME!
CLEAR THE ROAD OR THEY'LL GET AWAY!
FWAK
AH!
IF WE HAD A KIND KING...
...A *GENTLE* KING... MAYBE ALL THIS COULD STOP...
TMP
TMP
TMP
TMP
MP
!
KEEP OUT
THIS WILL DO IT!
IF WE FIGHT *HERE*, NO BYSTANDERS WILL GET HURT!

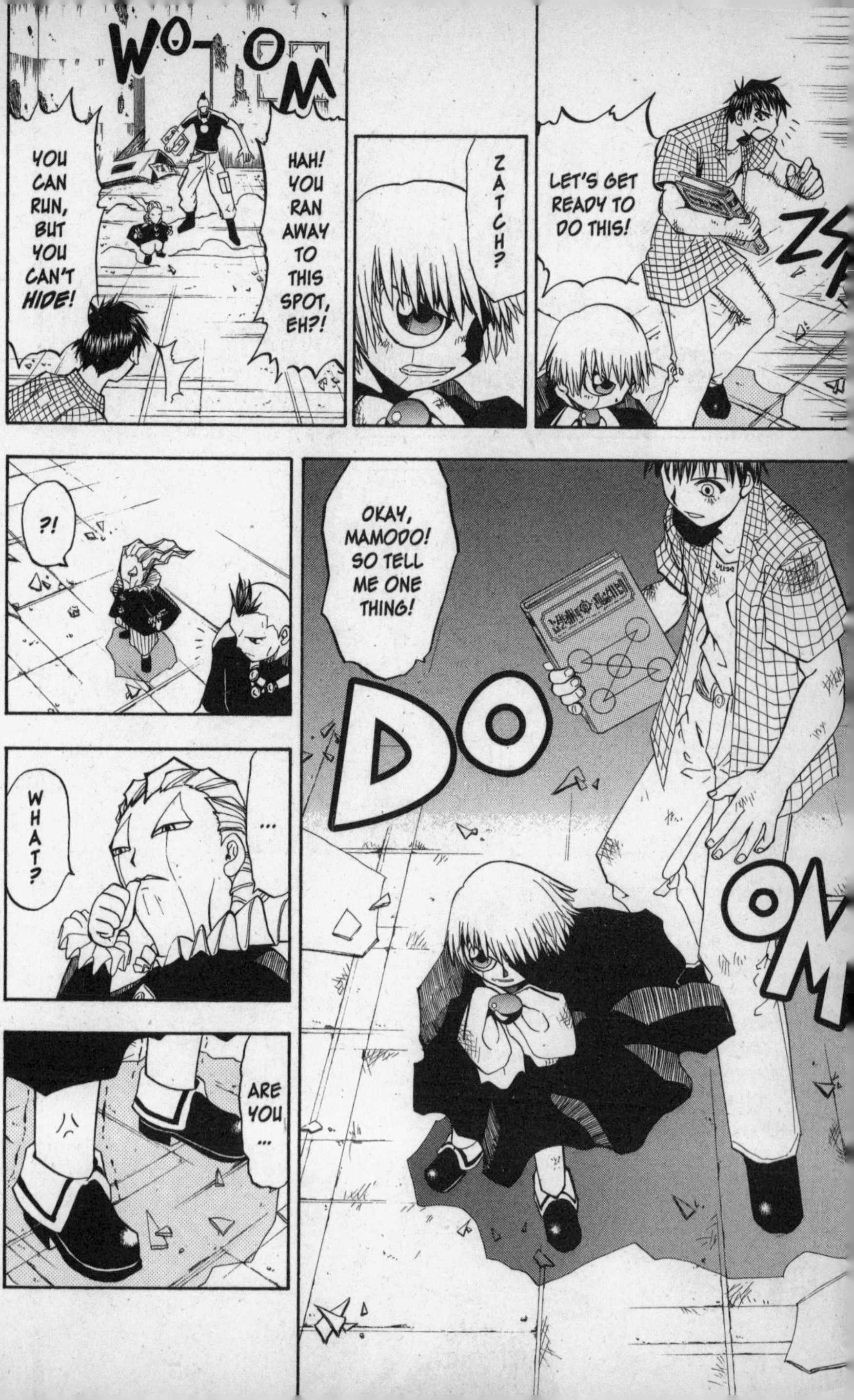
LET'S GET READY TO DO THIS!
ZS
ZATCH?
WO-OM
HAH! YOU RAN AWAY TO THIS SPOT, EH?!
YOU CAN RUN, BUT YOU CAN'T HIDE!
OKAY, MAMODO! SO TELL ME ONE THING!
DO
OM
?!
...
WHAT?
ARE YOU ...

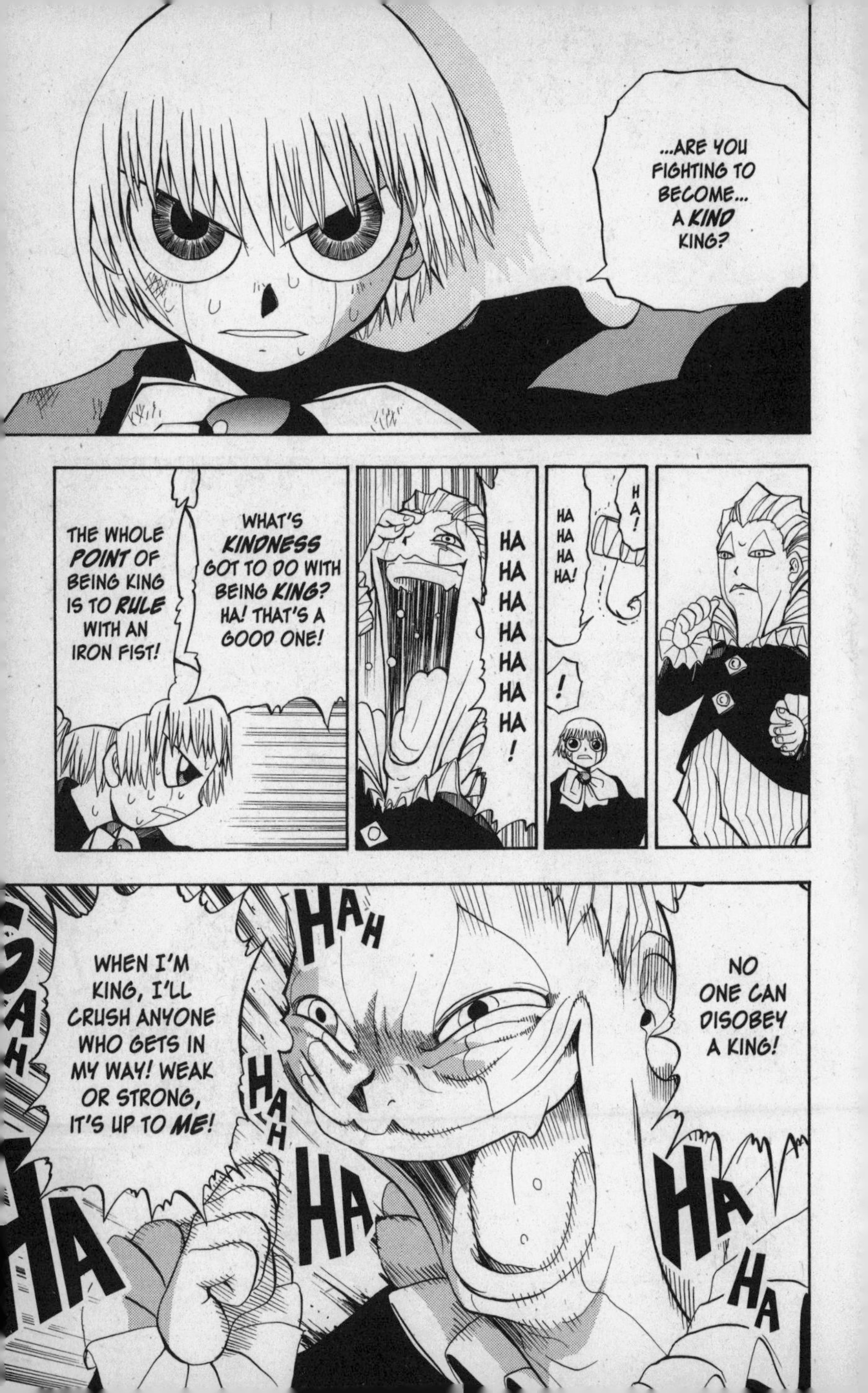
...ARE YOU FIGHTING TO BECOME... A KIND KING?
HA!
HA HA HA HA!
!
HA HA HA HA HA HA HA!
WHAT'S KINDNESS GOT TO DO WITH BEING KING? HA! THAT'S A GOOD ONE!
THE WHOLE POINT OF BEING KING IS TO RULE WITH AN IRON FIST!
NO ONE CAN DISOBEY A KING!
WHEN I'M KING, I'LL CRUSH ANYONE WHO GETS IN MY WAY! WEAK OR STRONG, IT'S UP TO ME!
HAH
HAH
HA
HA HA HA

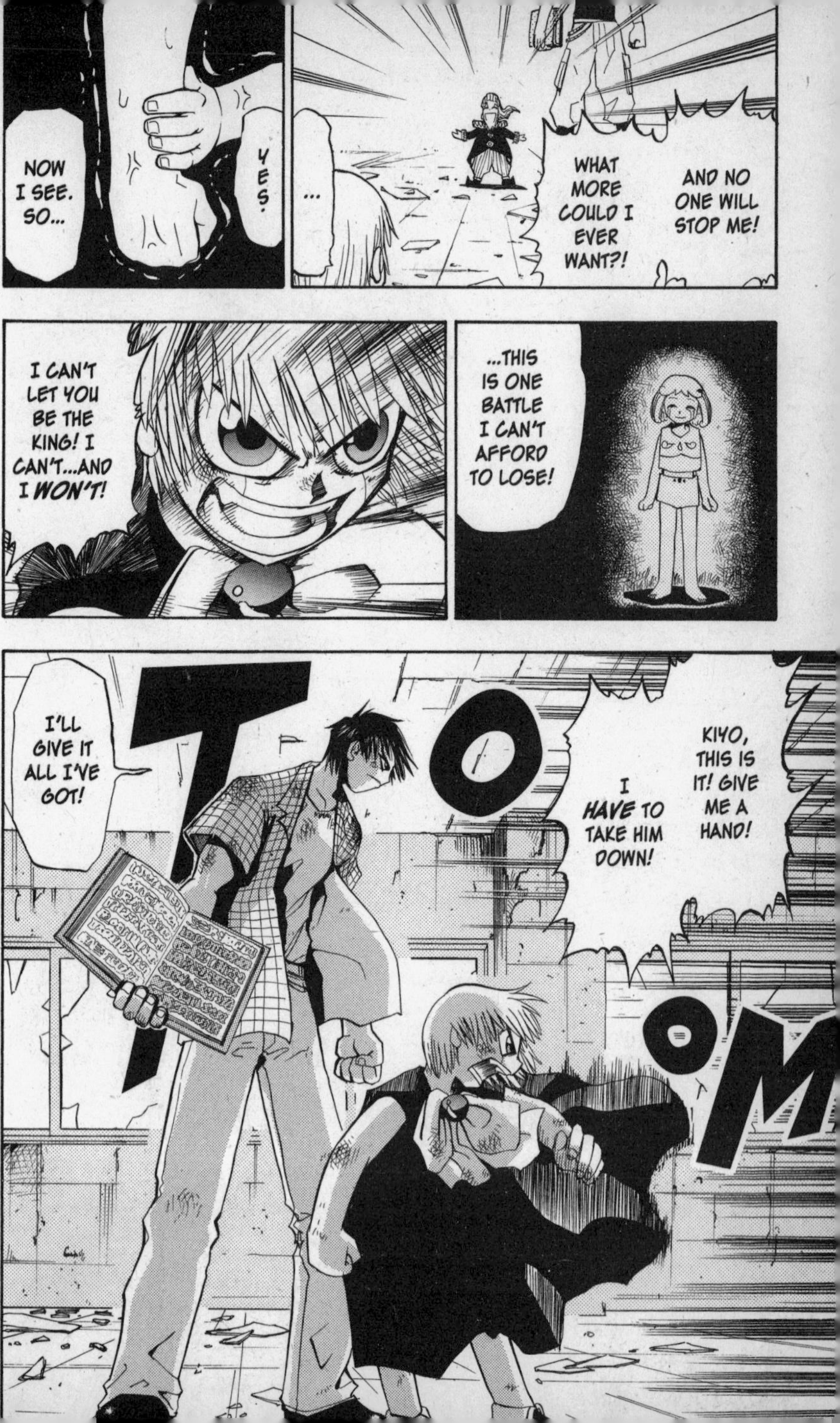
AND NO ONE WILL STOP ME!
WHAT MORE COULD I EVER WANT?!
...
YES.
NOW I SEE. SO...
...THIS IS ONE BATTLE I CAN'T AFFORD TO LOSE!
I CAN'T LET YOU BE THE KING! I CAN'T...AND I *WON'T*!
KIYO, THIS IS IT! GIVE ME A HAND!
I *HAVE* TO TAKE HIM DOWN!
TOOM
I'LL GIVE IT ALL I'VE GOT!

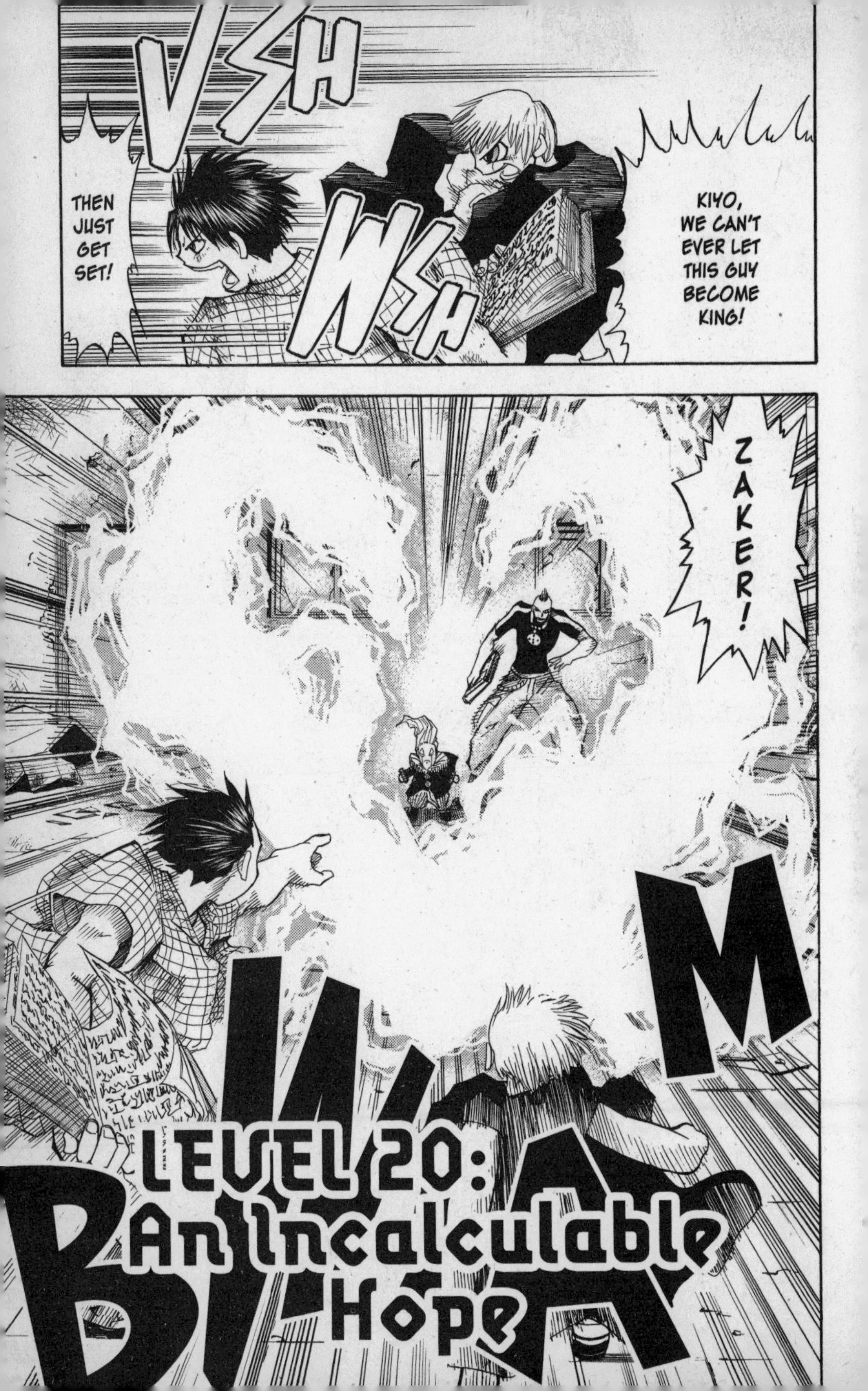
VSH
KIYO, WE CAN'T EVER LET THIS GUY BECOME KING!
WSH
THEN JUST GET SET!
ZAKER!

# LEVEL 20: An Incalculable Hope

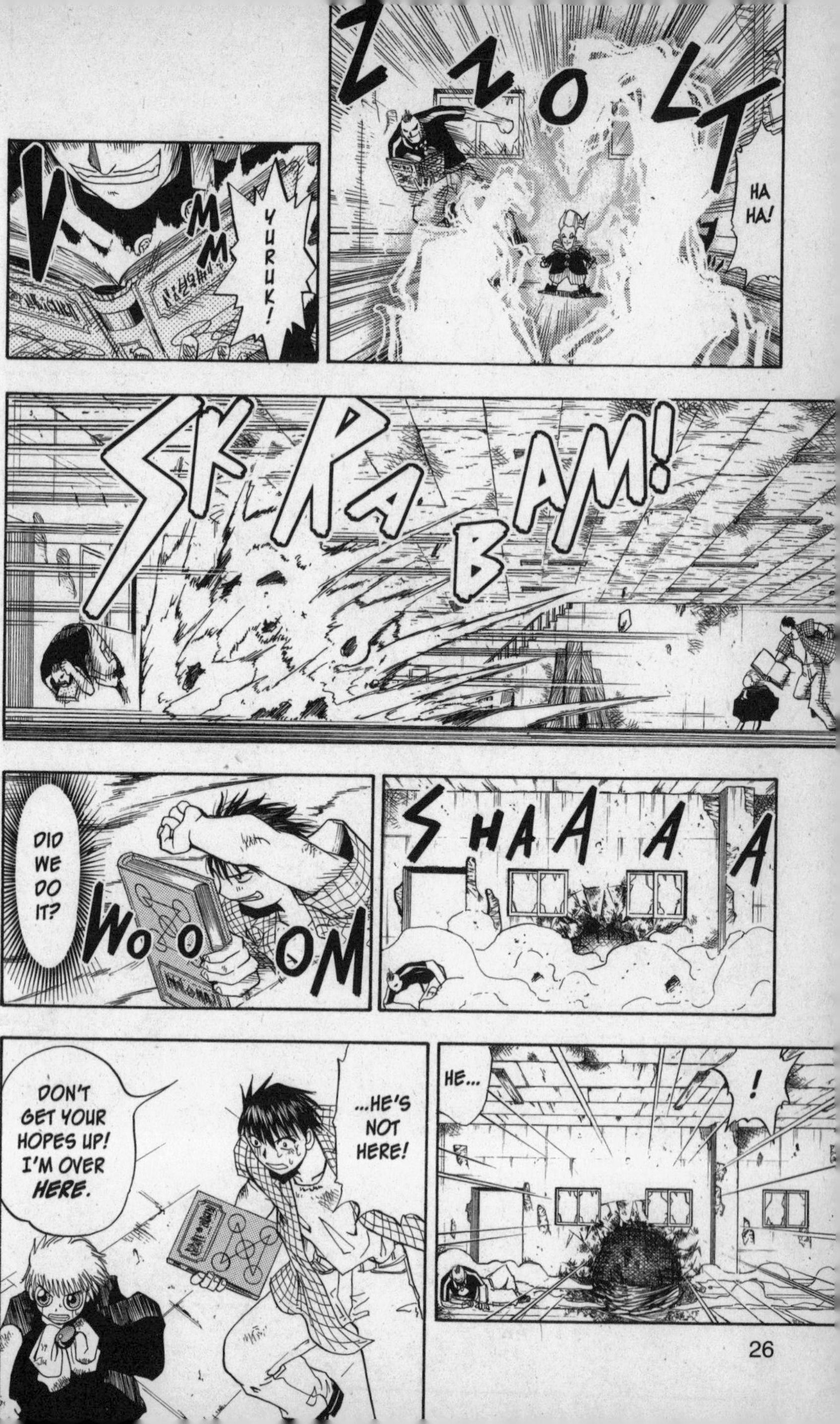

ZZOLT
HA HA!
VMM
YURUK!
SKRABAM!
SHAAAAA
DID WE DO IT?
WOOOM
HE...
!
...HE'S NOT HERE!
DON'T GET YOUR HOPES UP! I'M OVER **HERE**.

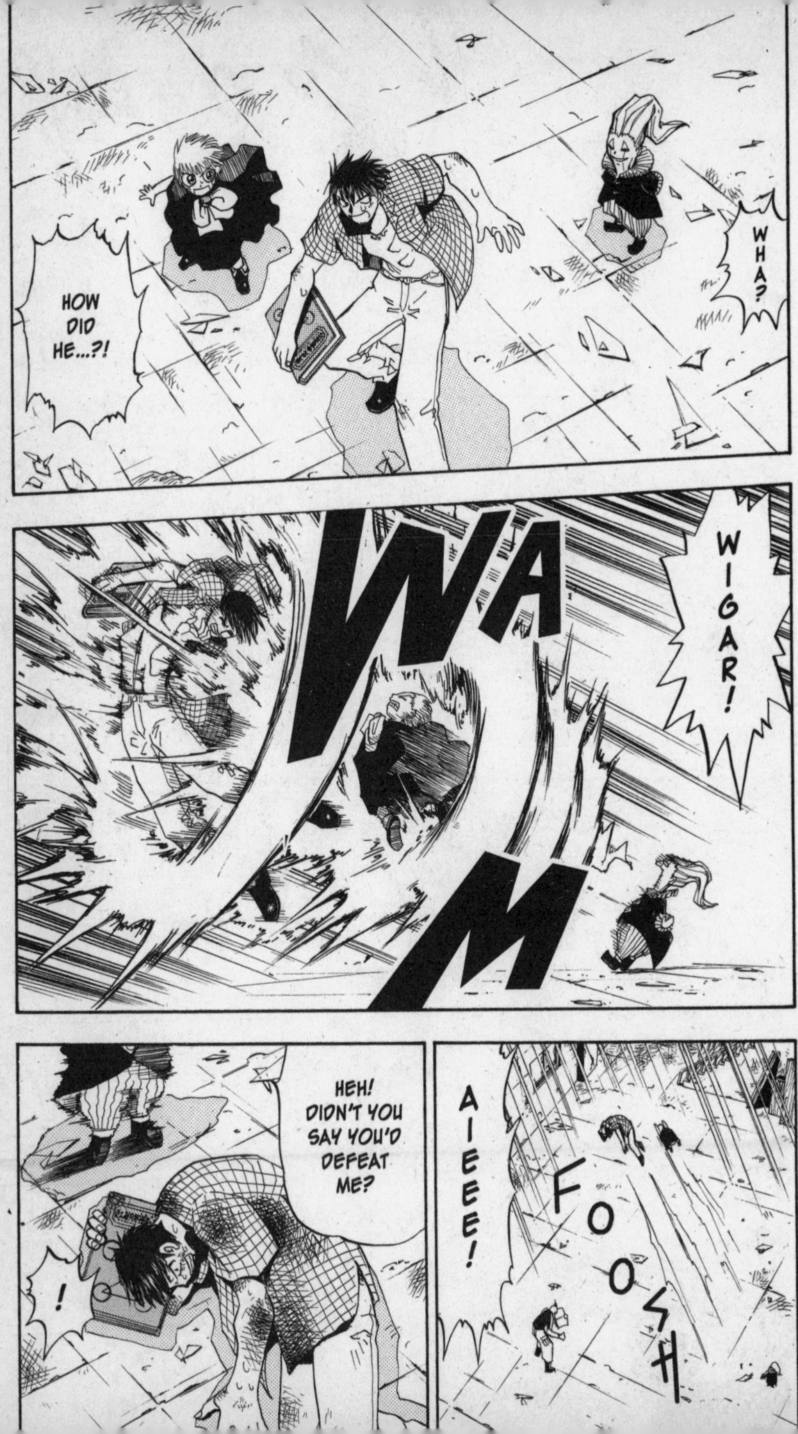
WHA?
HOW DID HE...?!
WIGAR!
WHAM
AIEEE!
FOOSH
HEH! DIDN'T YOU SAY YOU'D DEFEAT ME?
!

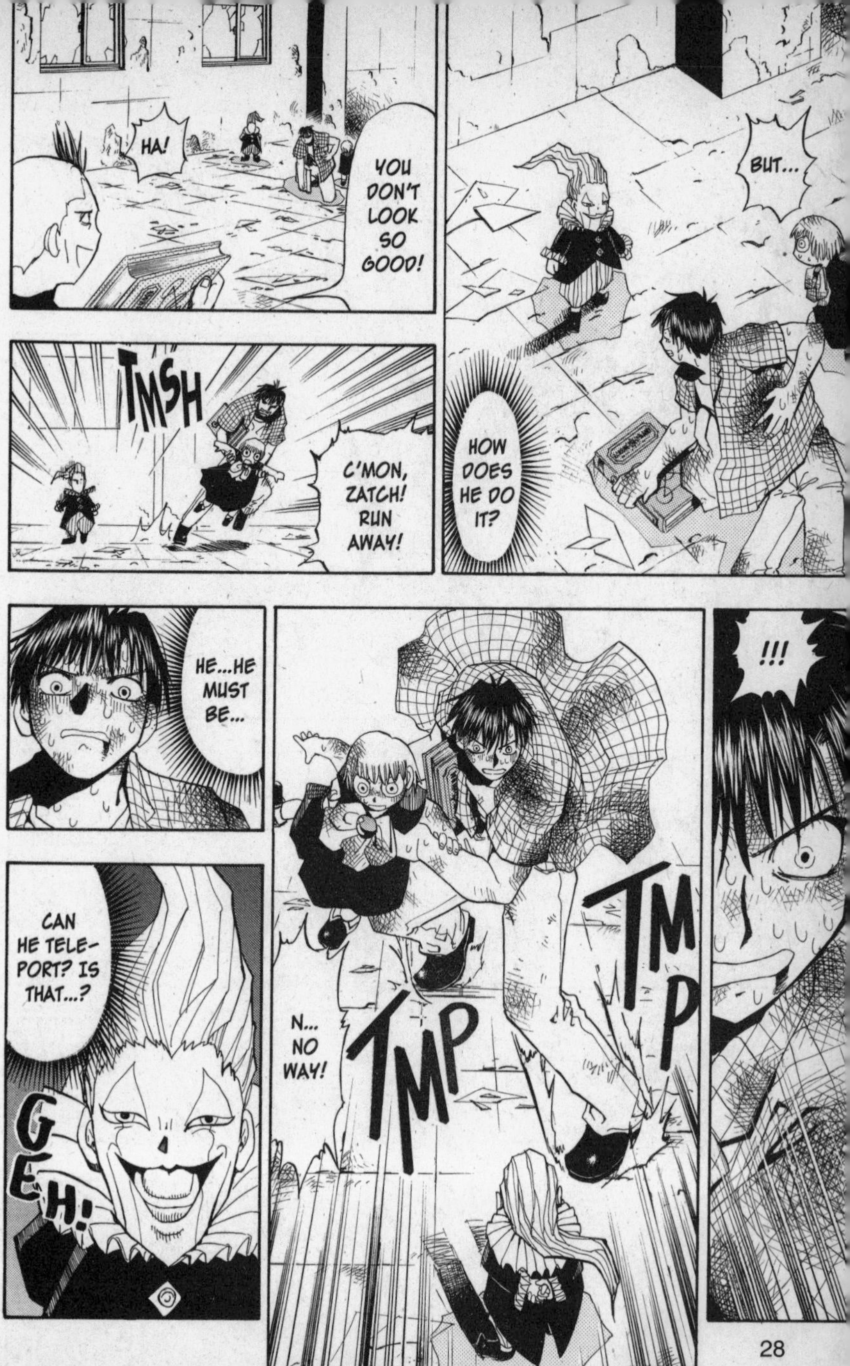

BUT...
HOW DOES HE DO IT?
HA!
YOU DON'T LOOK SO GOOD!
TMSH
C'MON, ZATCH! RUN AWAY!
!!!
TMP
N... NO WAY!
TMP
HE...HE MUST BE...
CAN HE TELE-PORT? IS THAT...?
GEH!

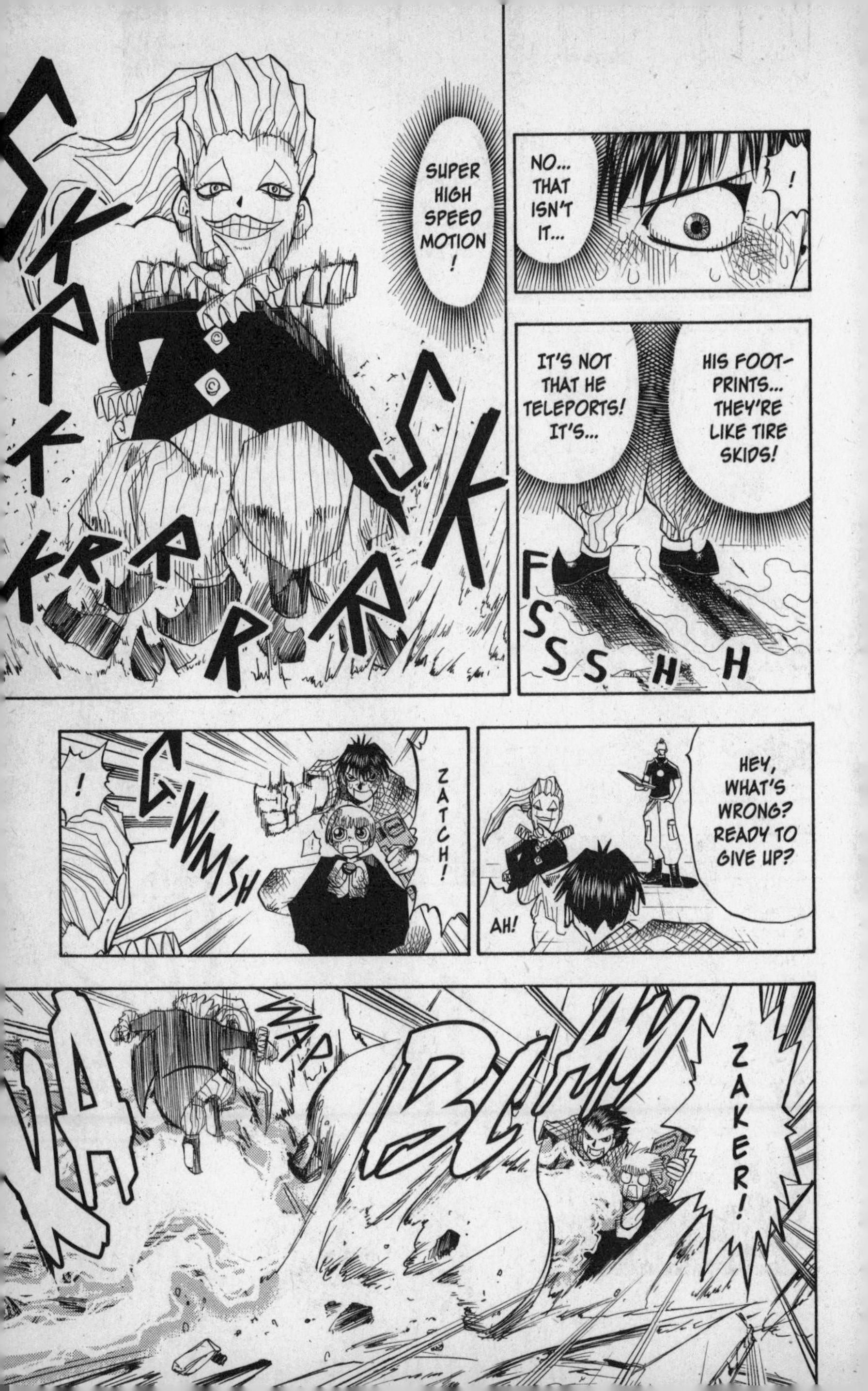
!
NO... THAT ISN'T IT...
HIS FOOT-PRINTS... THEY'RE LIKE TIRE SKIDS!
IT'S NOT THAT HE TELEPORTS! IT'S...
FSSSHH
SUPER HIGH SPEED MOTION!
SKRRR
SKRRR
HEY, WHAT'S WRONG? READY TO GIVE UP?
AH!
ZATCH!
GWMSH
!
ZAKER!
WAP

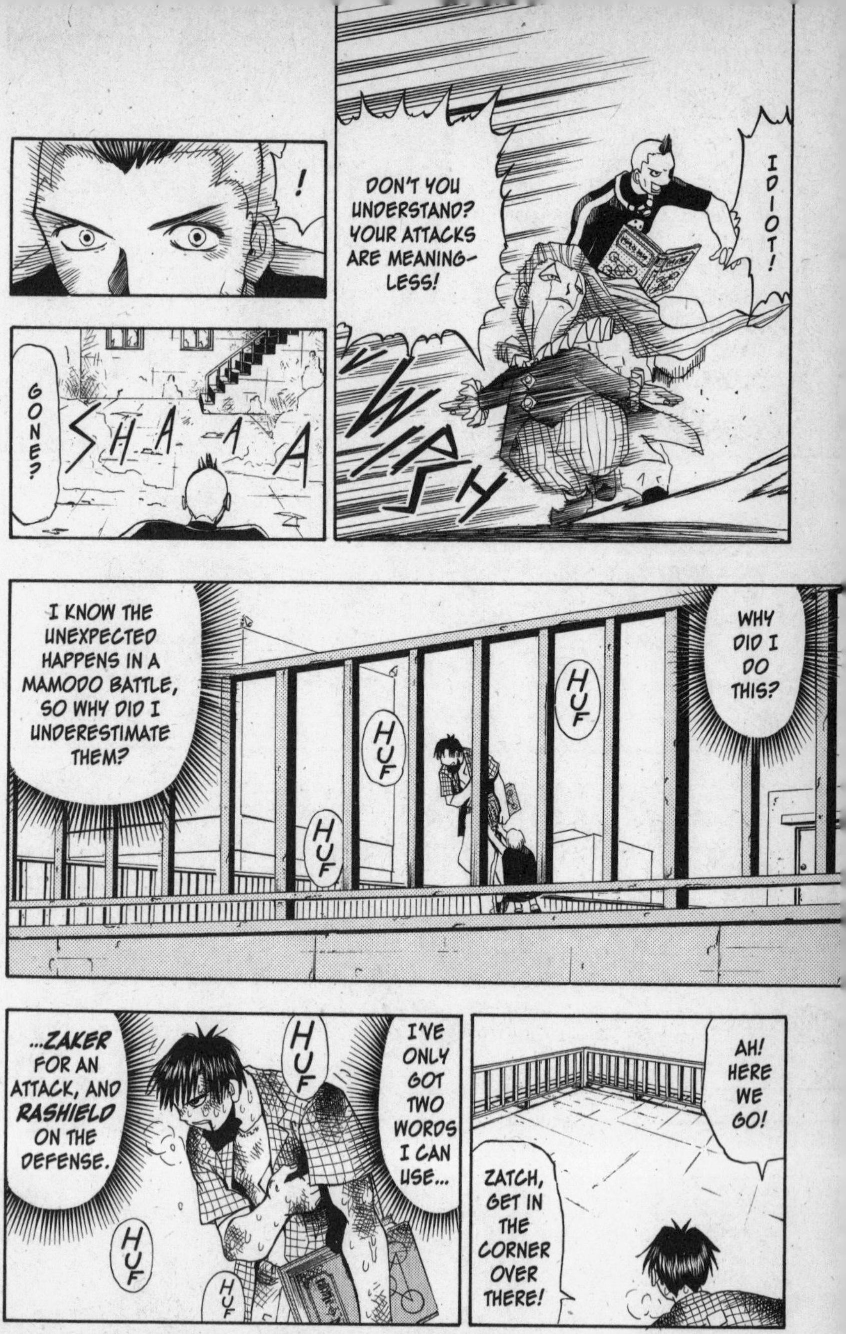
IDIOT!
DON'T YOU UNDERSTAND? YOUR ATTACKS ARE MEANINGLESS!
WHISH
!
GONE?
SHAAA
WHY DID I DO THIS?
HUF
HUF
HUF
I KNOW THE UNEXPECTED HAPPENS IN A MAMODO BATTLE, SO WHY DID I UNDERESTIMATE THEM?
AH! HERE WE GO!
ZATCH, GET IN THE CORNER OVER THERE!
I'VE ONLY GOT TWO WORDS I CAN USE...
HUF
...ZAKER FOR AN ATTACK, AND RASHIELD ON THE DEFENSE.
HUF
HUF

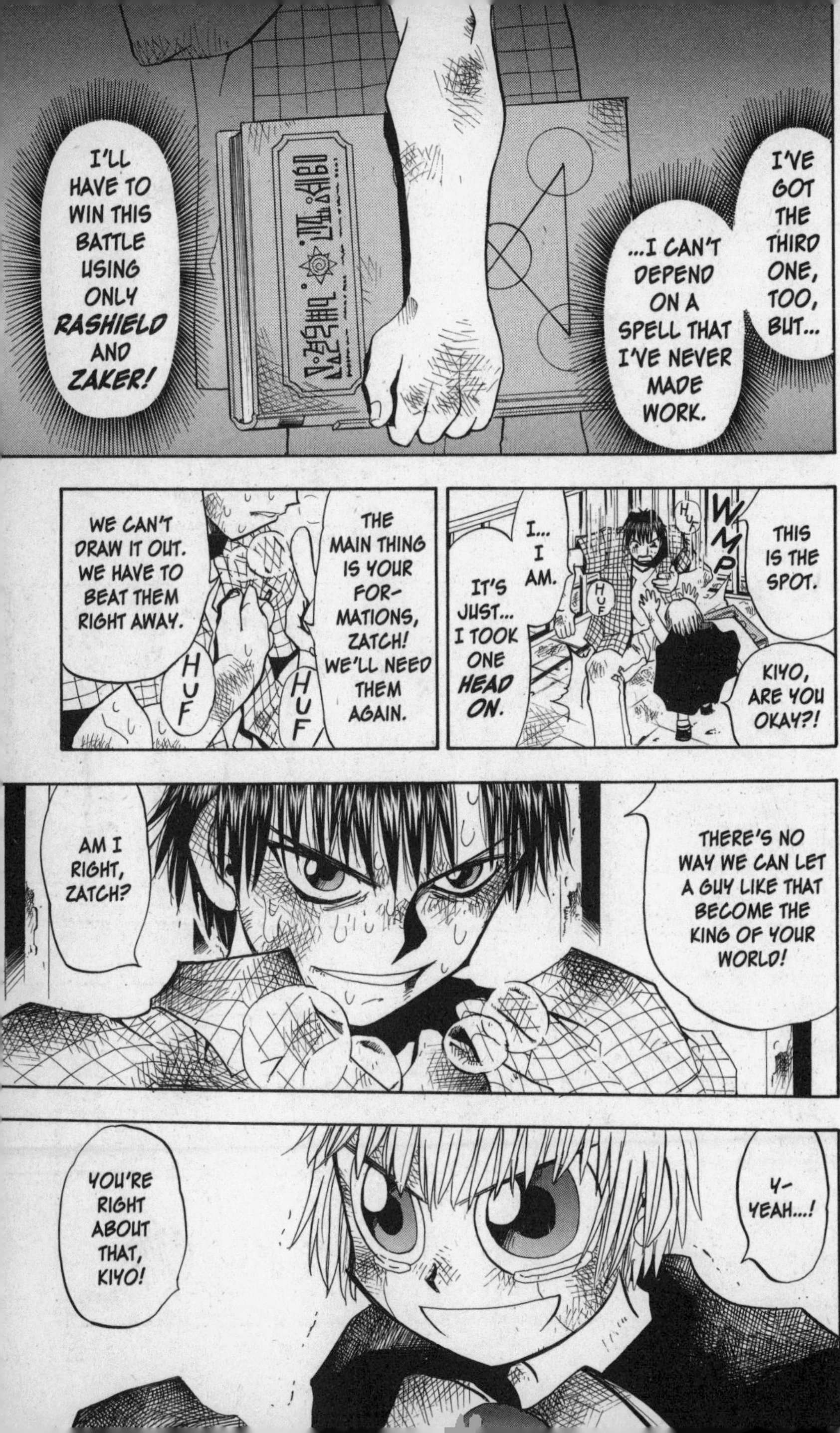
I'VE GOT THE THIRD ONE, TOO, BUT...
...I CAN'T DEPEND ON A SPELL THAT I'VE NEVER MADE WORK.
I'LL HAVE TO WIN THIS BATTLE USING ONLY *RASHIELD* AND *ZAKER!*
THIS IS THE SPOT.
WMP
HUF
HUF
KIYO, ARE YOU OKAY?!
I... I AM.
IT'S JUST... I TOOK ONE *HEAD ON.*
THE MAIN THING IS YOUR FOR-MATIONS, ZATCH! WE'LL NEED THEM AGAIN.
HUF
HUF
WE CAN'T DRAW IT OUT. WE HAVE TO BEAT THEM RIGHT AWAY.
THERE'S NO WAY WE CAN LET A GUY LIKE THAT BECOME THE KING OF YOUR WORLD!
AM I RIGHT, ZATCH?
Y-YEAH...!
YOU'RE RIGHT ABOUT THAT, KIYO!

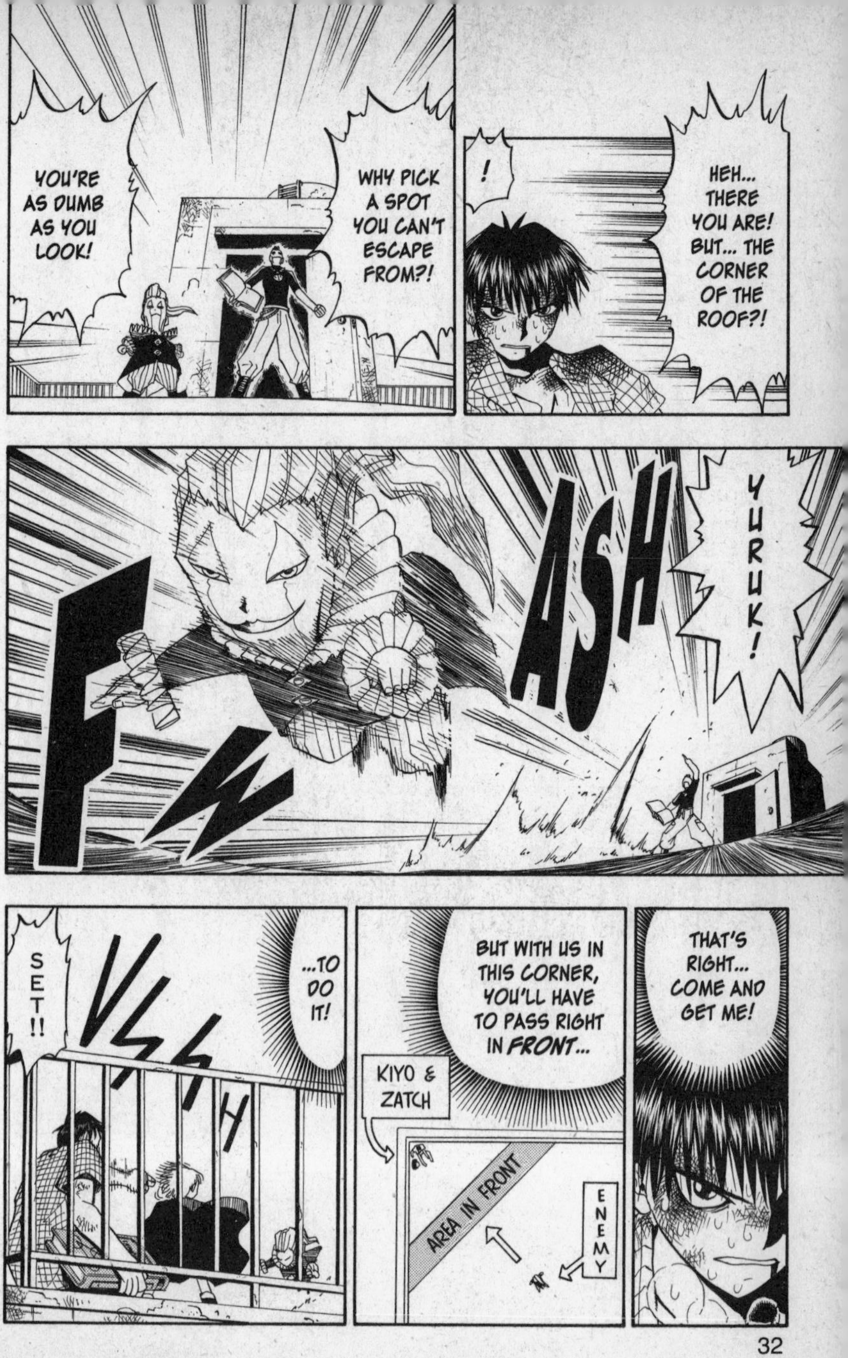
HEH... THERE YOU ARE! BUT... THE CORNER OF THE ROOF?!
!
WHY PICK A SPOT YOU CAN'T ESCAPE FROM?!
YOU'RE AS DUMB AS YOU LOOK!
YURUK!
FWASH
THAT'S RIGHT... COME AND GET ME!
BUT WITH US IN THIS CORNER, YOU'LL HAVE TO PASS RIGHT IN FRONT...
KIYO & ZATCH
AREA IN FRONT
ENEMY
...TO DO IT!
SET!!
VSSH

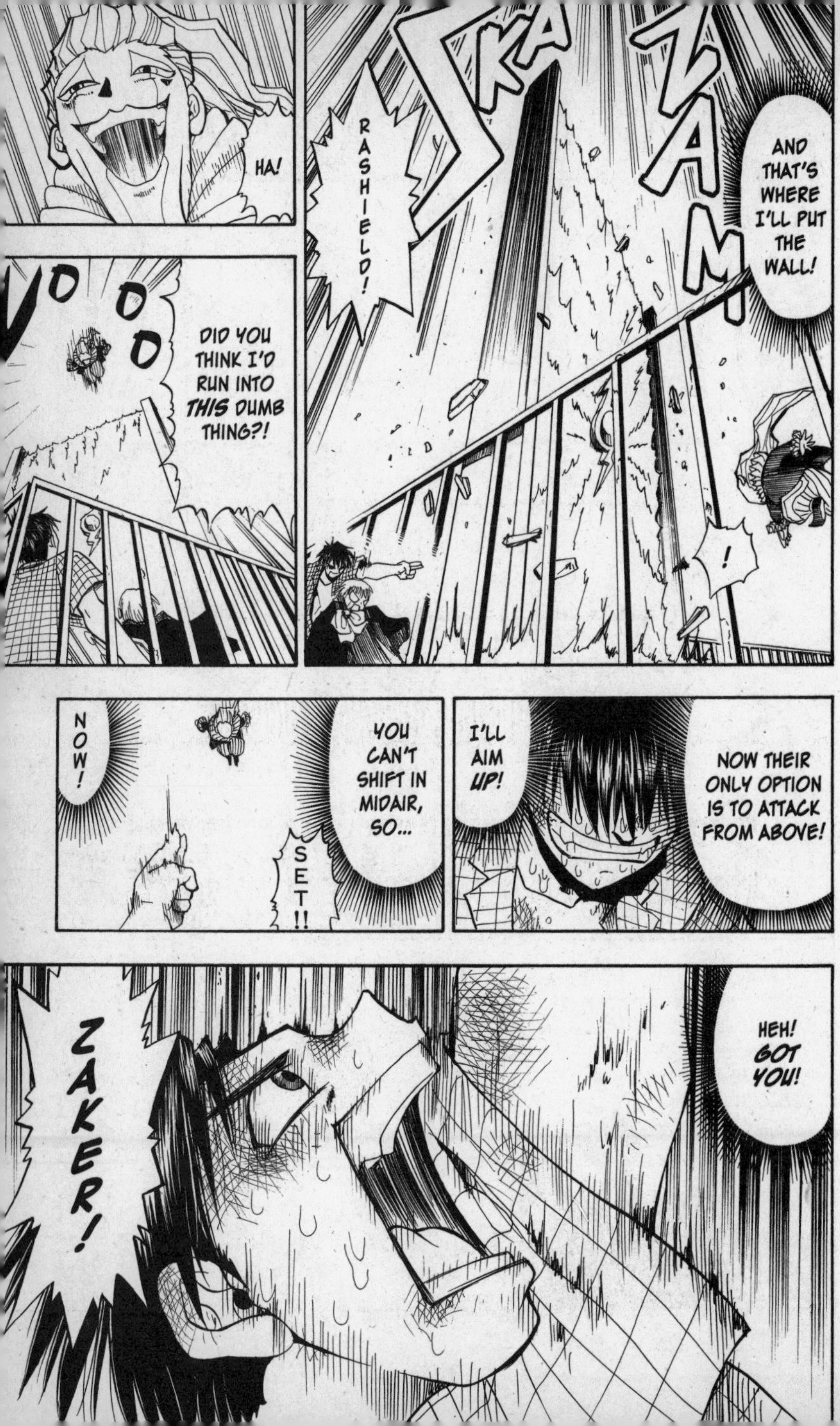
AND THAT'S WHERE I'LL PUT THE WALL!
ZAM
SKA
RASHIELD!
!
HA!
VOOO
DID YOU THINK I'D RUN INTO THIS DUMB THING?!
NOW THEIR ONLY OPTION IS TO ATTACK FROM ABOVE!
I'LL AIM UP!
YOU CAN'T SHIFT IN MIDAIR, SO...
SET!!
NOW!
HEH! GOT YOU!
ZAKER!

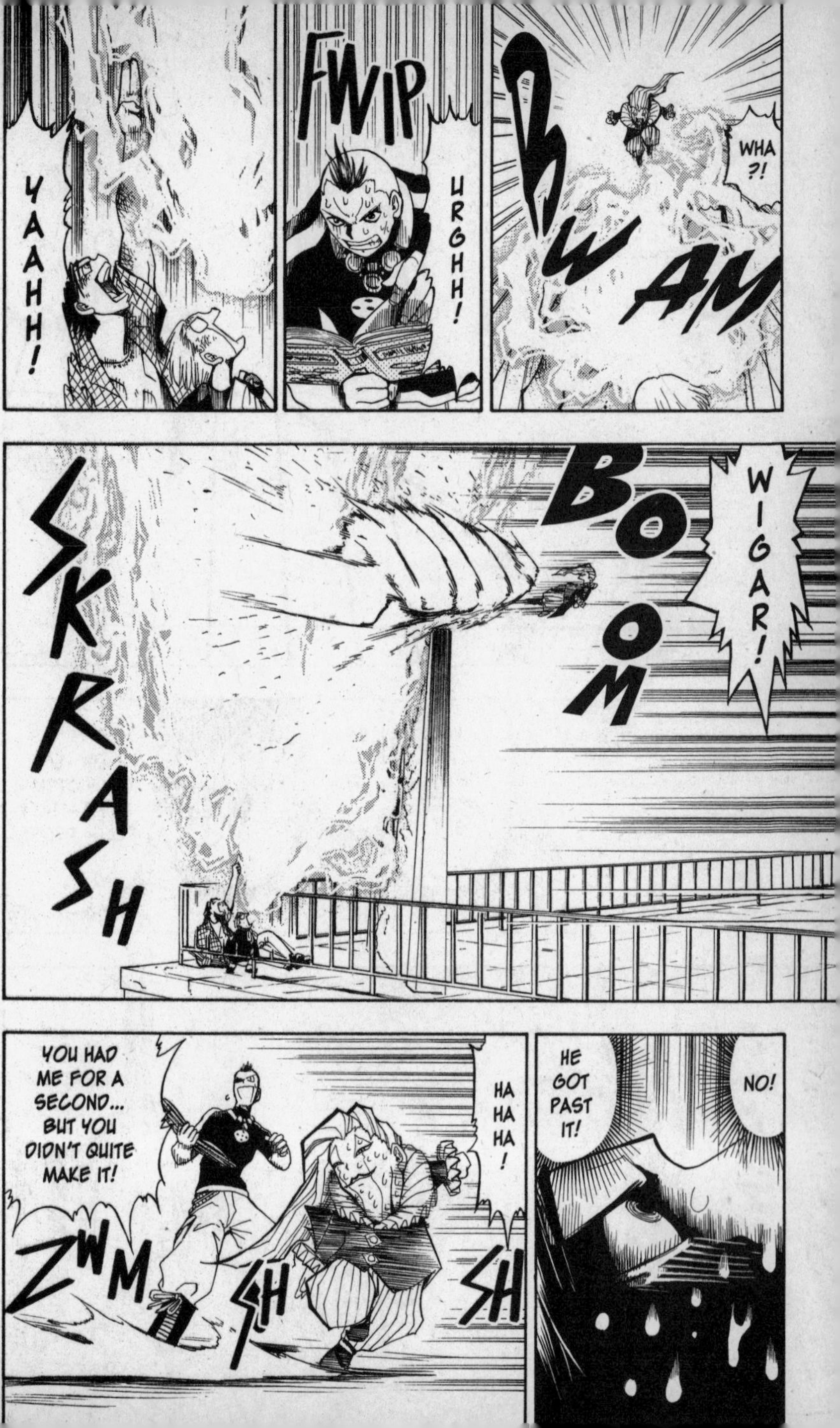
WHA ?!
BWAM
FWIP
URGHH!
YAAAHH!
WIGAR!
BOOM
SKRASH
NO!
HE GOT PAST IT!
HA HA HA!
YOU HAD ME FOR A SECOND... BUT YOU DIDN'T QUITE MAKE IT!
SH
SH
ZWM

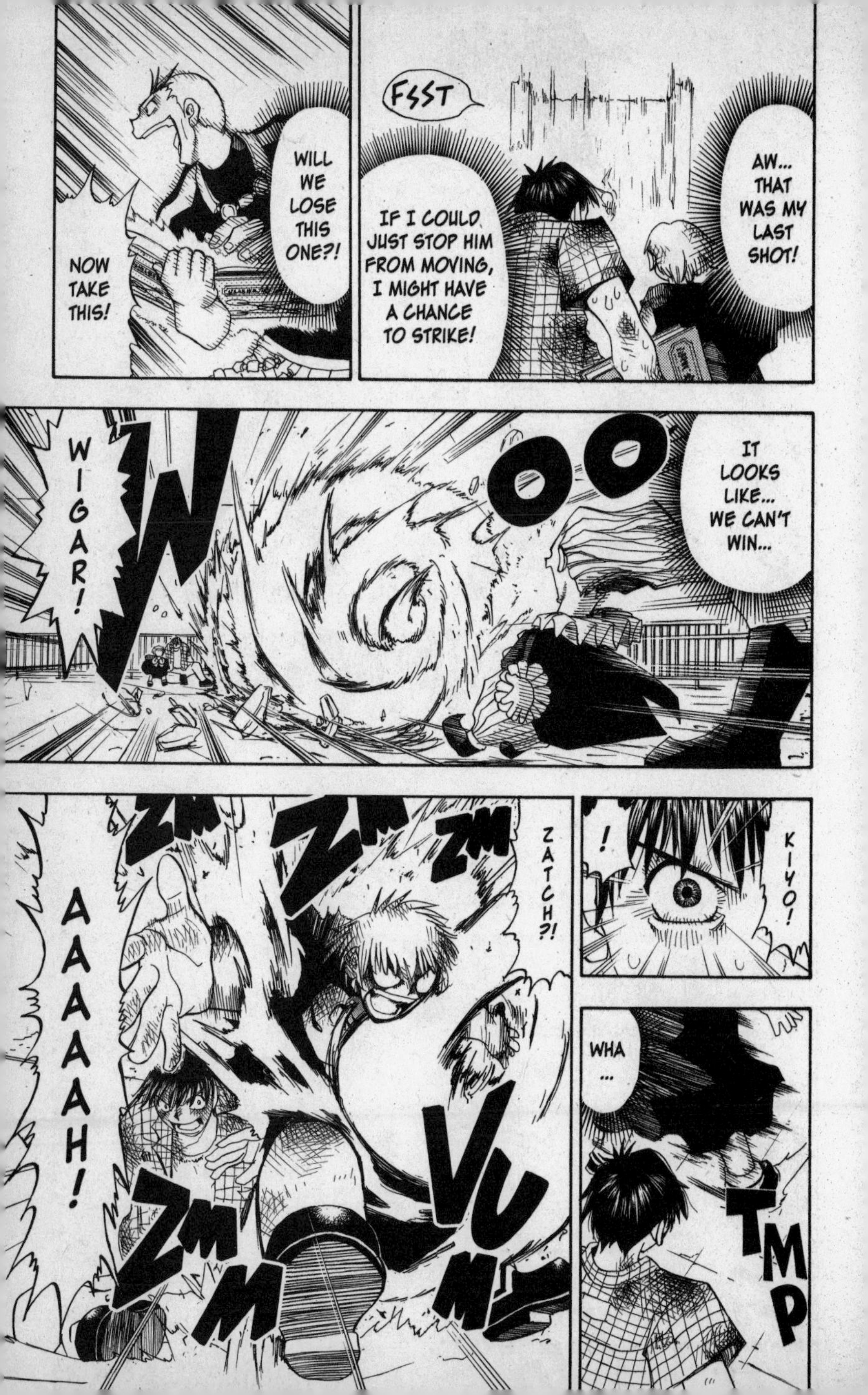

AW... THAT WAS MY LAST SHOT!
FSST
IF I COULD JUST STOP HIM FROM MOVING, I MIGHT HAVE A CHANCE TO STRIKE!
WILL WE LOSE THIS ONE?!
NOW TAKE THIS!
IT LOOKS LIKE... WE CAN'T WIN...
WOOO
WIGAR!
KIYO!
!
WHA ...
TMP
ZATCH?!
ZM
ZM
ZM
AAAAAAH!
VUM
ZM

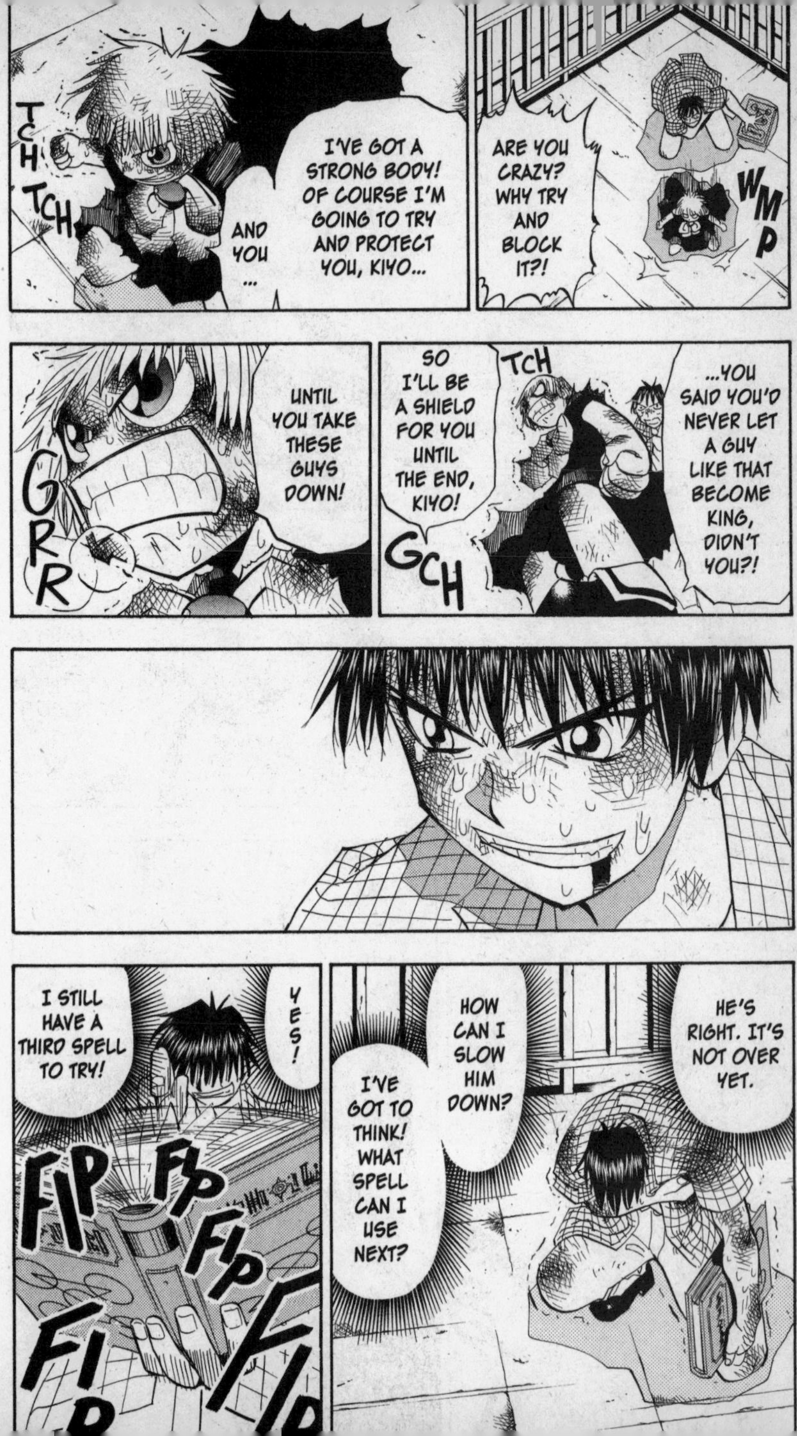

ARE YOU CRAZY? WHY TRY AND BLOCK IT?!
WMP
I'VE GOT A STRONG BODY! OF COURSE I'M GOING TO TRY AND PROTECT YOU, KIYO...
AND YOU ...
TCH TCH
...YOU SAID YOU'D NEVER LET A GUY LIKE THAT BECOME KING, DIDN'T YOU?!
TCH
SO I'LL BE A SHIELD FOR YOU UNTIL THE END, KIYO!
GCH
UNTIL YOU TAKE THESE GUYS DOWN!
GRR
HE'S RIGHT. IT'S NOT OVER YET.
HOW CAN I SLOW HIM DOWN?
I'VE GOT TO THINK! WHAT SPELL CAN I USE NEXT?
YES!
I STILL HAVE A THIRD SPELL TO TRY!
FSP
FIP
FIP

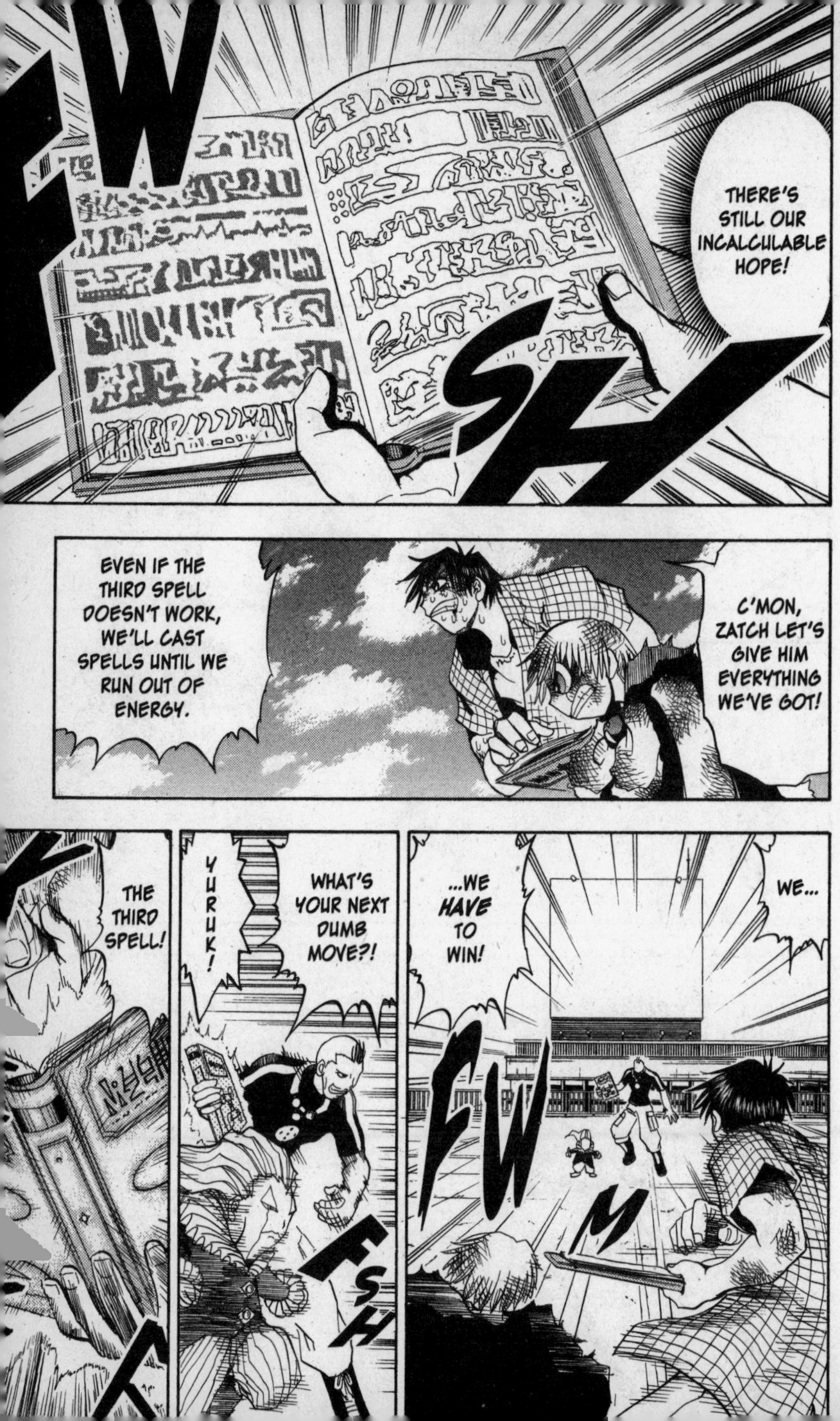
THERE'S STILL OUR INCALCULABLE HOPE!
SH
W
C'MON, ZATCH LET'S GIVE HIM EVERYTHING WE'VE GOT!
EVEN IF THE THIRD SPELL DOESN'T WORK, WE'LL CAST SPELLS UNTIL WE RUN OUT OF ENERGY.
WE...
...WE HAVE TO WIN!
FWM
WHAT'S YOUR NEXT DUMB MOVE?!
YURUK!
FSH
THE THIRD SPELL!

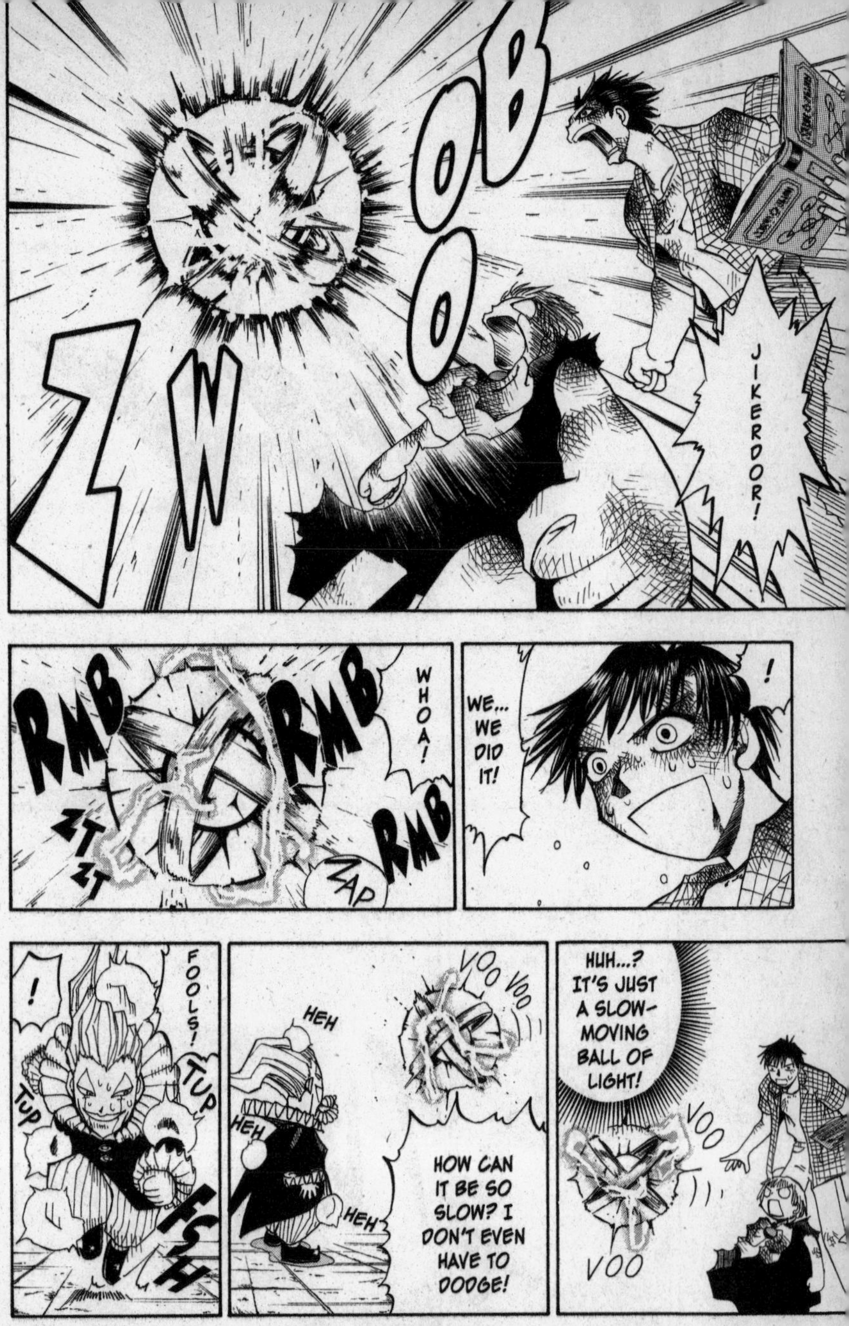
JIKERDOOR!
ZWOOB
!
WE... WE DID IT!
WHOA!
RMB
RMB
RMB
ZT ZT
ZAP
HUH...? IT'S JUST A SLOW-MOVING BALL OF LIGHT!
VOO
VOO
VOO VOO
HEH
HEH
HEH
HOW CAN IT BE SO SLOW? I DON'T EVEN HAVE TO DODGE!
FOOLS!
!
TUP
TUP
FSSH

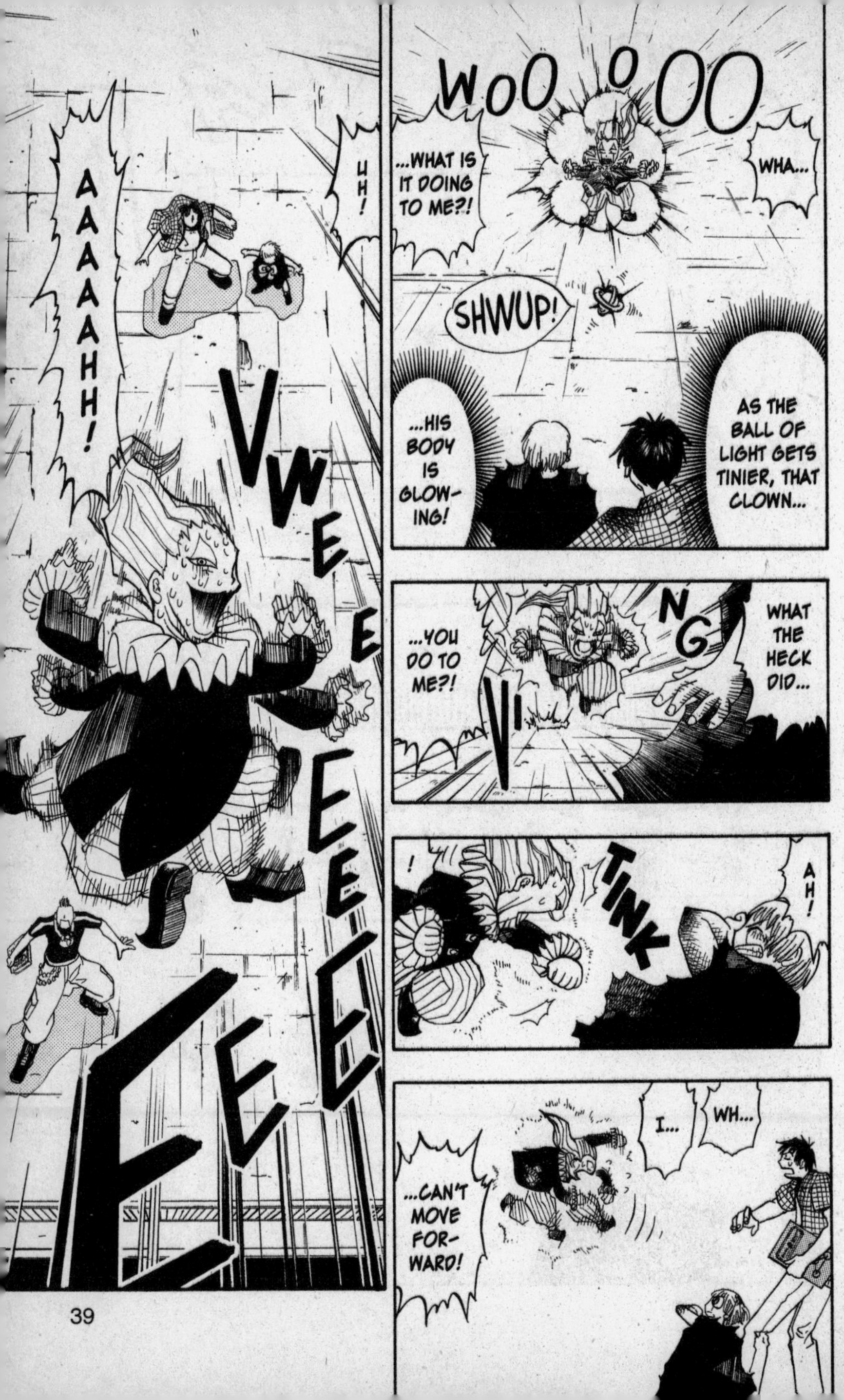
WHA...
WOOO OOO
...WHAT IS IT DOING TO ME?!
SHWUP!
AS THE BALL OF LIGHT GETS TINIER, THAT CLOWN...
...HIS BODY IS GLOWING!
WHAT THE HECK DID...
NG
...YOU DO TO ME?!
VI
AH!
TINK
!
WH...
I...
...CAN'T MOVE FORWARD!
UH!
VWEEEEEEE
AAAAAAHH!

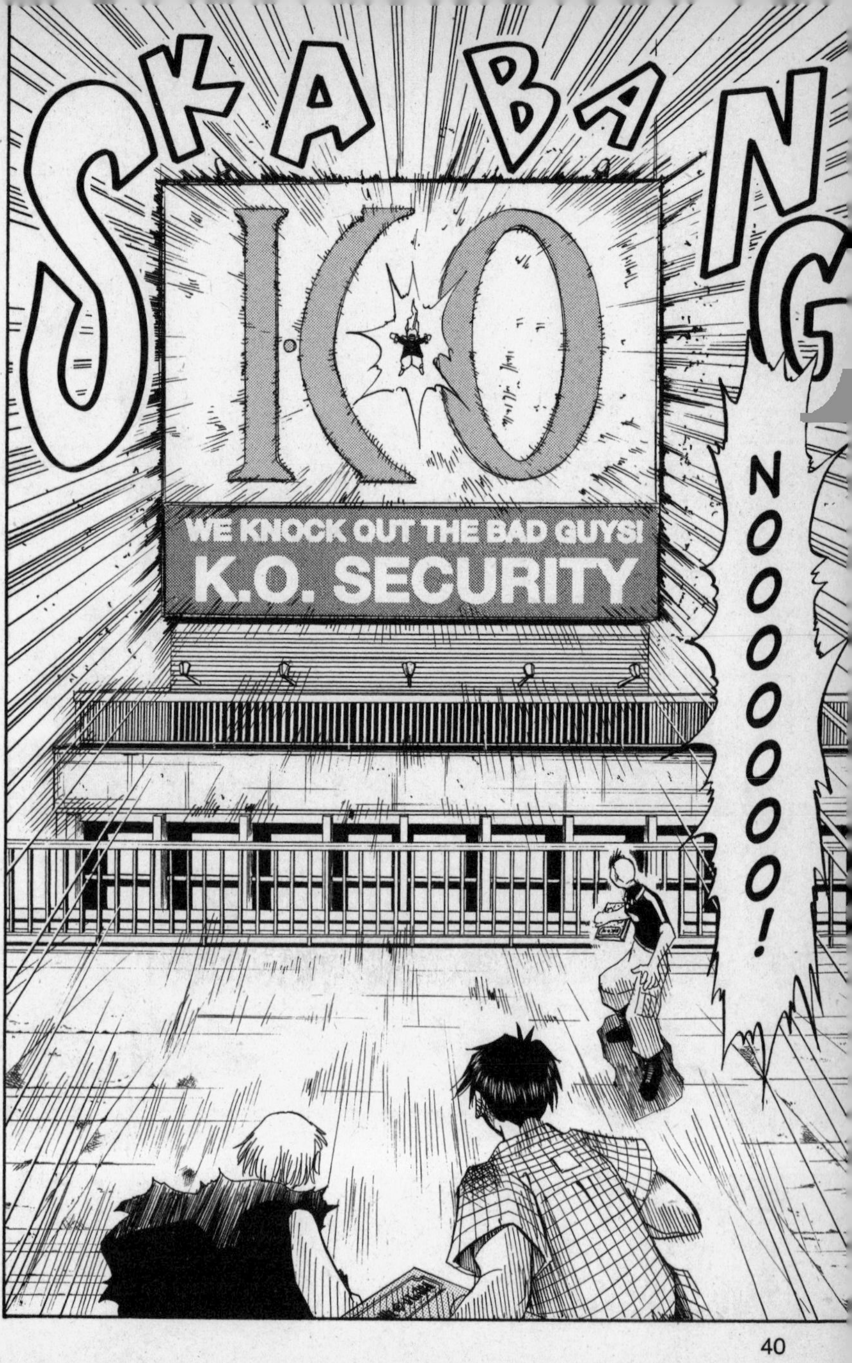
SKABANG
WE KNOCK OUT THE BAD GUYS!
K.O. SECURITY
NOOOOOOOO!

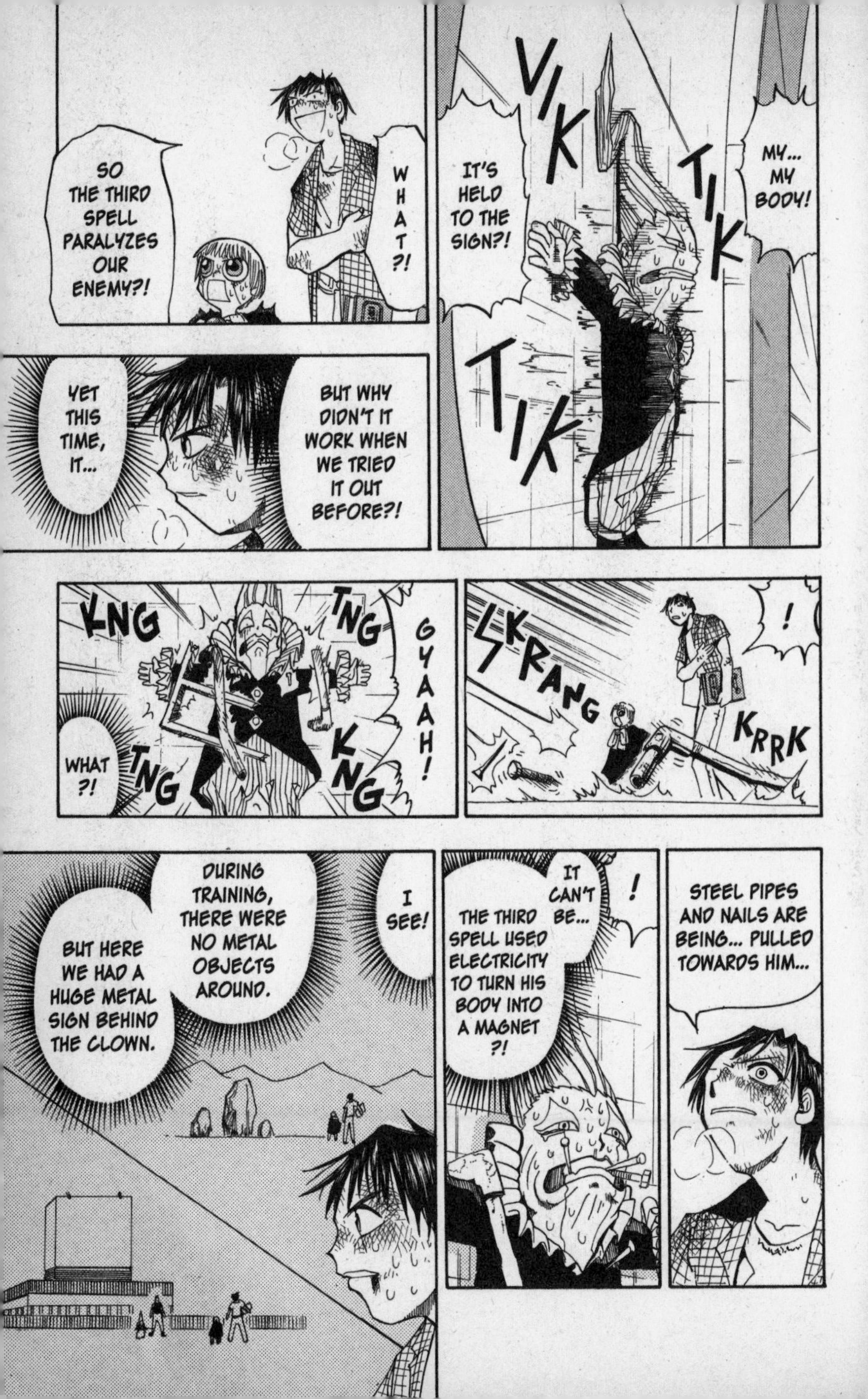
MY... MY BODY!
TIK
VIK
IT'S HELD TO THE SIGN?!
TIK
WHAT?!
SO THE THIRD SPELL PARALYZES OUR ENEMY?!
BUT WHY DIDN'T IT WORK WHEN WE TRIED IT OUT BEFORE?!
YET THIS TIME, IT...
!
SKRANG
KRRK
GYAAAH!
TNG
KNG
KNG
TNG
WHAT?!
STEEL PIPES AND NAILS ARE BEING... PULLED TOWARDS HIM...
!
IT CAN'T BE...
THE THIRD SPELL USED ELECTRICITY TO TURN HIS BODY INTO A MAGNET?!
I SEE!
DURING TRAINING, THERE WERE NO METAL OBJECTS AROUND.
BUT HERE WE HAD A HUGE METAL SIGN BEHIND THE CLOWN.

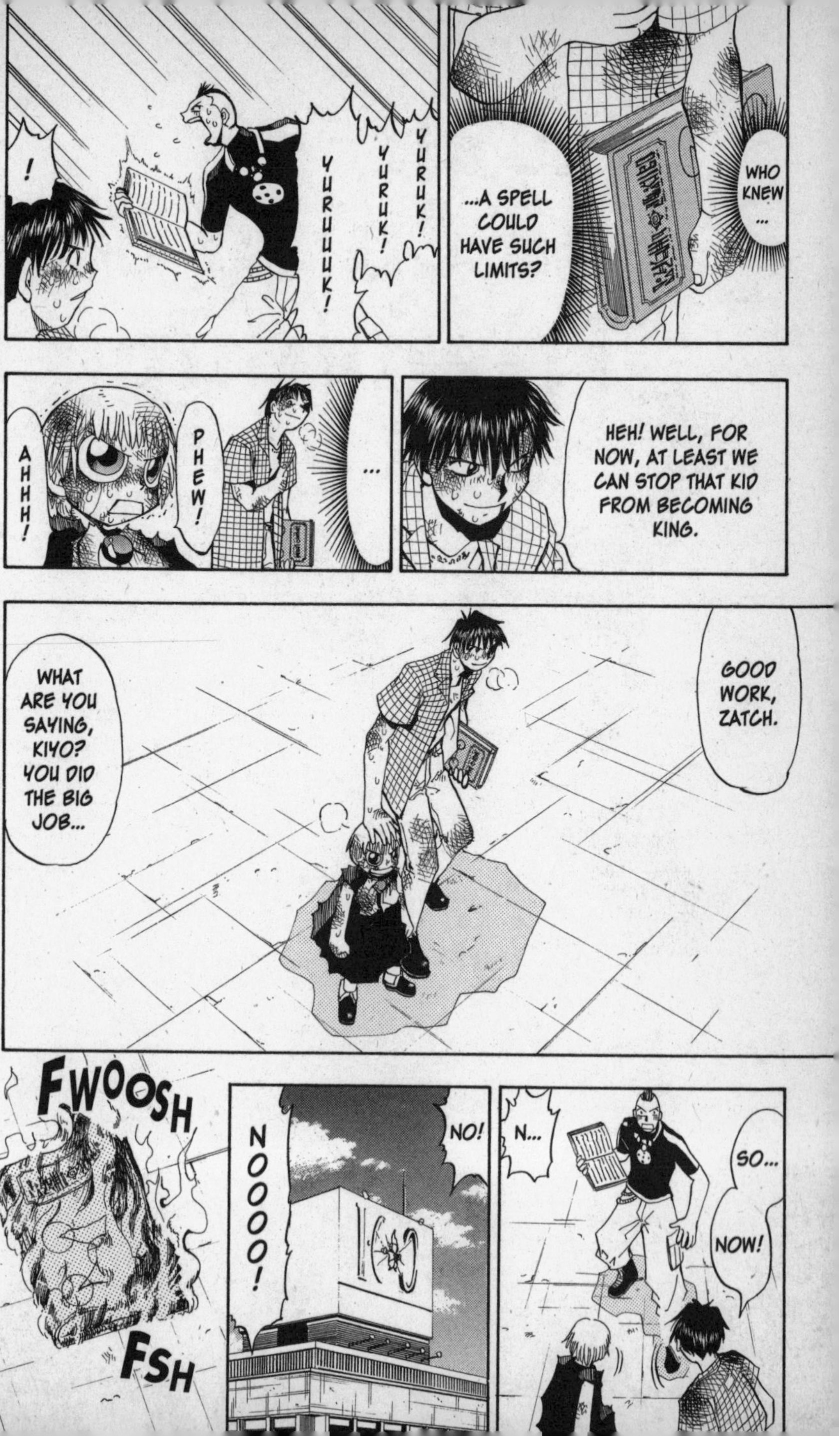
WHO KNEW ...
...A SPELL COULD HAVE SUCH LIMITS?
YURUK!
YURUK!
YURUUUK!
!
HEH! WELL, FOR NOW, AT LEAST WE CAN STOP THAT KID FROM BECOMING KING.
...
PHEW!
AHHH!
GOOD WORK, ZATCH.
WHAT ARE YOU SAYING, KIYO? YOU DID THE BIG JOB...
SO...
NOW!
N...
NO!
NOOOOO!
FWOOSH
FSH

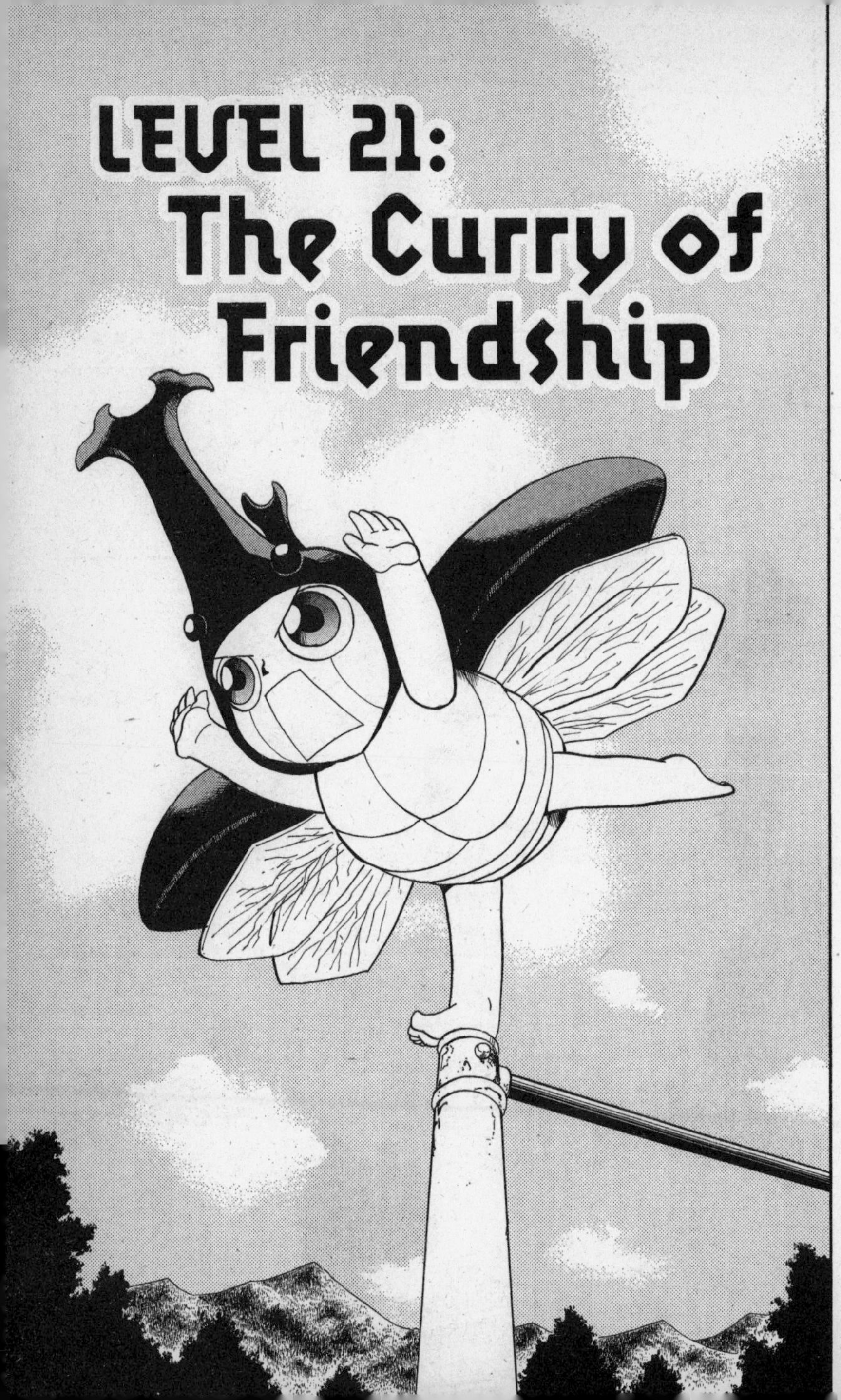
LEVEL 21:
The Curry of
Friendship

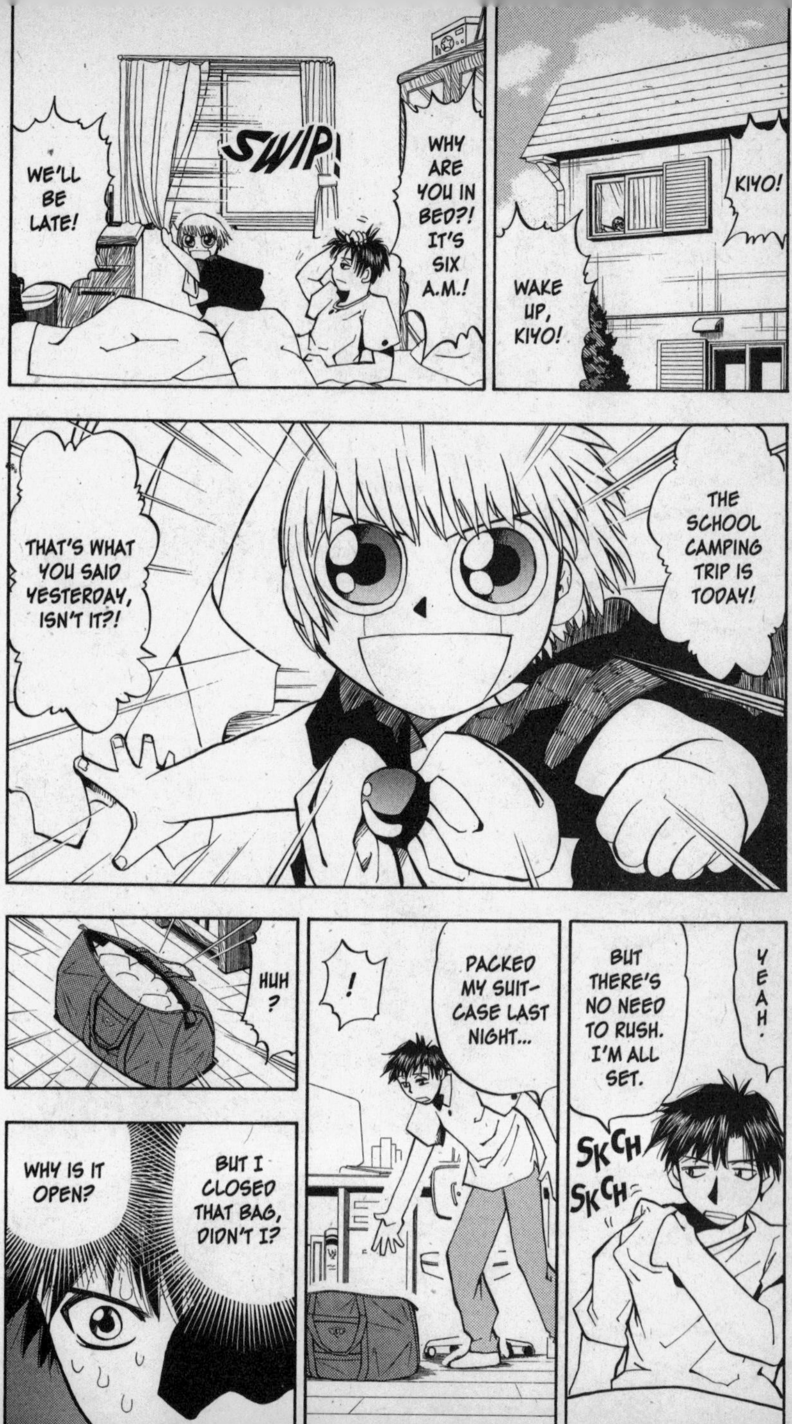
KIYO!
WAKE UP, KIYO!
WHY ARE YOU IN BED?! IT'S SIX A.M.!
SWIP!
WE'LL BE LATE!
THE SCHOOL CAMPING TRIP IS TODAY!
THAT'S WHAT YOU SAID YESTERDAY, ISN'T IT?!
YEAH.
BUT THERE'S NO NEED TO RUSH. I'M ALL SET.
SKCH SKCH
PACKED MY SUIT-CASE LAST NIGHT...
!
HUH?
BUT I CLOSED THAT BAG, DIDN'T I?
WHY IS IT OPEN?

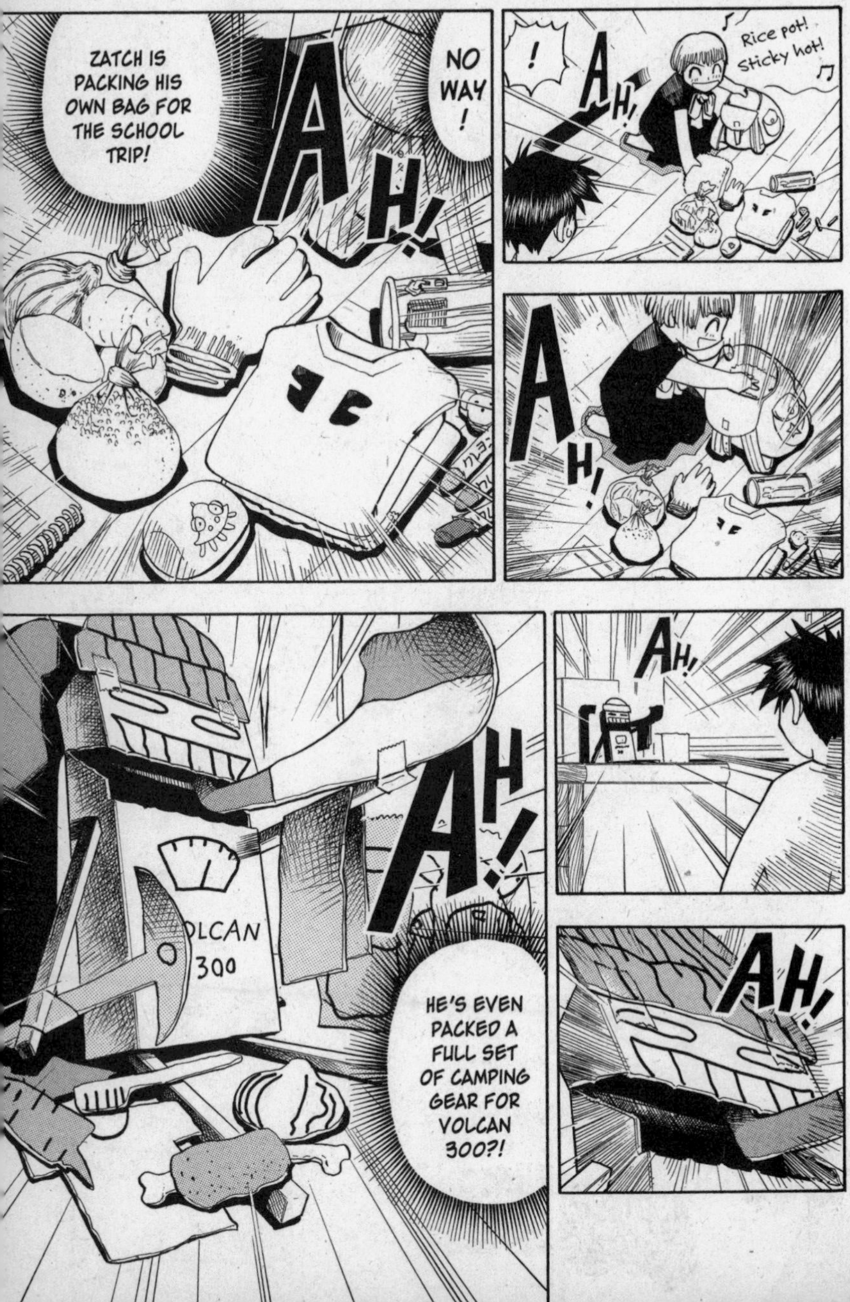
Rice pot! Sticky hot!
!
AH!
AH!
NO WAY!
AH!
ZATCH IS PACKING HIS OWN BAG FOR THE SCHOOL TRIP!
AH!
AH!
AH!
VOLCAN 300
HE'S EVEN PACKED A FULL SET OF CAMPING GEAR FOR VOLCAN 300?!

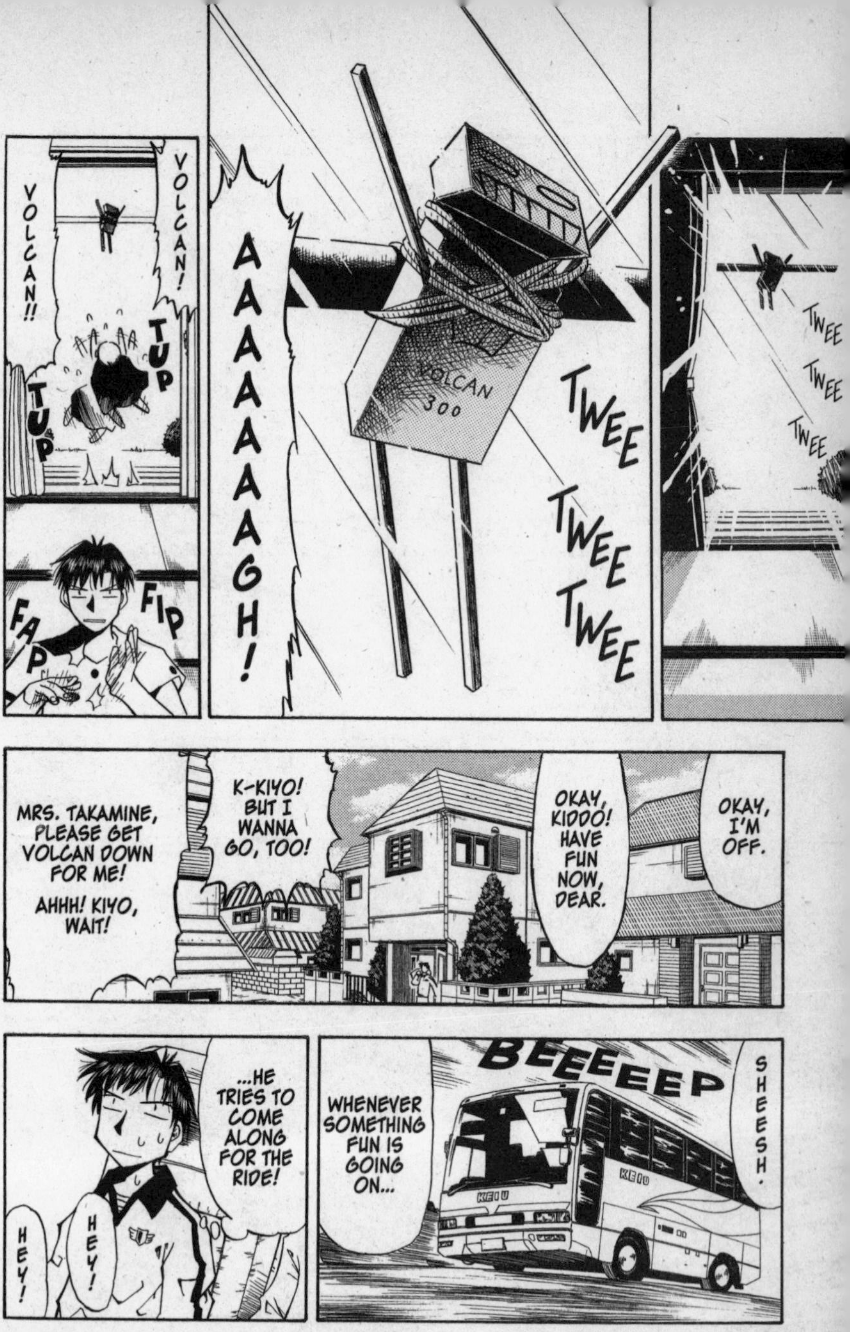
TWEE
TWEE
TWEE
AAAAAAAAAGH!
VOLCAN 300
TWEE
TWEE
TWEE
VOLCAN!
VOLCAN!!
TUP
TUP
FIP
FAP
OKAY, I'M OFF.
OKAY, KIDDO! HAVE FUN NOW, DEAR.
K-KIYO! BUT I WANNA GO, TOO!
MRS. TAKAMINE, PLEASE GET VOLCAN DOWN FOR ME!
AHHH! KIYO, WAIT!
SHEESH.
BEEEEEP
KEIU
WHENEVER SOMETHING FUN IS GOING ON...
...HE TRIES TO COME ALONG FOR THE RIDE!
HEY!
HEY!

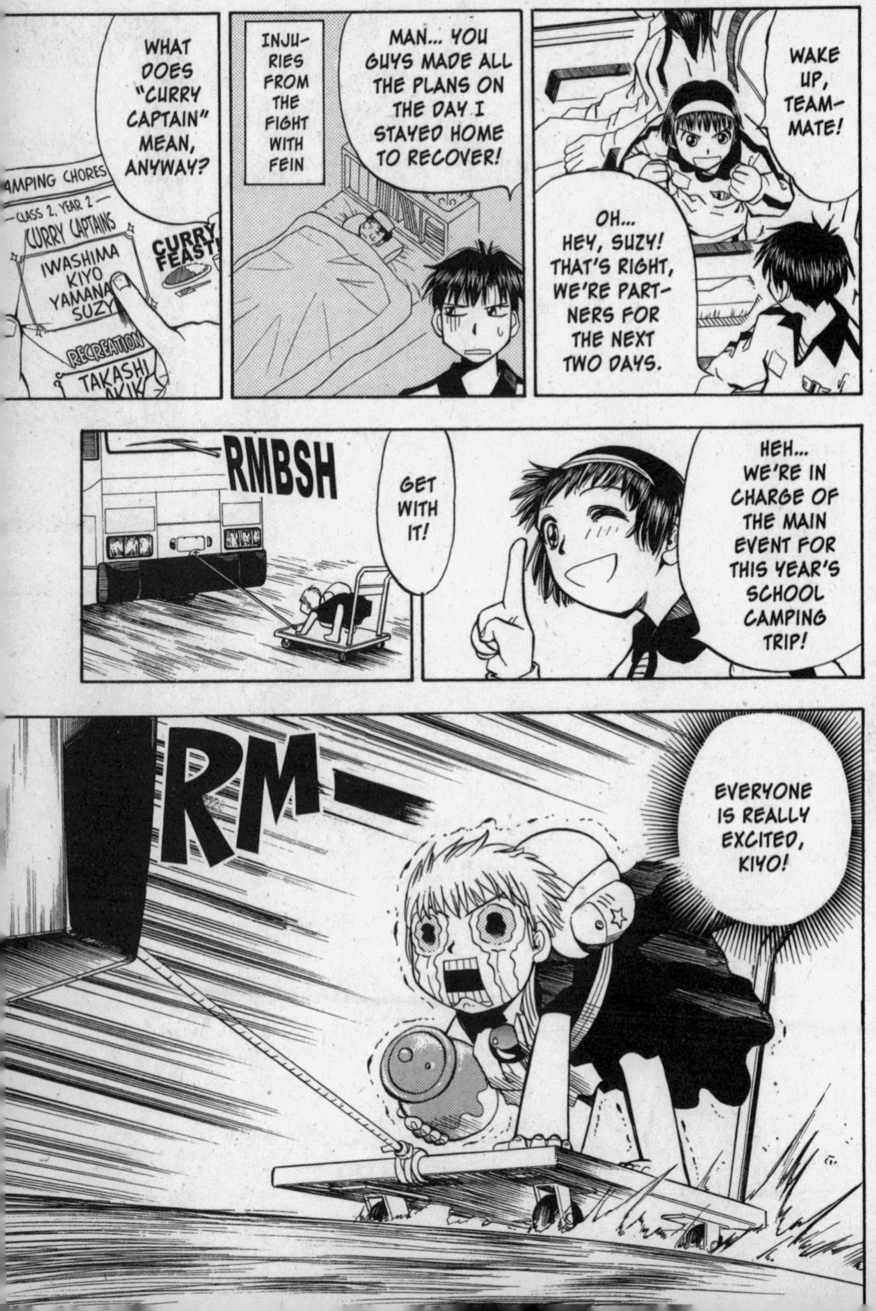
WAKE UP, TEAM-MATE!
OH... HEY, SUZY! THAT'S RIGHT, WE'RE PART-NERS FOR THE NEXT TWO DAYS.
MAN... YOU GUYS MADE ALL THE PLANS ON THE DAY I STAYED HOME TO RECOVER!
INJU-RIES FROM THE FIGHT WITH FEIN
WHAT DOES "CURRY CAPTAIN" MEAN, ANYWAY?
AMPING CHORES
CLASS 2, YEAR 2
CURRY CAPTAINS
IWASHIMA KIYO
YAMANA SUZY
CURRY FEAST!
RECREATION
TAKASHI
HEH... WE'RE IN CHARGE OF THE MAIN EVENT FOR THIS YEAR'S SCHOOL CAMPING TRIP!
GET WITH IT!
RMBSH
EVERYONE IS REALLY EXCITED, KIYO!
RM—

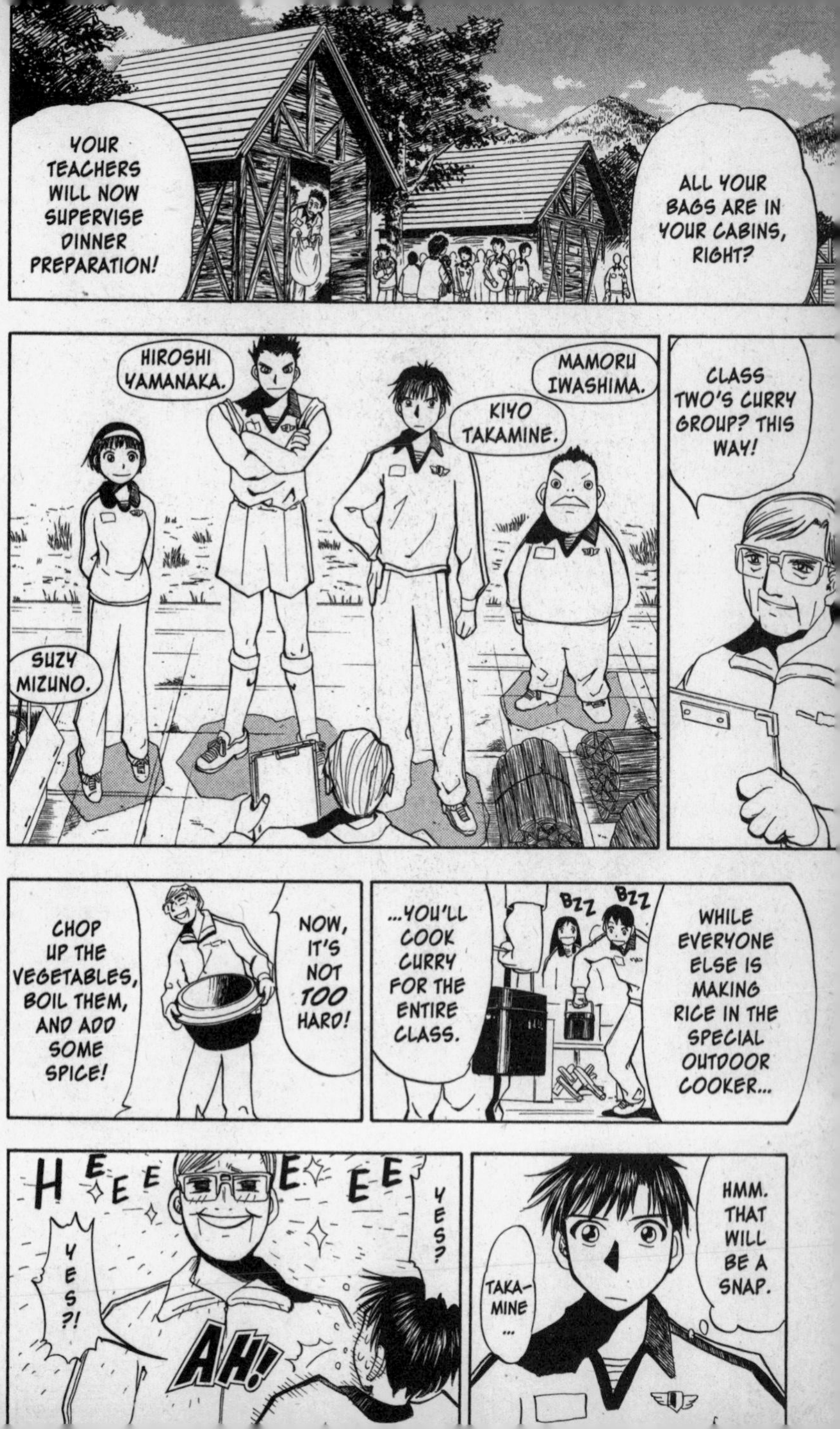

ALL YOUR BAGS ARE IN YOUR CABINS, RIGHT?
YOUR TEACHERS WILL NOW SUPERVISE DINNER PREPARATION!
CLASS TWO'S CURRY GROUP? THIS WAY!
MAMORU IWASHIMA.
KIYO TAKAMINE.
HIROSHI YAMANAKA.
SUZY MIZUNO.
WHILE EVERYONE ELSE IS MAKING RICE IN THE SPECIAL OUTDOOR COOKER...
BZZ
BZZ
...YOU'LL COOK CURRY FOR THE ENTIRE CLASS.
NOW, IT'S NOT *TOO* HARD!
CHOP UP THE VEGETABLES, BOIL THEM, AND ADD SOME SPICE!
HMM. THAT WILL BE A SNAP.
TAKA-MINE...
YES?
HEEEEEE
YES?!
AH!

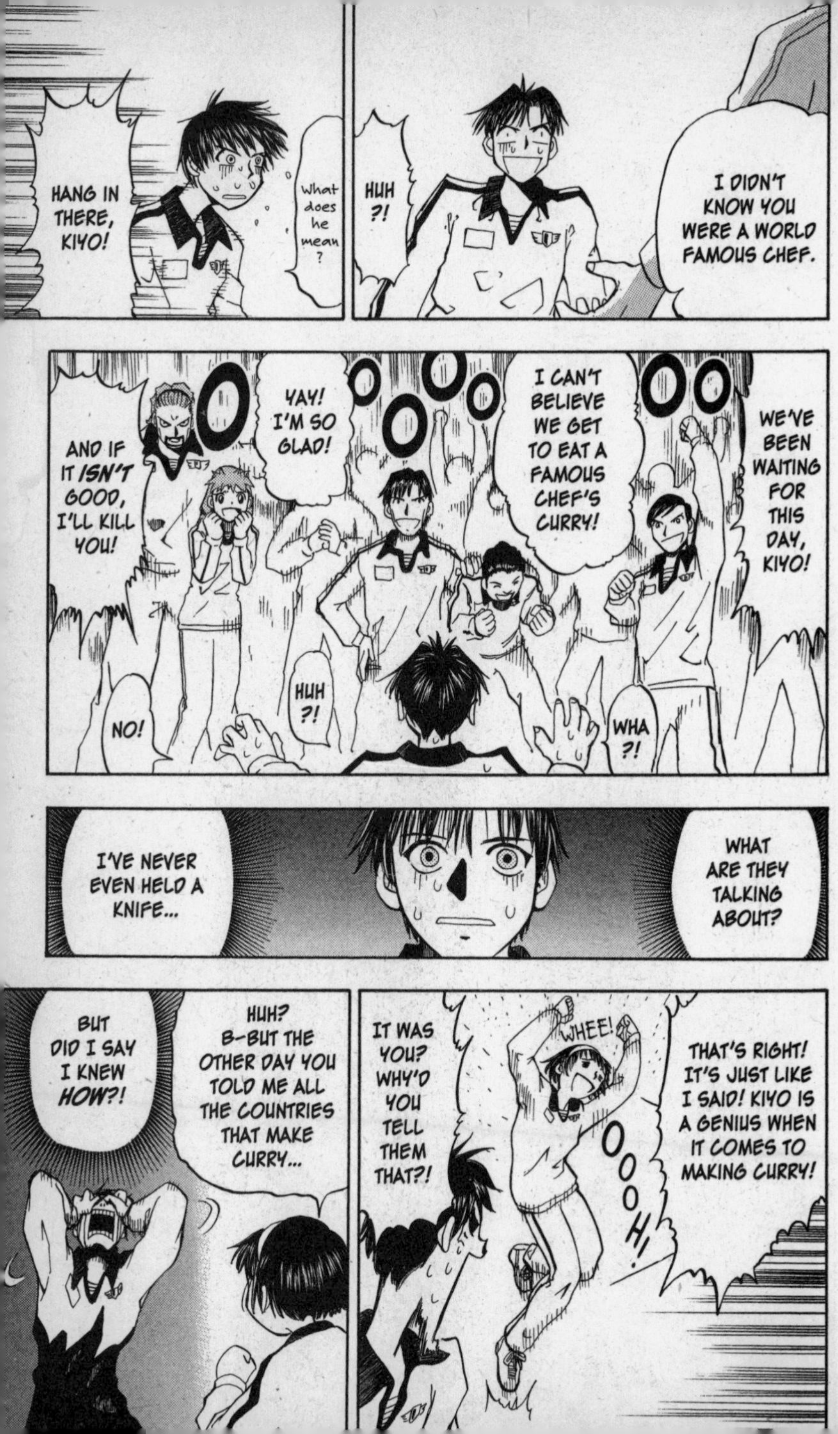
I DIDN'T KNOW YOU WERE A WORLD FAMOUS CHEF.
HUH ?!
What does he mean ?
HANG IN THERE, KIYO!
WE'VE BEEN WAITING FOR THIS DAY, KIYO!
I CAN'T BELIEVE WE GET TO EAT A FAMOUS CHEF'S CURRY!
YAY! I'M SO GLAD!
AND IF IT ISN'T GOOD, I'LL KILL YOU!
WHA ?!
HUH ?!
NO!
WHAT ARE THEY TALKING ABOUT?
I'VE NEVER EVEN HELD A KNIFE...
THAT'S RIGHT! IT'S JUST LIKE I SAID! KIYO IS A GENIUS WHEN IT COMES TO MAKING CURRY!
WHEE!
OOOH!
IT WAS YOU? WHY'D YOU TELL THEM THAT?!
HUH? B-BUT THE OTHER DAY YOU TOLD ME ALL THE COUNTRIES THAT MAKE CURRY...
BUT DID I SAY I KNEW HOW?!

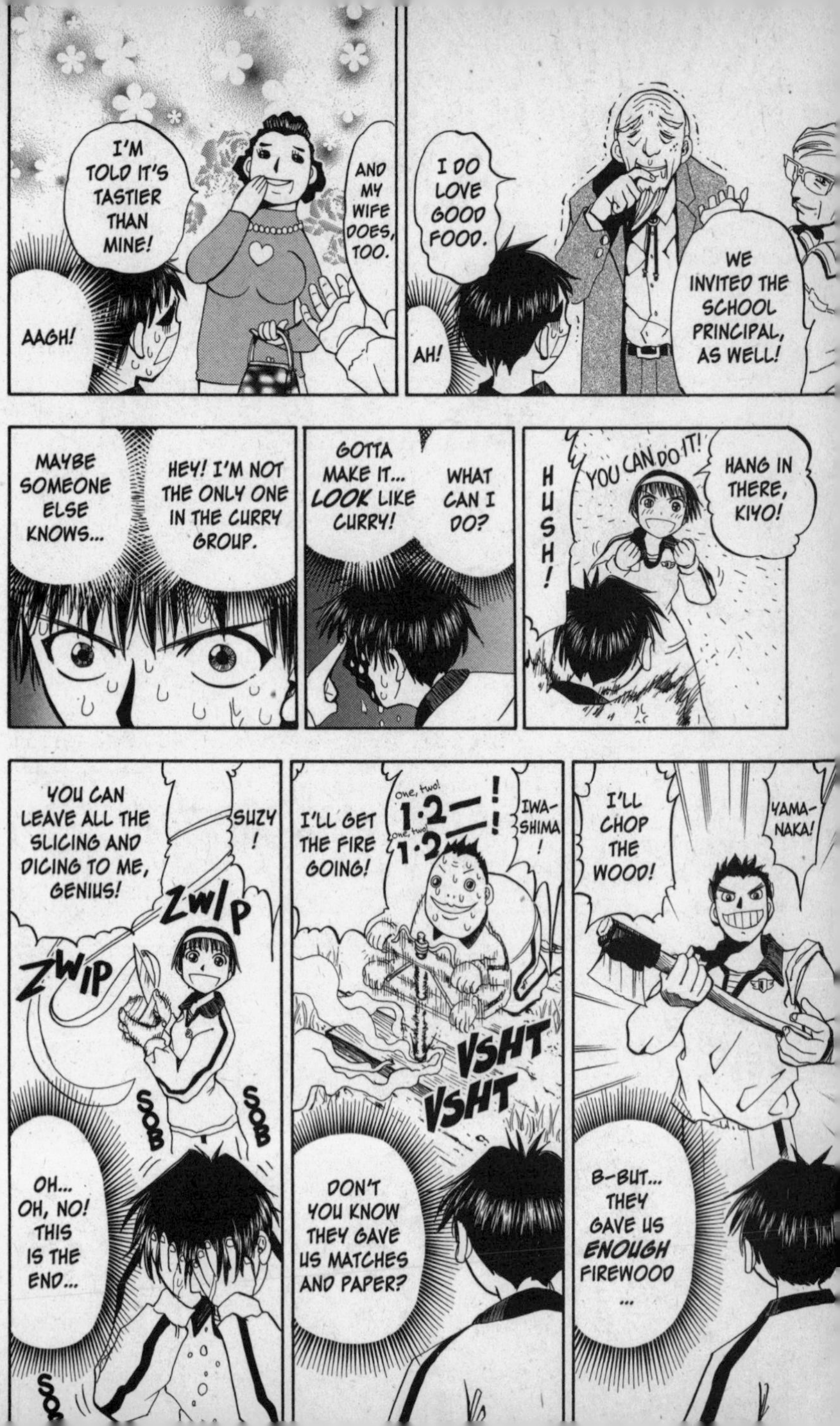
WE INVITED THE SCHOOL PRINCIPAL, AS WELL!
I DO LOVE GOOD FOOD.
AH!
AND MY WIFE DOES, TOO.
I'M TOLD IT'S TASTIER THAN MINE!
AAGH!
HANG IN THERE, KIYO!
YOU CAN DO IT!
HUSH!
WHAT CAN I DO?
GOTTA MAKE IT... LOOK LIKE CURRY!
HEY! I'M NOT THE ONLY ONE IN THE CURRY GROUP.
MAYBE SOMEONE ELSE KNOWS...
YAMANAKA!
I'LL CHOP THE WOOD!
B-BUT... THEY GAVE US ENOUGH FIREWOOD ...
IWASHIMA!
one, two!
1·2—!
one, two!
1·2—!
I'LL GET THE FIRE GOING!
VSHT
VSHT
DON'T YOU KNOW THEY GAVE US MATCHES AND PAPER?
SUZY!
YOU CAN LEAVE ALL THE SLICING AND DICING TO ME, GENIUS!
ZWIP
ZWIP
SOB
SOB
OH... OH, NO! THIS IS THE END...

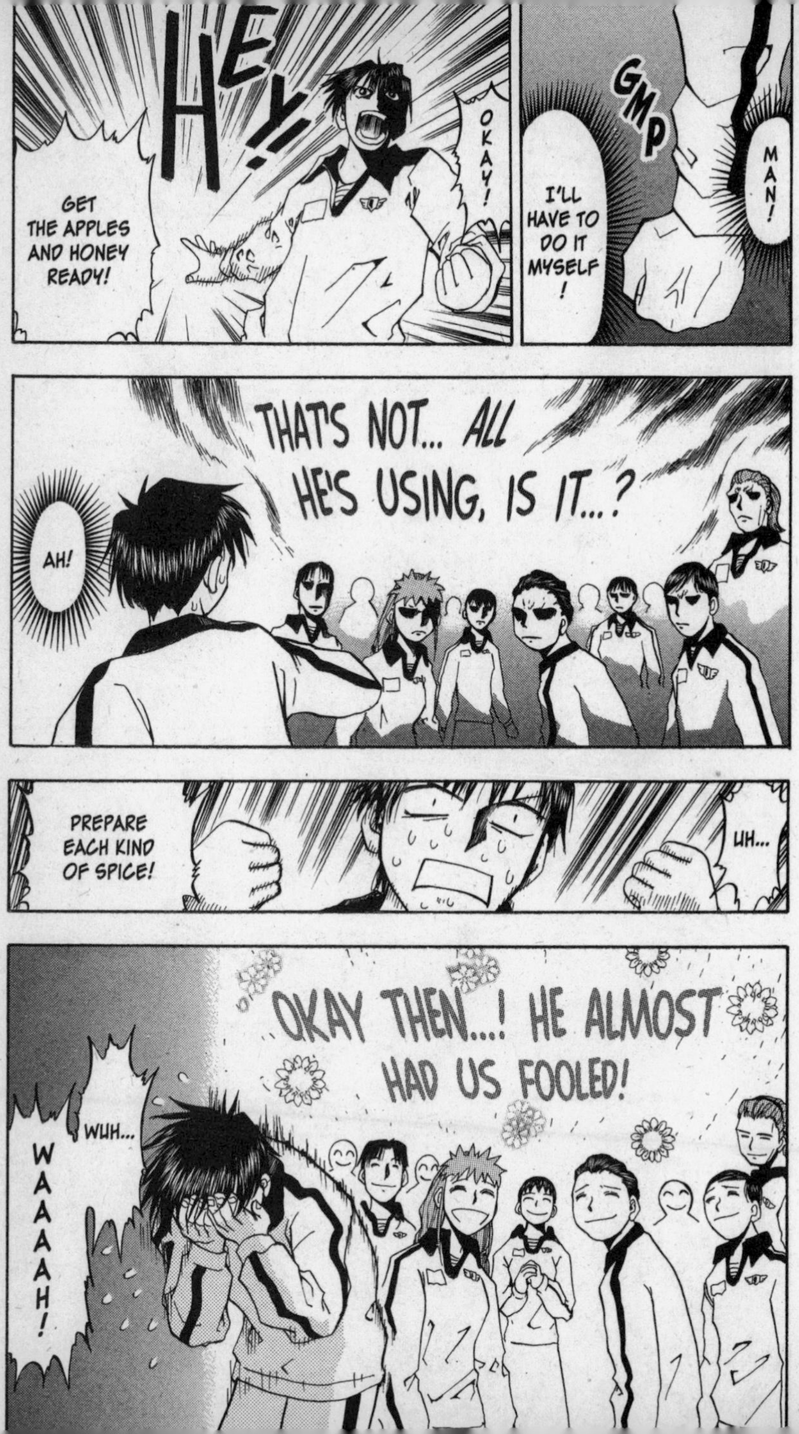
MAN!
GMP
I'LL HAVE TO DO IT MYSELF!
OKAY!
HEY!!
GET THE APPLES AND HONEY READY!
THAT'S NOT... ALL HE'S USING, IS IT...?
AH!
UH...
PREPARE EACH KIND OF SPICE!
OKAY THEN...! HE ALMOST HAD US FOOLED!
WUH...
WAAAAAH!

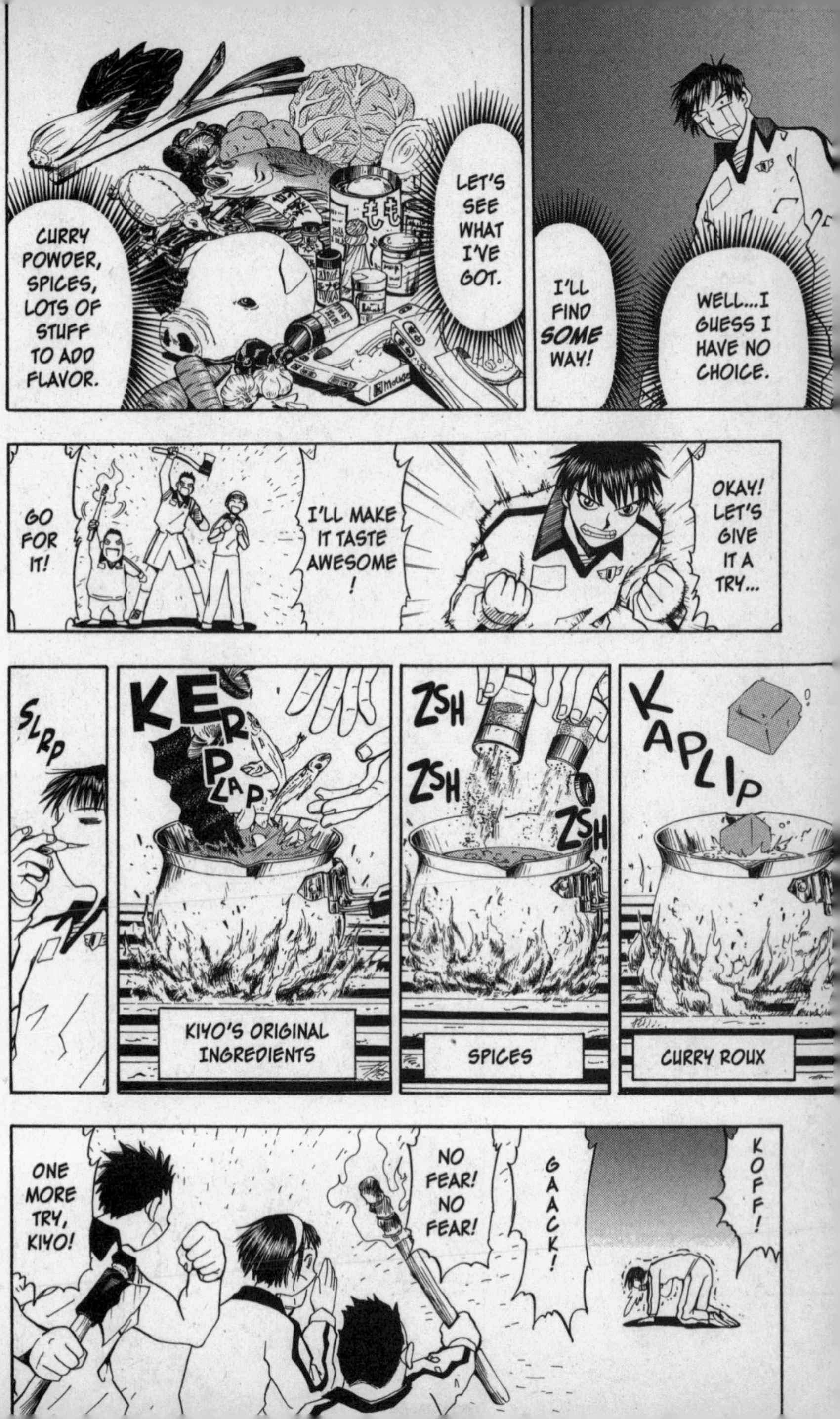
WELL...I GUESS I HAVE NO CHOICE.
I'LL FIND SOME WAY!
LET'S SEE WHAT I'VE GOT.
CURRY POWDER, SPICES, LOTS OF STUFF TO ADD FLAVOR.
OKAY! LET'S GIVE IT A TRY...
I'LL MAKE IT TASTE AWESOME!
GO FOR IT!
KAPLIP
CURRY ROUX
ZSH
ZSH
ZSH
SPICES
KERPLAP
KIYO'S ORIGINAL INGREDIENTS
SLRP
KOFF!
GAACK!
NO FEAR! NO FEAR!
ONE MORE TRY, KIYO!

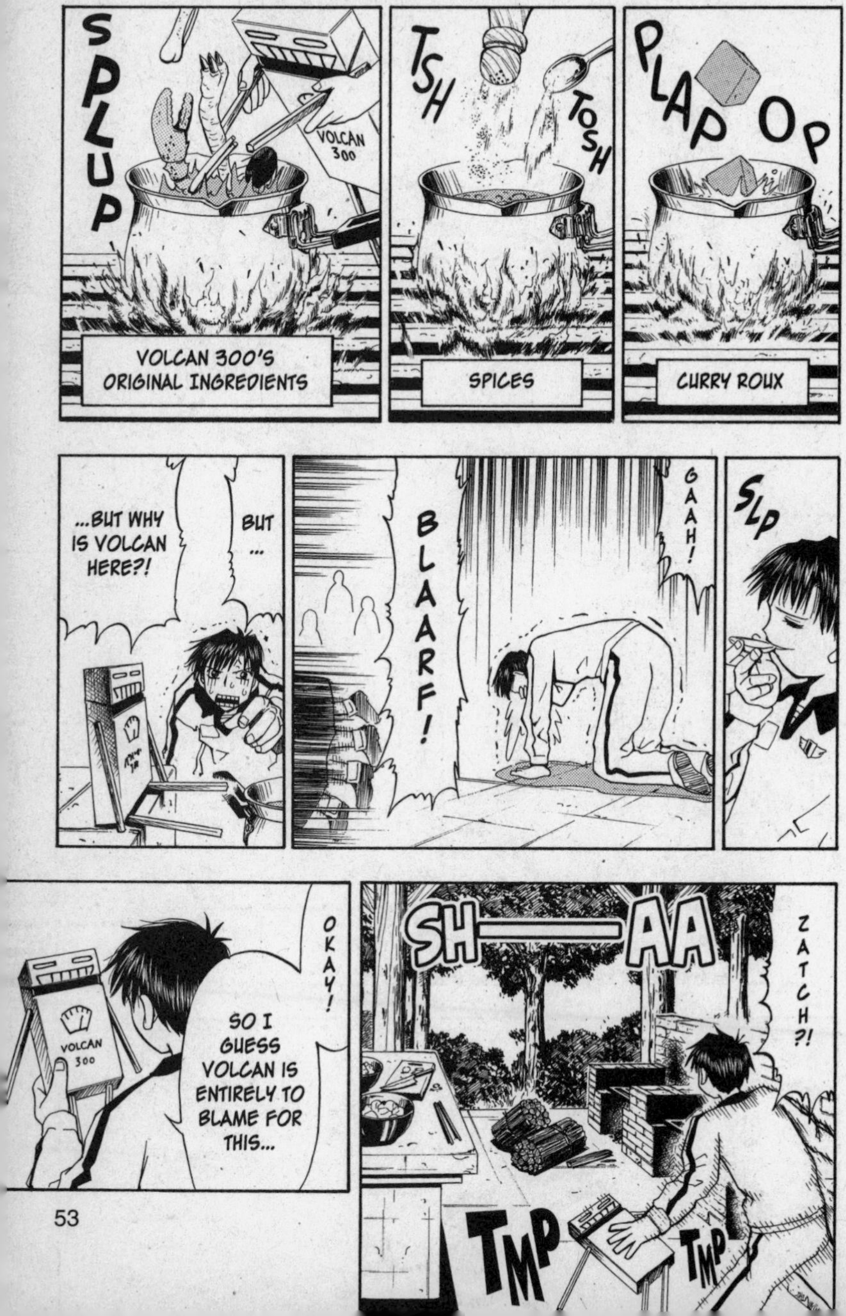
PLAP
OP
CURRY ROUX
TSH
TOSH
SPICES
SPLUP
VOLCAN 300
VOLCAN 300'S ORIGINAL INGREDIENTS
SLP
GAAH!
BLAARF!
BUT ...
...BUT WHY IS VOLCAN HERE?!
ZATCH?!
SH—AA
TMP
TMP
OKAY!
SO I GUESS VOLCAN IS ENTIRELY TO BLAME FOR THIS...
VOLCAN 300

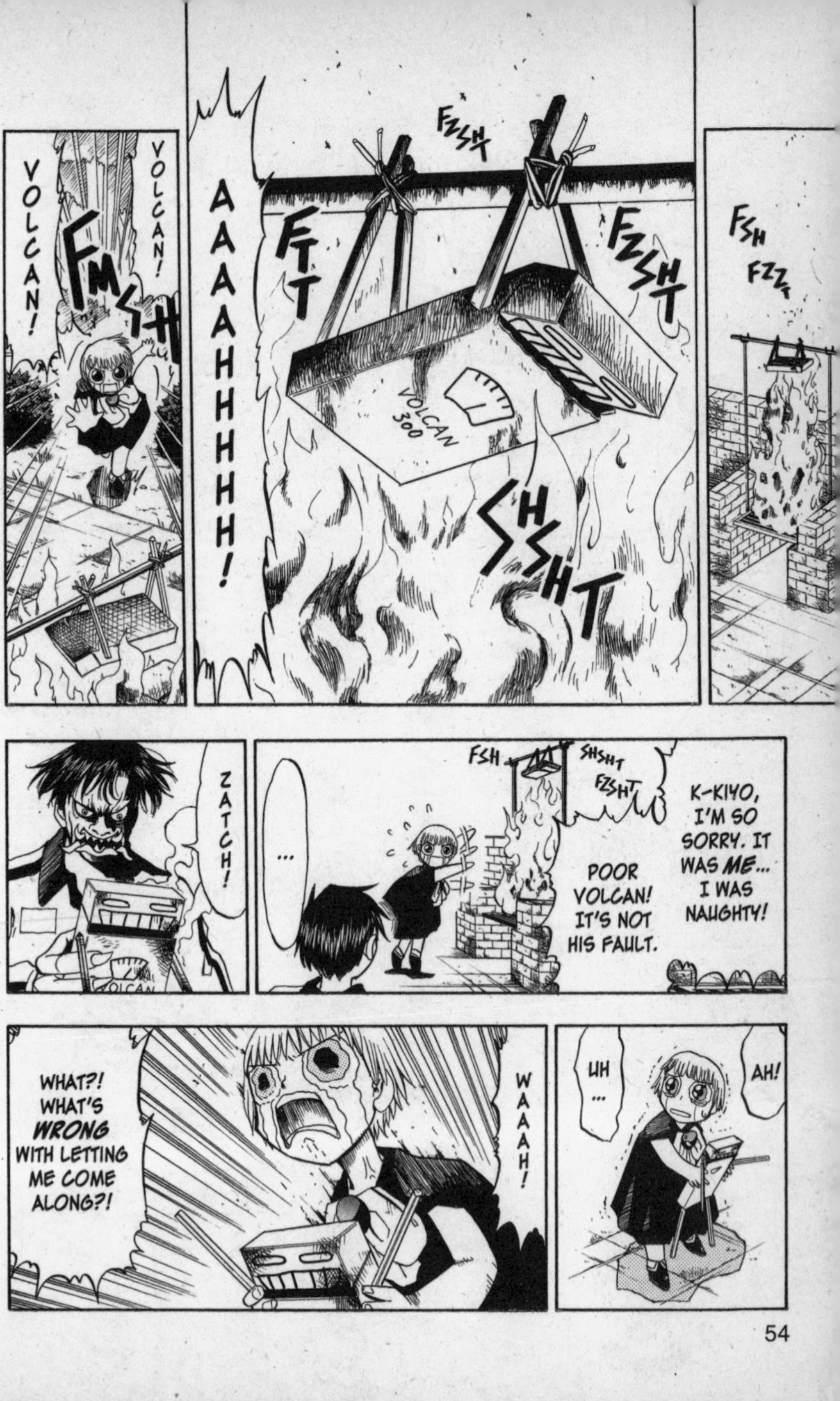
FSH
FZZ
FZSHT
FZSHT
AAAAAHHHHHHH!
FTT
VOLCAN 300
SHSHT
VOLCAN!
VOLCAN!
FMSHH
FSH
SHSHT
FZSHT
K-KIYO, I'M SO SORRY. IT WAS ME... I WAS NAUGHTY!
POOR VOLCAN! IT'S NOT HIS FAULT.
...
ZATCH!
AH!
UH...
WAAAAH!
WHAT?! WHAT'S WRONG WITH LETTING ME COME ALONG?!

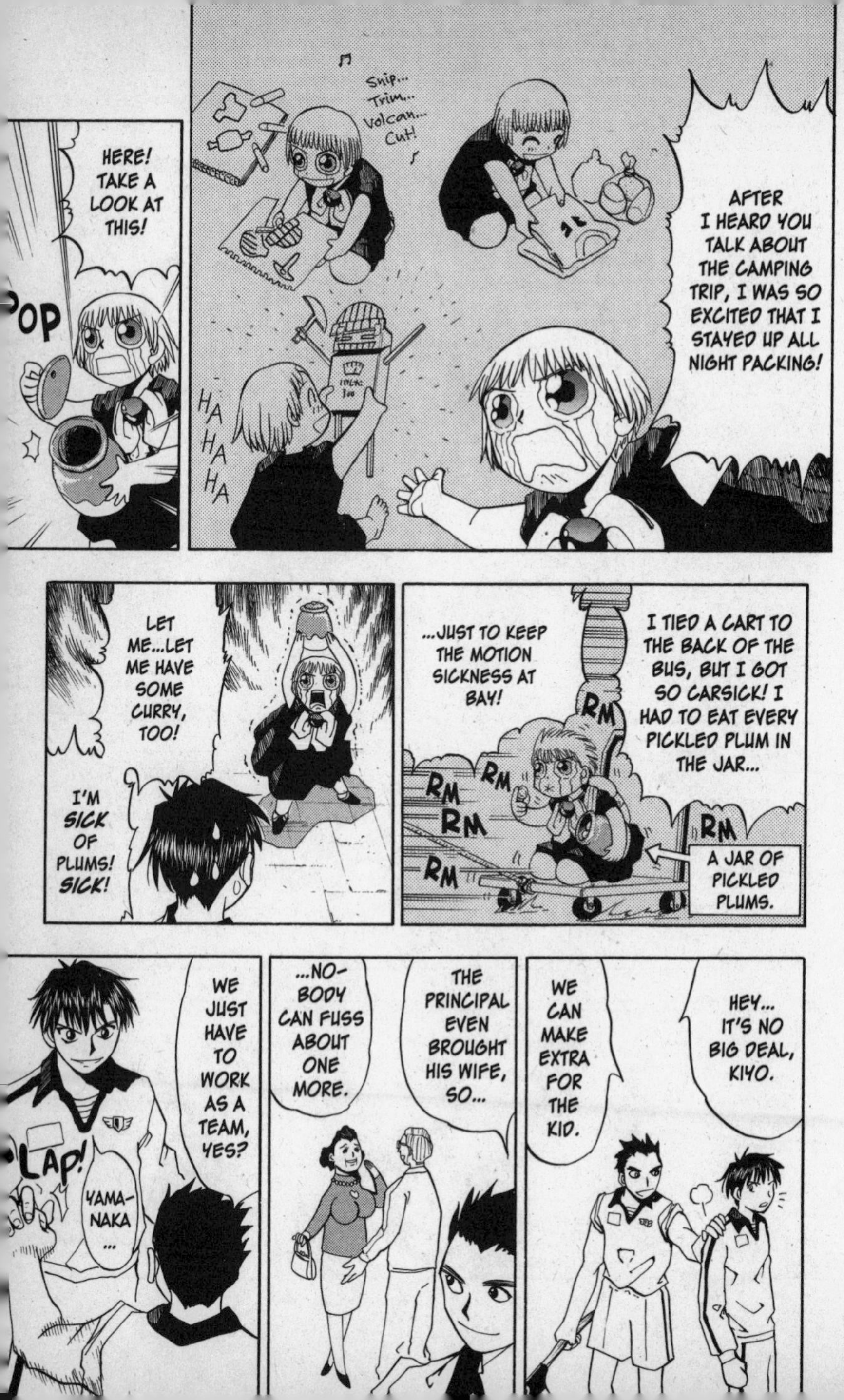
AFTER I HEARD YOU TALK ABOUT THE CAMPING TRIP, I WAS SO EXCITED THAT I STAYED UP ALL NIGHT PACKING!
Snip... Trim... Volcan... Cut!
HAHAHAHA
HERE! TAKE A LOOK AT THIS!
POP
I TIED A CART TO THE BACK OF THE BUS, BUT I GOT SO CARSICK! I HAD TO EAT EVERY PICKLED PLUM IN THE JAR...
...JUST TO KEEP THE MOTION SICKNESS AT BAY!
RM
RM
RM
RM
RM
A JAR OF PICKLED PLUMS.
LET ME...LET ME HAVE SOME CURRY, TOO!
I'M SICK OF PLUMS! SICK!
HEY... IT'S NO BIG DEAL, KIYO.
WE CAN MAKE EXTRA FOR THE KID.
THE PRINCIPAL EVEN BROUGHT HIS WIFE, SO...
...NOBODY CAN FUSS ABOUT ONE MORE.
WE JUST HAVE TO WORK AS A TEAM, YES?
LAP!
YAMANAKA...

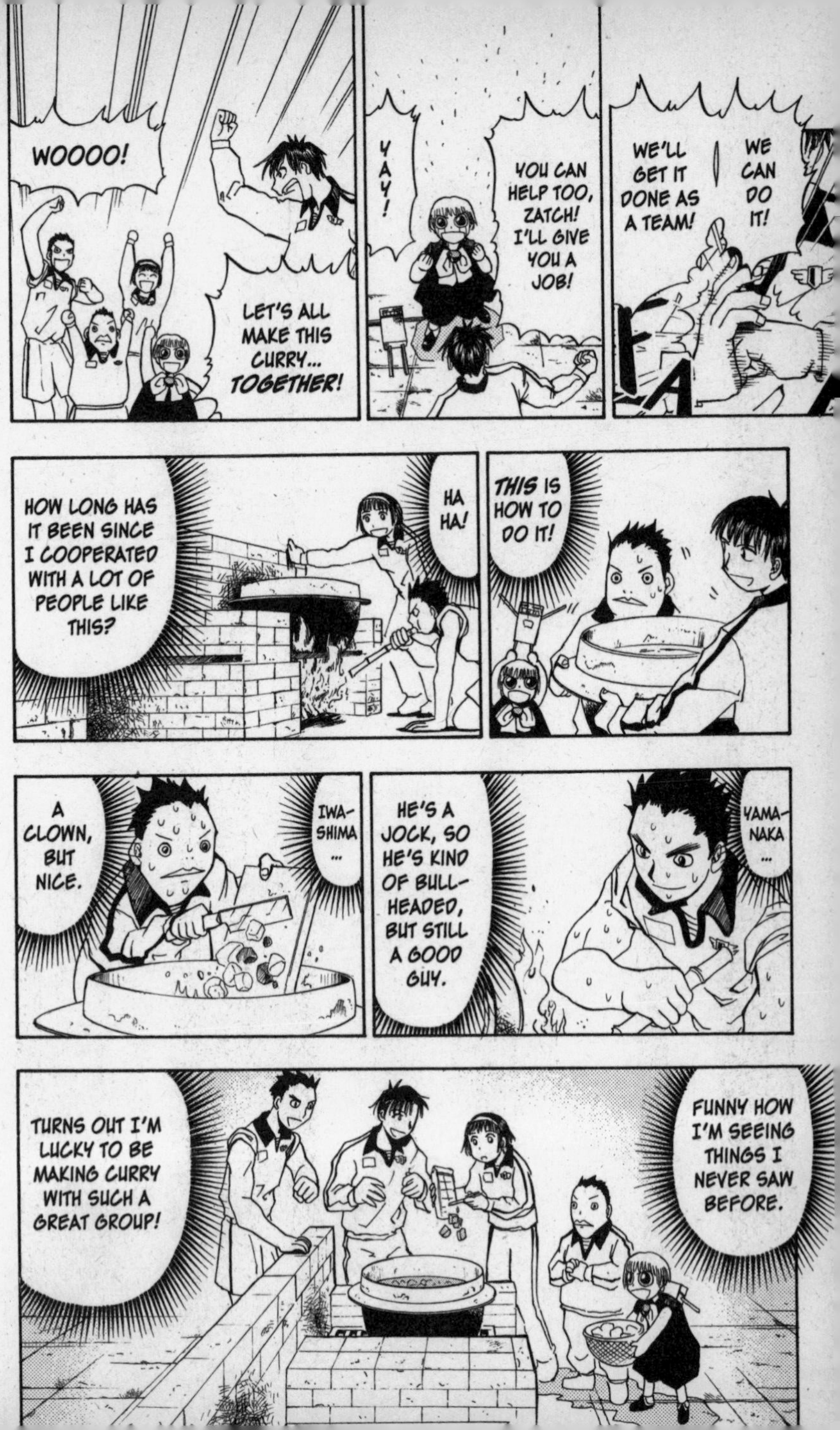
WE CAN DO IT!
WE'LL GET IT DONE AS A TEAM!
YOU CAN HELP TOO, ZATCH! I'LL GIVE YOU A JOB!
YAY!
LET'S ALL MAKE THIS CURRY... TOGETHER!
WOOOO!
THIS IS HOW TO DO IT!
HA HA!
HOW LONG HAS IT BEEN SINCE I COOPERATED WITH A LOT OF PEOPLE LIKE THIS?
YAMA-NAKA...
HE'S A JOCK, SO HE'S KIND OF BULL-HEADED, BUT STILL A GOOD GUY.
IWA-SHIMA...
A CLOWN, BUT NICE.
FUNNY HOW I'M SEEING THINGS I NEVER SAW BEFORE.
TURNS OUT I'M LUCKY TO BE MAKING CURRY WITH SUCH A GREAT GROUP!

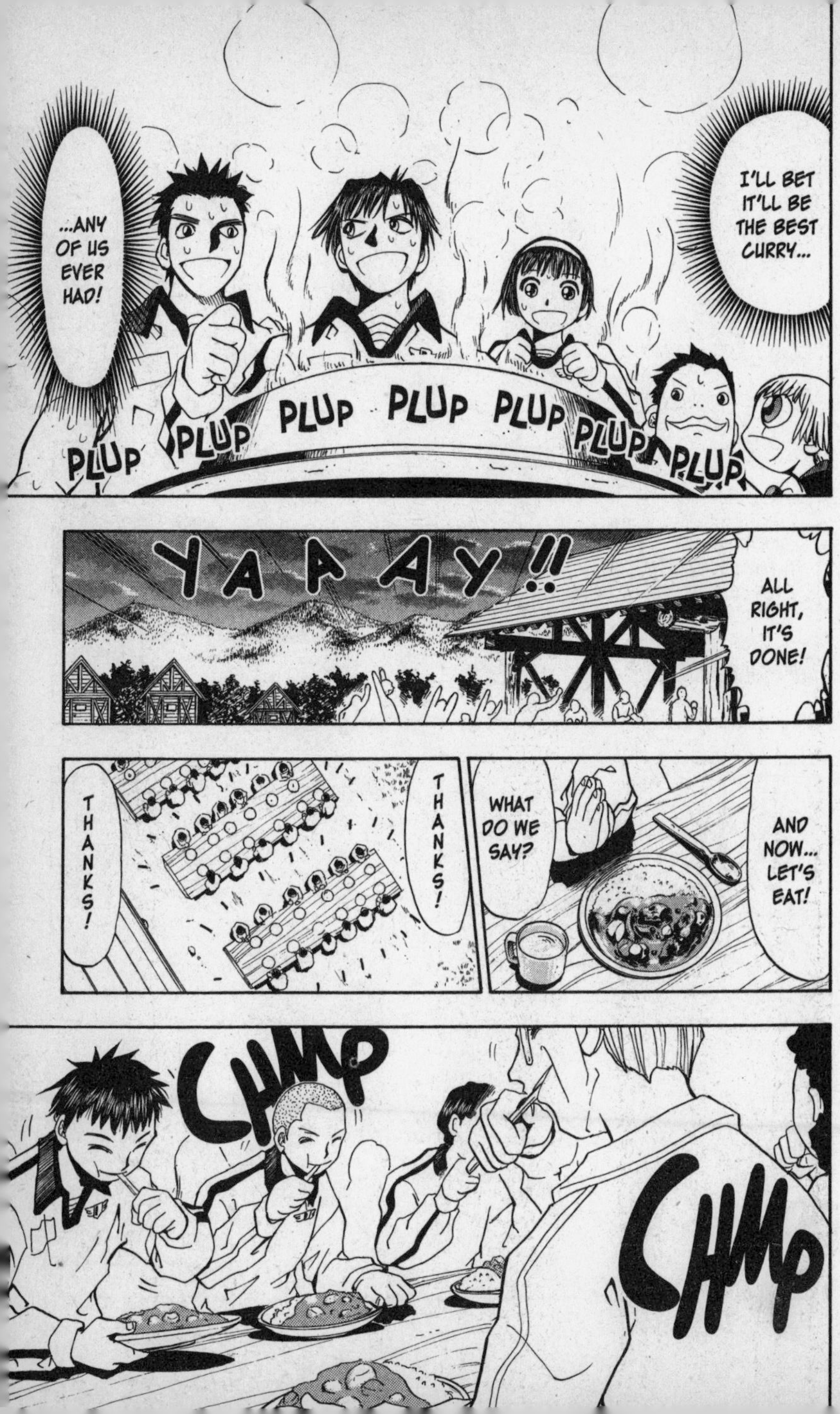
I'LL BET IT'LL BE THE BEST CURRY...
...ANY OF US EVER HAD!
PLUP PLUP PLUP PLUP PLUP PLUP PLUP
ALL RIGHT, IT'S DONE!
YAAAY!!
AND NOW... LET'S EAT!
WHAT DO WE SAY?
THANKS!
THANKS!
CHMP
CHMP

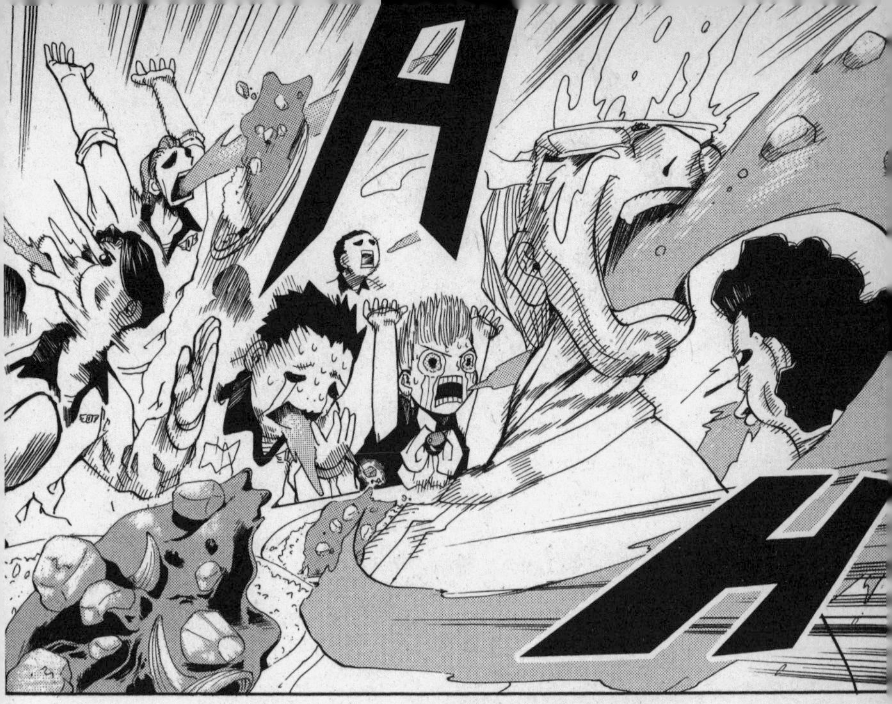
AH

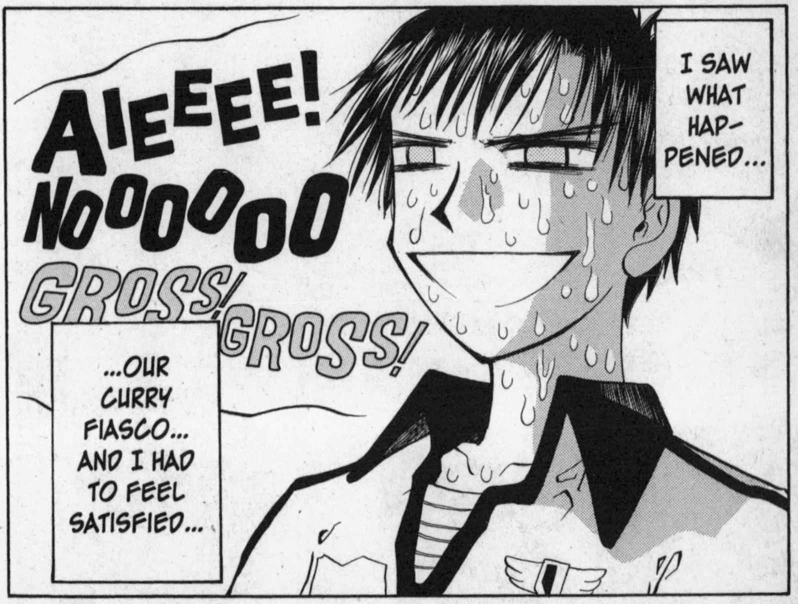
I SAW WHAT HAP-PENED...
AIEEEEE! NOOOOOOO
GROSS! GROSS!
...OUR CURRY FIASCO... AND I HAD TO FEEL SATISFIED...

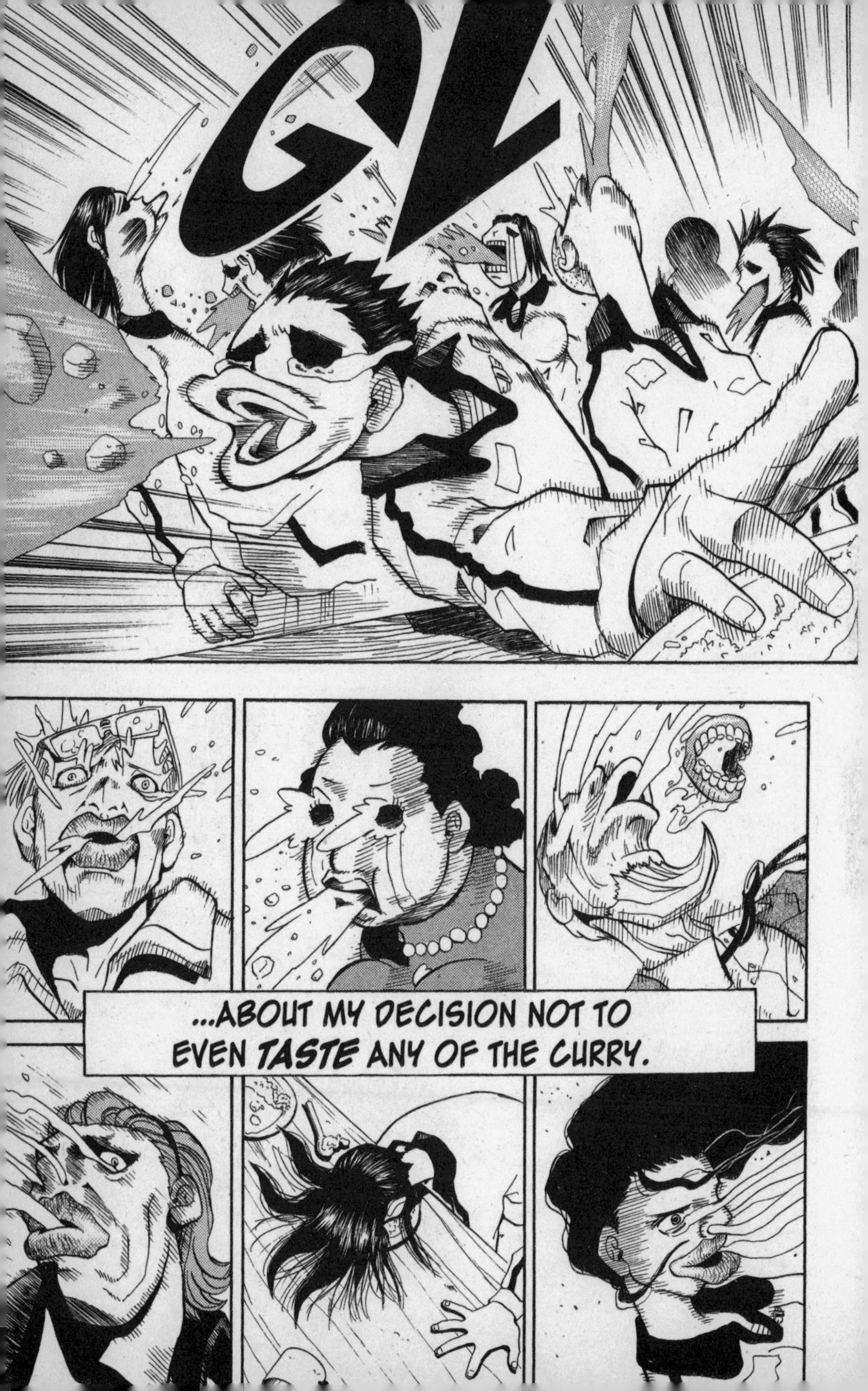
GL
...ABOUT MY DECISION NOT TO EVEN TASTE ANY OF THE CURRY.

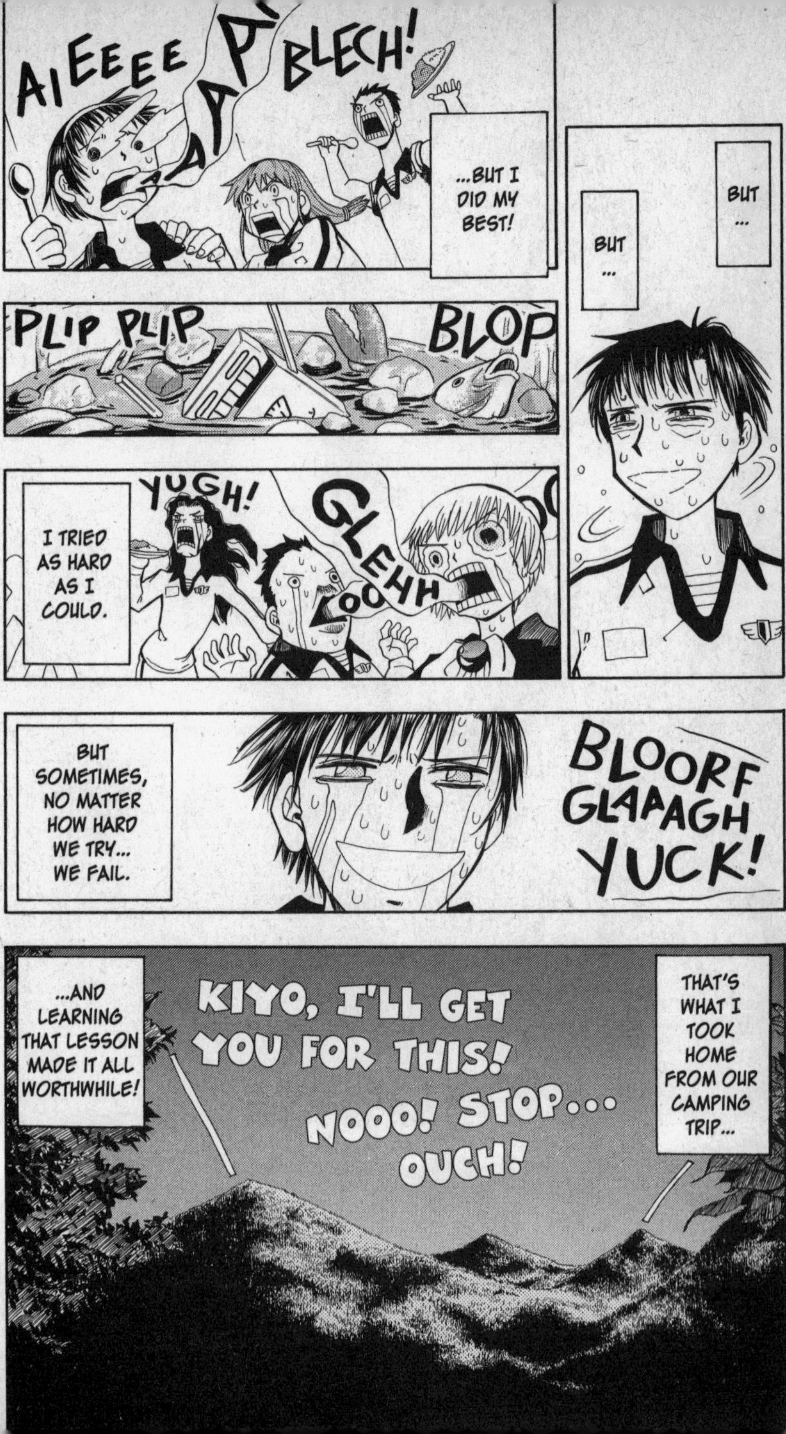
...BUT I DID MY BEST!
BLECH!
AAA
AIEEEEE
BUT ...
BUT ...
BLOP
PLIP PLIP
GLEHH
OOHH
YUGH!
I TRIED AS HARD AS I COULD.
BLOORF GLAAAGH YUCK!
BUT SOMETIMES, NO MATTER HOW HARD WE TRY... WE FAIL.
THAT'S WHAT I TOOK HOME FROM OUR CAMPING TRIP...
KIYO, I'LL GET YOU FOR THIS!
NOOO! STOP...
OUCH!
...AND LEARNING THAT LESSON MADE IT ALL WORTHWHILE!

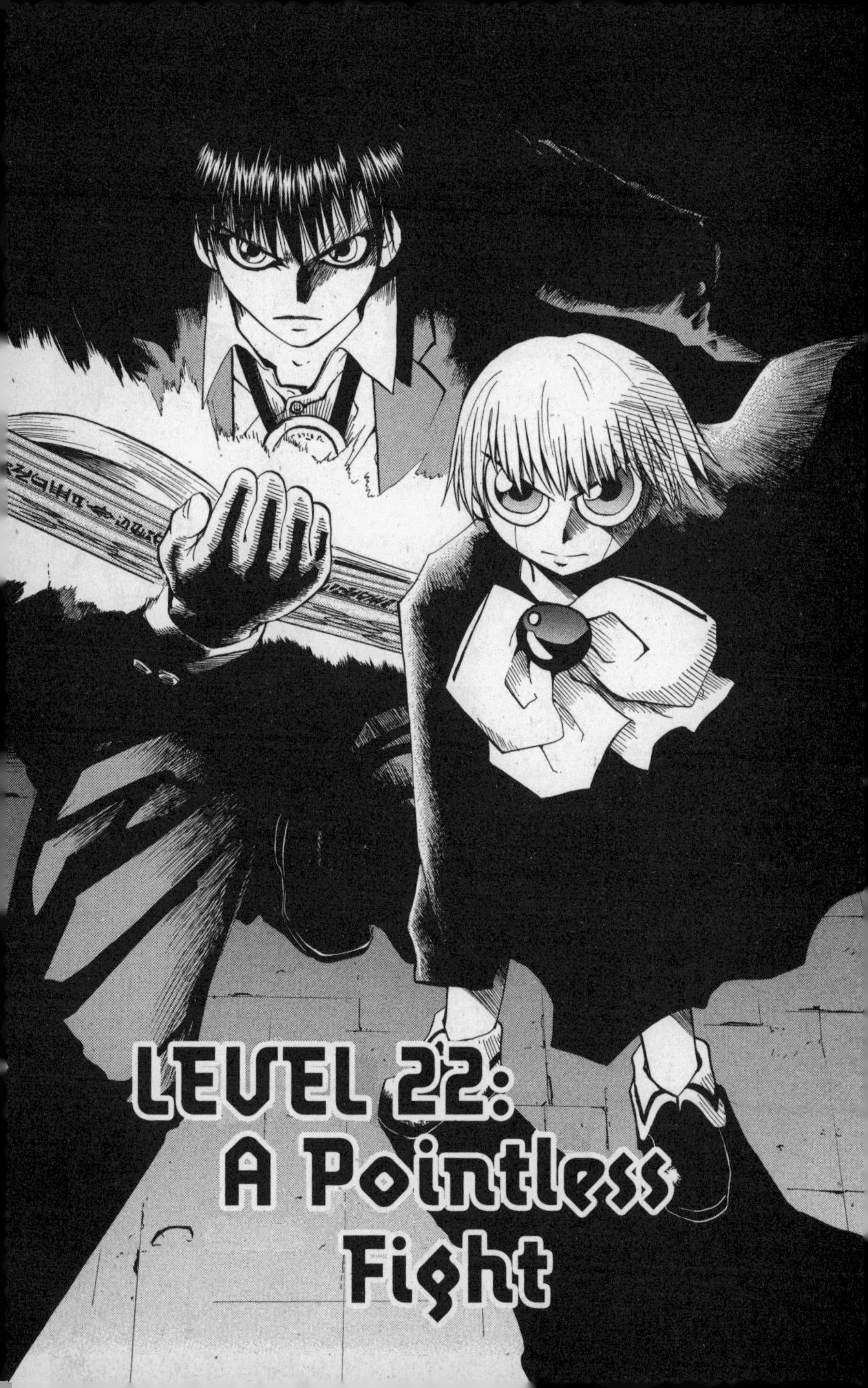
LEVEL 22:
A Pointless
Fight

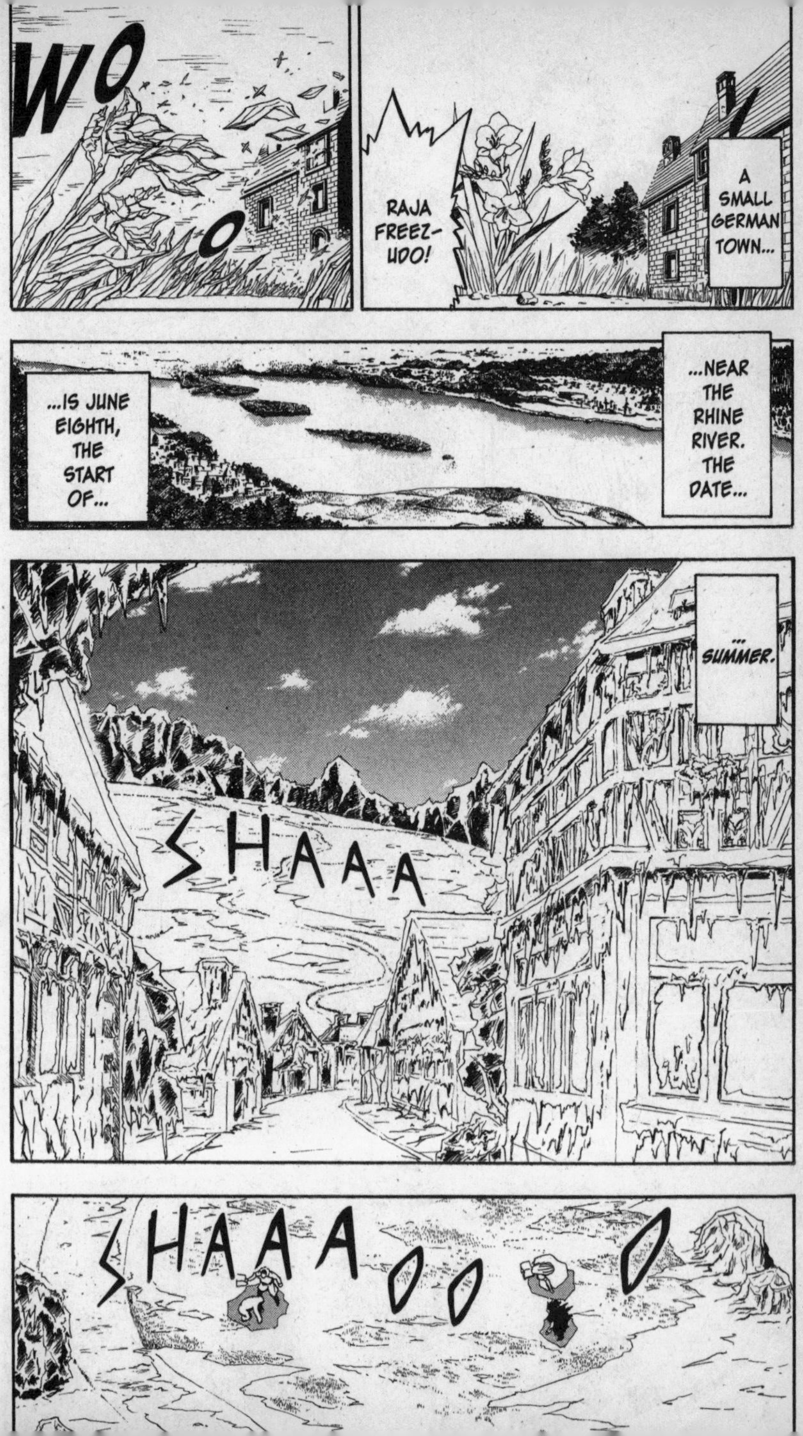
A SMALL GERMAN TOWN...
RAJA FREEZ-UDO!
WO O
...NEAR THE RHINE RIVER. THE DATE...
...IS JUNE EIGHTH, THE START OF...
... SUMMER.
SHAAA
SHAAAOOO

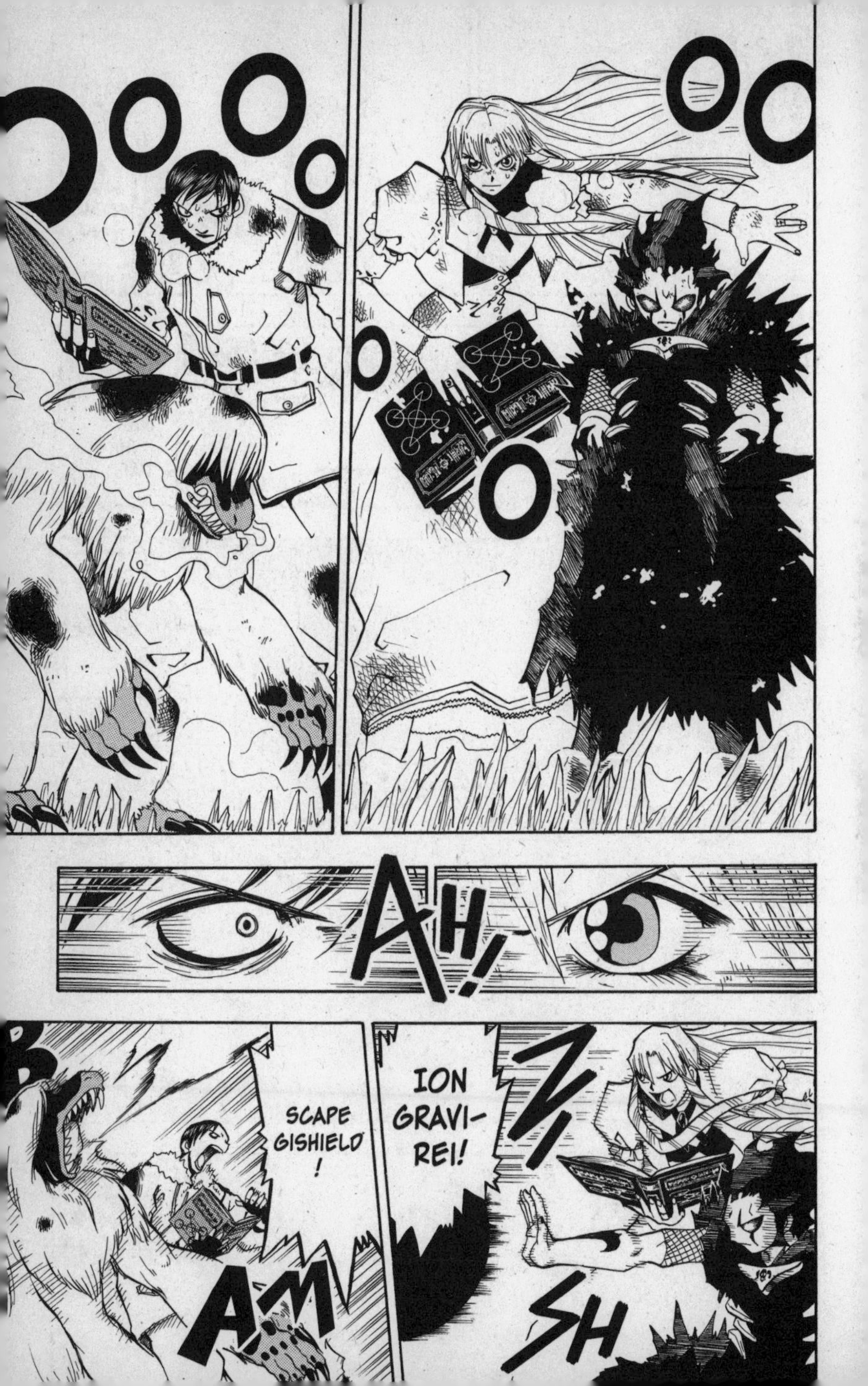
AH!
ION
GRAVI-
REI!
SCAPE
GISHIELD
!

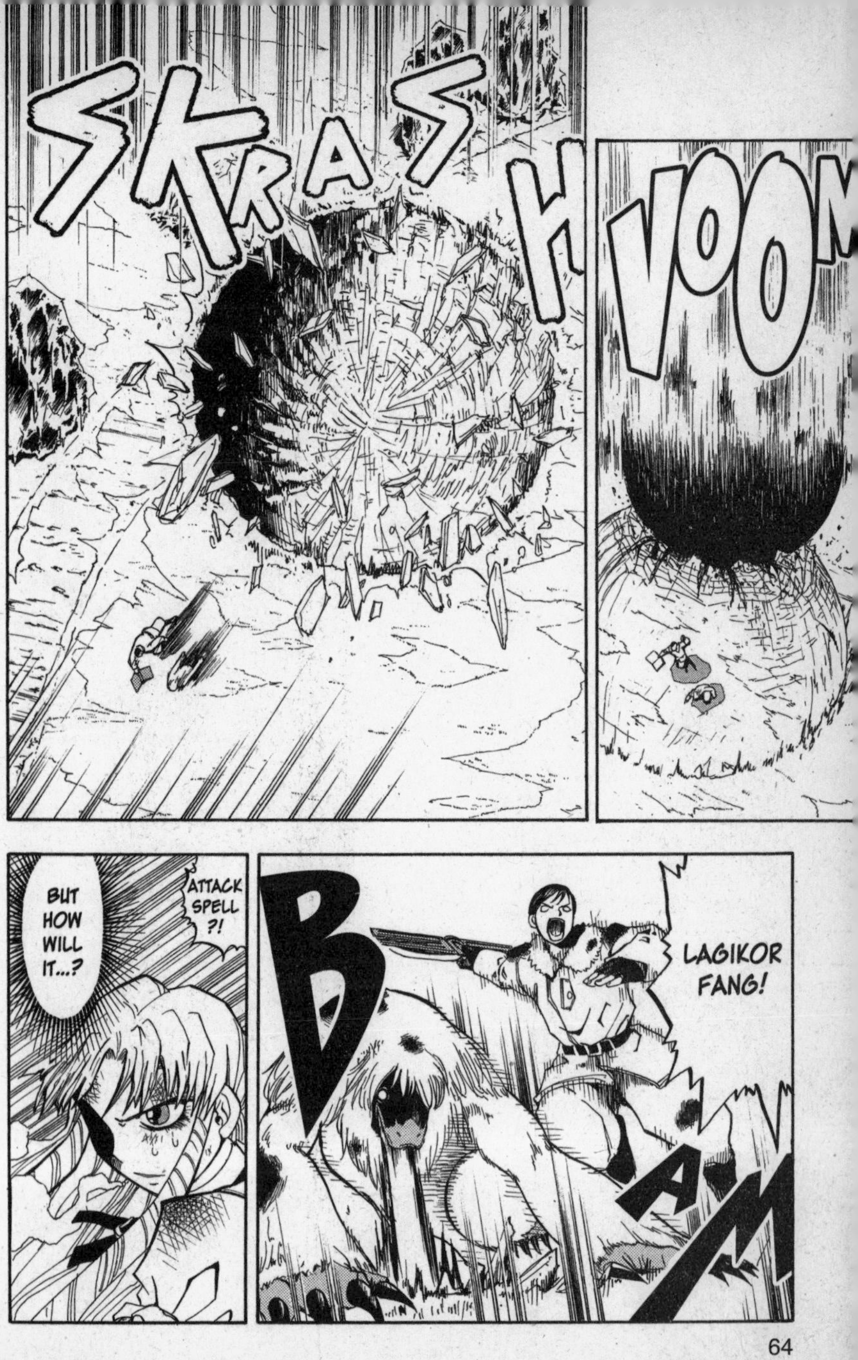
VOOM
SKRASH
LAGIKOR FANG!
BAM
ATTACK SPELL ?!
BUT HOW WILL IT...?

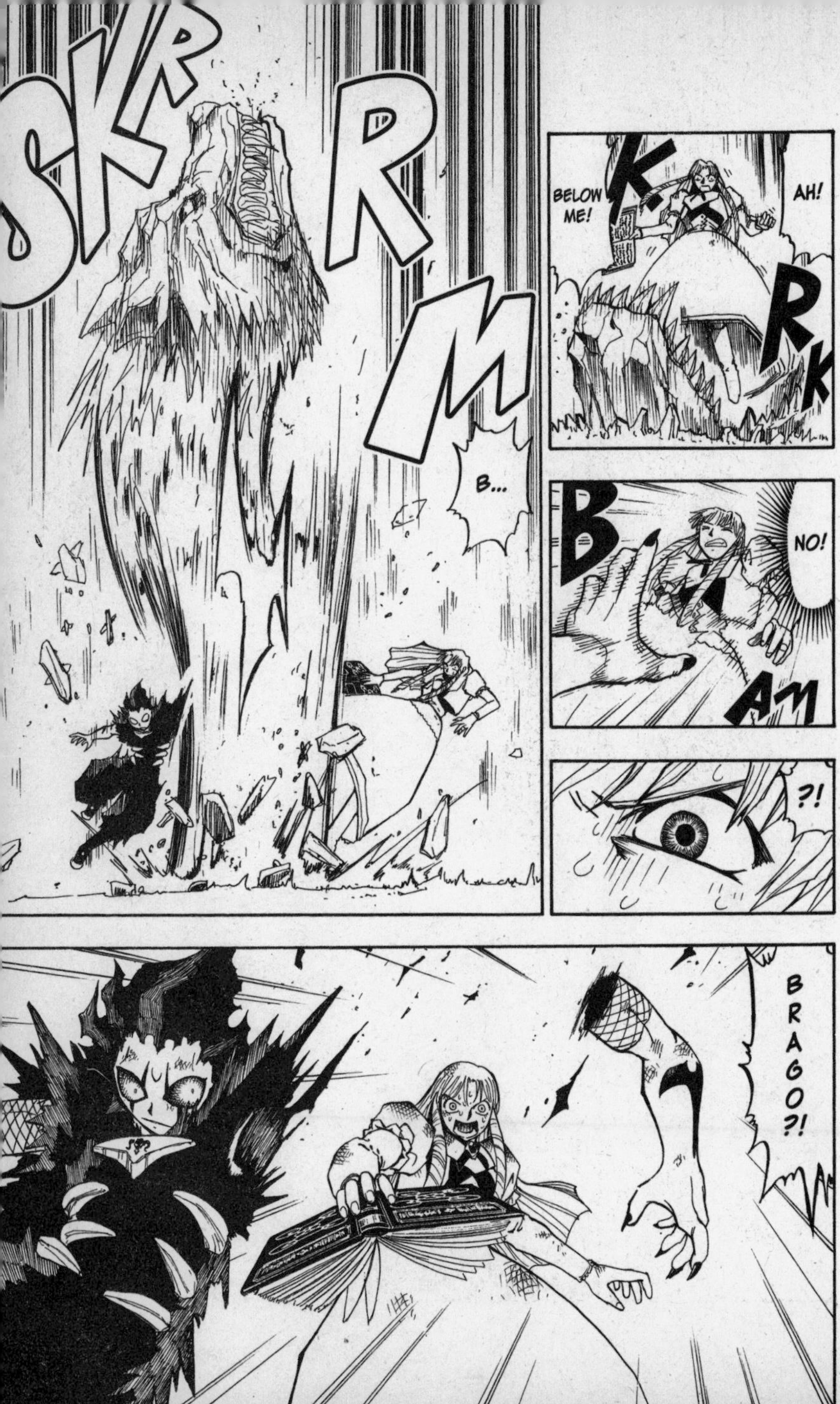
AH!
BELOW ME!
K
RK
RK
NO!
B
AM
?!
SKR
R
M
B...
BRAGO?!

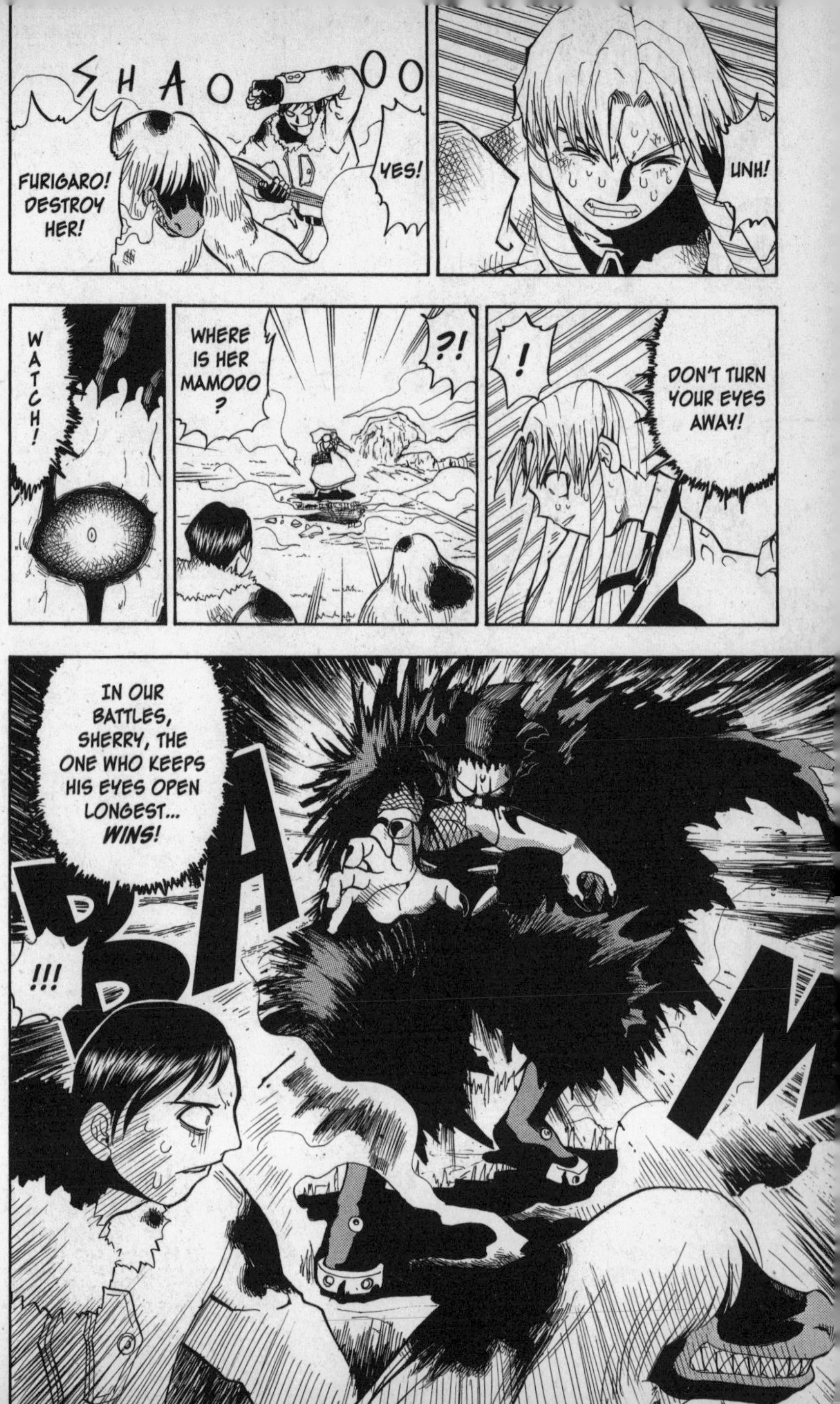
UNH!
SHAOOO
FURIGARO! DESTROY HER!
YES!
!
DON'T TURN YOUR EYES AWAY!
?!
WHERE IS HER MAMODO ?
WATCH!
IN OUR BATTLES, SHERRY, THE ONE WHO KEEPS HIS EYES OPEN LONGEST... WINS!
BAM
!!!

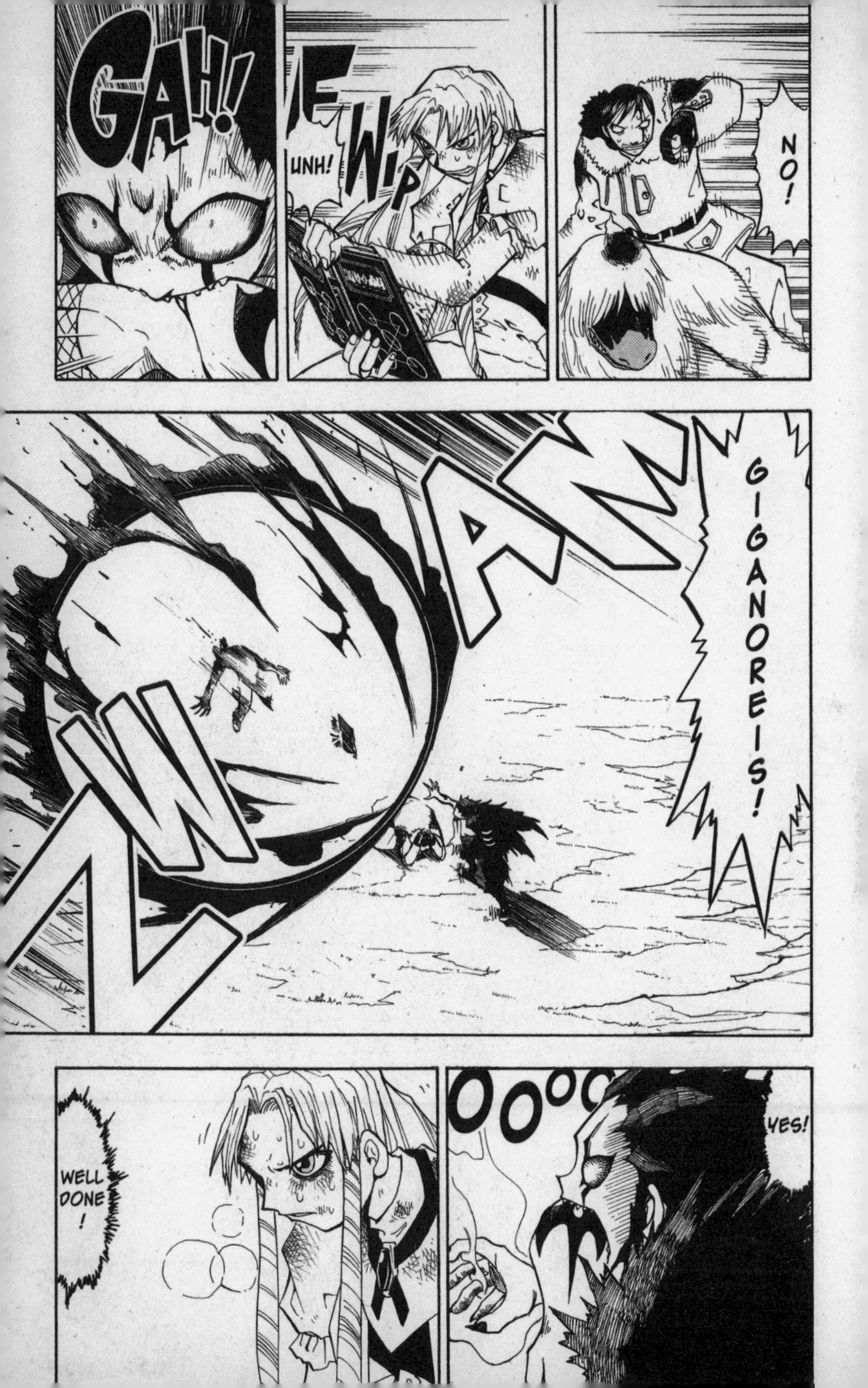

NO!
UNH!
FWIP
GAH!!
GIGANOREIS!
OOOO
YES!
WELL DONE!

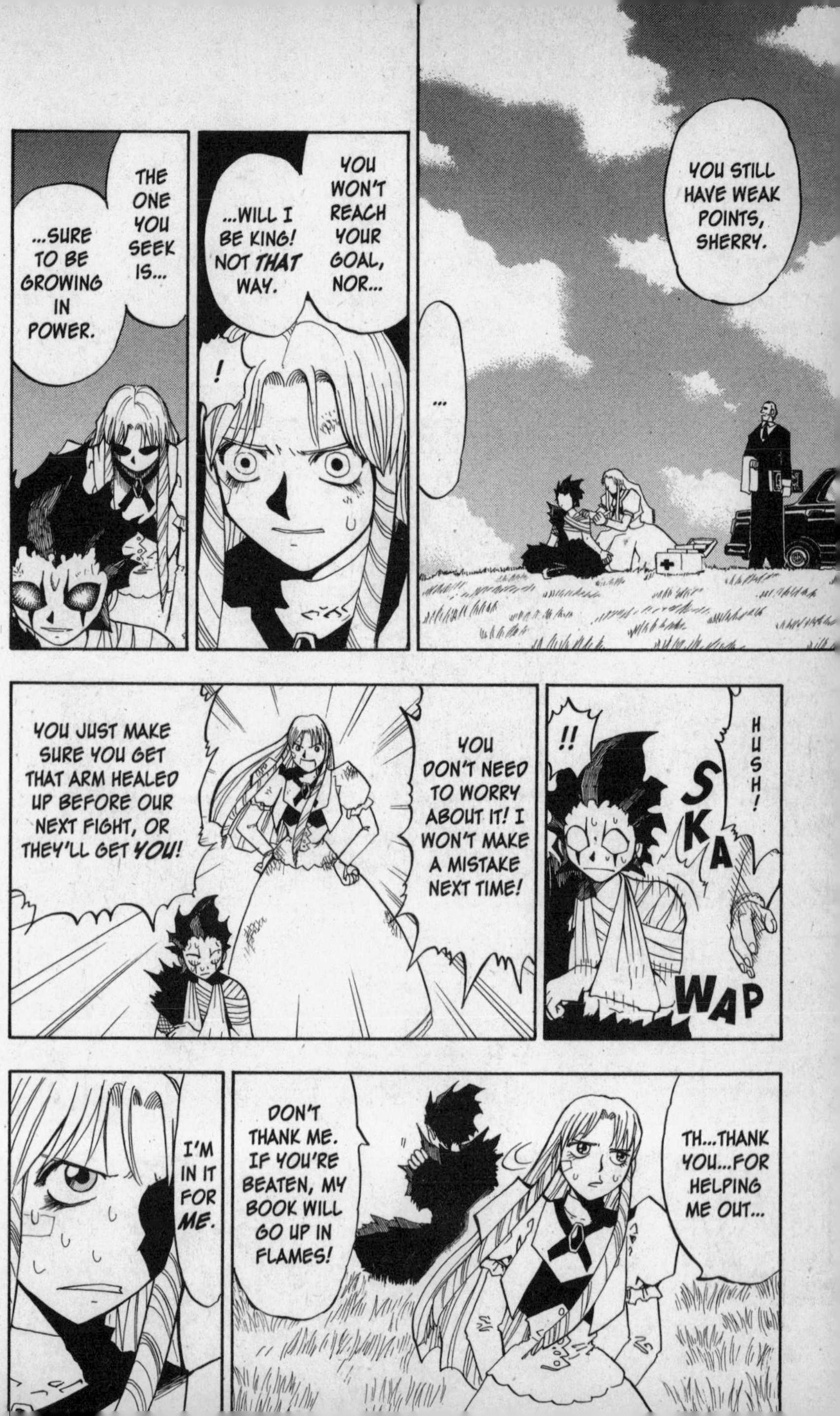
YOU STILL HAVE WEAK POINTS, SHERRY.
...
YOU WON'T REACH YOUR GOAL, NOR...
...WILL I BE KING! NOT THAT WAY.
!
THE ONE YOU SEEK IS...
...SURE TO BE GROWING IN POWER.
HUSH!
!!
SKA
WAP
YOU DON'T NEED TO WORRY ABOUT IT! I WON'T MAKE A MISTAKE NEXT TIME!
YOU JUST MAKE SURE YOU GET THAT ARM HEALED UP BEFORE OUR NEXT FIGHT, OR THEY'LL GET YOU!
TH...THANK YOU...FOR HELPING ME OUT...
DON'T THANK ME. IF YOU'RE BEATEN, MY BOOK WILL GO UP IN FLAMES!
I'M IN IT FOR ME.

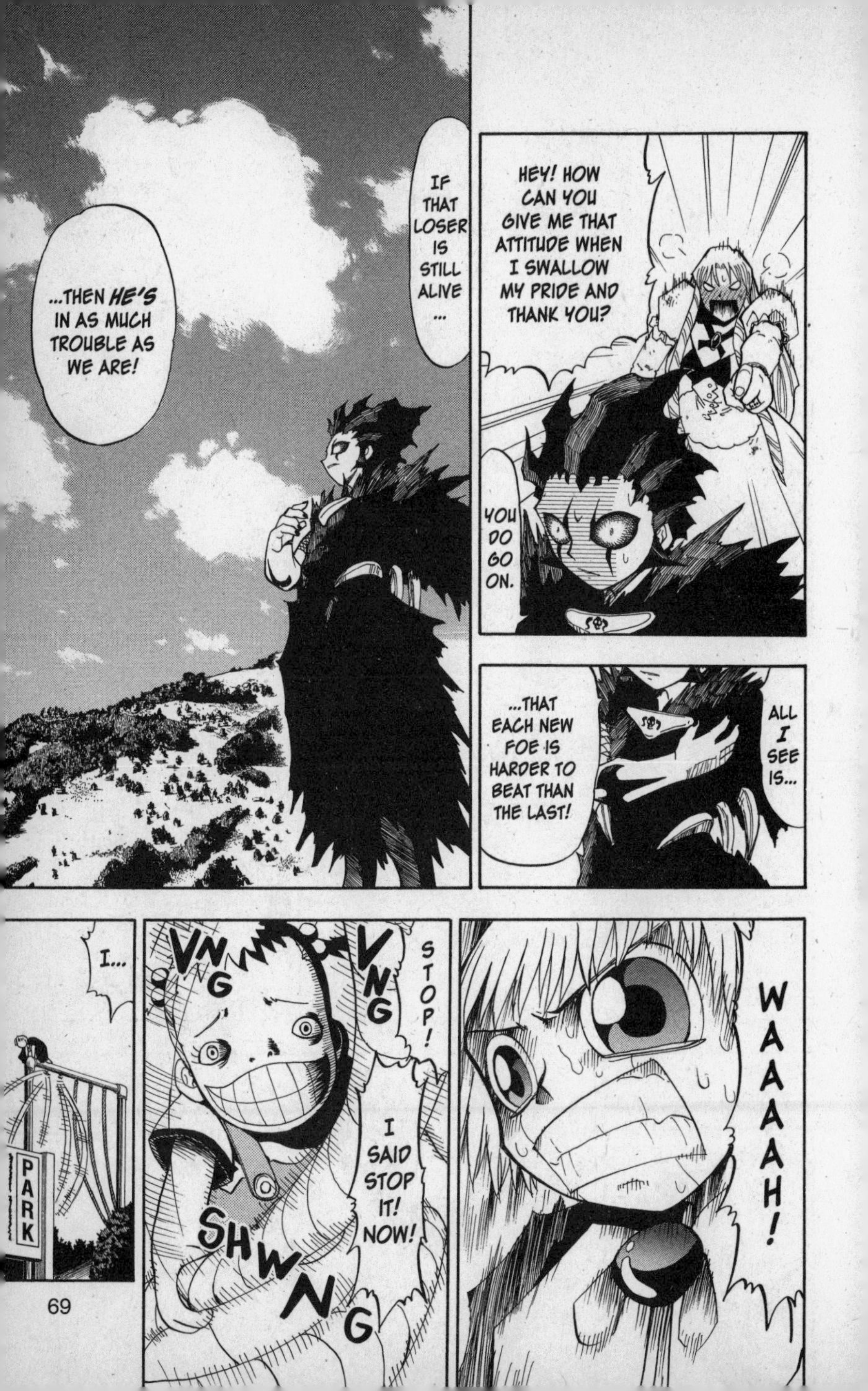
HEY! HOW CAN YOU GIVE ME THAT ATTITUDE WHEN I SWALLOW MY PRIDE AND THANK YOU?
YOU DO GO ON.
ALL I SEE IS...
...THAT EACH NEW FOE IS HARDER TO BEAT THAN THE LAST!
IF THAT LOSER IS STILL ALIVE...
...THEN HE'S IN AS MUCH TROUBLE AS WE ARE!
WAAAAAH!
VNG
VNG
STOP!
I SAID STOP IT! NOW!
SHWNG
I...
PARK

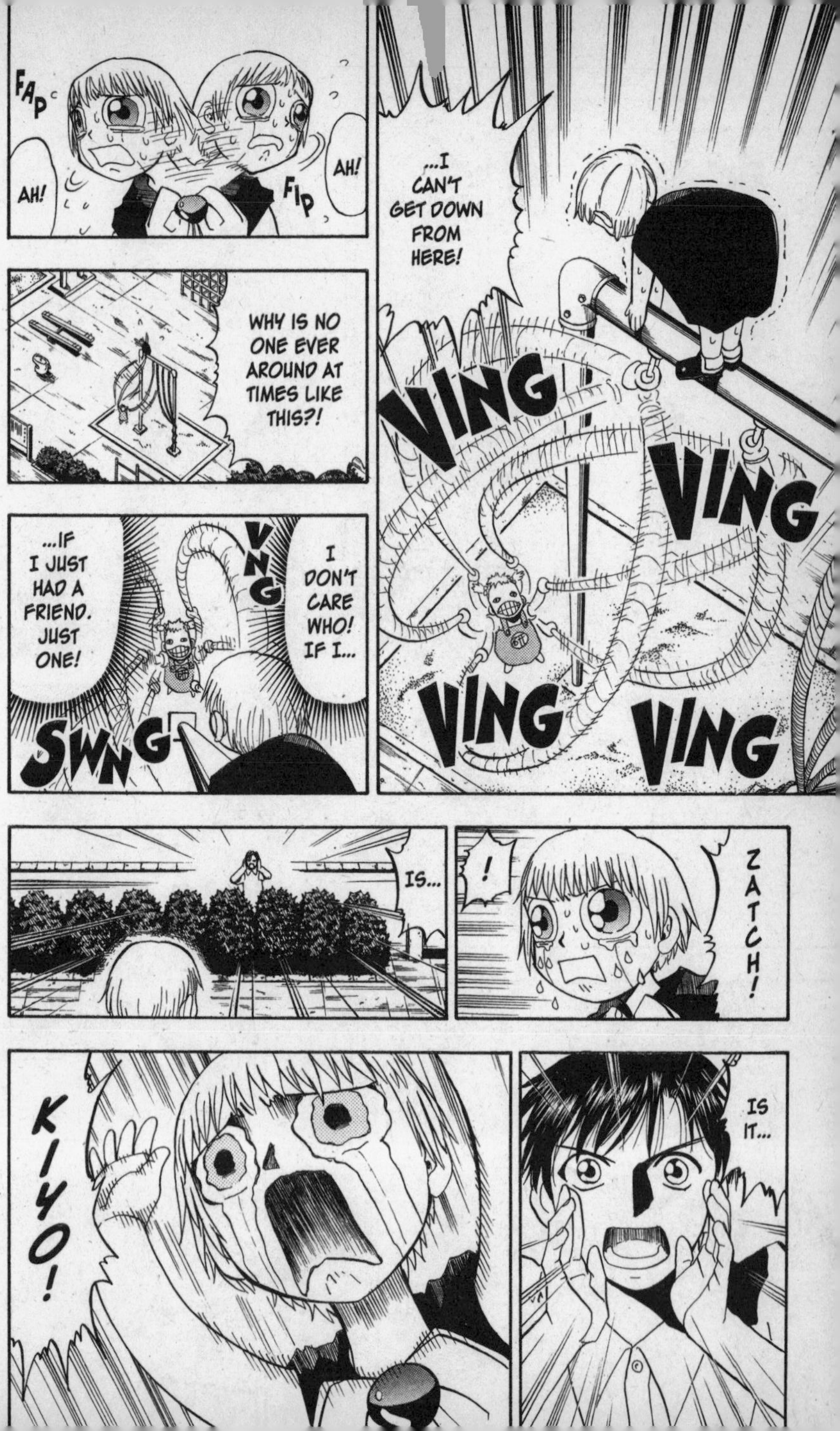
...I CAN'T GET DOWN FROM HERE!
VING
VING
VING
VING
AH!
FLIP
FAP
AH!
WHY IS NO ONE EVER AROUND AT TIMES LIKE THIS?!
I DON'T CARE WHO! IF I...
VNG
...IF I JUST HAD A FRIEND. JUST ONE!
SWNG
ZATCH!
!
IS...
IS IT...
KIYO!

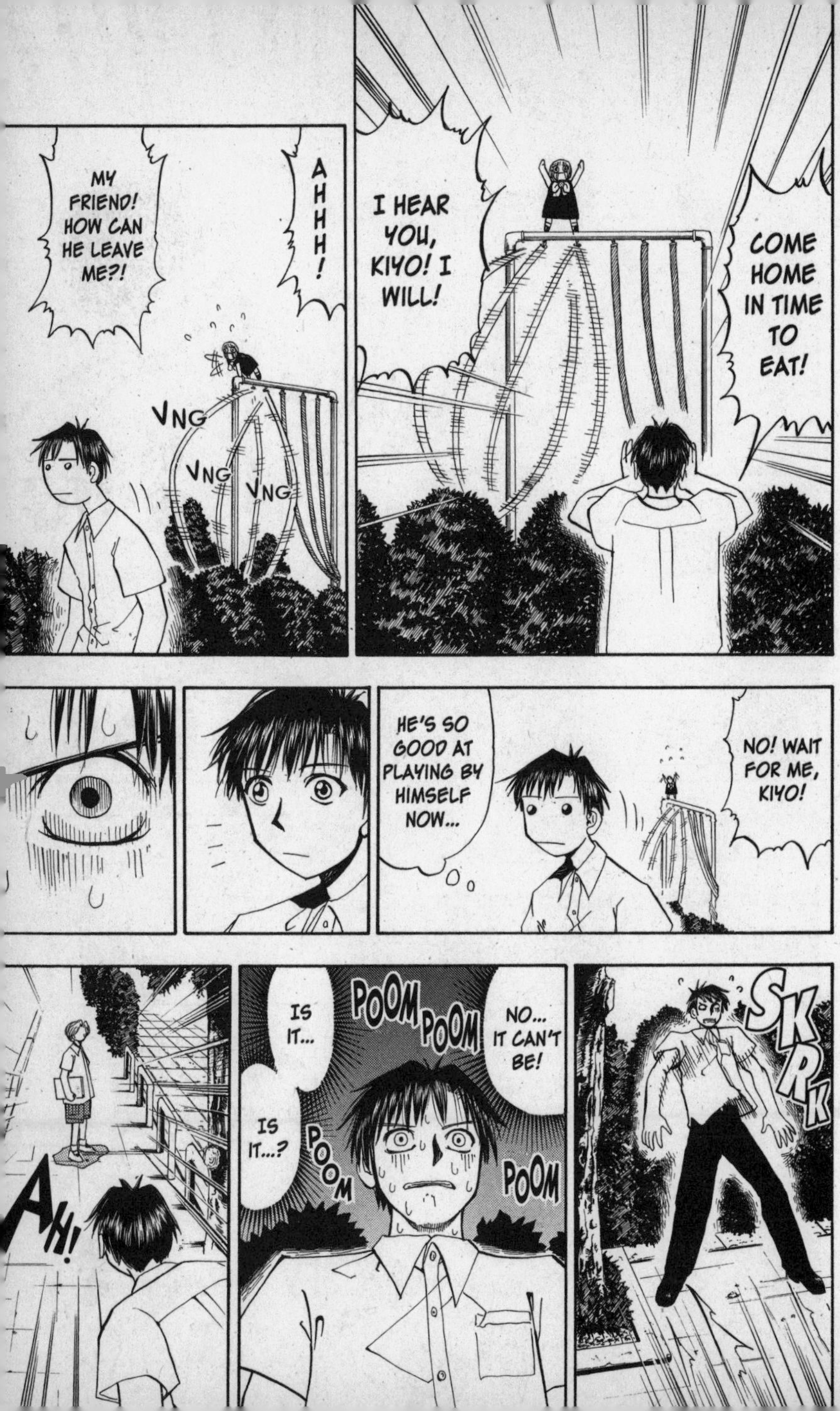
COME HOME IN TIME TO EAT!
I HEAR YOU, KIYO! I WILL!
AHHHH!
MY FRIEND! HOW CAN HE LEAVE ME?!
VNG
VNG
VNG
NO! WAIT FOR ME, KIYO!
HE'S SO GOOD AT PLAYING BY HIMSELF NOW...
SKRK
NO... IT CAN'T BE!
POOM POOM
IS IT...
IS IT...?
POOM
POOM
AH!

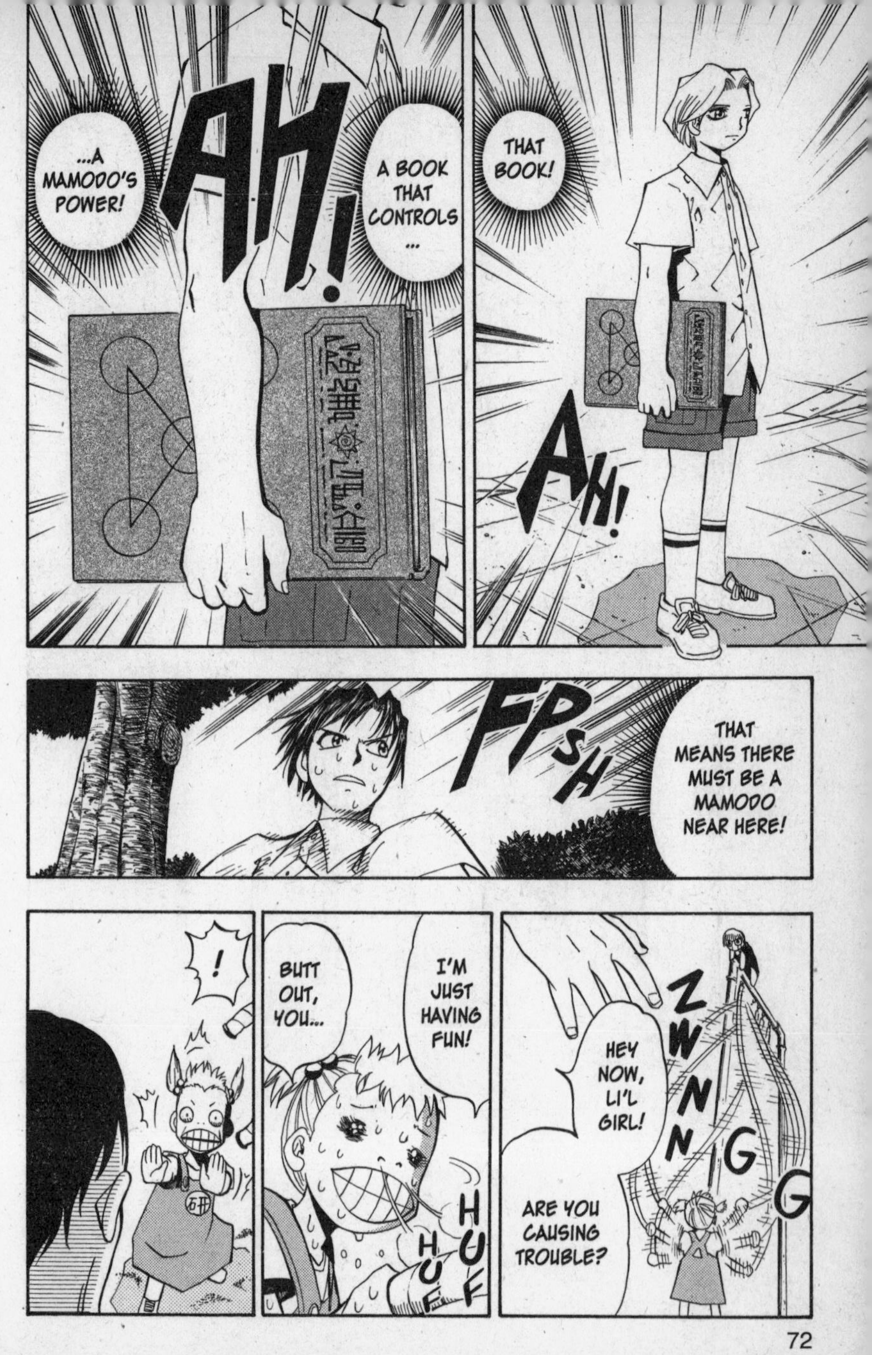
THAT BOOK!
AH!
A BOOK THAT CONTROLS ...
AH!
...A MAMODO'S POWER!
THAT MEANS THERE MUST BE A MAMODO NEAR HERE!
FPSH
ZWNNGG
HEY NOW, LI'L GIRL!
ARE YOU CAUSING TROUBLE?
I'M JUST HAVING FUN!
BUTT OUT, YOU...
HUF
HUF
!

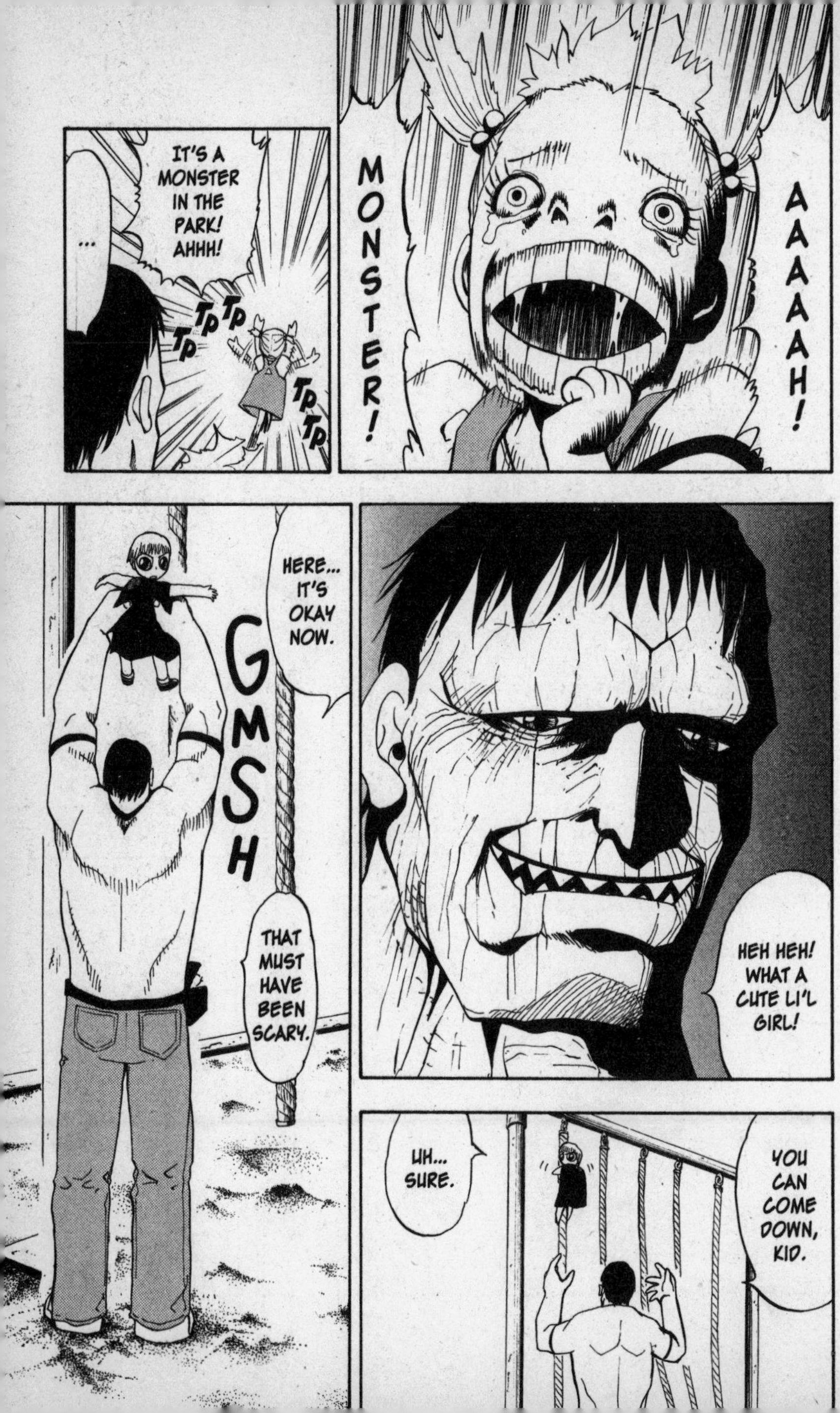
AAAAAAH!
MONSTER!
IT'S A MONSTER IN THE PARK! AHHH!
...
TP TP TP TP
TP TP TP
HEH HEH! WHAT A CUTE LI'L GIRL!
YOU CAN COME DOWN, KID.
UH... SURE.
HERE... IT'S OKAY NOW.
GMSH
THAT MUST HAVE BEEN SCARY.

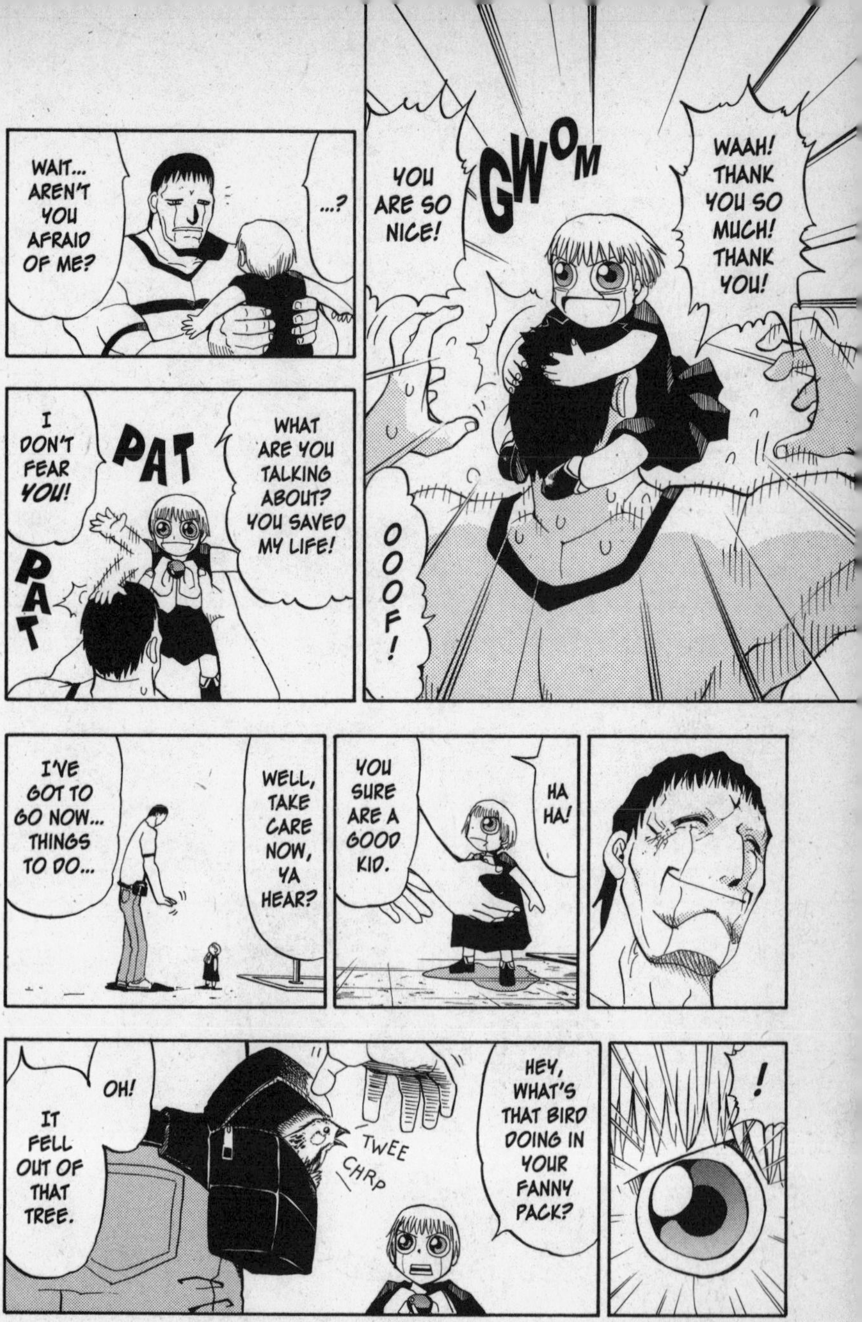
WAAH! THANK YOU SO MUCH! THANK YOU!
GWOM
YOU ARE SO NICE!
OOOF!
...?
WAIT... AREN'T YOU AFRAID OF ME?
WHAT ARE YOU TALKING ABOUT? YOU SAVED MY LIFE!
PAT
I DON'T FEAR YOU!
PAT
PAT
HA HA!
YOU SURE ARE A GOOD KID.
WELL, TAKE CARE NOW, YA HEAR?
I'VE GOT TO GO NOW... THINGS TO DO...
!
HEY, WHAT'S THAT BIRD DOING IN YOUR FANNY PACK?
TWEE
CHRP
OH!
IT FELL OUT OF THAT TREE.

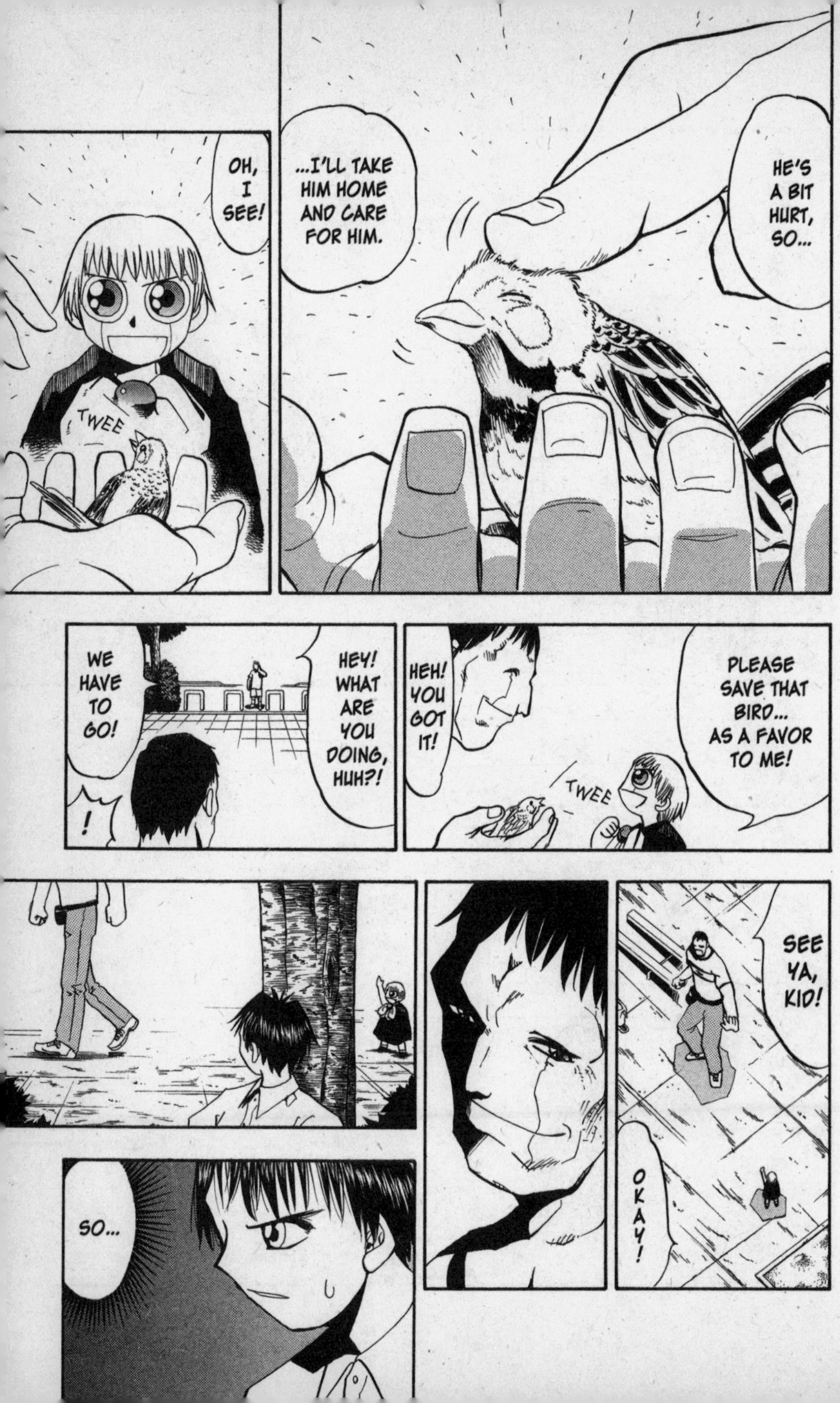
HE'S A BIT HURT, SO...
...I'LL TAKE HIM HOME AND CARE FOR HIM.
OH, I SEE!
TWEE
PLEASE SAVE THAT BIRD... AS A FAVOR TO ME!
TWEE
HEH! YOU GOT IT!
HEY! WHAT ARE YOU DOING, HUH?!
WE HAVE TO GO!
!
SEE YA, KID!
OKAY!
SO...

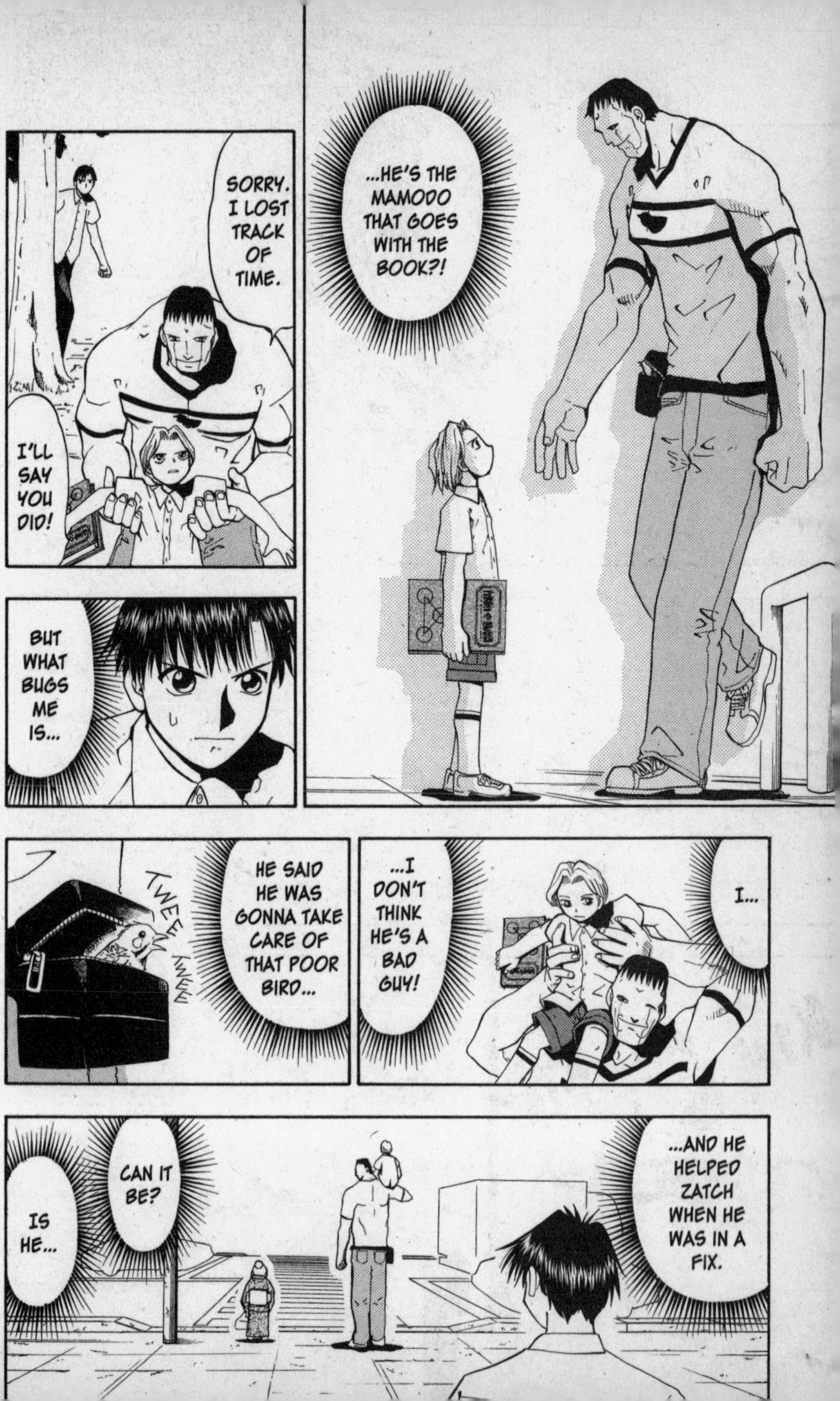
...HE'S THE MAMODO THAT GOES WITH THE BOOK?!
SORRY. I LOST TRACK OF TIME.
I'LL SAY YOU DID!
BUT WHAT BUGS ME IS...
I...
...I DON'T THINK HE'S A BAD GUY!
HE SAID HE WAS GONNA TAKE CARE OF THAT POOR BIRD...
TWEE
TWEE
...AND HE HELPED ZATCH WHEN HE WAS IN A FIX.
CAN IT BE?
IS HE...

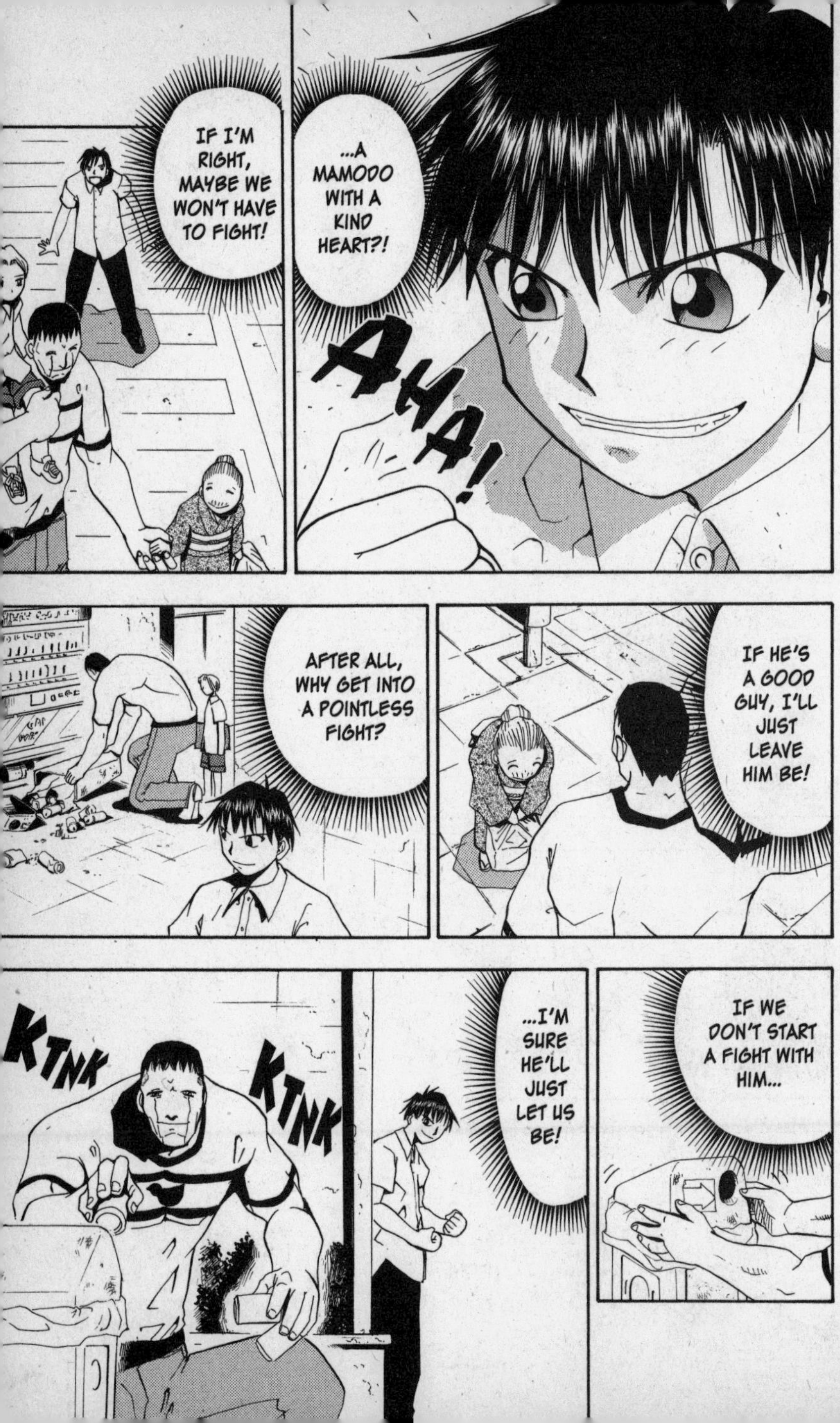
...A MAMODO WITH A KIND HEART?!
AHA!
IF I'M RIGHT, MAYBE WE WON'T HAVE TO FIGHT!
IF HE'S A GOOD GUY, I'LL JUST LEAVE HIM BE!
AFTER ALL, WHY GET INTO A POINTLESS FIGHT?
IF WE DON'T START A FIGHT WITH HIM...
...I'M SURE HE'LL JUST LET US BE!
KTNK
KTNK

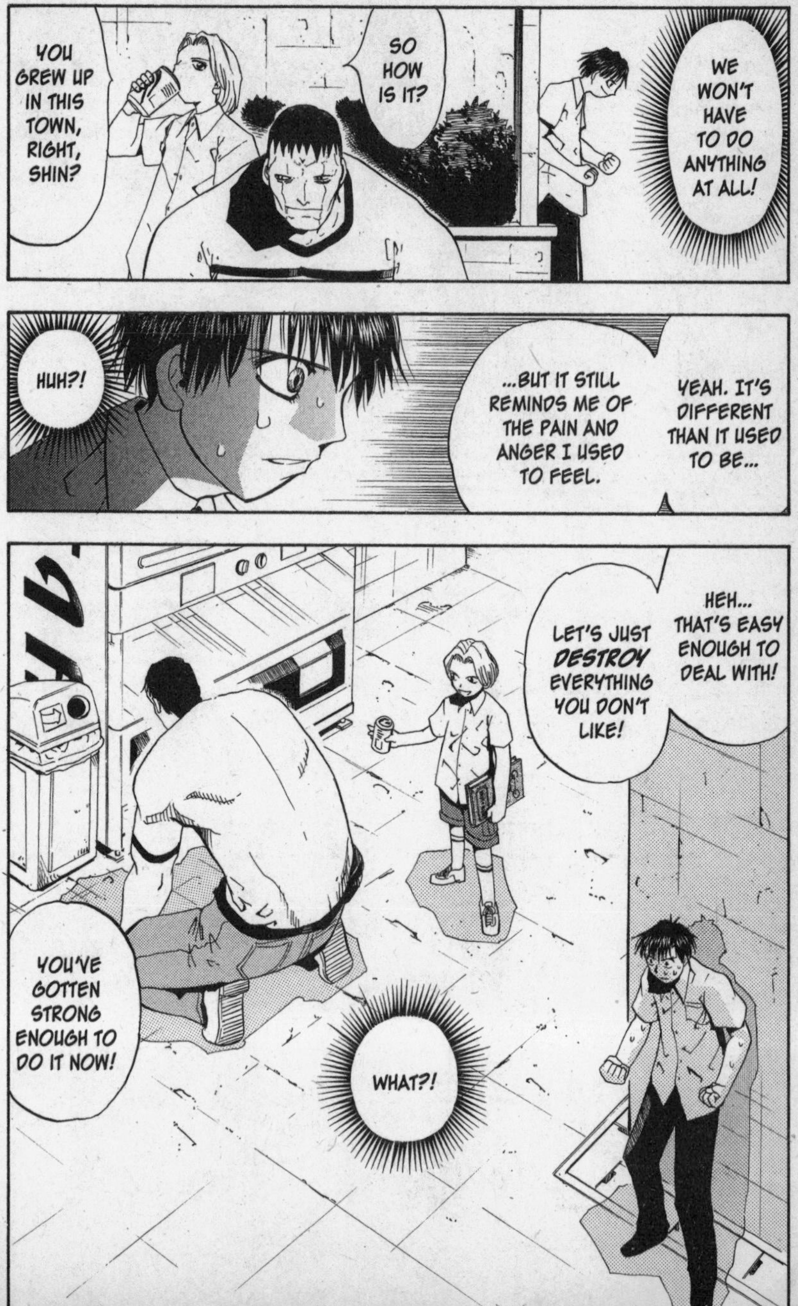
WE WON'T HAVE TO DO ANYTHING AT ALL!
SO HOW IS IT?
YOU GREW UP IN THIS TOWN, RIGHT, SHIN?
YEAH. IT'S DIFFERENT THAN IT USED TO BE...
...BUT IT STILL REMINDS ME OF THE PAIN AND ANGER I USED TO FEEL.
HUH?!
HEH... THAT'S EASY ENOUGH TO DEAL WITH!
LET'S JUST DESTROY EVERYTHING YOU DON'T LIKE!
YOU'VE GOTTEN STRONG ENOUGH TO DO IT NOW!
WHAT?!

# LEVEL 23: A Mother's Wish

YOU GREW UP IN THIS TOWN, RIGHT, SHIN?

?!

?!

IT STILL REMINDS ME OF THE PAIN AND ANGER I USED TO FEEL...

?!

WELL, THAT'S WHAT I'M HERE FOR! YOU AND ME...

...WE'LL RIP THIS WHOLE TOWN TO BITS!

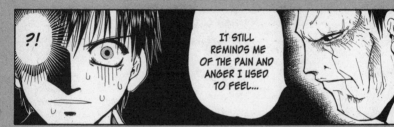

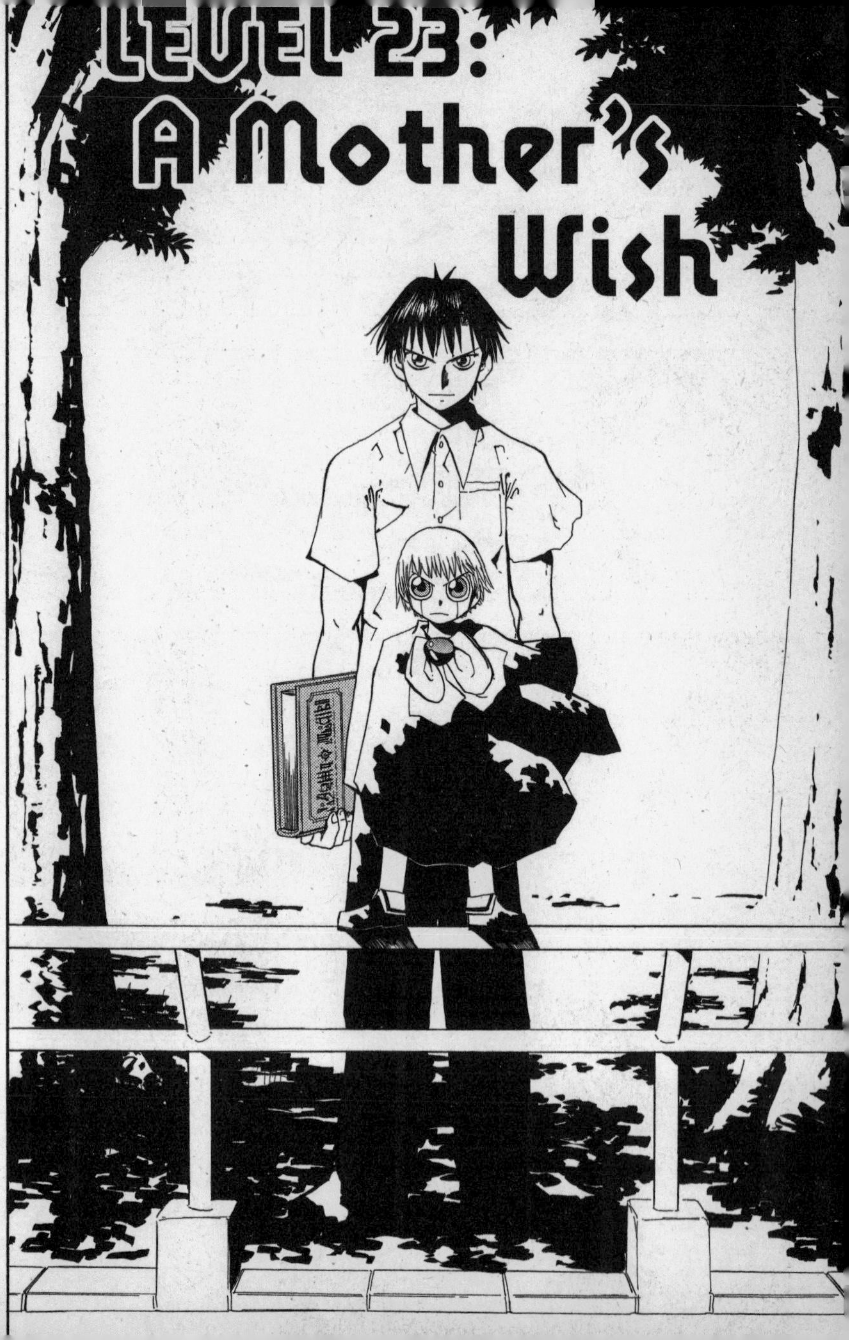
LEVEL 23:
A Mother's Wish

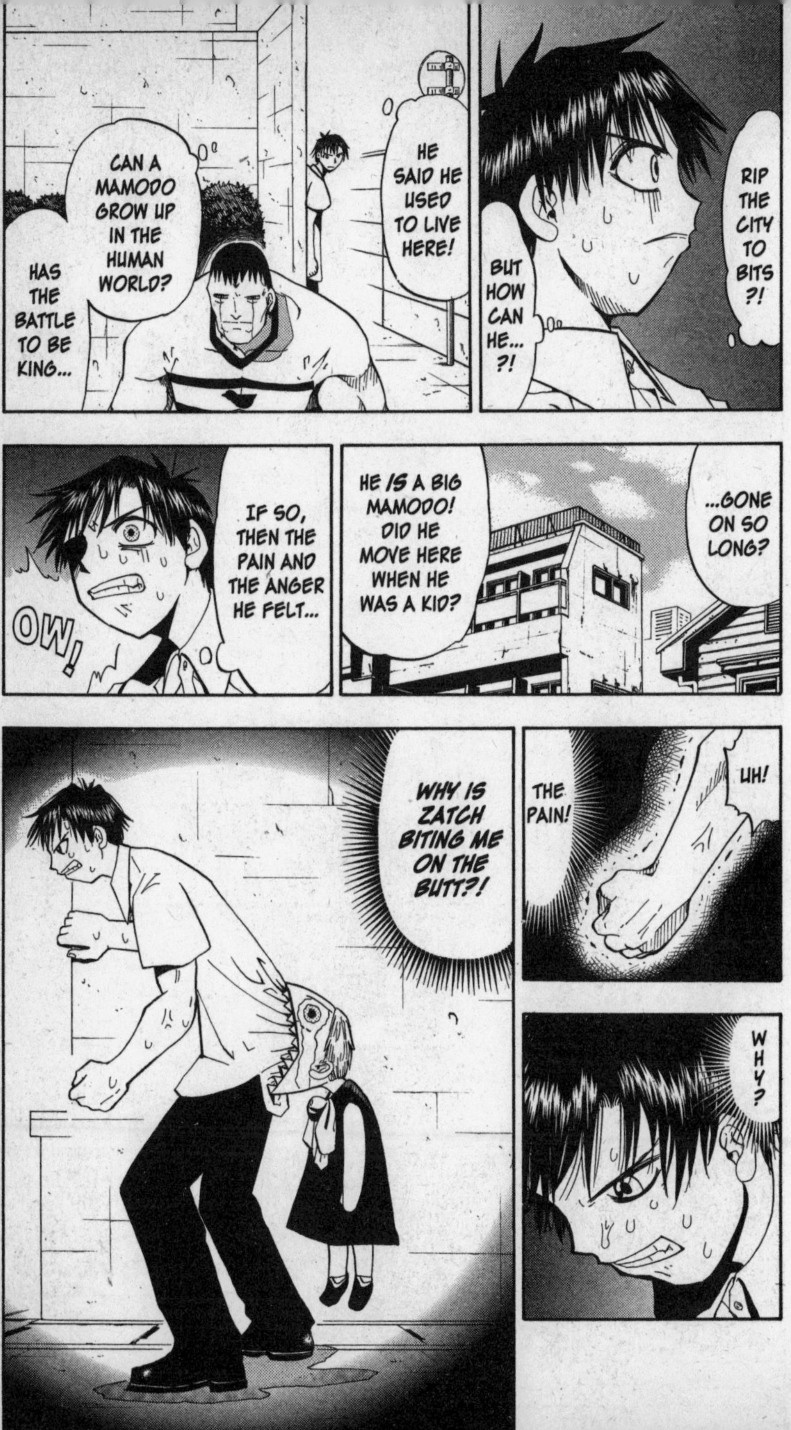
RIP THE CITY TO BITS?!
BUT HOW CAN HE...?!
HE SAID HE USED TO LIVE HERE!
CAN A MAMODO GROW UP IN THE HUMAN WORLD?
HAS THE BATTLE TO BE KING...
...GONE ON SO LONG?
HE IS A BIG MAMODO! DID HE MOVE HERE WHEN HE WAS A KID?
IF SO, THEN THE PAIN AND THE ANGER HE FELT...
OW!
UH!
THE PAIN!
WHY?
WHY IS ZATCH BITING ME ON THE BUTT?!

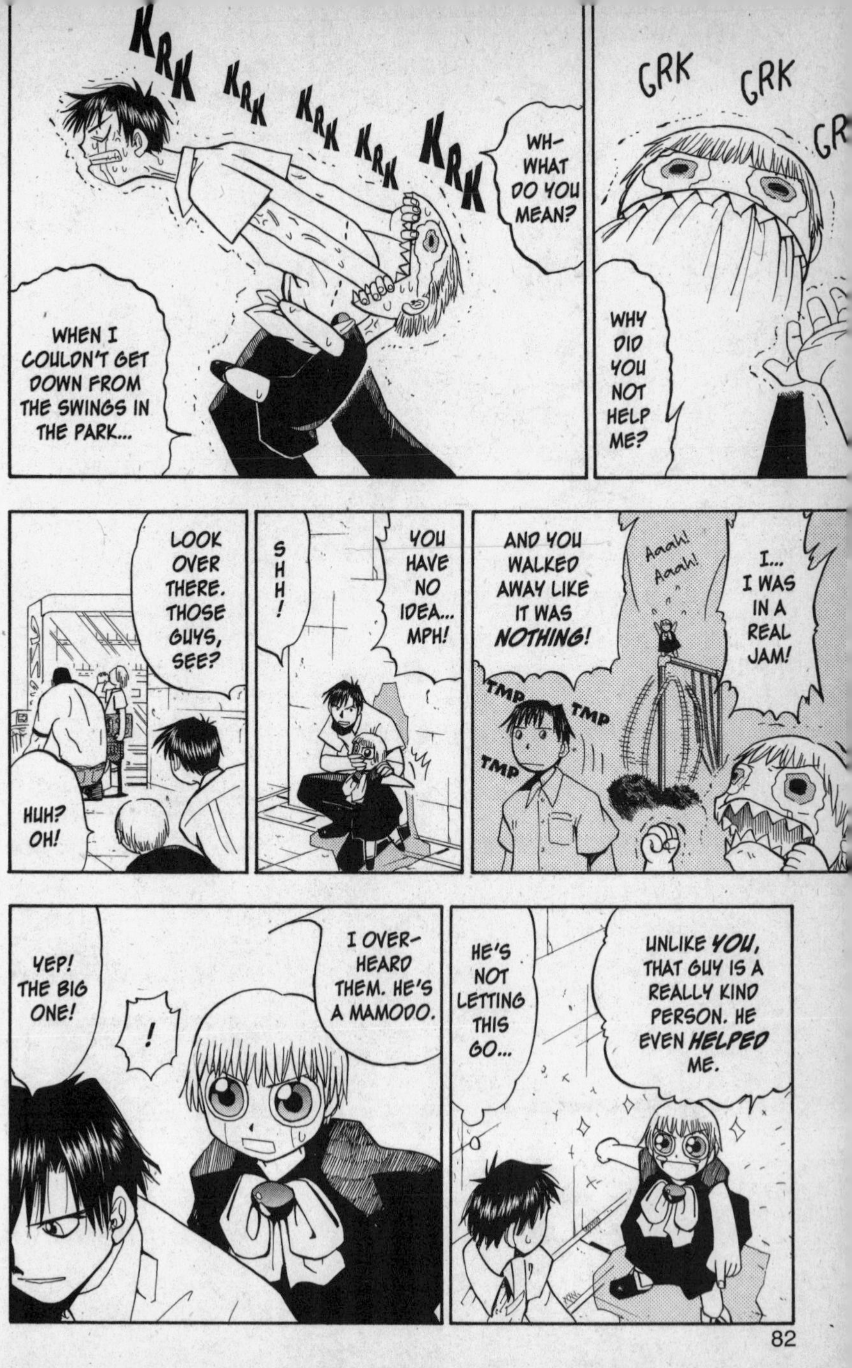
GRK GRK GR
WHY DID YOU NOT HELP ME?
WH- WHAT DO YOU MEAN?
KRK KRK KRK KRK KRK
WHEN I COULDN'T GET DOWN FROM THE SWINGS IN THE PARK...
I... I WAS IN A REAL JAM!
Aaah! Aaah!
AND YOU WALKED AWAY LIKE IT WAS NOTHING!
TMP TMP TMP
YOU HAVE NO IDEA... MPH!
SHH!
LOOK OVER THERE. THOSE GUYS, SEE?
HUH? OH!
UNLIKE YOU, THAT GUY IS A REALLY KIND PERSON. HE EVEN HELPED ME.
HE'S NOT LETTING THIS GO...
I OVER-HEARD THEM. HE'S A MAMODO.
!
YEP! THE BIG ONE!

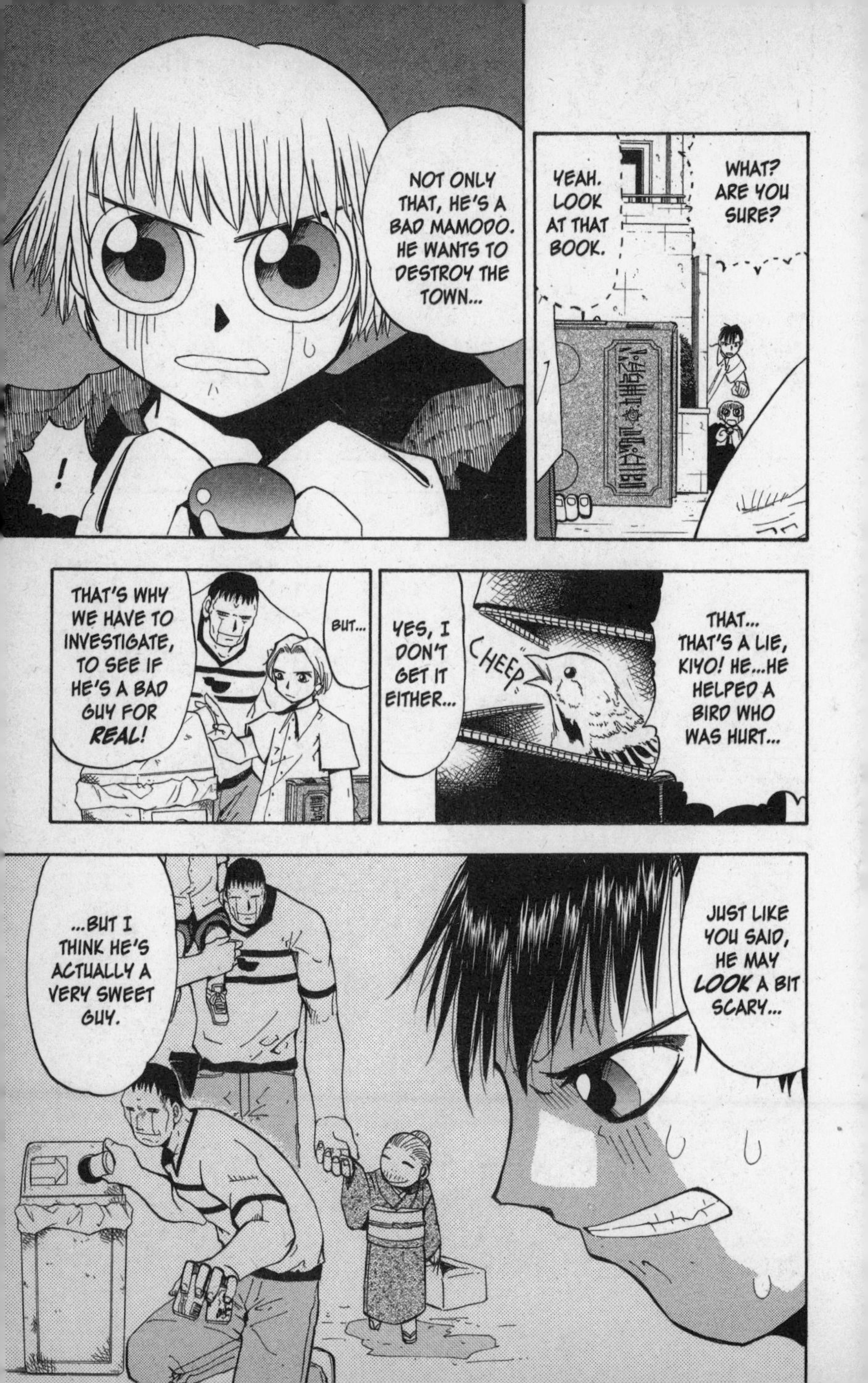
WHAT? ARE YOU SURE?
YEAH. LOOK AT THAT BOOK.
NOT ONLY THAT, HE'S A BAD MAMODO. HE WANTS TO DESTROY THE TOWN...
!
THAT... THAT'S A LIE, KIYO! HE...HE HELPED A BIRD WHO WAS HURT...
CHEEP
YES, I DON'T GET IT EITHER...
BUT...
THAT'S WHY WE HAVE TO INVESTIGATE, TO SEE IF HE'S A BAD GUY FOR REAL!
JUST LIKE YOU SAID, HE MAY LOOK A BIT SCARY...
...BUT I THINK HE'S ACTUALLY A VERY SWEET GUY.

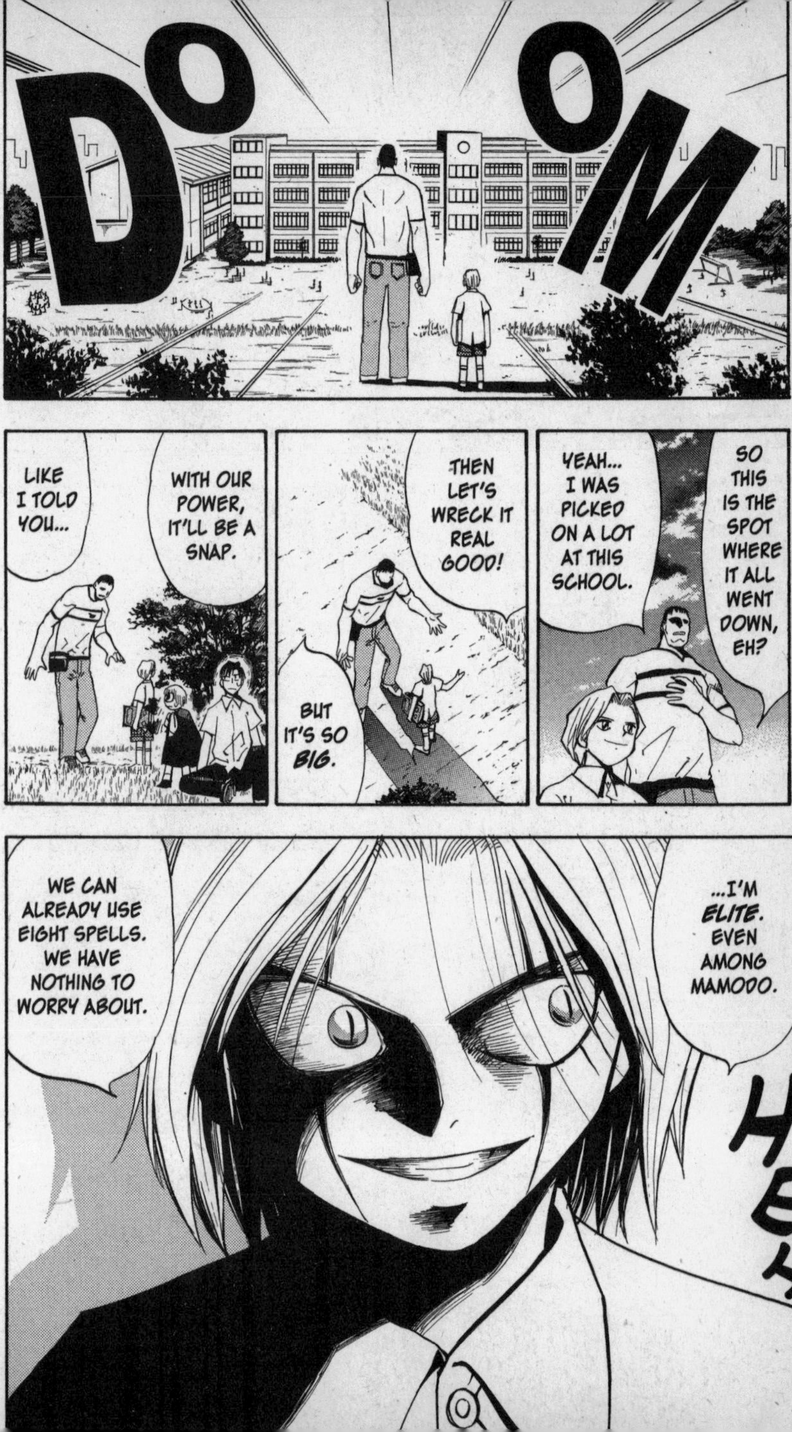
DOOM
SO THIS IS THE SPOT WHERE IT ALL WENT DOWN, EH?
YEAH... I WAS PICKED ON A LOT AT THIS SCHOOL.
THEN LET'S WRECK IT REAL GOOD!
BUT IT'S SO *BIG*.
WITH OUR POWER, IT'LL BE A SNAP.
LIKE I TOLD YOU...
...I'M *ELITE*. EVEN AMONG MAMODO.
WE CAN ALREADY USE EIGHT SPELLS. WE HAVE NOTHING TO WORRY ABOUT.
HEH

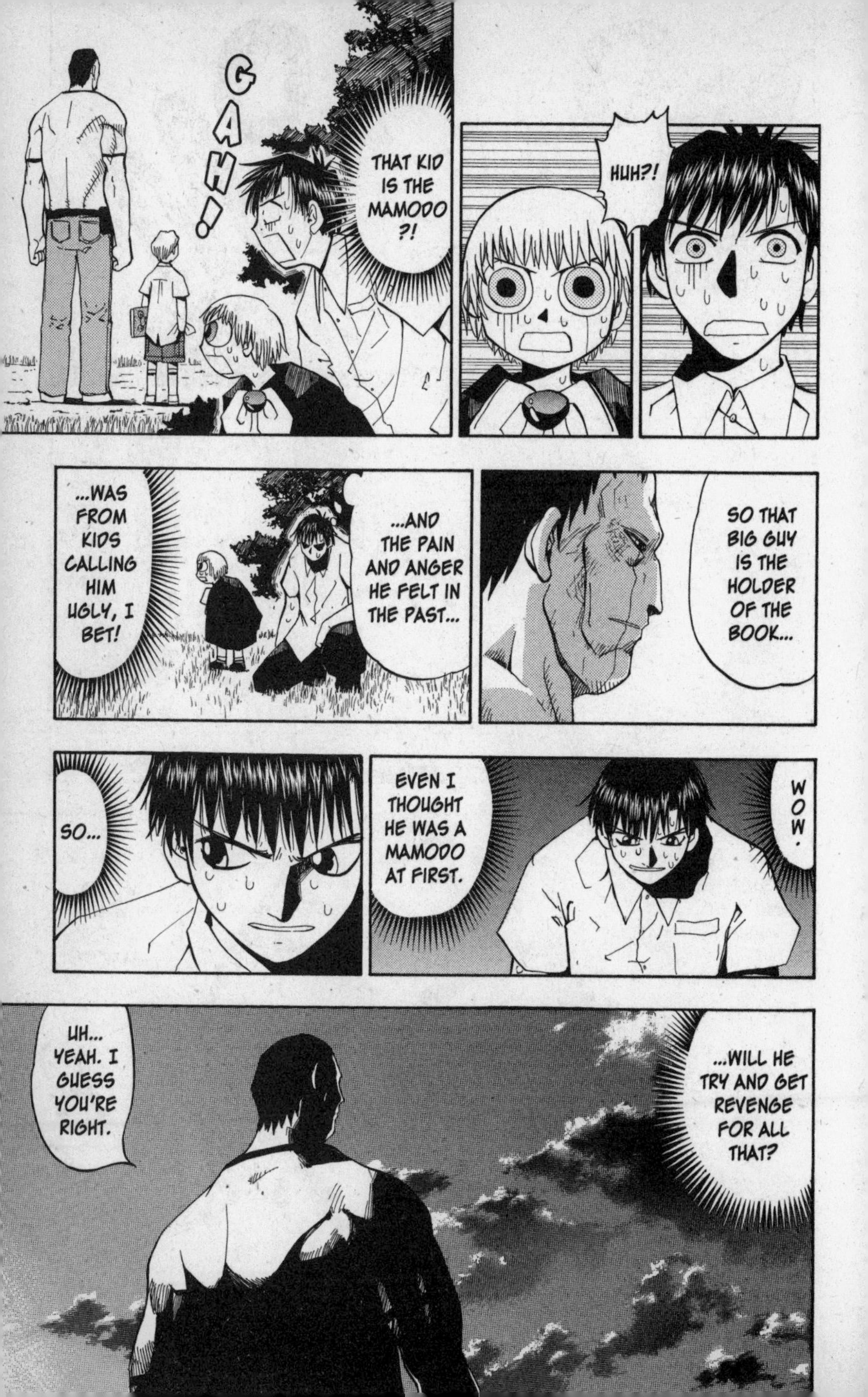
HUH?!
THAT KID IS THE MAMODO ?!
GAH!
SO THAT BIG GUY IS THE HOLDER OF THE BOOK...
...AND THE PAIN AND ANGER HE FELT IN THE PAST...
...WAS FROM KIDS CALLING HIM UGLY, I BET!
WOW.
EVEN I THOUGHT HE WAS A MAMODO AT FIRST.
SO...
...WILL HE TRY AND GET REVENGE FOR ALL THAT?
UH... YEAH. I GUESS YOU'RE RIGHT.

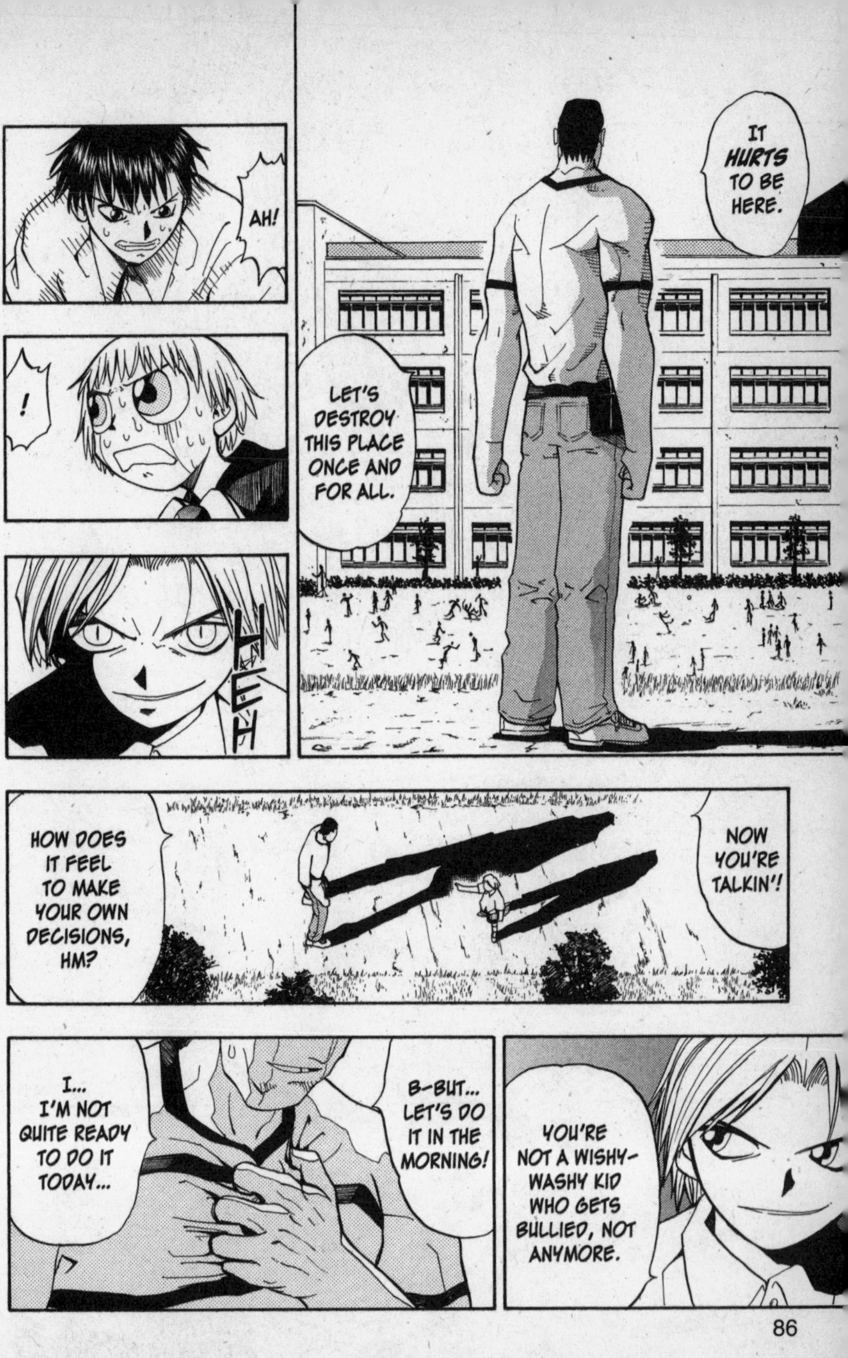
IT HURTS TO BE HERE.
LET'S DESTROY THIS PLACE ONCE AND FOR ALL.
AH!
!
HEH
NOW YOU'RE TALKIN'!
HOW DOES IT FEEL TO MAKE YOUR OWN DECISIONS, HM?
YOU'RE NOT A WISHY-WASHY KID WHO GETS BULLIED, NOT ANYMORE.
I... I'M NOT QUITE READY TO DO IT TODAY...
B-BUT... LET'S DO IT IN THE MORNING!

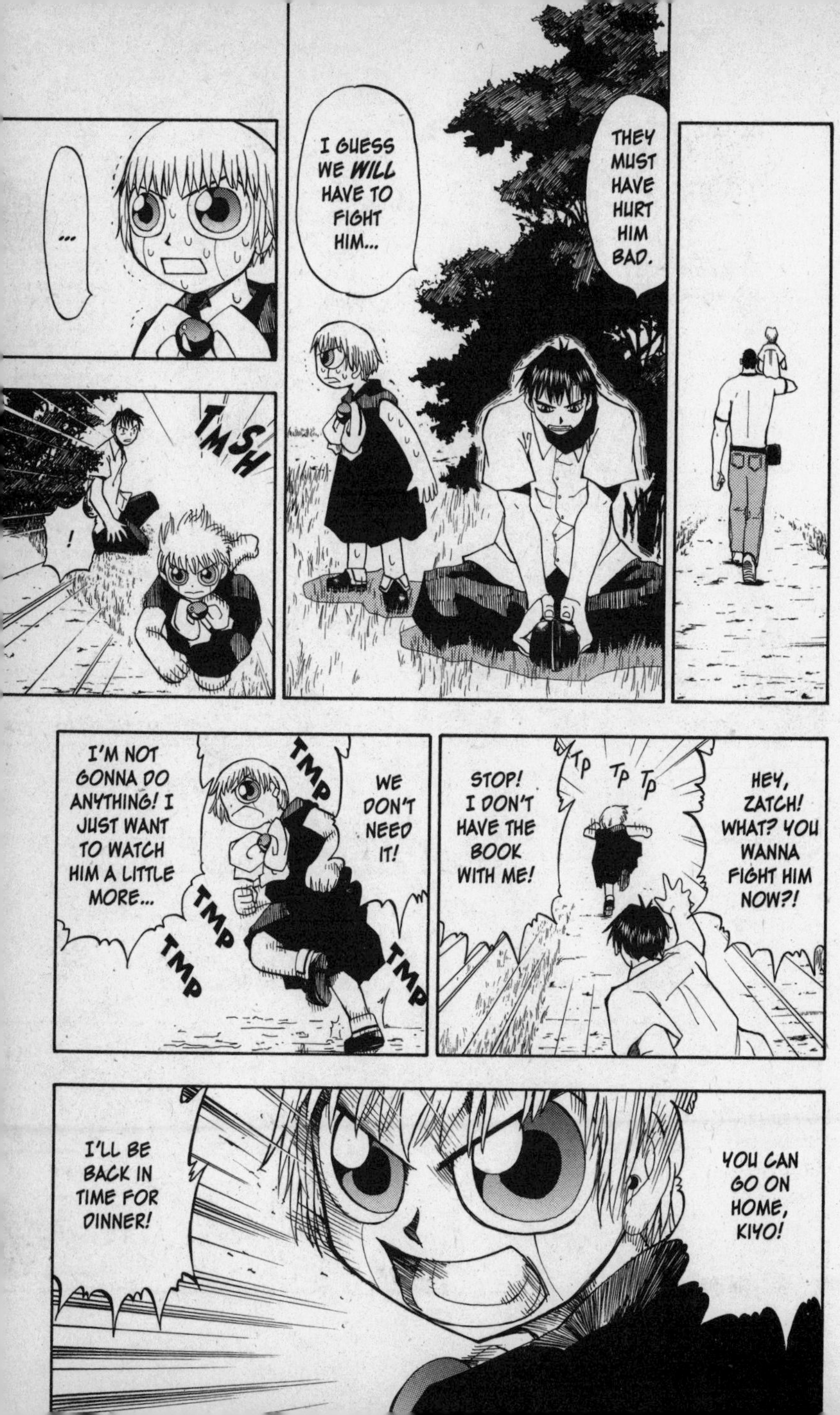
THEY MUST HAVE HURT HIM BAD.
I GUESS WE WILL HAVE TO FIGHT HIM...
...
TMSH
!
HEY, ZATCH! WHAT? YOU WANNA FIGHT HIM NOW?!
TP TP TP
STOP! I DON'T HAVE THE BOOK WITH ME!
WE DON'T NEED IT!
TMP
I'M NOT GONNA DO ANYTHING! I JUST WANT TO WATCH HIM A LITTLE MORE...
TMP
TMP
TMP
YOU CAN GO ON HOME, KIYO!
I'LL BE BACK IN TIME FOR DINNER!

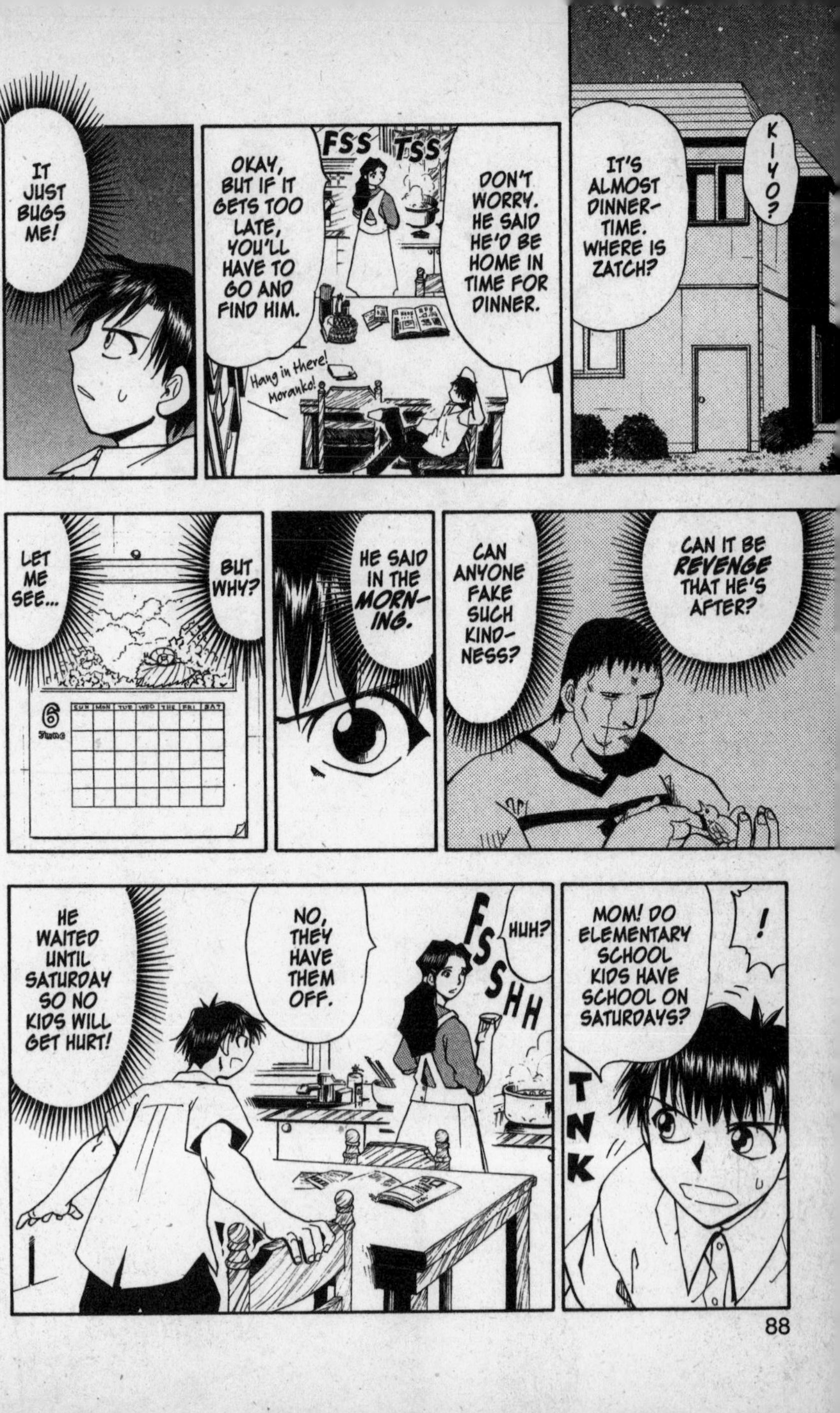

KIYO?
IT'S ALMOST DINNER-TIME. WHERE IS ZATCH?
DON'T WORRY. HE SAID HE'D BE HOME IN TIME FOR DINNER.
FSS TSS
OKAY, BUT IF IT GETS TOO LATE, YOU'LL HAVE TO GO AND FIND HIM.
Hang in there! Moranko!
IT JUST BUGS ME!
CAN IT BE REVENGE THAT HE'S AFTER?
CAN ANYONE FAKE SUCH KINDNESS?
HE SAID IN THE MORNING.
BUT WHY?
LET ME SEE...
!
MOM! DO ELEMENTARY SCHOOL KIDS HAVE SCHOOL ON SATURDAYS?
TNK
HUH?
FSSHH
NO, THEY HAVE THEM OFF.
HE WAITED UNTIL SATURDAY SO NO KIDS WILL GET HURT!

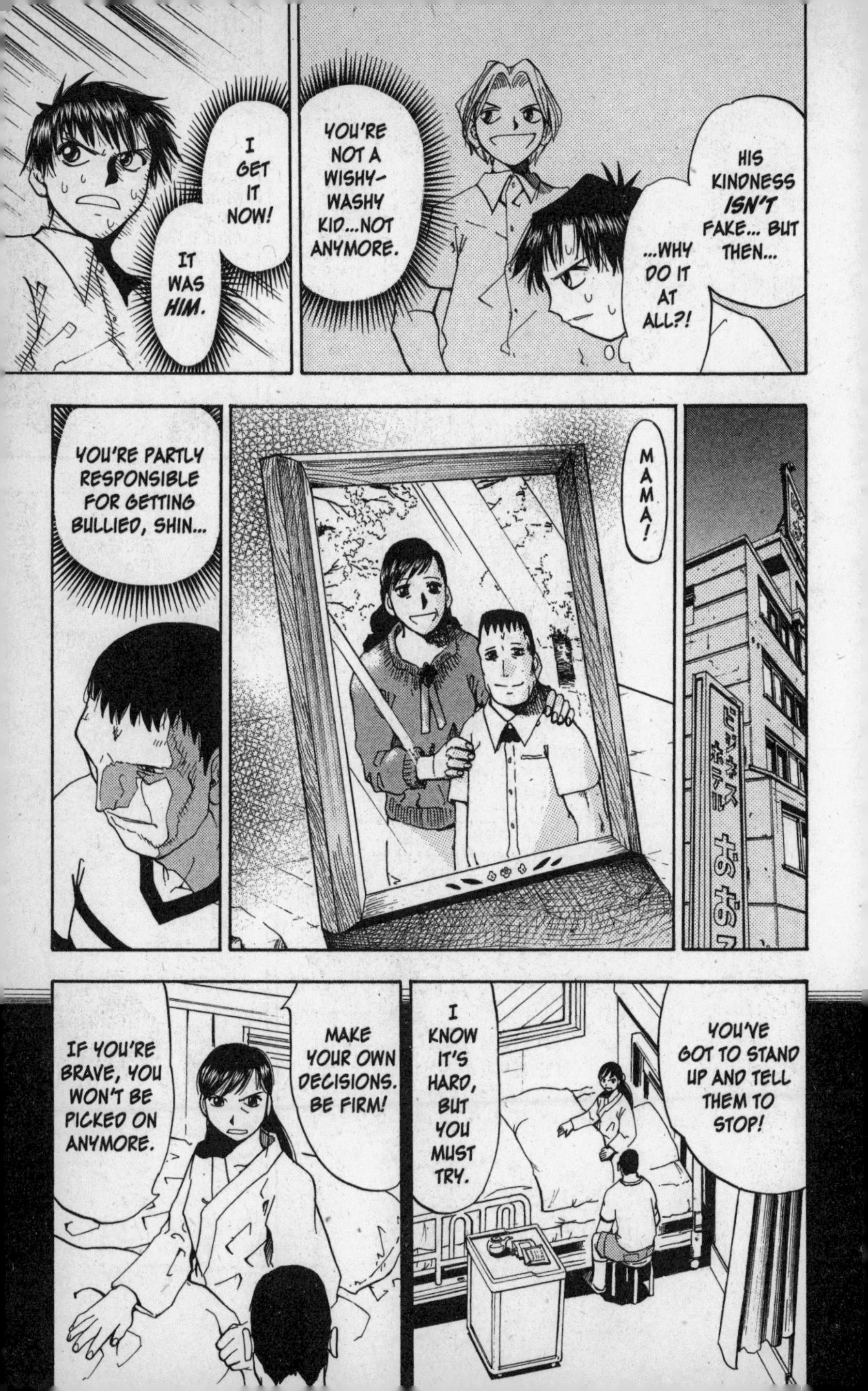
HIS KINDNESS ISN'T FAKE... BUT THEN...
...WHY DO IT AT ALL?!
YOU'RE NOT A WISHY-WASHY KID...NOT ANYMORE.
I GET IT NOW!
IT WAS HIM.
ビジネスホテル
MAMA!
YOU'RE PARTLY RESPONSIBLE FOR GETTING BULLIED, SHIN...
YOU'VE GOT TO STAND UP AND TELL THEM TO STOP!
I KNOW IT'S HARD, BUT YOU MUST TRY.
MAKE YOUR OWN DECISIONS. BE FIRM!
IF YOU'RE BRAVE, YOU WON'T BE PICKED ON ANYMORE.

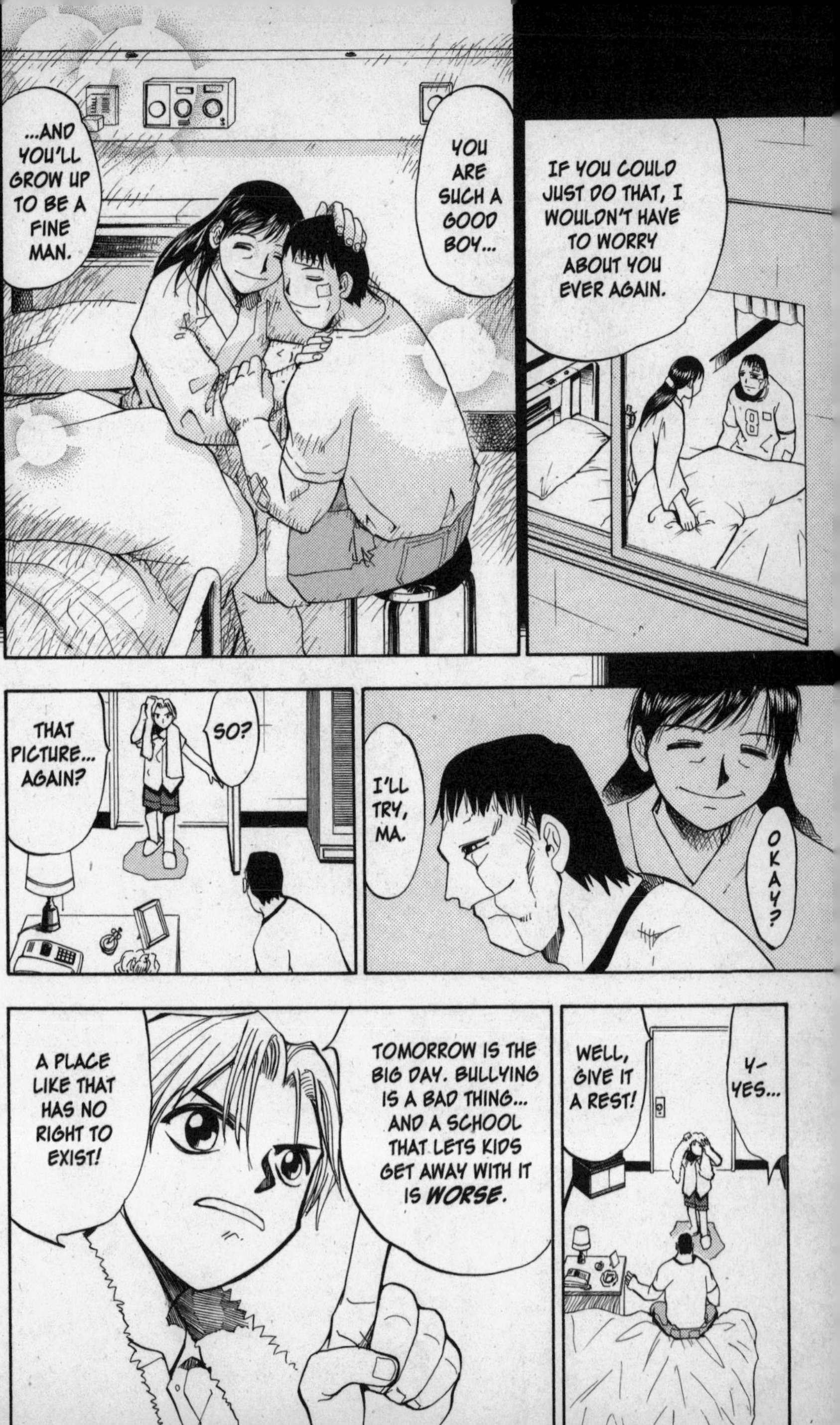
IF YOU COULD JUST DO THAT, I WOULDN'T HAVE TO WORRY ABOUT YOU EVER AGAIN.
YOU ARE SUCH A GOOD BOY...
...AND YOU'LL GROW UP TO BE A FINE MAN.
OKAY?
I'LL TRY, MA.
SO?
THAT PICTURE... AGAIN?
Y-YES...
WELL, GIVE IT A REST!
TOMORROW IS THE BIG DAY. BULLYING IS A BAD THING... AND A SCHOOL THAT LETS KIDS GET AWAY WITH IT IS *WORSE*.
A PLACE LIKE THAT HAS NO RIGHT TO EXIST!

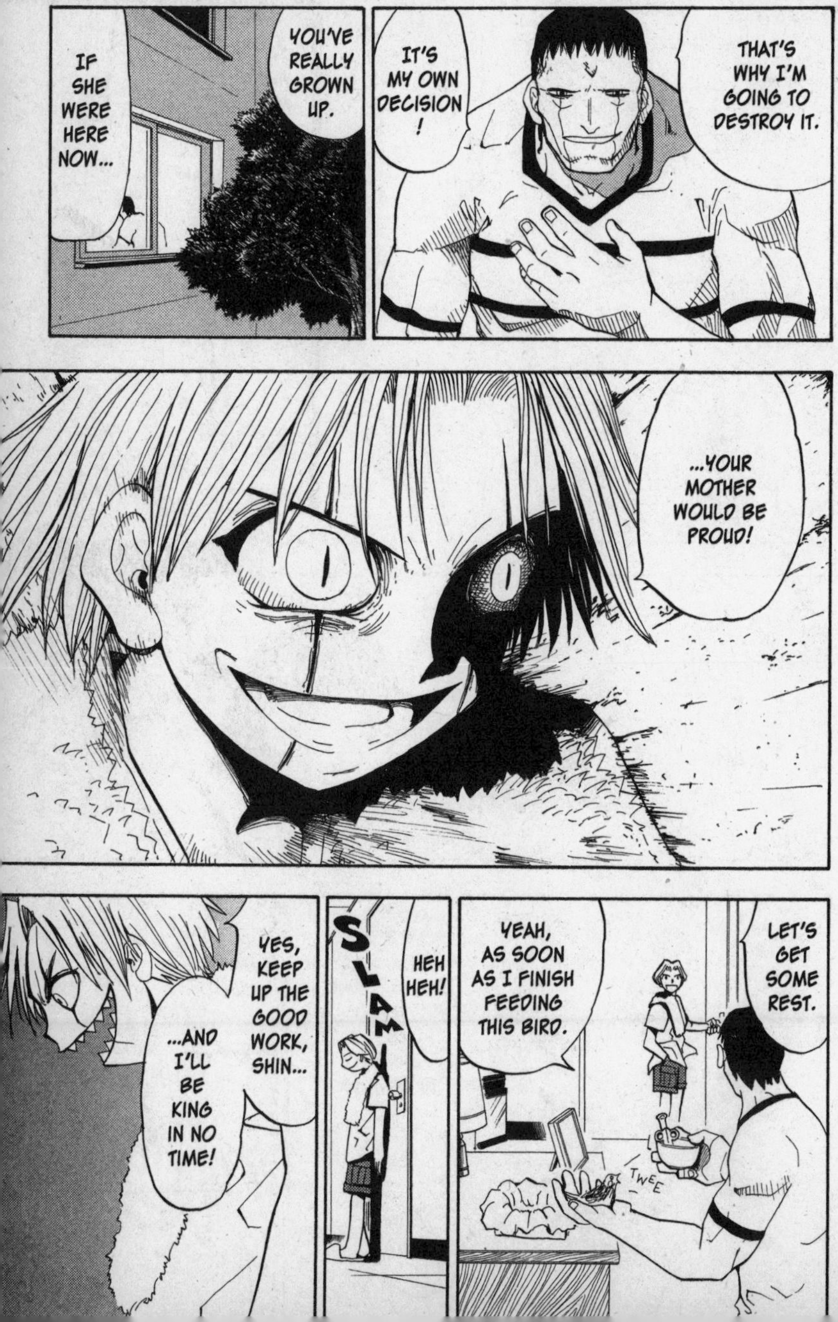
THAT'S WHY I'M GOING TO DESTROY IT.
IT'S MY OWN DECISION!
YOU'VE REALLY GROWN UP.
IF SHE WERE HERE NOW...
...YOUR MOTHER WOULD BE PROUD!
LET'S GET SOME REST.
YEAH, AS SOON AS I FINISH FEEDING THIS BIRD.
TWEE
HEH HEH!
SLAM
YES, KEEP UP THE GOOD WORK, SHIN...
...AND I'LL BE KING IN NO TIME!

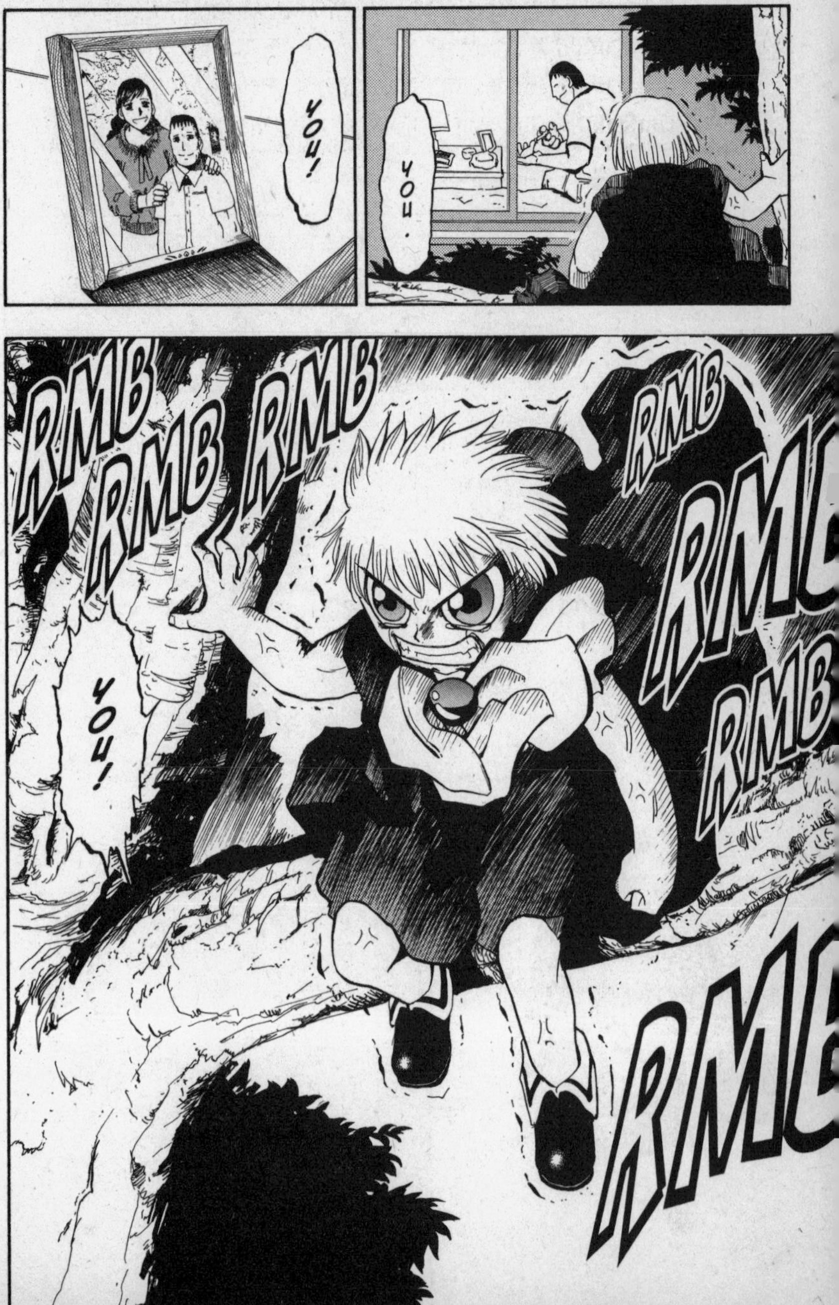
YOU.
YOU!
RMB
RMB
RMB
RMB
RMB
RMB
RMB
RMB
YOU!

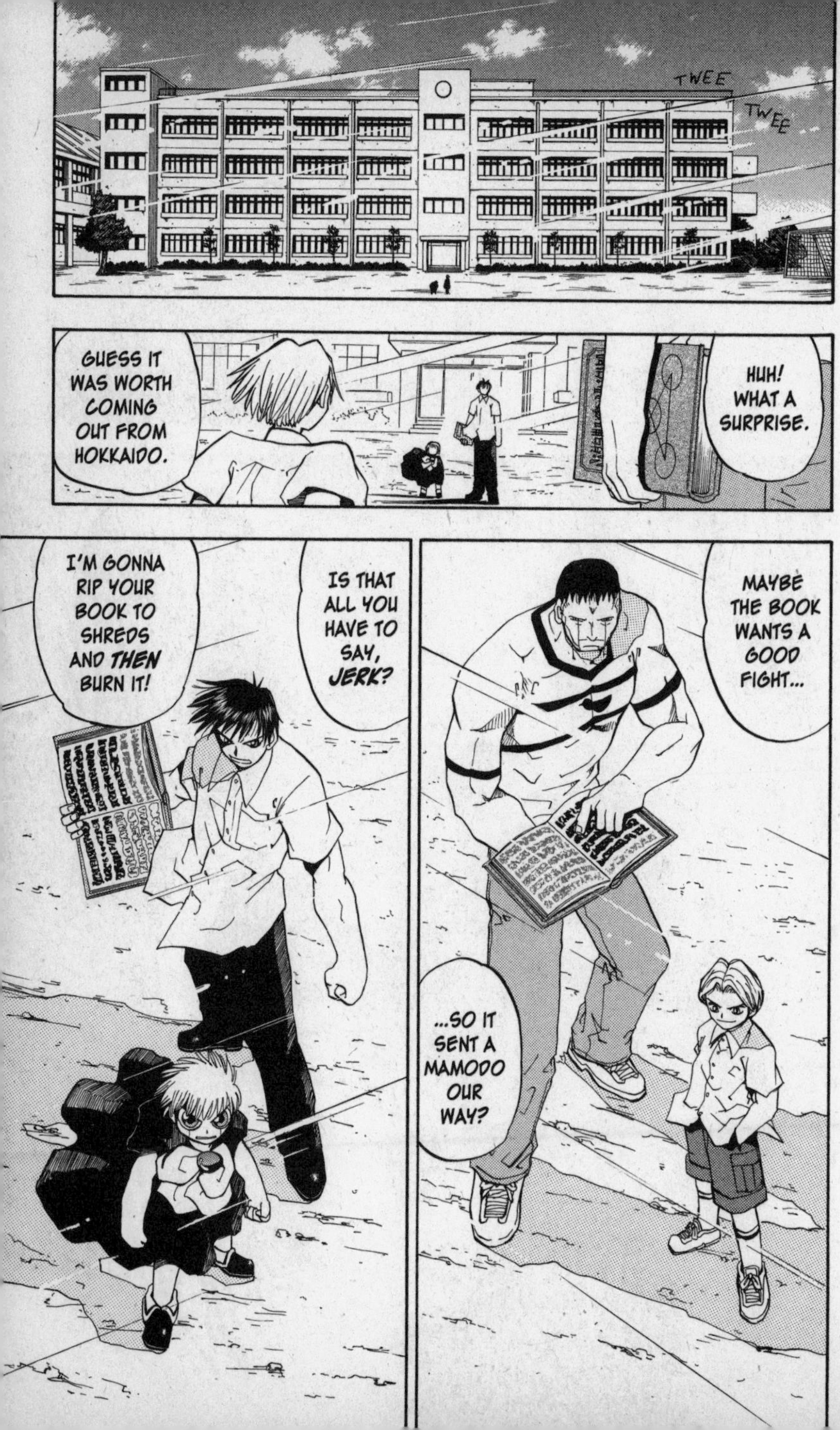
TWEE
TWEE
HUH! WHAT A SURPRISE.
GUESS IT WAS WORTH COMING OUT FROM HOKKAIDO.
MAYBE THE BOOK WANTS A GOOD FIGHT...
...SO IT SENT A MAMODO OUR WAY?
IS THAT ALL YOU HAVE TO SAY, *JERK?*
I'M GONNA RIP YOUR BOOK TO SHREDS AND *THEN* BURN IT!

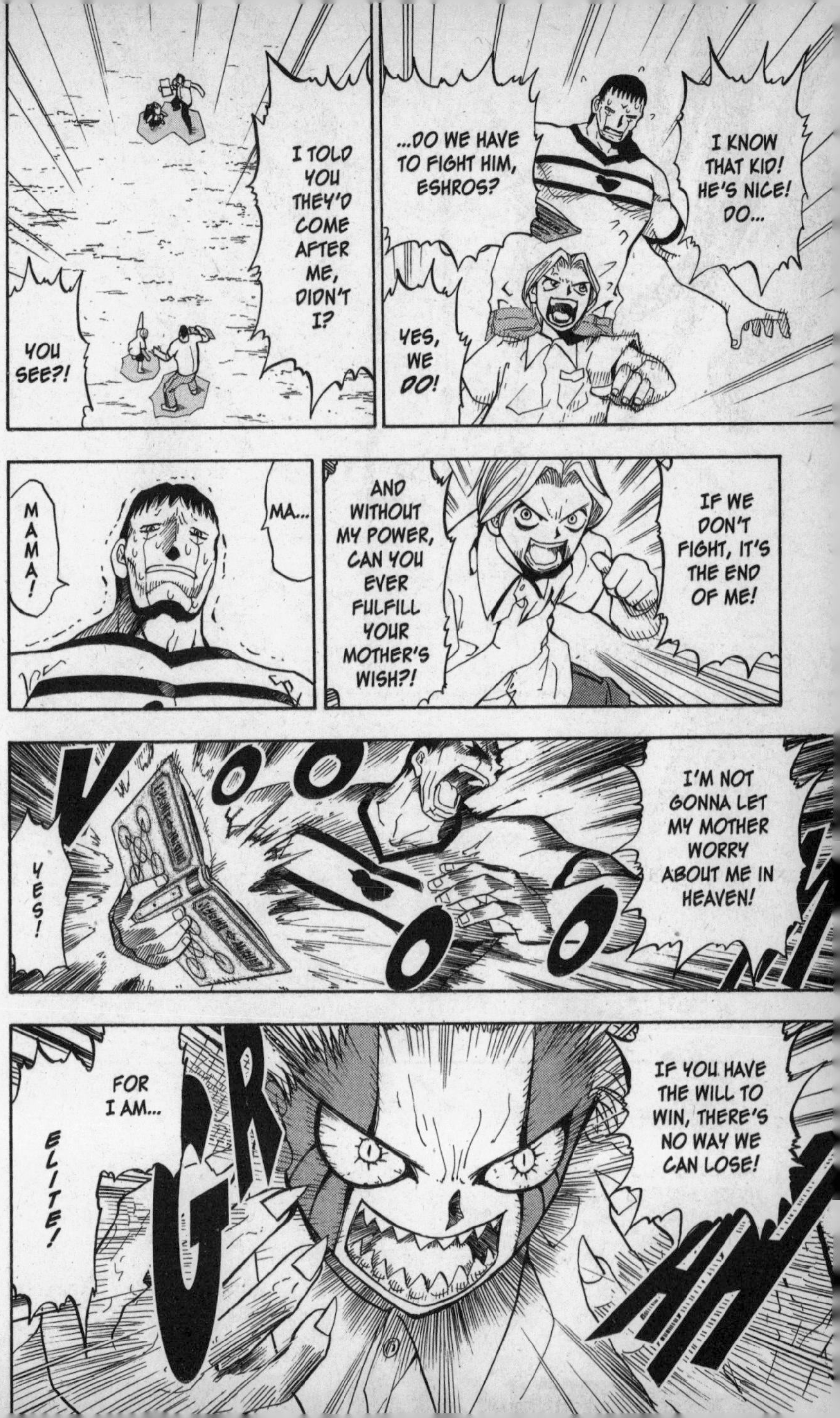
I KNOW THAT KID! HE'S NICE! DO...
...DO WE HAVE TO FIGHT HIM, ESHROS?
YES, WE DO!
I TOLD YOU THEY'D COME AFTER ME, DIDN'T I?
YOU SEE?!
IF WE DON'T FIGHT, IT'S THE END OF ME!
AND WITHOUT MY POWER, CAN YOU EVER FULFILL YOUR MOTHER'S WISH?!
MA...
MAMA!
I'M NOT GONNA LET MY MOTHER WORRY ABOUT ME IN HEAVEN!
YES!
IF YOU HAVE THE WILL TO WIN, THERE'S NO WAY WE CAN LOSE!
FOR I AM...
ELITE!

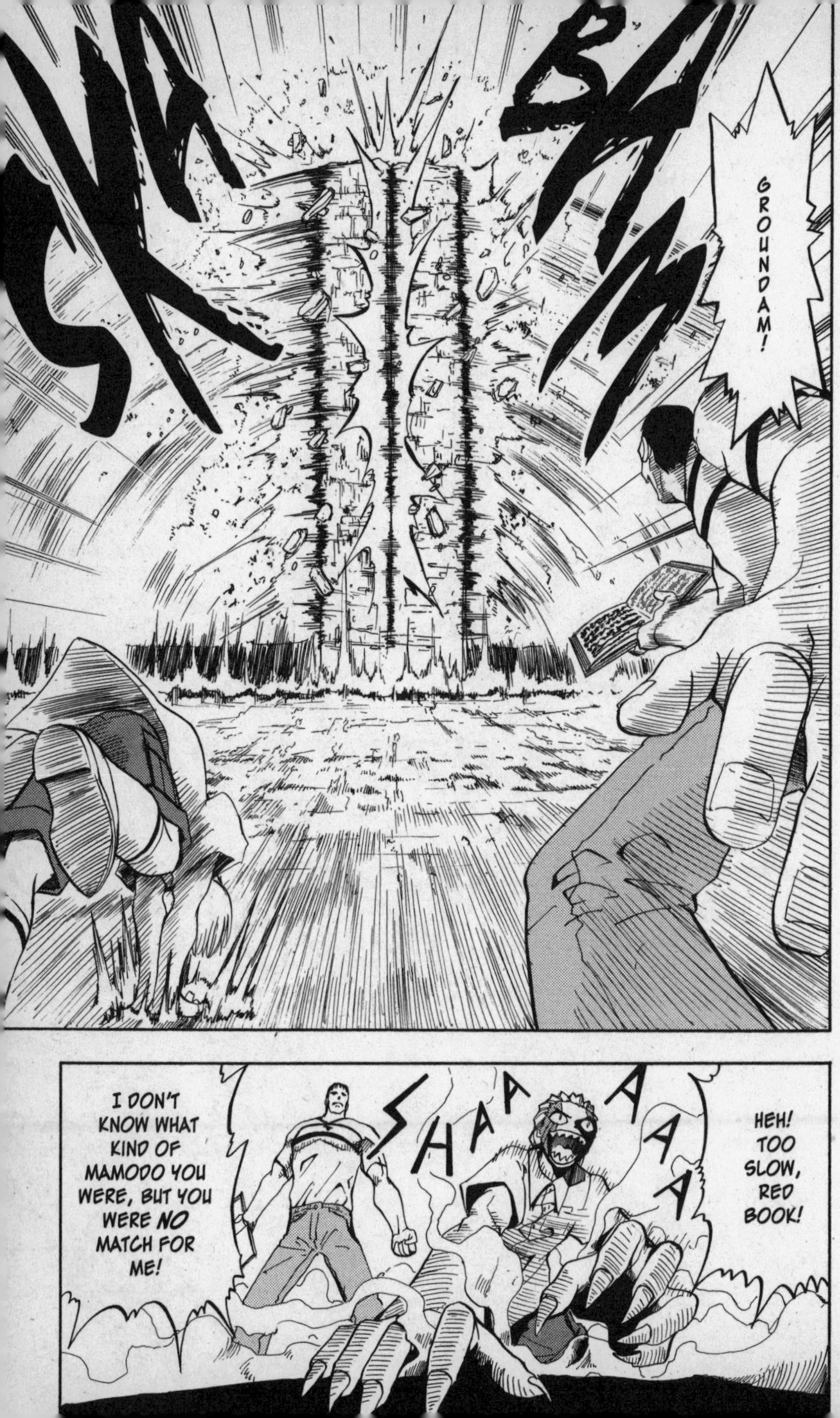
BAM
GROUNDAM!
HEH! TOO SLOW, RED BOOK!
SHAAAAA
I DON'T KNOW WHAT KIND OF MAMODO YOU WERE, BUT YOU WERE NO MATCH FOR ME!

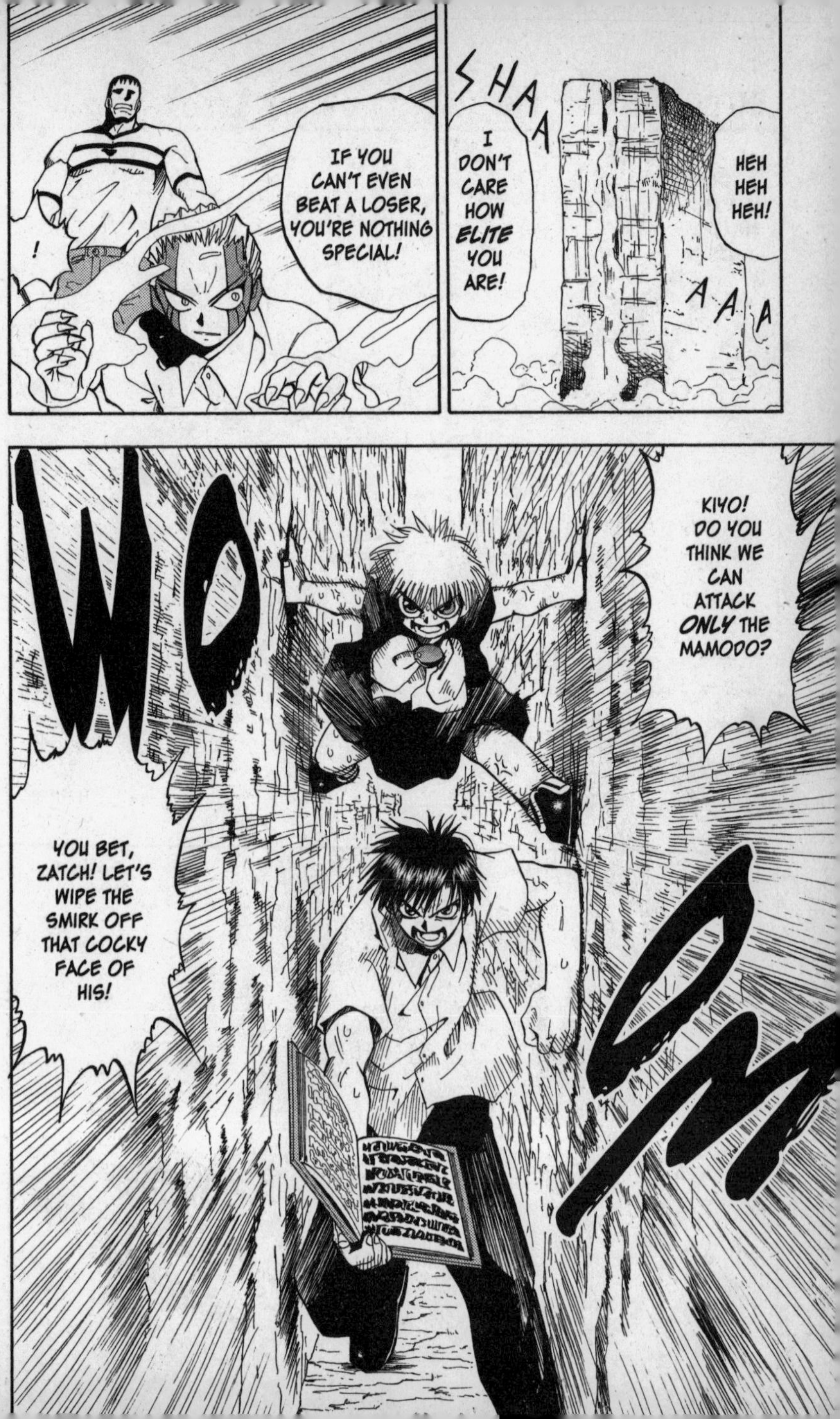
HEH HEH HEH!
SHAAAAA
I DON'T CARE HOW ELITE YOU ARE!
IF YOU CAN'T EVEN BEAT A LOSER, YOU'RE NOTHING SPECIAL!
!
KIYO! DO YOU THINK WE CAN ATTACK ONLY THE MAMODO?
WO
OM
YOU BET, ZATCH! LET'S WIPE THE SMIRK OFF THAT COCKY FACE OF HIS!

# LEVEL 24: The Appearance of Strength

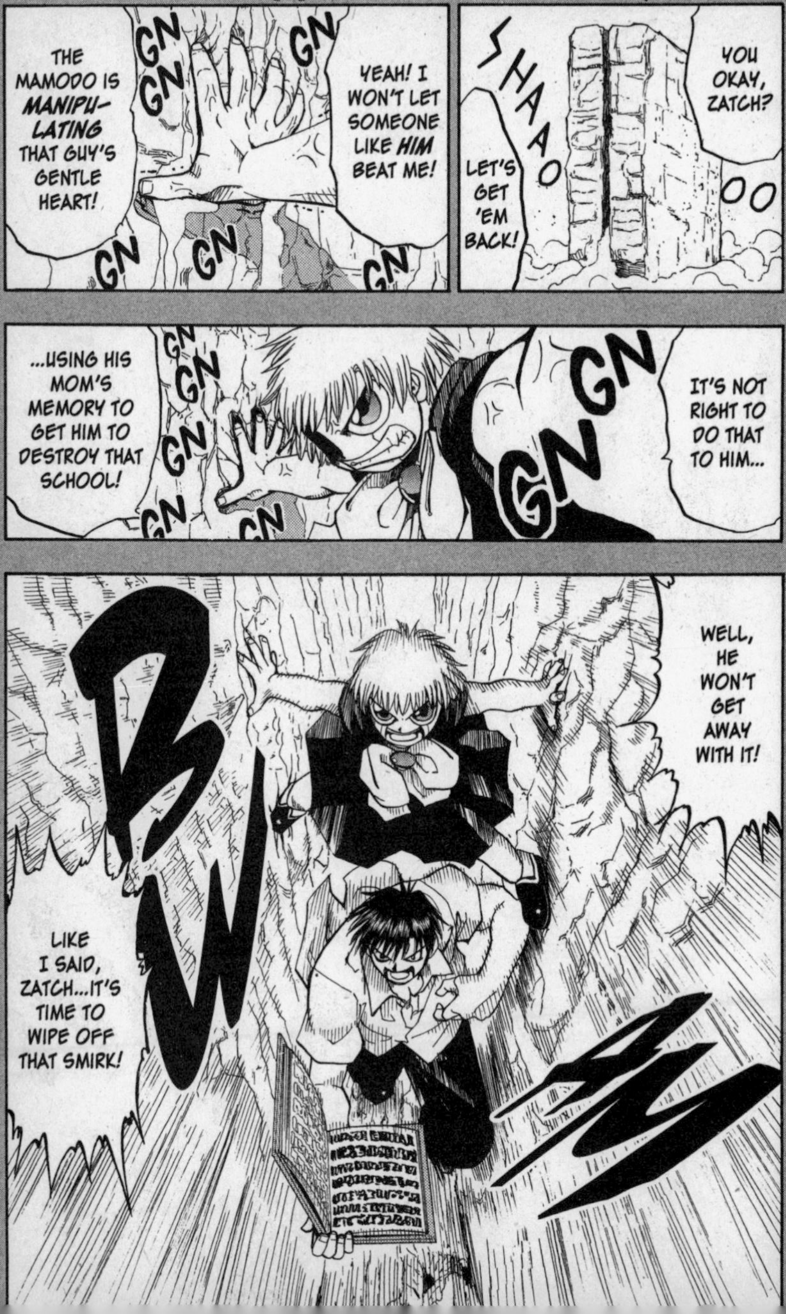
YOU OKAY, ZATCH?
SHAAO
OO
LET'S GET 'EM BACK!
YEAH! I WON'T LET SOMEONE LIKE **HIM** BEAT ME!
THE MAMODO IS **MANIPU-LATING** THAT GUY'S GENTLE HEART!
GN GN GN GN GN GN
IT'S NOT RIGHT TO DO THAT TO HIM...
GN GN GN
...USING HIS MOM'S MEMORY TO GET HIM TO DESTROY THAT SCHOOL!
GN GN GN GN GN
WELL, HE WON'T GET AWAY WITH IT!
BWAM
LIKE I SAID, ZATCH...IT'S TIME TO WIPE OFF THAT SMIRK!

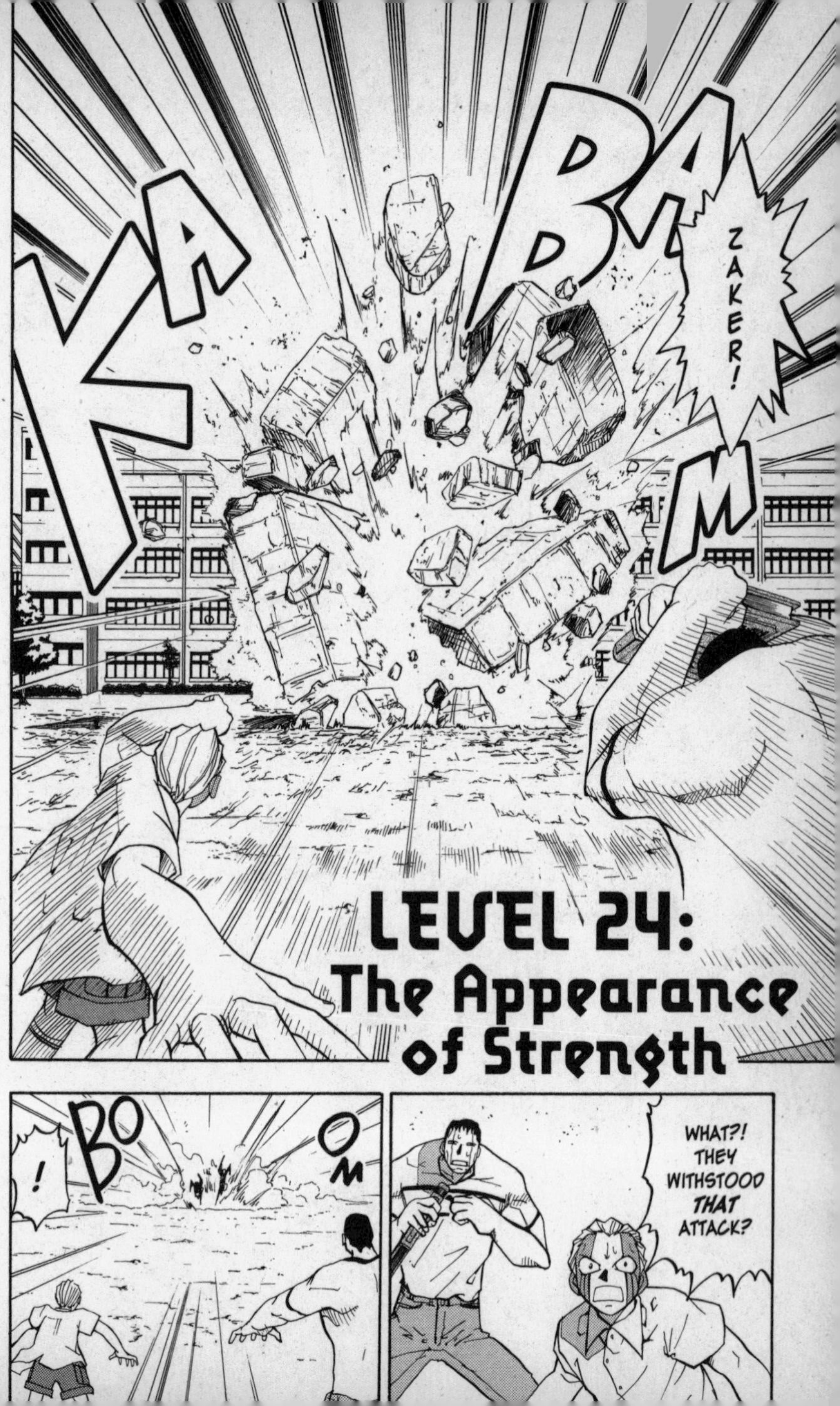
KABAM
ZAKER!
LEVEL 24:
The Appearance of Strength
WHAT?! THEY WITHSTOOD *THAT* ATTACK?
BOOM
!

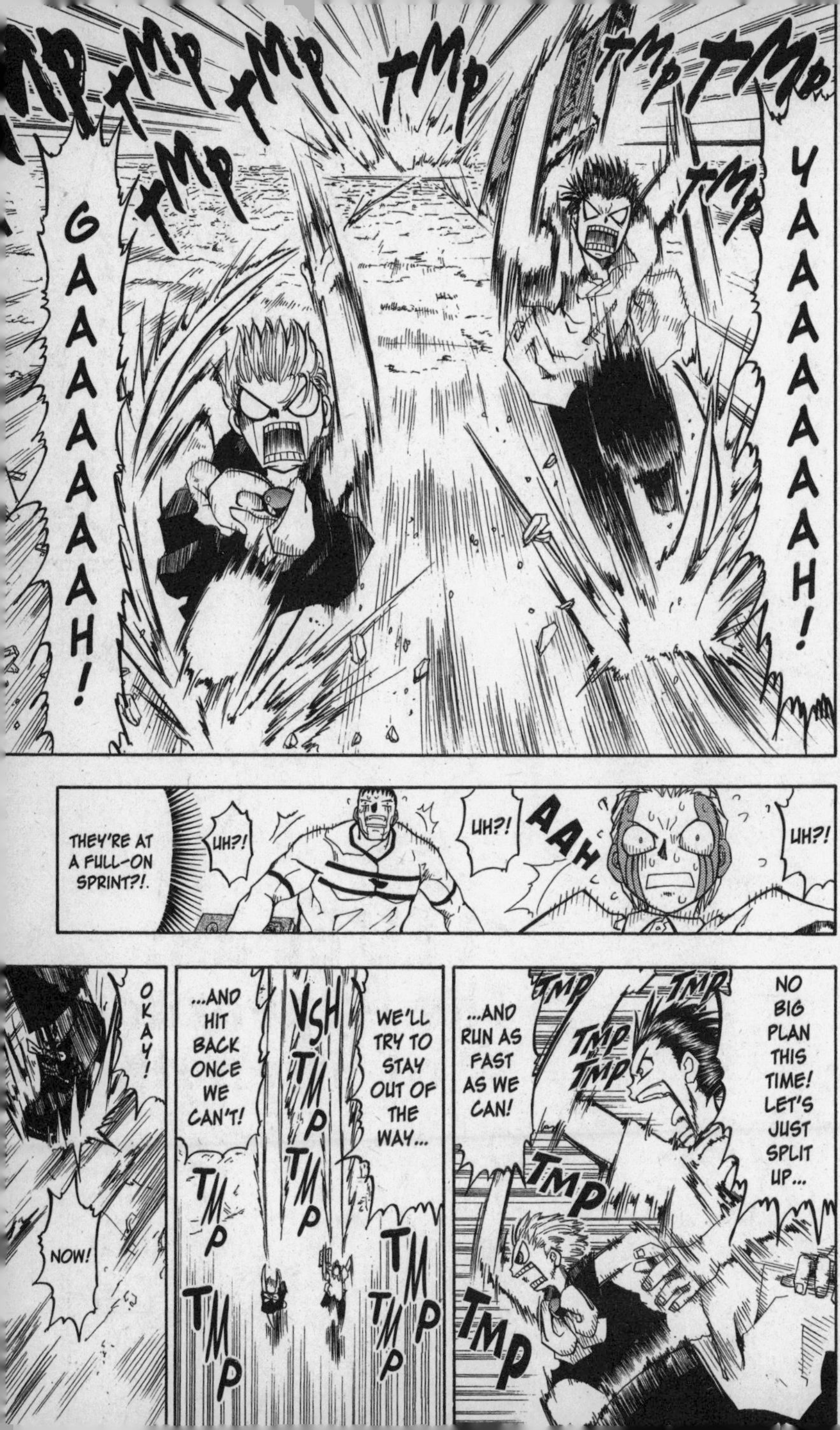
TMP TMP TMP TMP TMP TMP TMP TMP TMP
YAAAAAAAAAH!
GAAAAAAAAH!
UH?!
AAH
UH?!
UH?!
THEY'RE AT A FULL-ON SPRINT?!.
NO BIG PLAN THIS TIME! LET'S JUST SPLIT UP...
TMP TMP TMP TMP TMP TMP
...AND RUN AS FAST AS WE CAN!
WE'LL TRY TO STAY OUT OF THE WAY...
VSH
TMP TMP TMP TMP TMP TMP TMP
...AND HIT BACK ONCE WE CAN'T!
OKAY!
NOW!

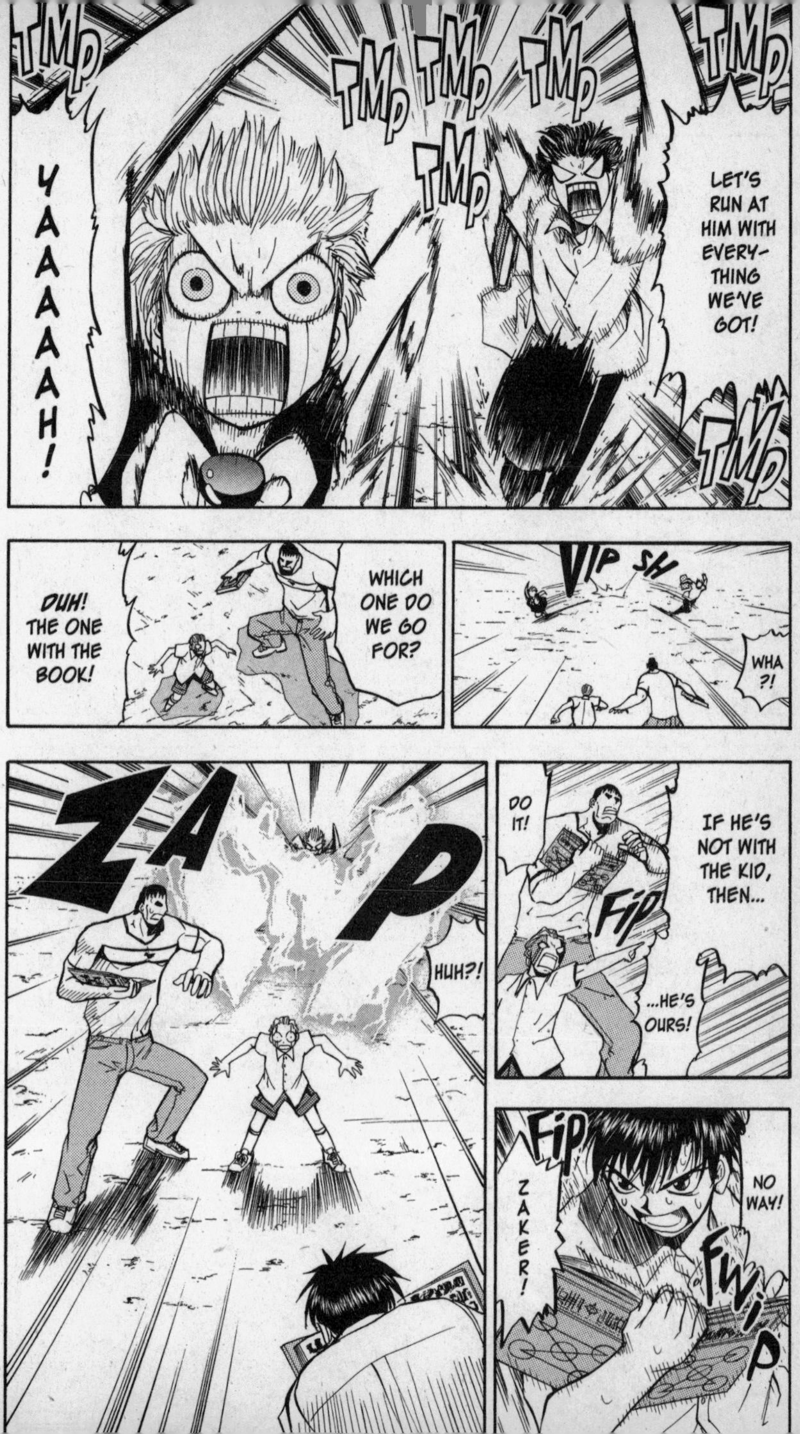
TMP
TMP
TMP
TMP
TMP
TMP
LET'S RUN AT HIM WITH EVERY-THING WE'VE GOT!
YAAAAAAAH!
TMP
VIP
SH
WHA?!
WHICH ONE DO WE GO FOR?
DUH! THE ONE WITH THE BOOK!
IF HE'S NOT WITH THE KID, THEN...
DO IT!
FIP
...HE'S OURS!
NO WAY!
FIP
ZAKER!
FWIP
ZAP
HUH?!

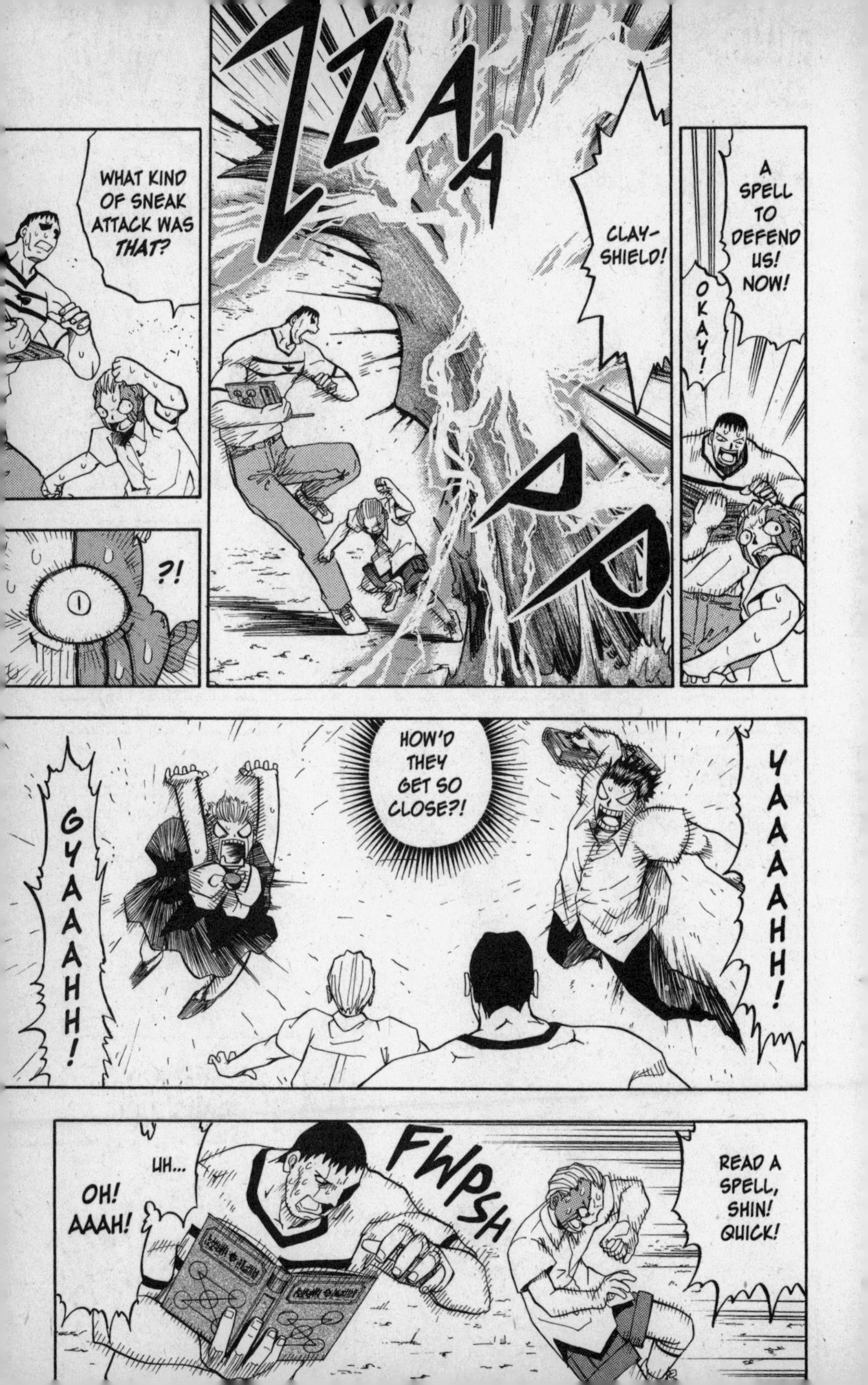
A SPELL TO DEFEND US! NOW!
OKAY!
CLAY-SHIELD!
ZZAAAPP
WHAT KIND OF SNEAK ATTACK WAS *THAT*?
?!
YAAAAAHH!
HOW'D THEY GET SO CLOSE?!
GYAAAAHH!
READ A SPELL, SHIN! QUICK!
FWPSH
UH...
OH! AAAH!

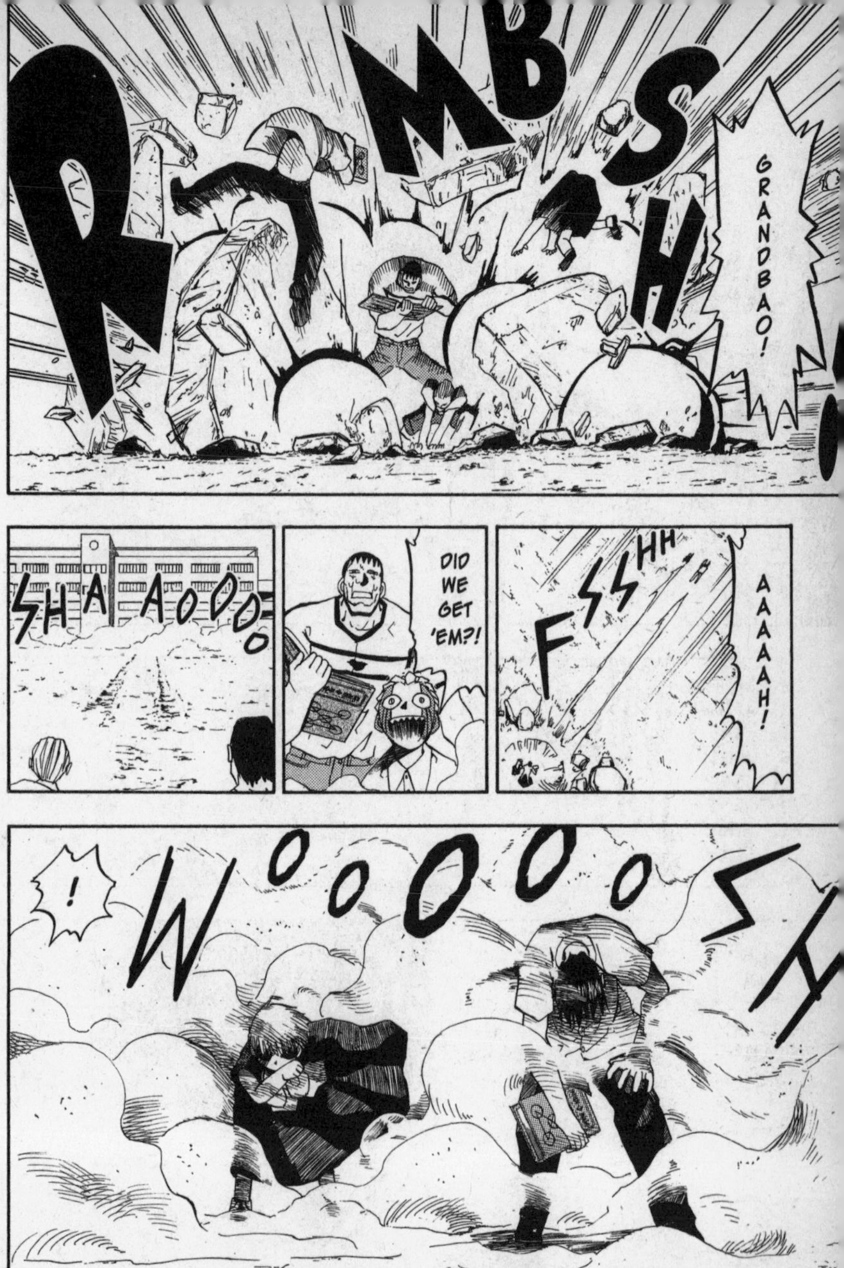
GRANDBAO!
RMBSH
AAAAAAH!
FSSHH
DID WE GET 'EM?!
SHA AODDDO
!
WOOOOOSH

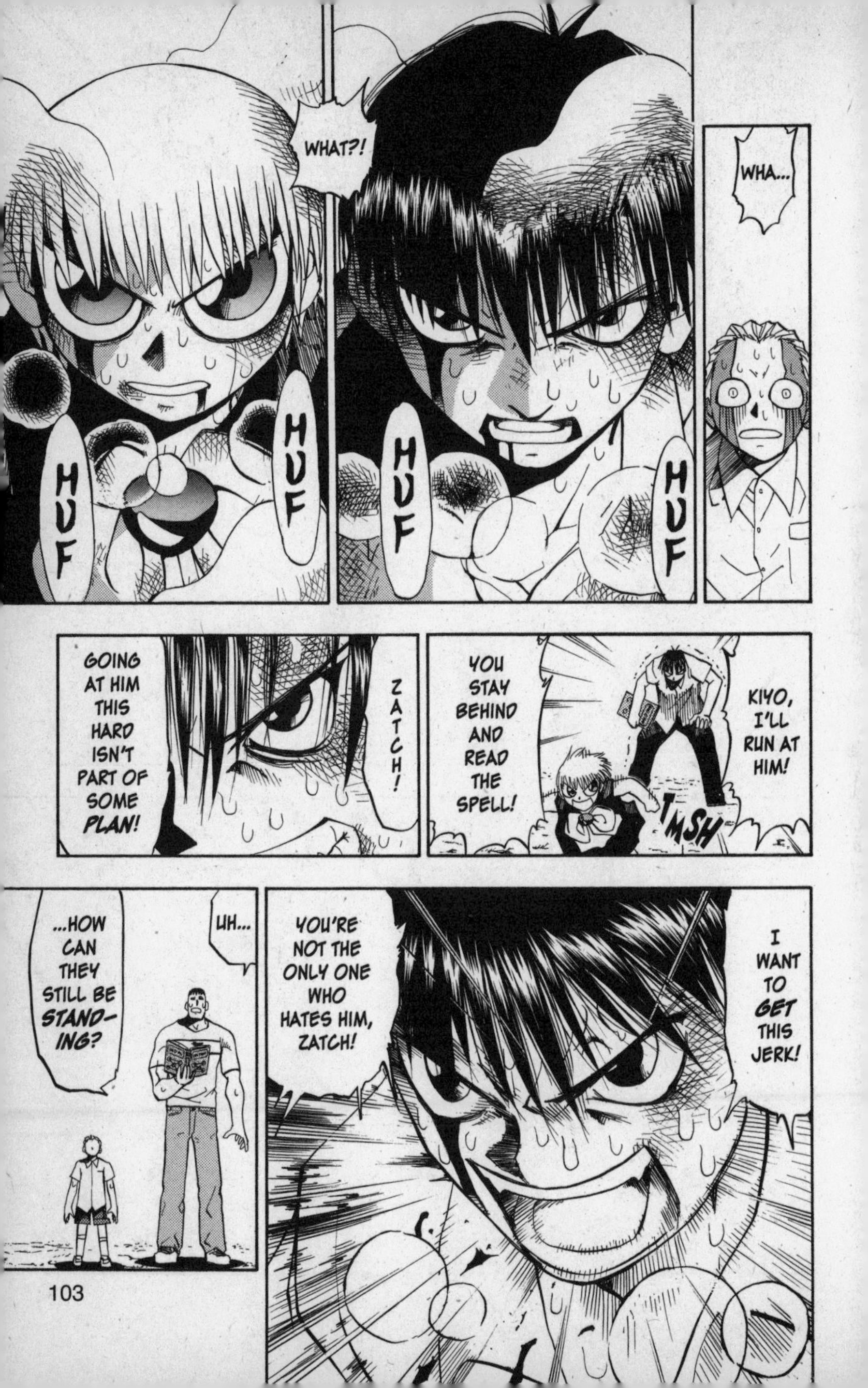
WHA...
WHAT?!
HUF
HUF
HUF
HUF
KIYO, I'LL RUN AT HIM!
YOU STAY BEHIND AND READ THE SPELL!
TMSH
ZATCH!
GOING AT HIM THIS HARD ISN'T PART OF SOME *PLAN*!
I WANT TO *GET* THIS JERK!
YOU'RE NOT THE ONLY ONE WHO HATES HIM, ZATCH!
UH...
...HOW CAN THEY STILL BE *STANDING?*

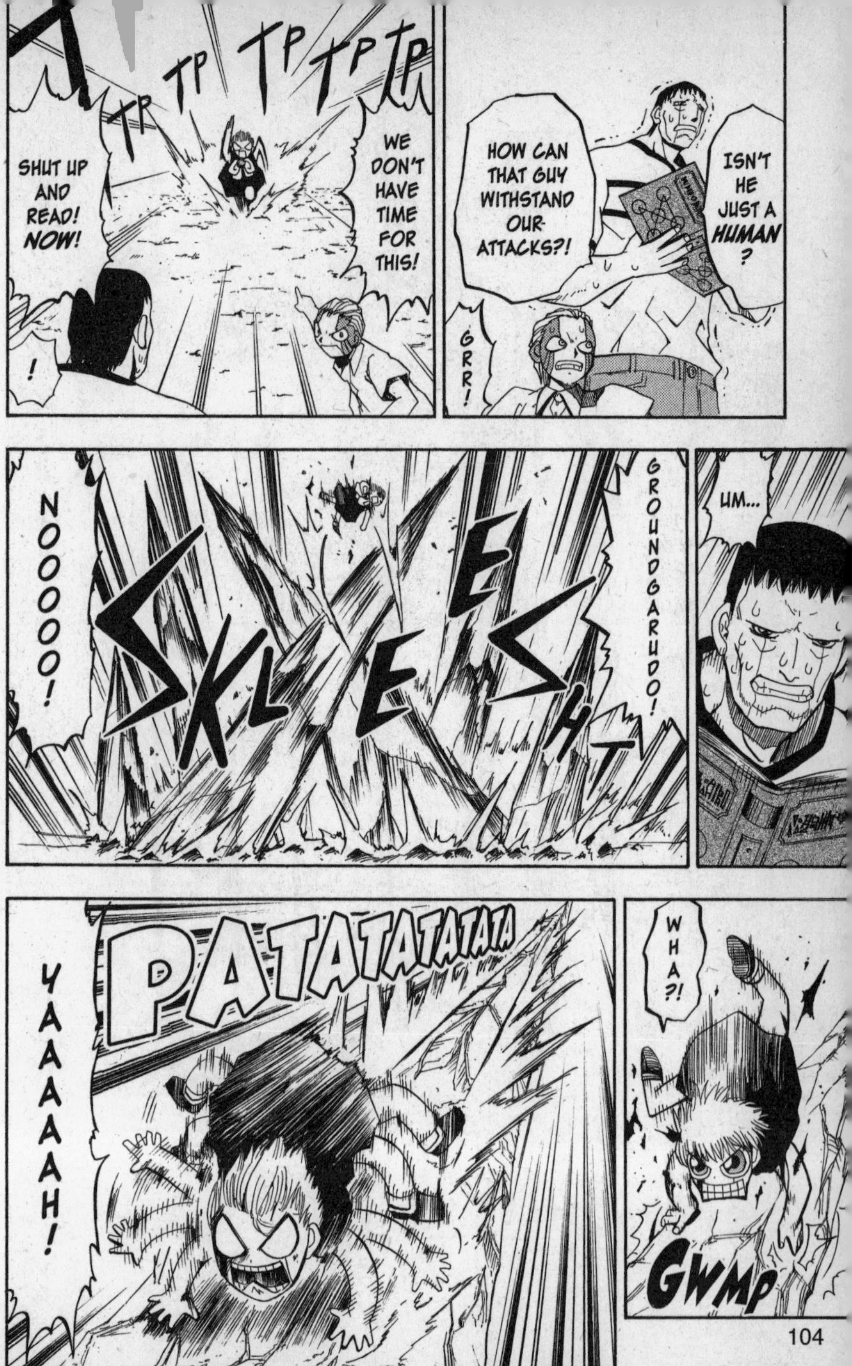
ISN'T HE JUST A HUMAN?
HOW CAN THAT GUY WITHSTAND OUR ATTACKS?!
GRR!
TP TP TP TP TP TP
WE DON'T HAVE TIME FOR THIS!
SHUT UP AND READ! NOW!
!
UM...
GROUNDGARUDO!
SKLEESHT
NOOOOOO!
WHA?!
GWMP
PATATATATATA
YAAAAAAH!

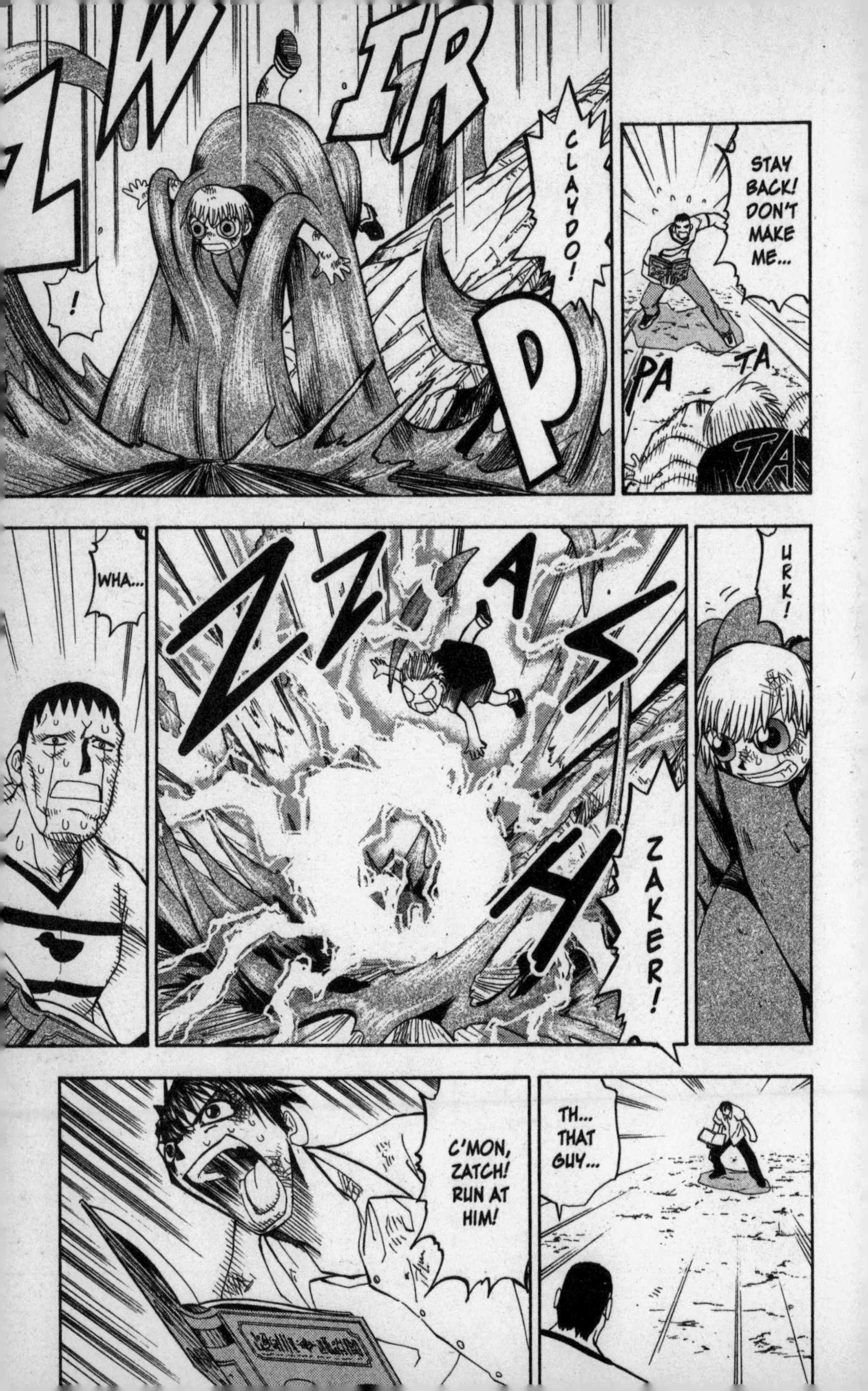
STAY BACK! DON'T MAKE ME...
PA
TA
TA
CLAYDO!
ZW
IR
P
!
URK!
ZAKER!
ZZASH
WHA...
TH... THAT GUY...
C'MON, ZATCH! RUN AT HIM!

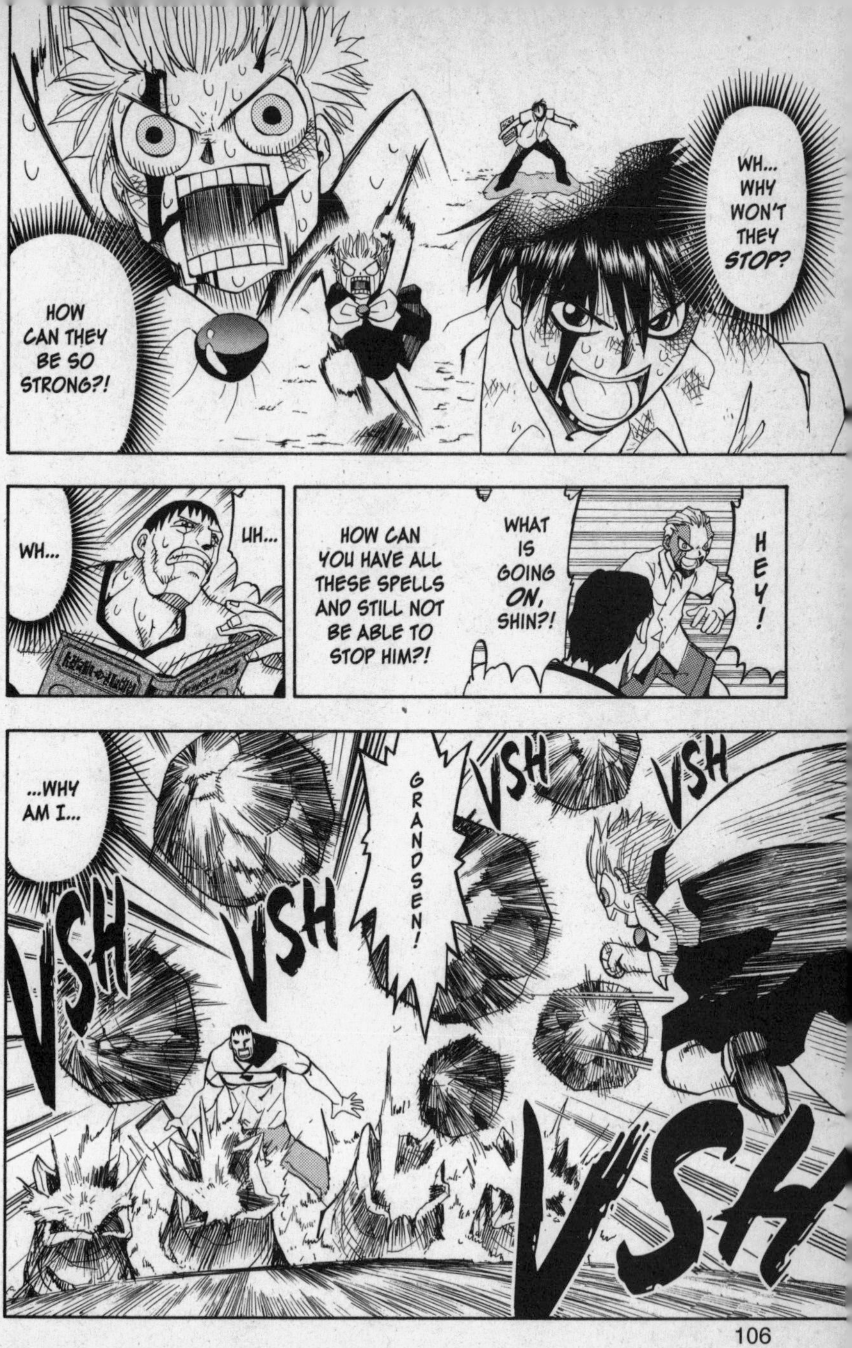
WH... WHY WON'T THEY STOP?
HOW CAN THEY BE SO STRONG?!
HEY!
WHAT IS GOING ON, SHIN?!
HOW CAN YOU HAVE ALL THESE SPELLS AND STILL NOT BE ABLE TO STOP HIM?!
UH...
WH...
VSH
VSH
GRANDSEN!
...WHY AM I...
VSH
VSH
VSH

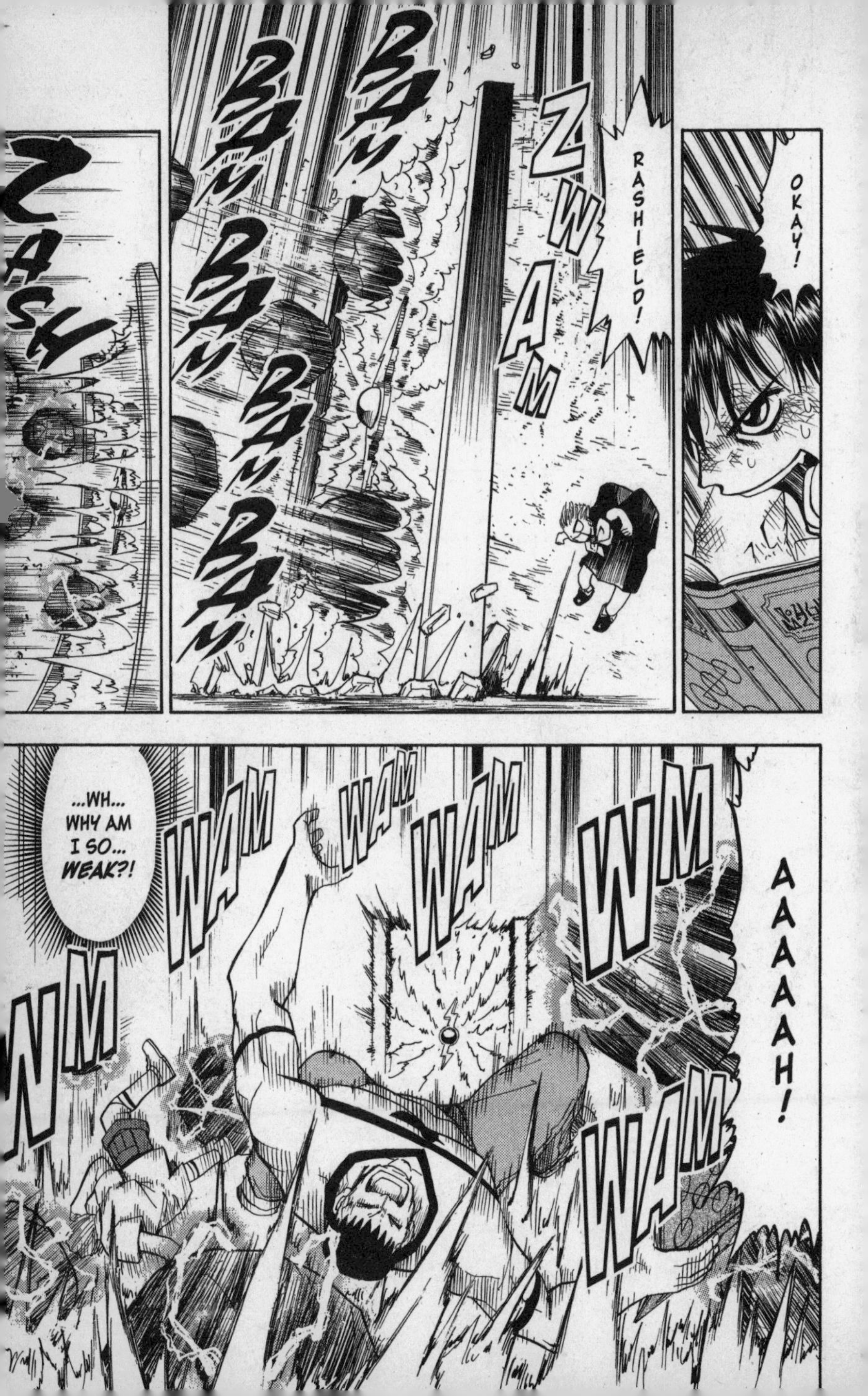
OKAY!
RASHIELD!
ZWAAM
BAM BAM BAM
BAM BAM BAM
ZASH
AAAAAAH!
WAM
WM
WAM
WAM
WAM
...WH... WHY AM I SO... WEAK?!
WM

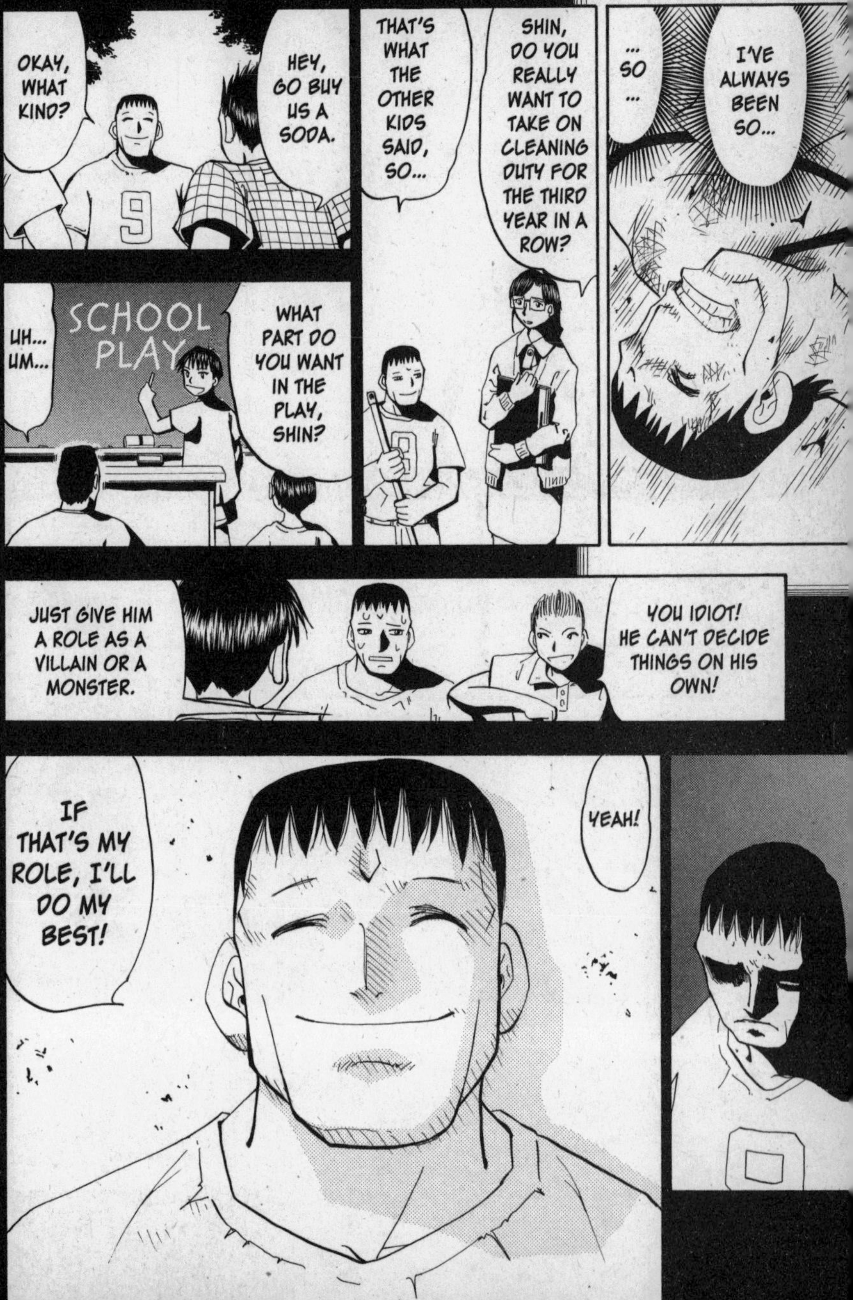
I'VE ALWAYS BEEN SO...
... SO ...
SHIN, DO YOU REALLY WANT TO TAKE ON CLEANING DUTY FOR THE THIRD YEAR IN A ROW?
THAT'S WHAT THE OTHER KIDS SAID, SO...
HEY, GO BUY US A SODA.
OKAY, WHAT KIND?
WHAT PART DO YOU WANT IN THE PLAY, SHIN?
SCHOOL PLAY
UH... UM...
YOU IDIOT! HE CAN'T DECIDE THINGS ON HIS OWN!
JUST GIVE HIM A ROLE AS A VILLAIN OR A MONSTER.
YEAH!
IF THAT'S MY ROLE, I'LL DO MY BEST!

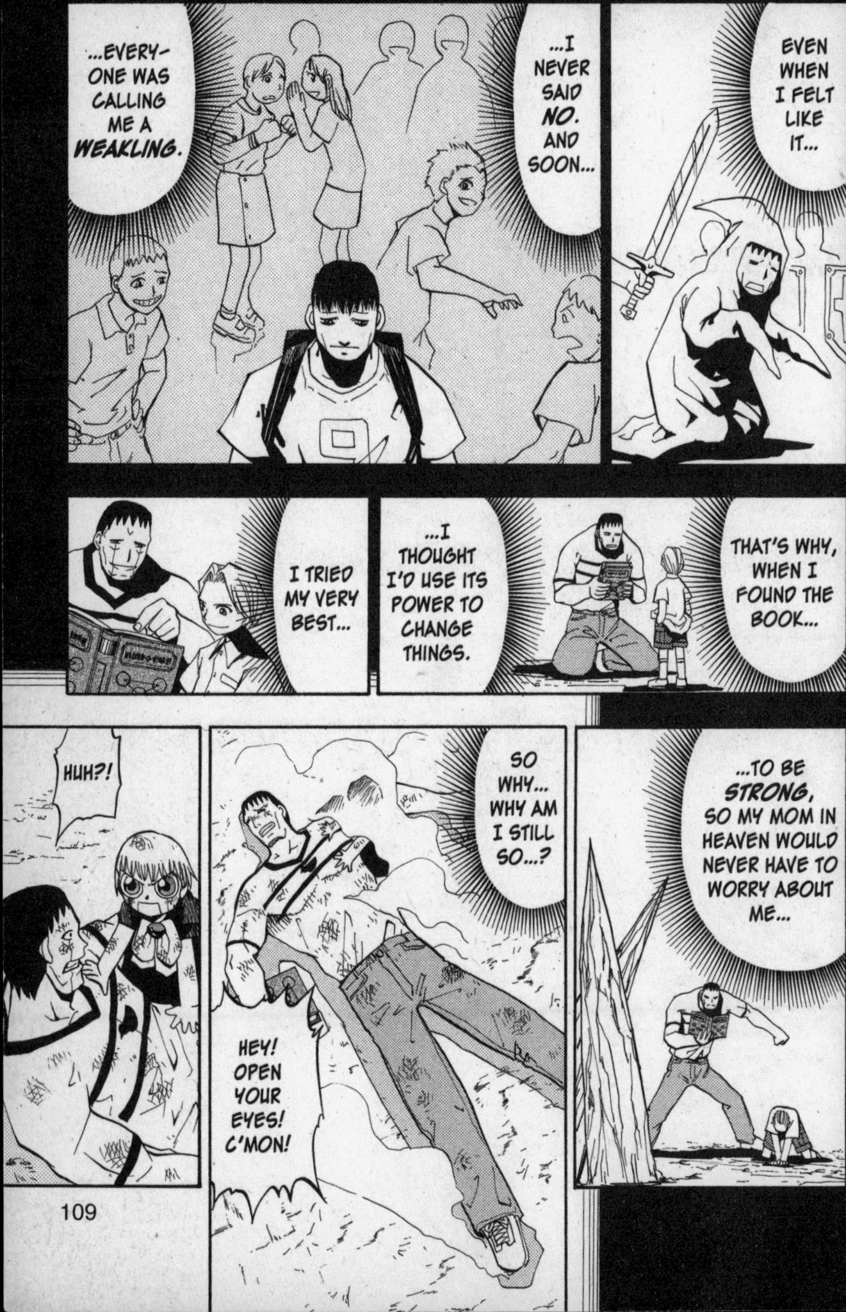
EVEN WHEN I FELT LIKE IT...
...I NEVER SAID NO. AND SOON...
...EVERY-ONE WAS CALLING ME A WEAKLING.
THAT'S WHY, WHEN I FOUND THE BOOK...
...I THOUGHT I'D USE ITS POWER TO CHANGE THINGS.
I TRIED MY VERY BEST...
...TO BE STRONG, SO MY MOM IN HEAVEN WOULD NEVER HAVE TO WORRY ABOUT ME...
SO WHY... WHY AM I STILL SO...?
HEY! OPEN YOUR EYES! C'MON!
HUH?!

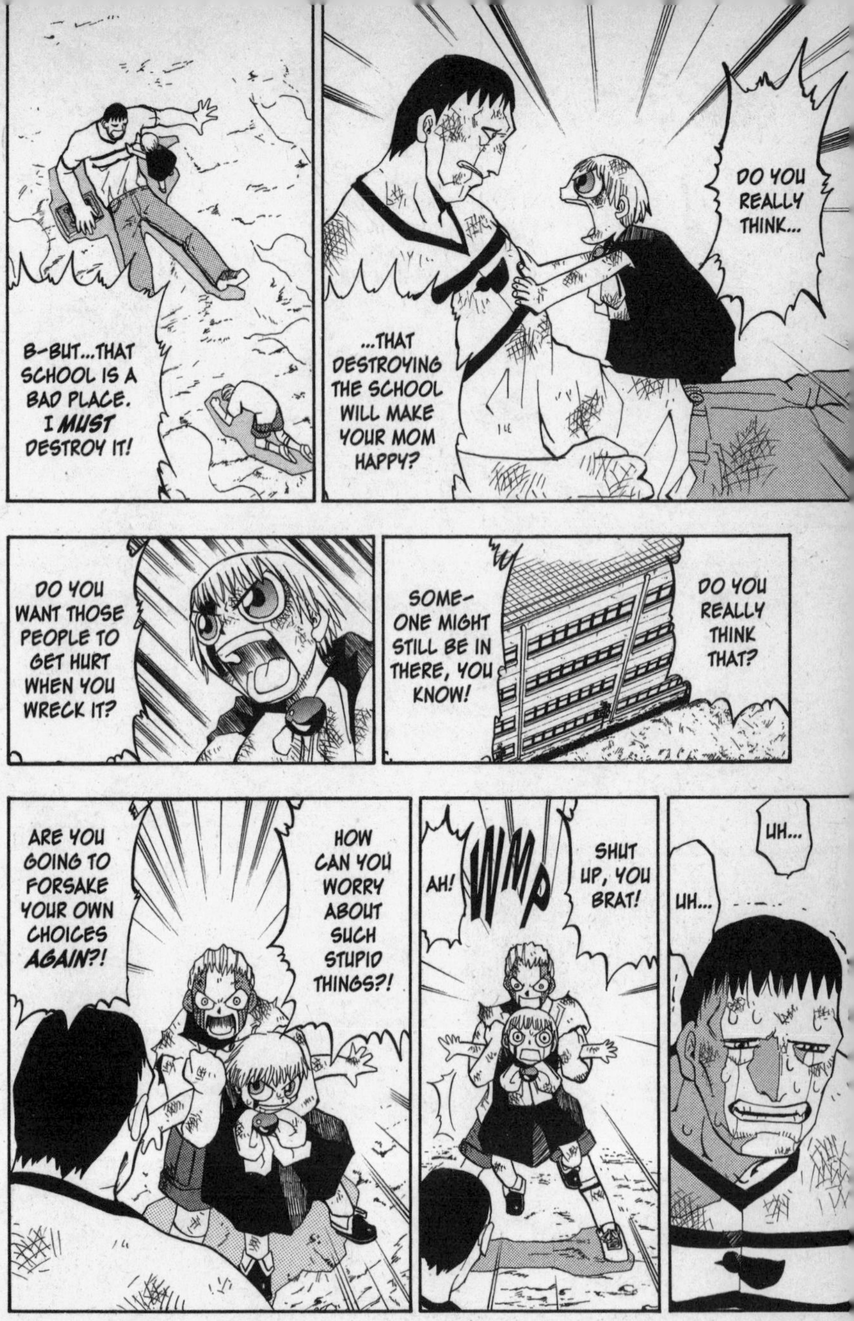
DO YOU REALLY THINK...
...THAT DESTROYING THE SCHOOL WILL MAKE YOUR MOM HAPPY?
B-BUT...THAT SCHOOL IS A BAD PLACE. I *MUST* DESTROY IT!
DO YOU REALLY THINK THAT?
SOME-ONE MIGHT STILL BE IN THERE, YOU KNOW!
DO YOU WANT THOSE PEOPLE TO GET HURT WHEN YOU WRECK IT?
UH...
UH...
SHUT UP, YOU BRAT!
WMP
AH!
HOW CAN YOU WORRY ABOUT SUCH STUPID THINGS?!
ARE YOU GOING TO FORSAKE YOUR OWN CHOICES *AGAIN*?!

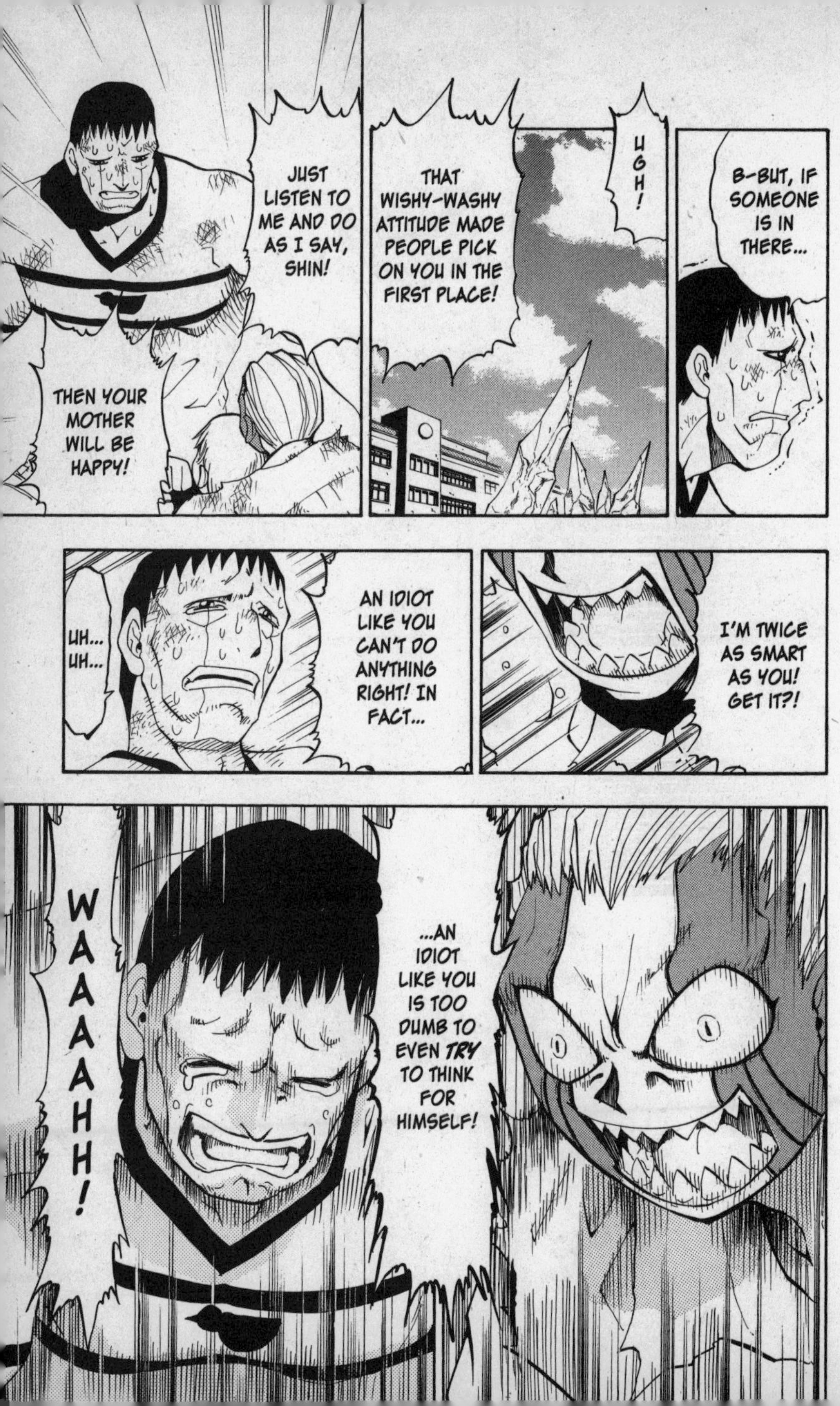
B-BUT, IF SOMEONE IS IN THERE...
UGH!
THAT WISHY-WASHY ATTITUDE MADE PEOPLE PICK ON YOU IN THE FIRST PLACE!
JUST LISTEN TO ME AND DO AS I SAY, SHIN!
THEN YOUR MOTHER WILL BE HAPPY!
I'M TWICE AS SMART AS YOU! GET IT?!
AN IDIOT LIKE YOU CAN'T DO ANYTHING RIGHT! IN FACT...
UH... UH...
...AN IDIOT LIKE YOU IS TOO DUMB TO EVEN TRY TO THINK FOR HIMSELF!
WAAAAAHH!

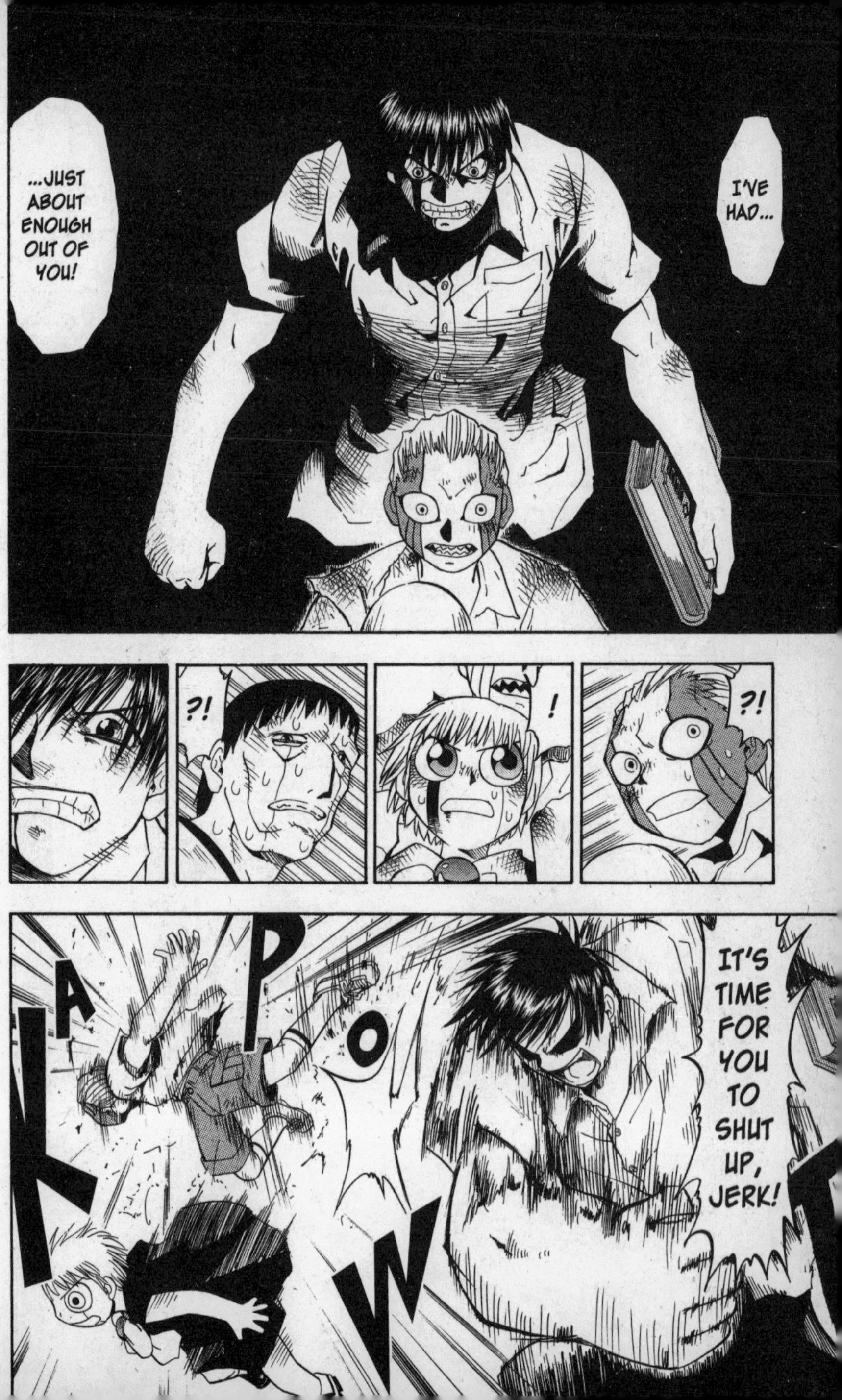
I'VE HAD...
...JUST ABOUT ENOUGH OUT OF YOU!
?!
!
?!
IT'S TIME FOR YOU TO SHUT UP, JERK!

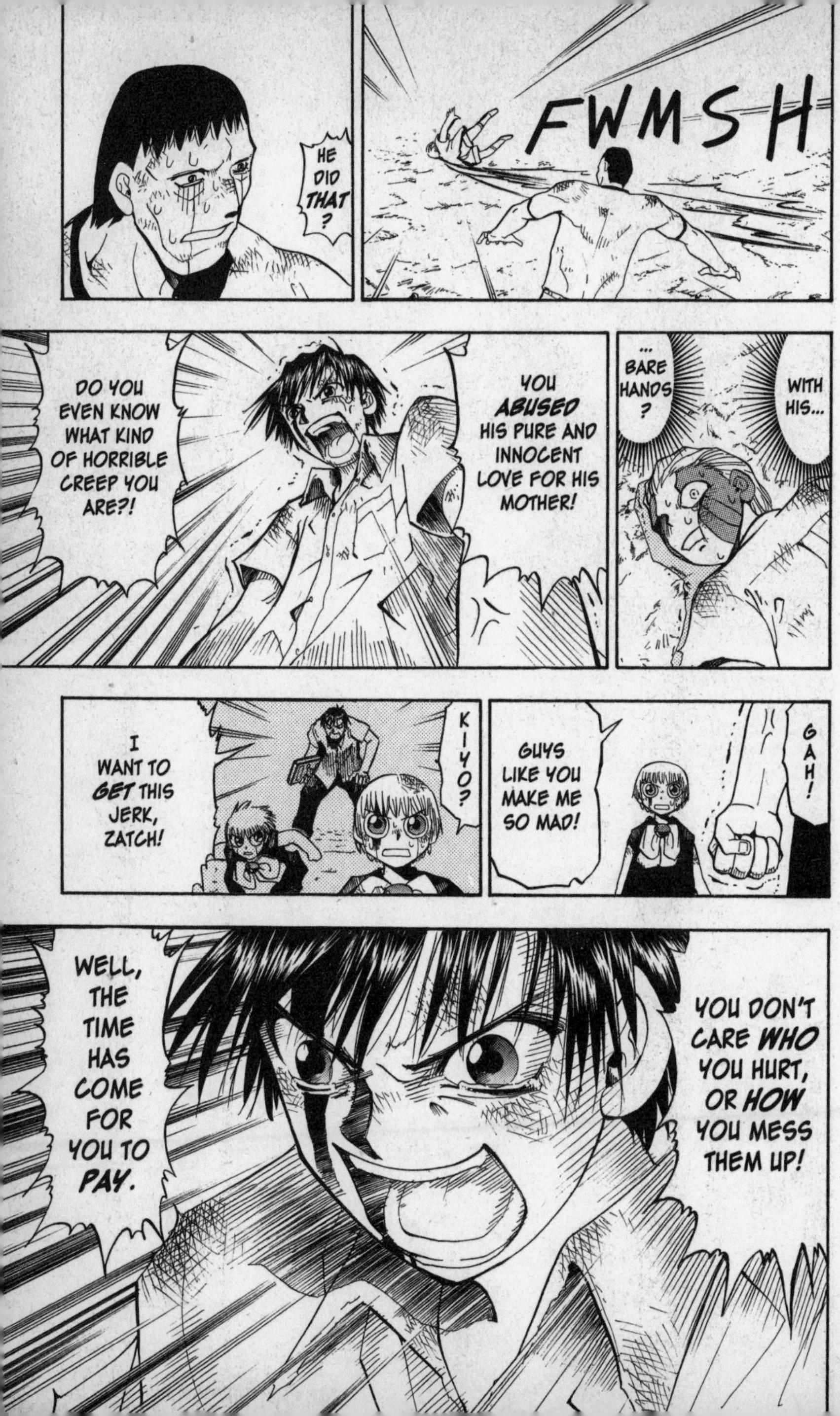
FWMSH
HE DID THAT?
WITH HIS...
...BARE HANDS?
YOU ABUSED HIS PURE AND INNOCENT LOVE FOR HIS MOTHER!
DO YOU EVEN KNOW WHAT KIND OF HORRIBLE CREEP YOU ARE?!
GAH!
GUYS LIKE YOU MAKE ME SO MAD!
KIYO?
I WANT TO GET THIS JERK, ZATCH!
YOU DON'T CARE WHO YOU HURT, OR HOW YOU MESS THEM UP!
WELL, THE TIME HAS COME FOR YOU TO PAY.

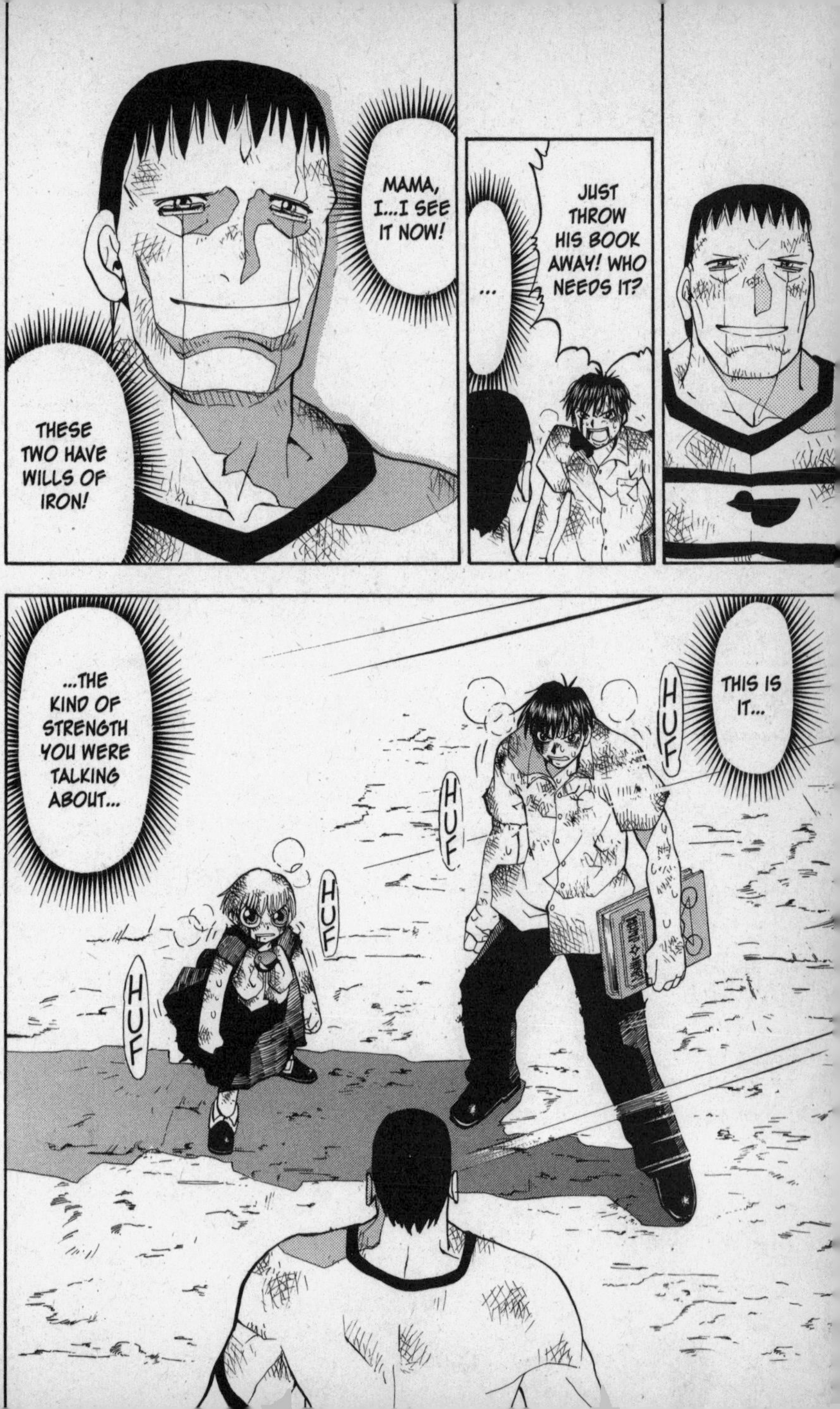
JUST THROW HIS BOOK AWAY! WHO NEEDS IT?
...
MAMA, I...I SEE IT NOW!
THESE TWO HAVE WILLS OF IRON!
THIS IS IT...
HUF
...THE KIND OF STRENGTH YOU WERE TALKING ABOUT...
HUF
HUF
HUF

# LEVEL 25: My Will

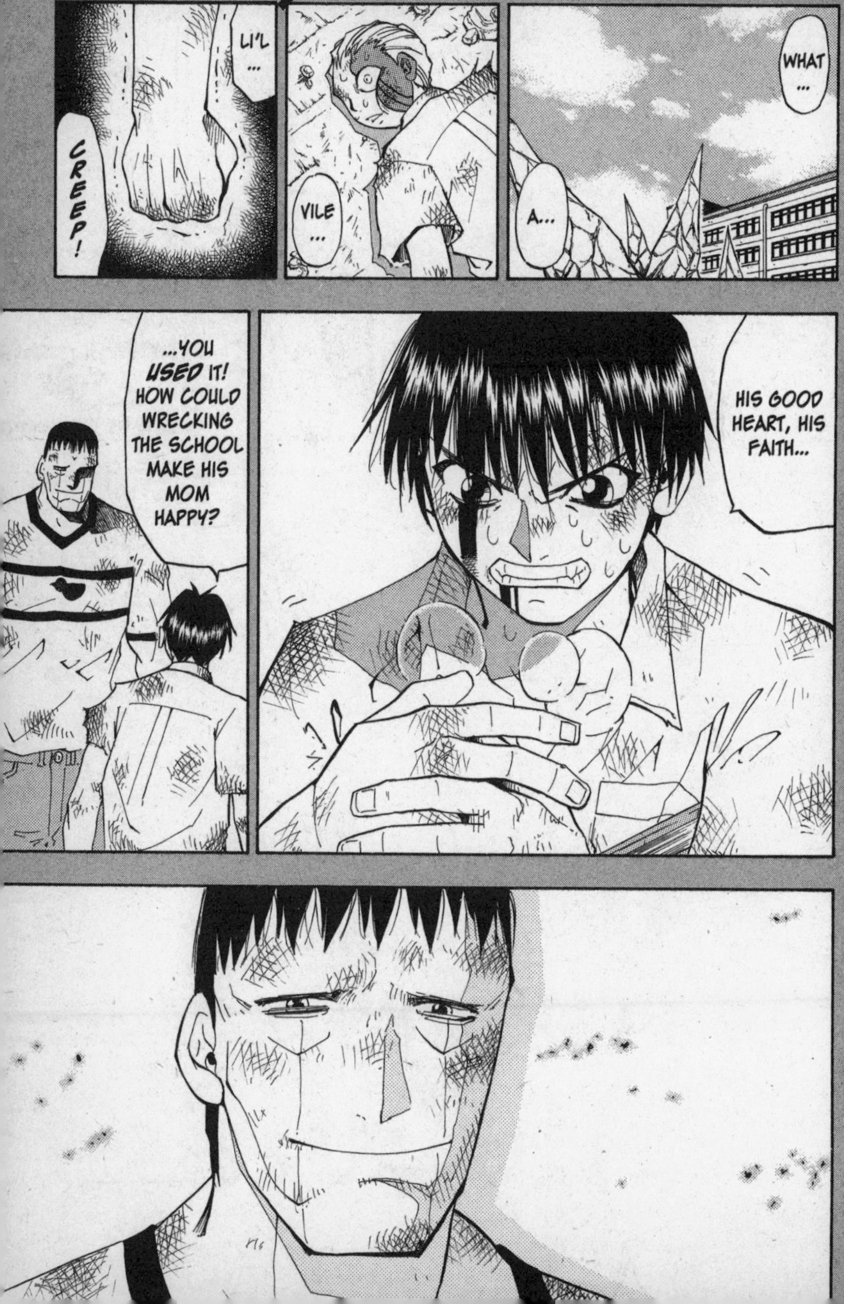
WHAT ...
A...
VILE ...
LI'L ...
CREEP!
HIS GOOD HEART, HIS FAITH...
...YOU USED IT! HOW COULD WRECKING THE SCHOOL MAKE HIS MOM HAPPY?

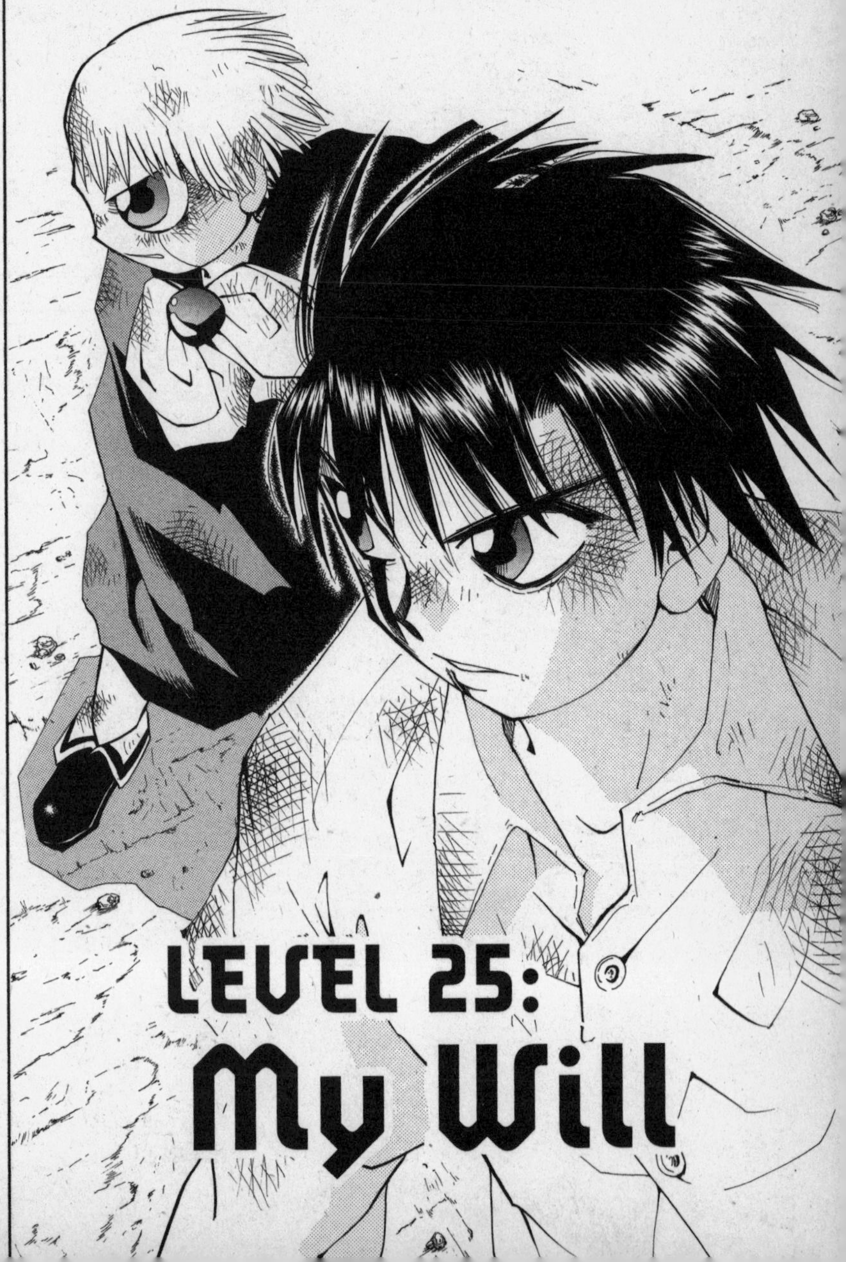
LEVEL 25:
My Will

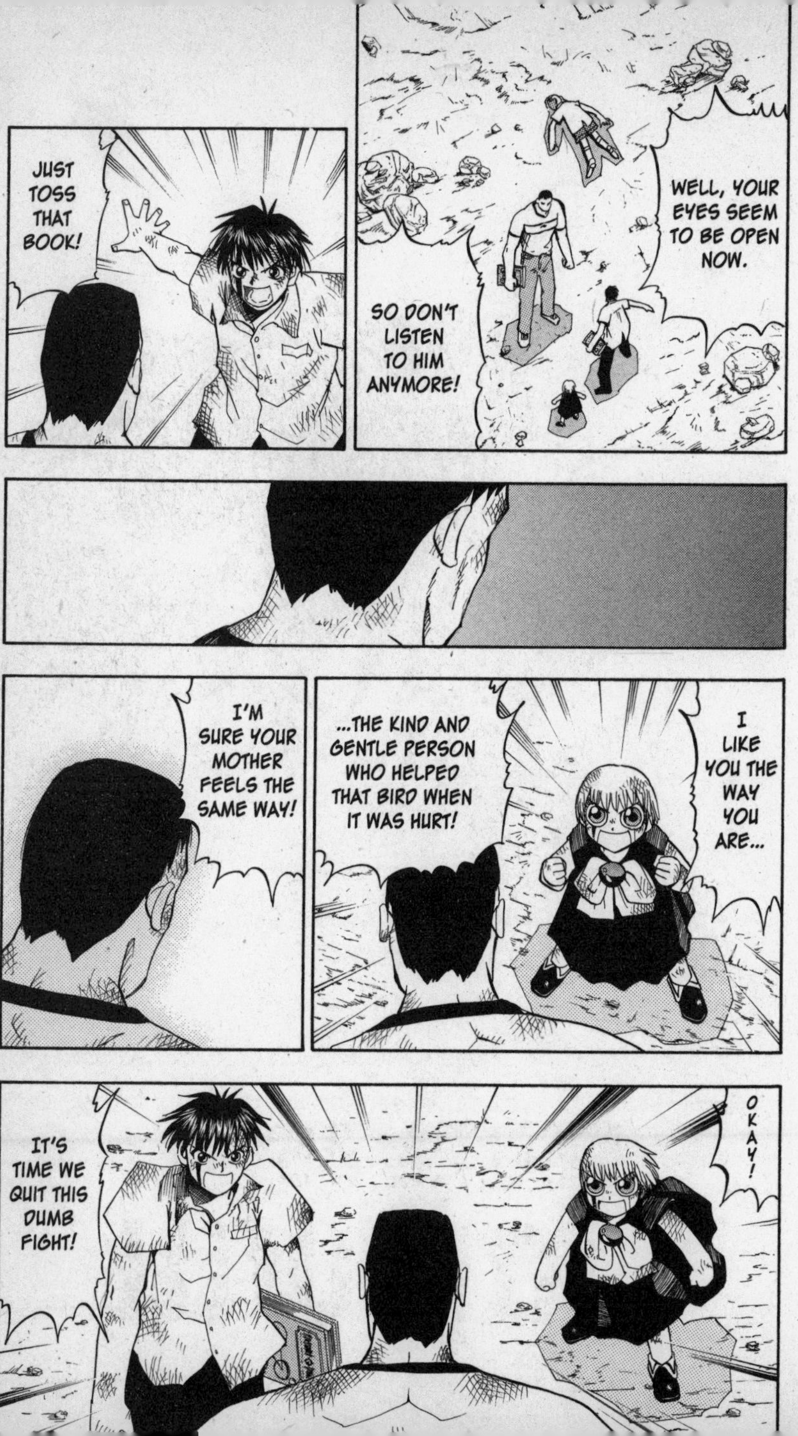
WELL, YOUR EYES SEEM TO BE OPEN NOW.
SO DON'T LISTEN TO HIM ANYMORE!
JUST TOSS THAT BOOK!
I LIKE YOU THE WAY YOU ARE...
...THE KIND AND GENTLE PERSON WHO HELPED THAT BIRD WHEN IT WAS HURT!
I'M SURE YOUR MOTHER FEELS THE SAME WAY!
OKAY!
IT'S TIME WE QUIT THIS DUMB FIGHT!

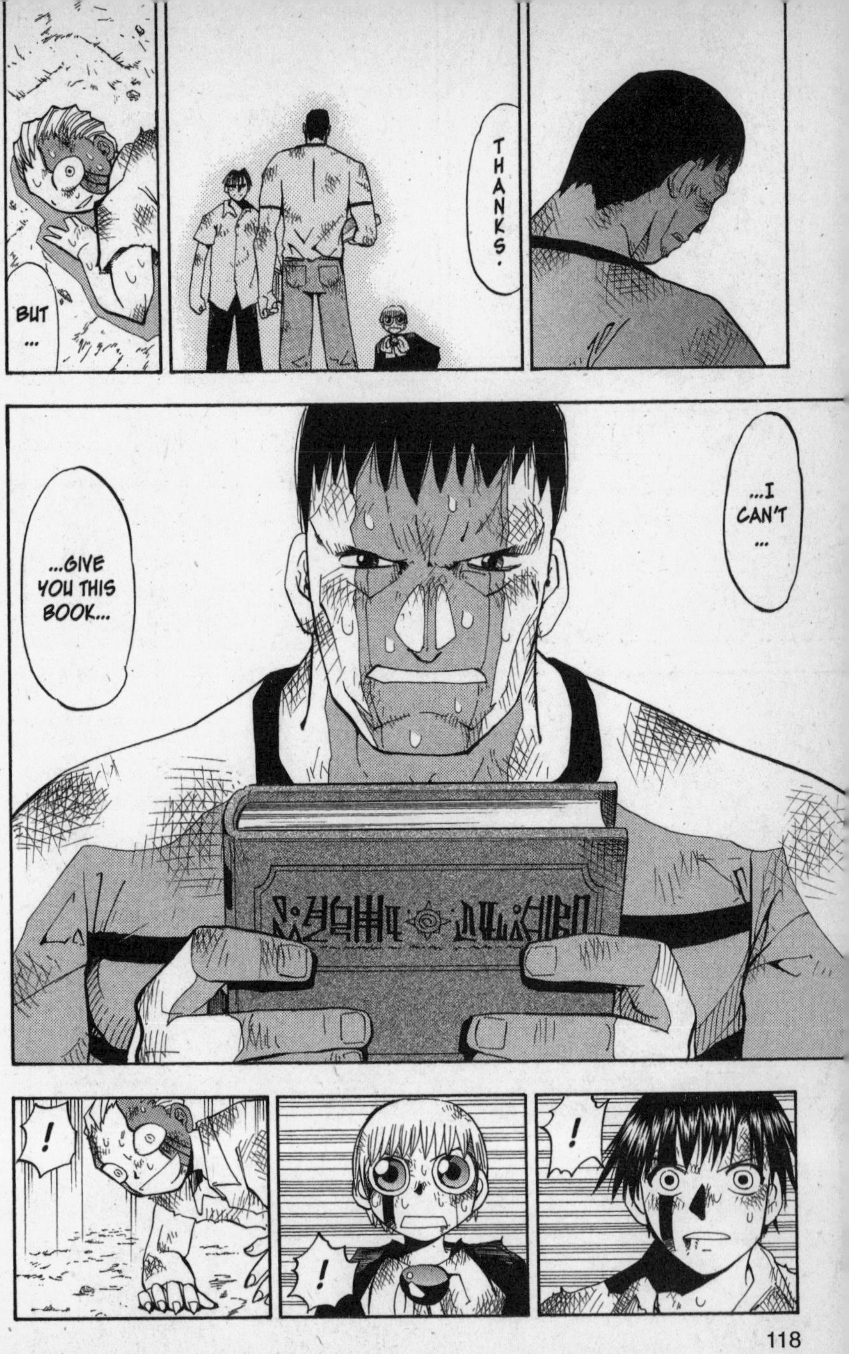
THANKS.
BUT ...
...I CAN'T ...
...GIVE YOU THIS BOOK...
!
!
!
!

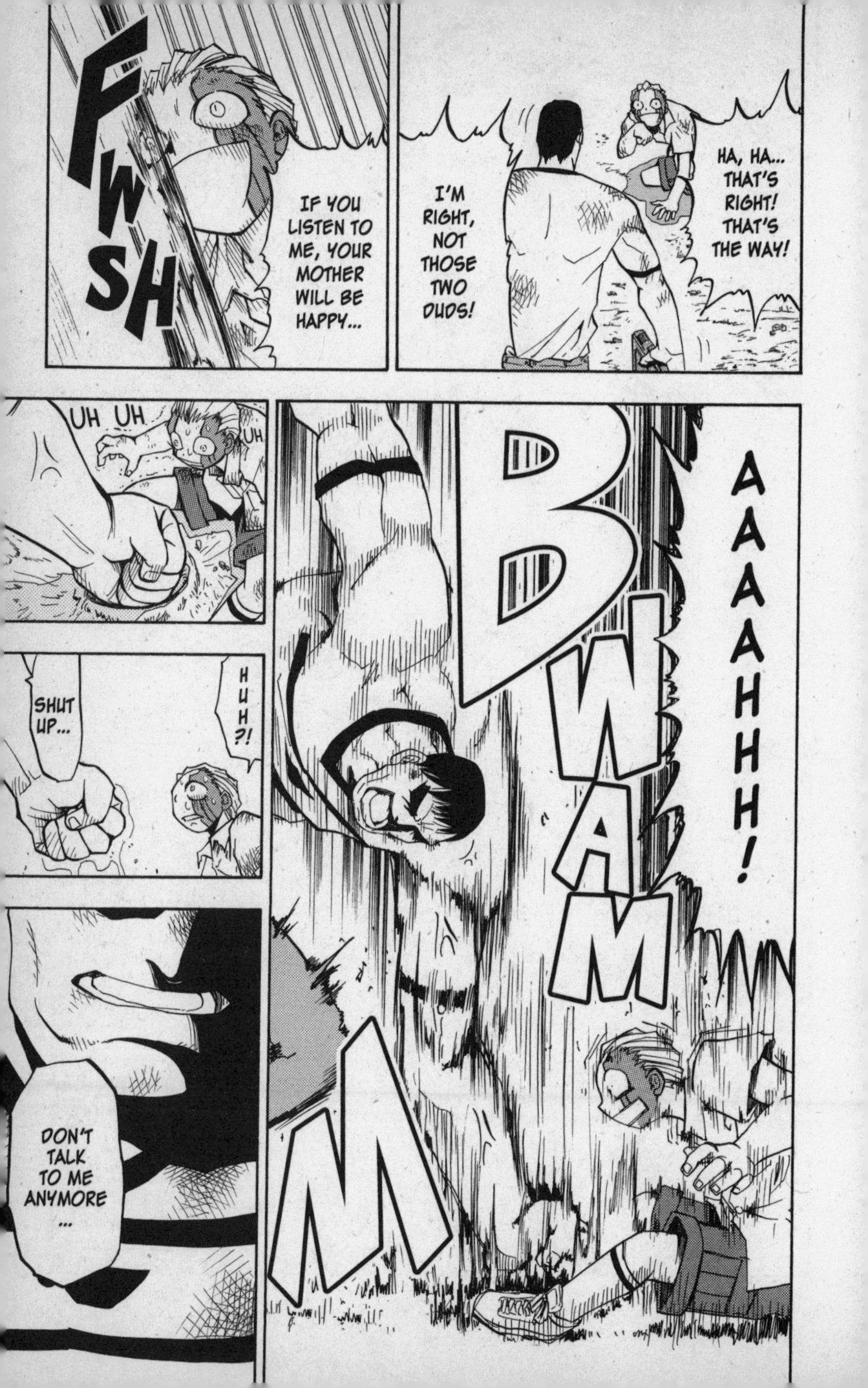
HA, HA... THAT'S RIGHT! THAT'S THE WAY!
I'M RIGHT, NOT THOSE TWO DUDS!
IF YOU LISTEN TO ME, YOUR MOTHER WILL BE HAPPY...
FWSH
AAAAHHH!
BWAMM
UH UH UH
HUH?!
SHUT UP...
DON'T TALK TO ME ANYMORE ...

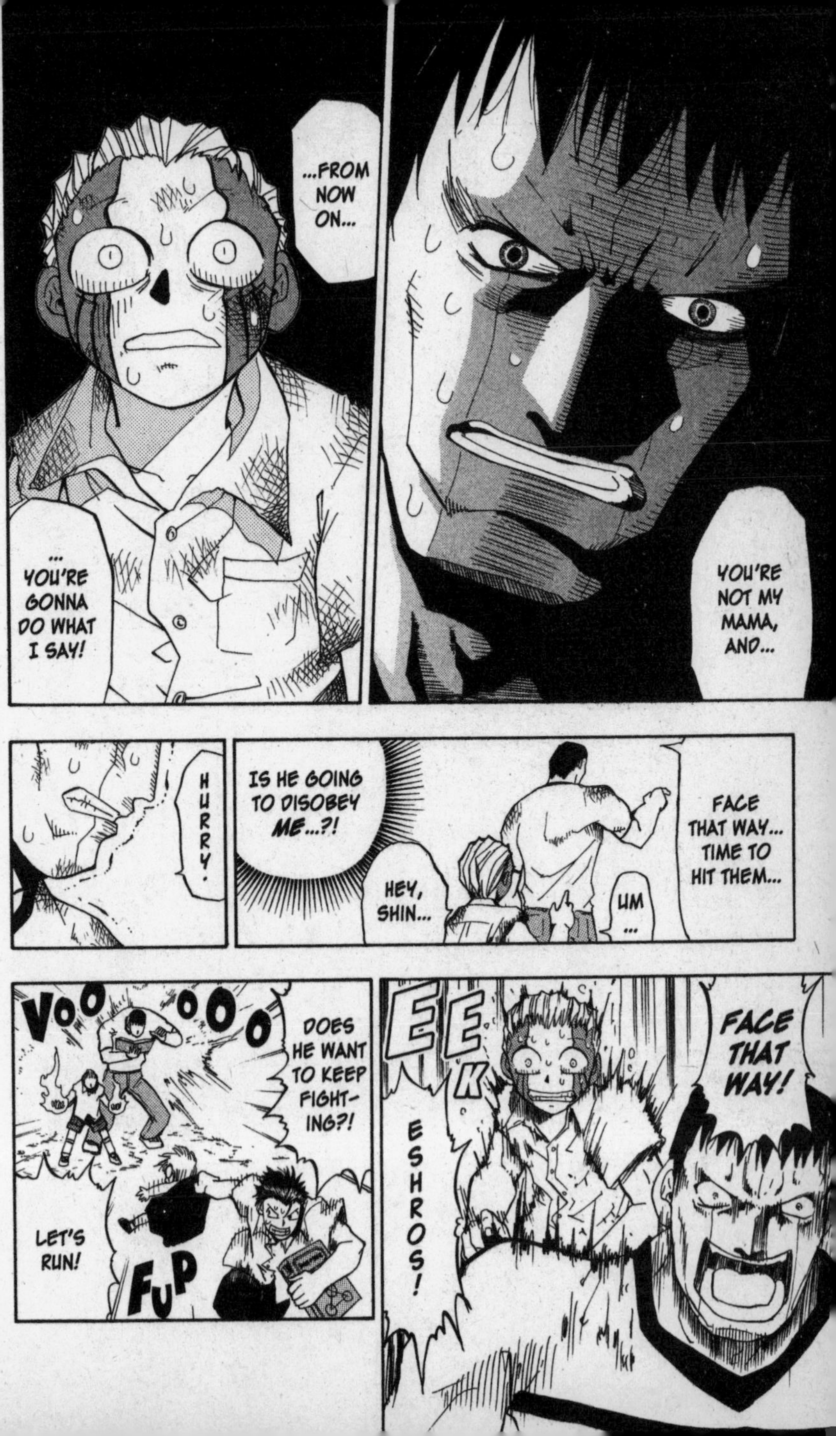
YOU'RE NOT MY MAMA, AND...
...FROM NOW ON...
... YOU'RE GONNA DO WHAT I SAY!
FACE THAT WAY... TIME TO HIT THEM...
UM ...
HEY, SHIN...
IS HE GOING TO DISOBEY ME...?!
HURRY.
FACE THAT WAY!
EEK
ESHROS!
DOES HE WANT TO KEEP FIGHTING?!
VOOOOO
LET'S RUN!
FUP

GROUNDCRAG!
BOOM
KA
AAAAAHH!
TP TP TP TP
AW, MAN!
CRAZY!
WHAT'S GOING ON?! DOESN'T HE SEE THAT HE'S BEING USED?!
SORRY!
I HATE TO STAB YOU IN THE BACK AFTER YOU TRIED TO HELP ME...
BUT...BUT I HAVE TO CHANGE MY LIFE!

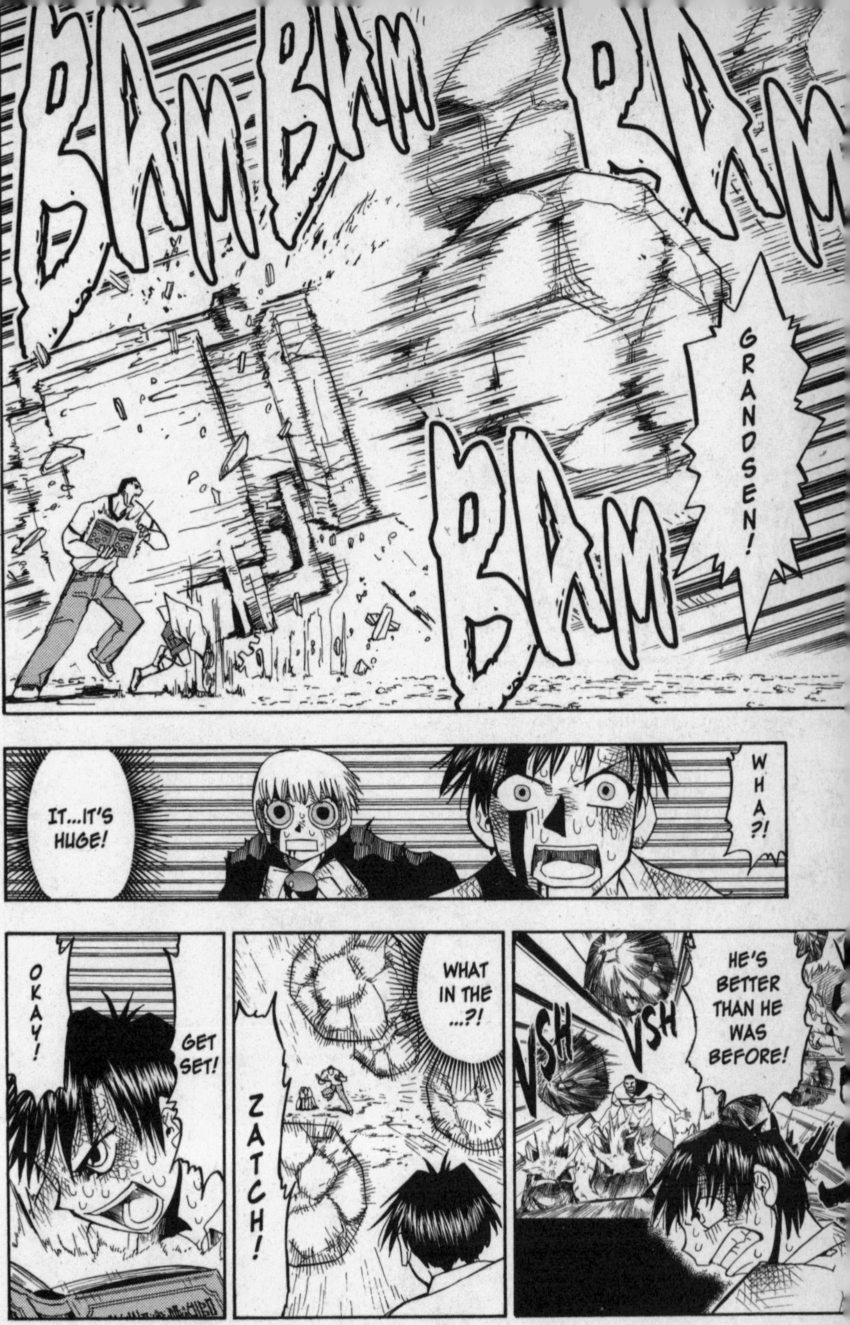
BAM
GRANDSEN!
BAM
BAM
BAM
WHA?!
IT...IT'S HUGE!
HE'S BETTER THAN HE WAS BEFORE!
VSH
VSH
WHAT IN THE ...?!
ZATCH!
OKAY!
GET SET!

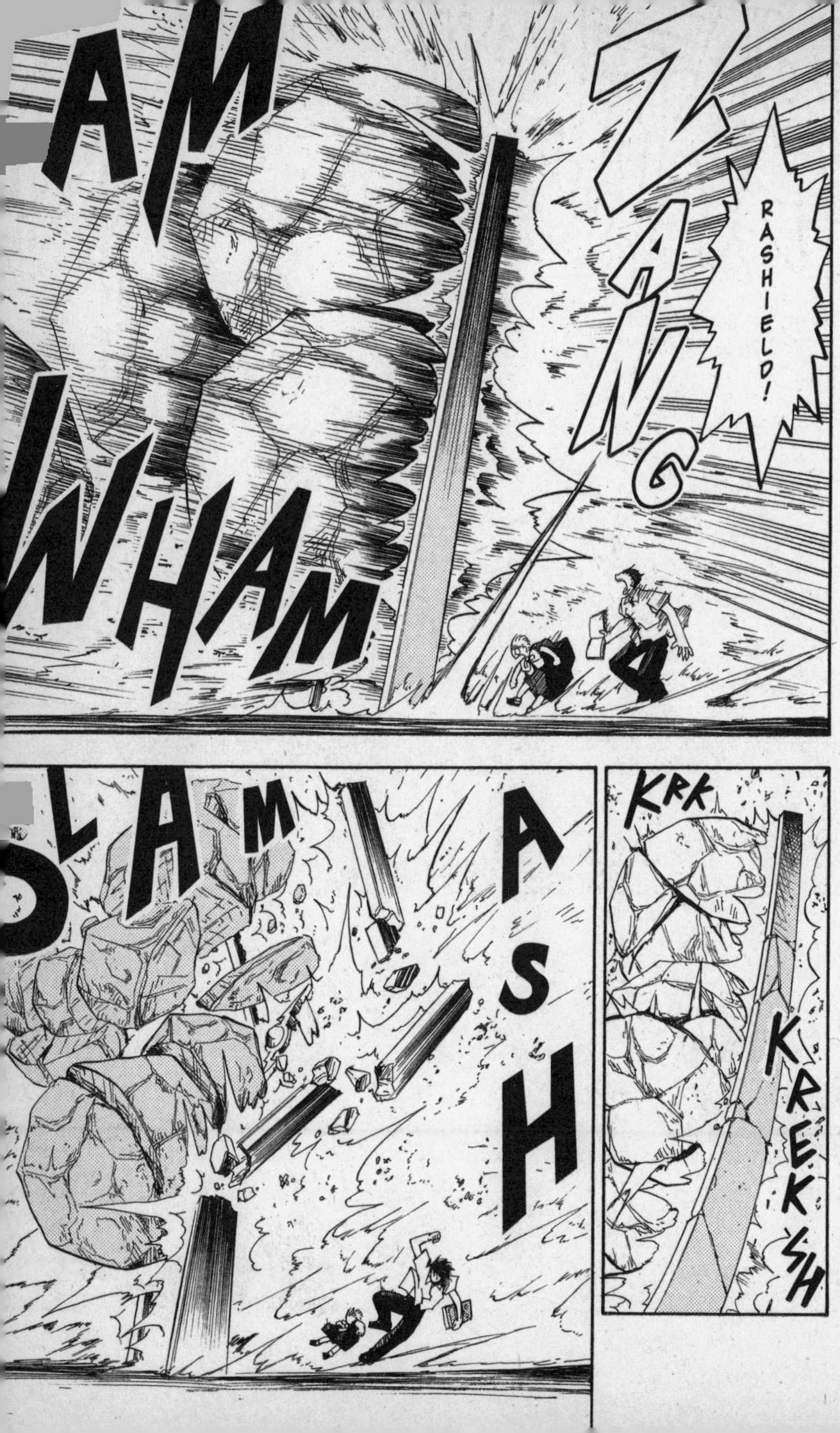
ZANG
RASHIELD!
AM
WHAM
KRK
KREKSH
ASH
SLAM

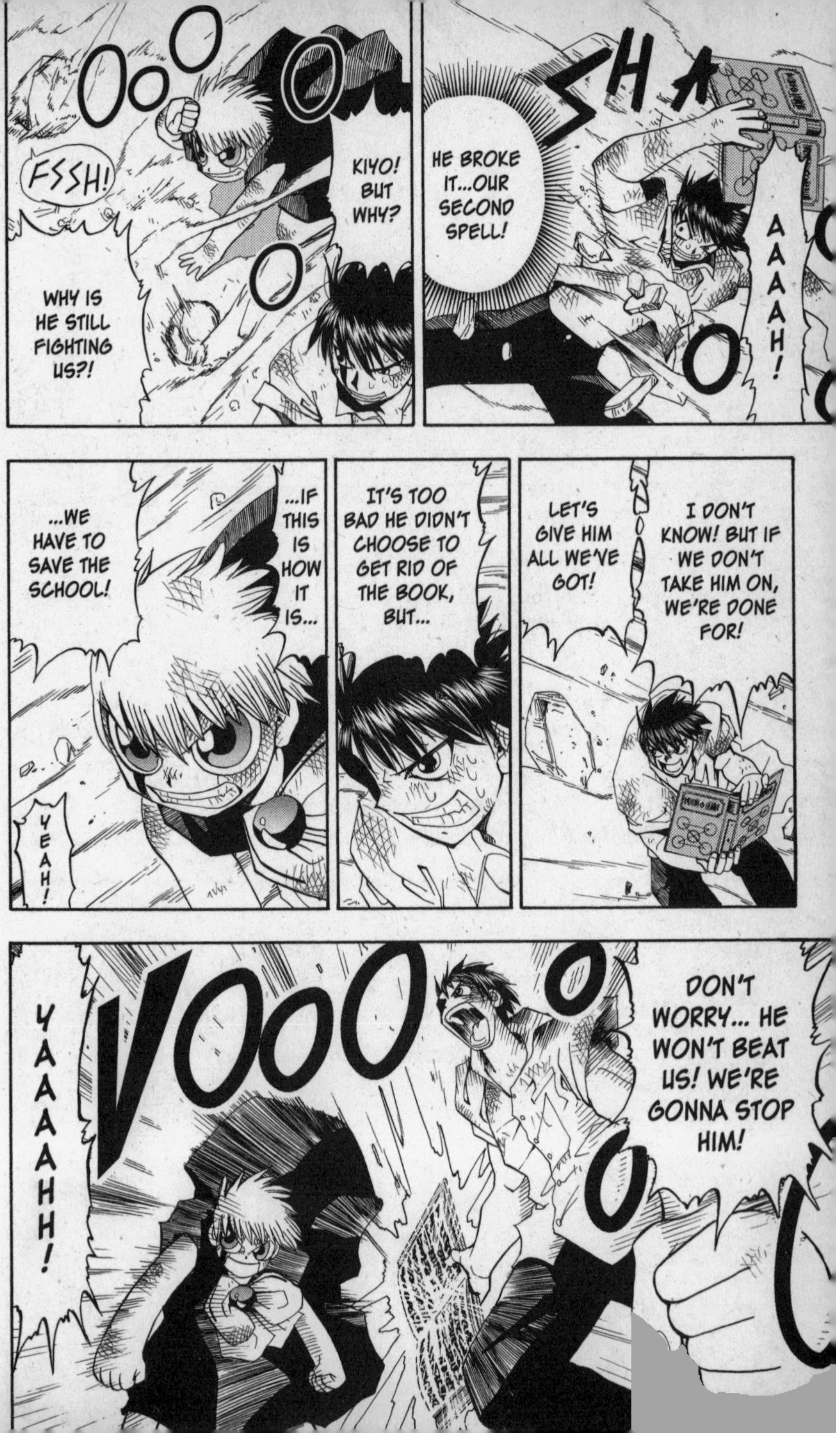
SHA
AAAAAH!
HE BROKE IT...OUR SECOND SPELL!
KIYO! BUT WHY?
OOOO
FSSH!
WHY IS HE STILL FIGHTING US?!
I DON'T KNOW! BUT IF WE DON'T TAKE HIM ON, WE'RE DONE FOR!
LET'S GIVE HIM ALL WE'VE GOT!
IT'S TOO BAD HE DIDN'T CHOOSE TO GET RID OF THE BOOK, BUT...
...IF THIS IS HOW IT IS...
...WE HAVE TO SAVE THE SCHOOL!
YEAH!
DON'T WORRY... HE WON'T BEAT US! WE'RE GONNA STOP HIM!
VOOOO
YAAAAAHH!

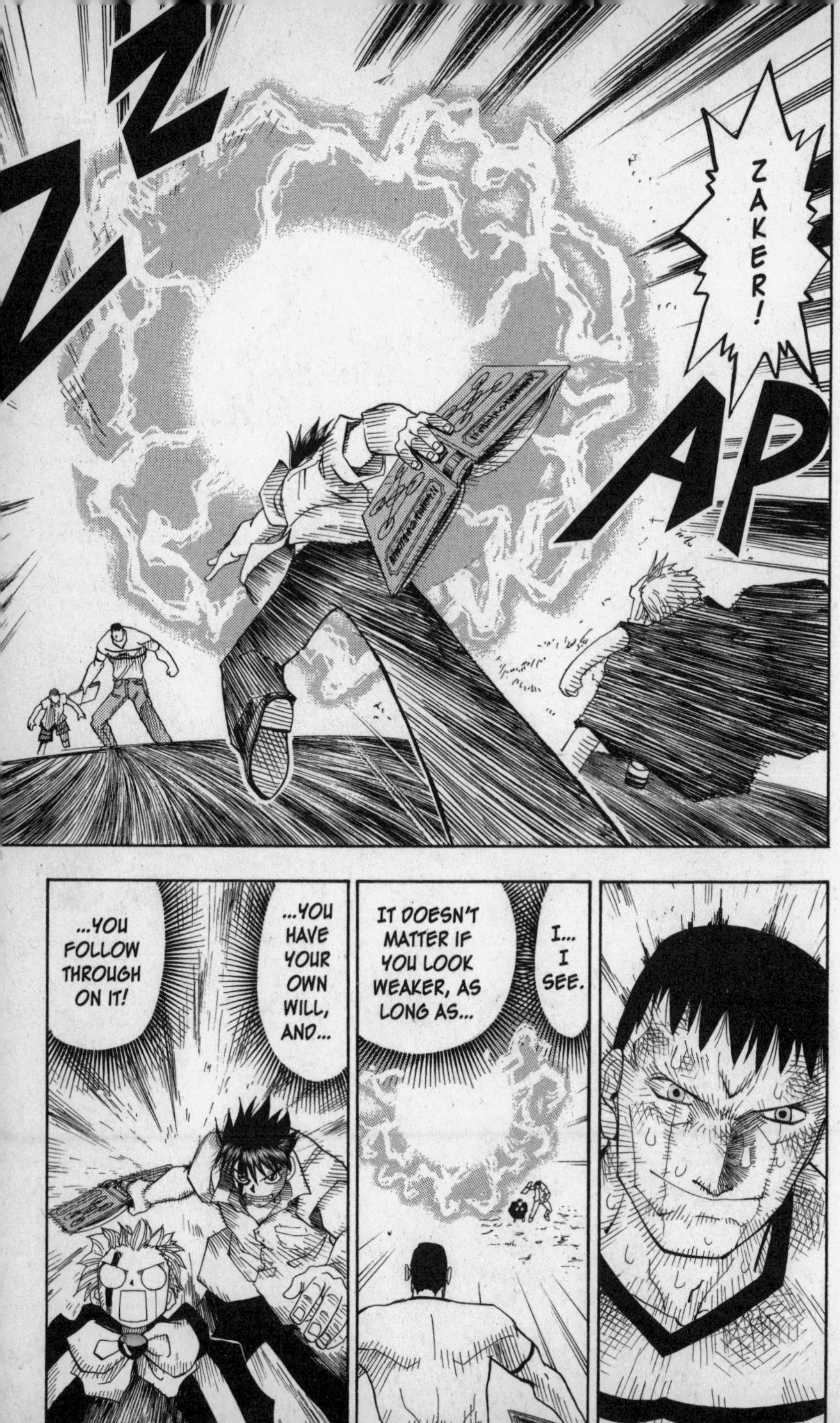
ZAKER!
ZZAP
I... I SEE.
IT DOESN'T MATTER IF YOU LOOK WEAKER, AS LONG AS...
...YOU HAVE YOUR OWN WILL, AND...
...YOU FOLLOW THROUGH ON IT!

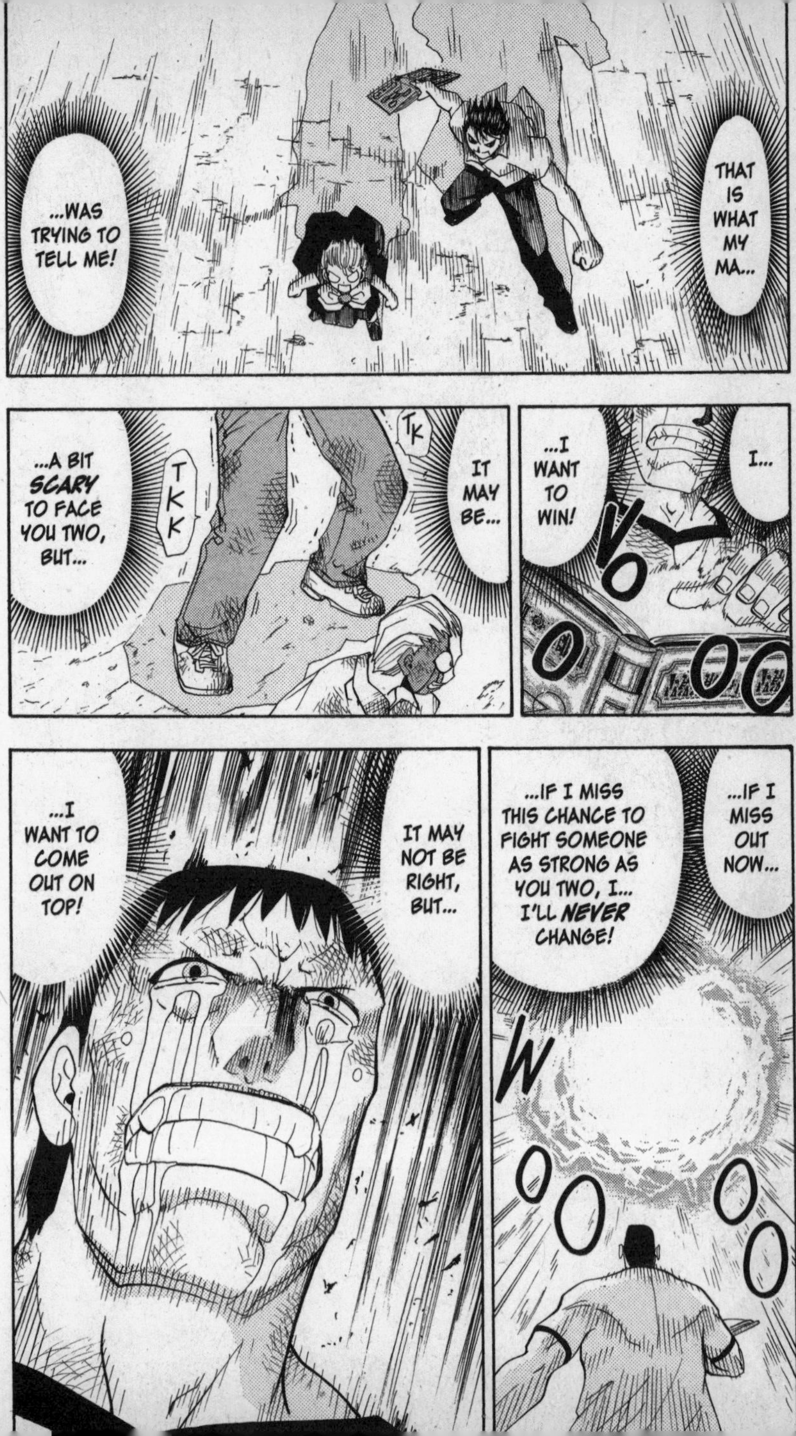
THAT IS WHAT MY MA...
...WAS TRYING TO TELL ME!
I...
...I WANT TO WIN!
VOOOO
IT MAY BE...
TK
TKK
...A BIT **SCARY** TO FACE YOU TWO, BUT...
...IF I MISS OUT NOW...
...IF I MISS THIS CHANCE TO FIGHT SOMEONE AS STRONG AS YOU TWO, I... I'LL **NEVER** CHANGE!
WOOOOO
IT MAY NOT BE RIGHT, BUT...
...I WANT TO COME OUT ON TOP!

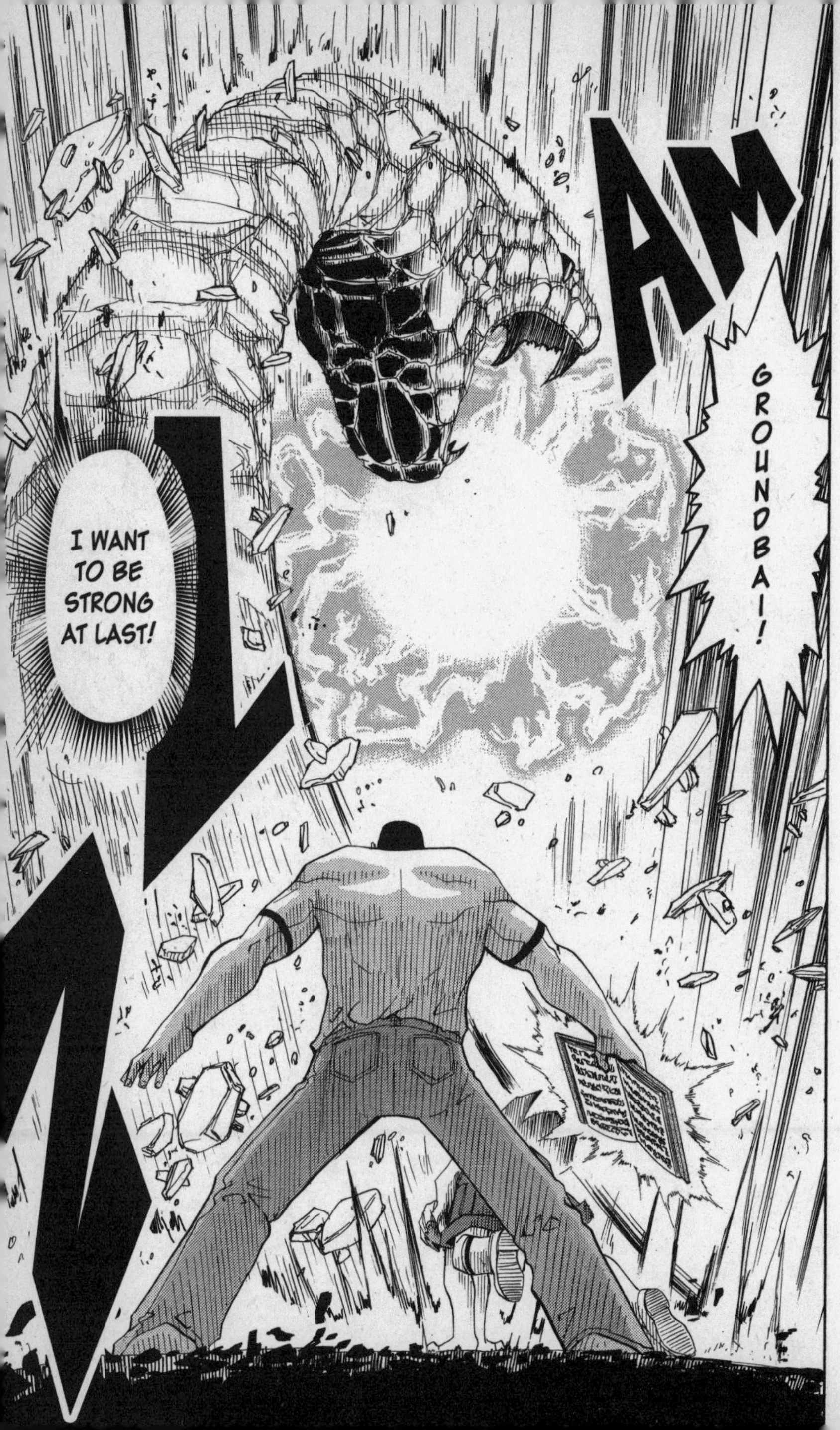
GROUNDBAI!
AM
I WANT TO BE STRONG AT LAST!

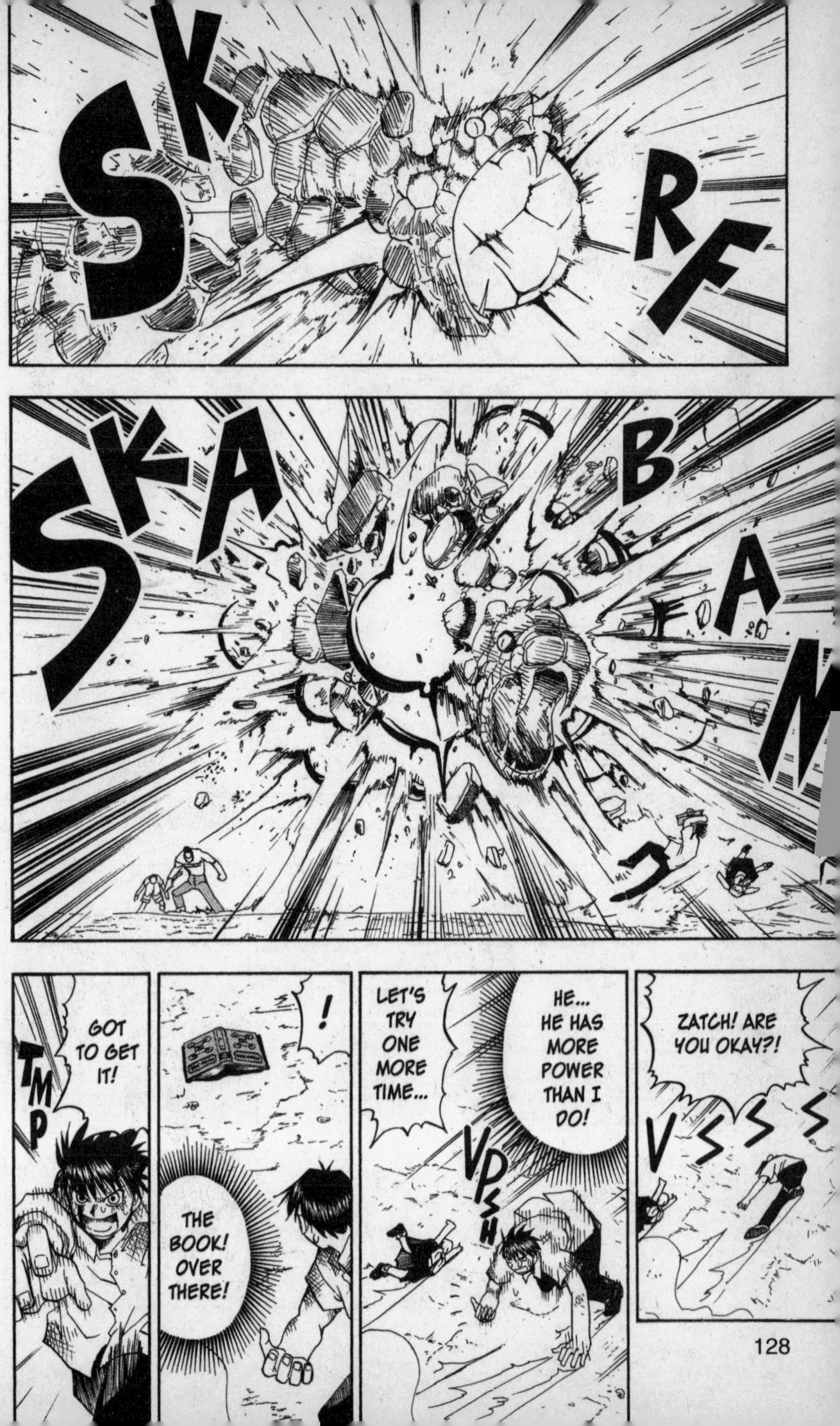
SKRF
SKABAM
ZATCH! ARE YOU OKAY?!
VSSS
HE... HE HAS MORE POWER THAN I DO!
VPSH
LET'S TRY ONE MORE TIME...
!
THE BOOK! OVER THERE!
GOT TO GET IT!
TMP

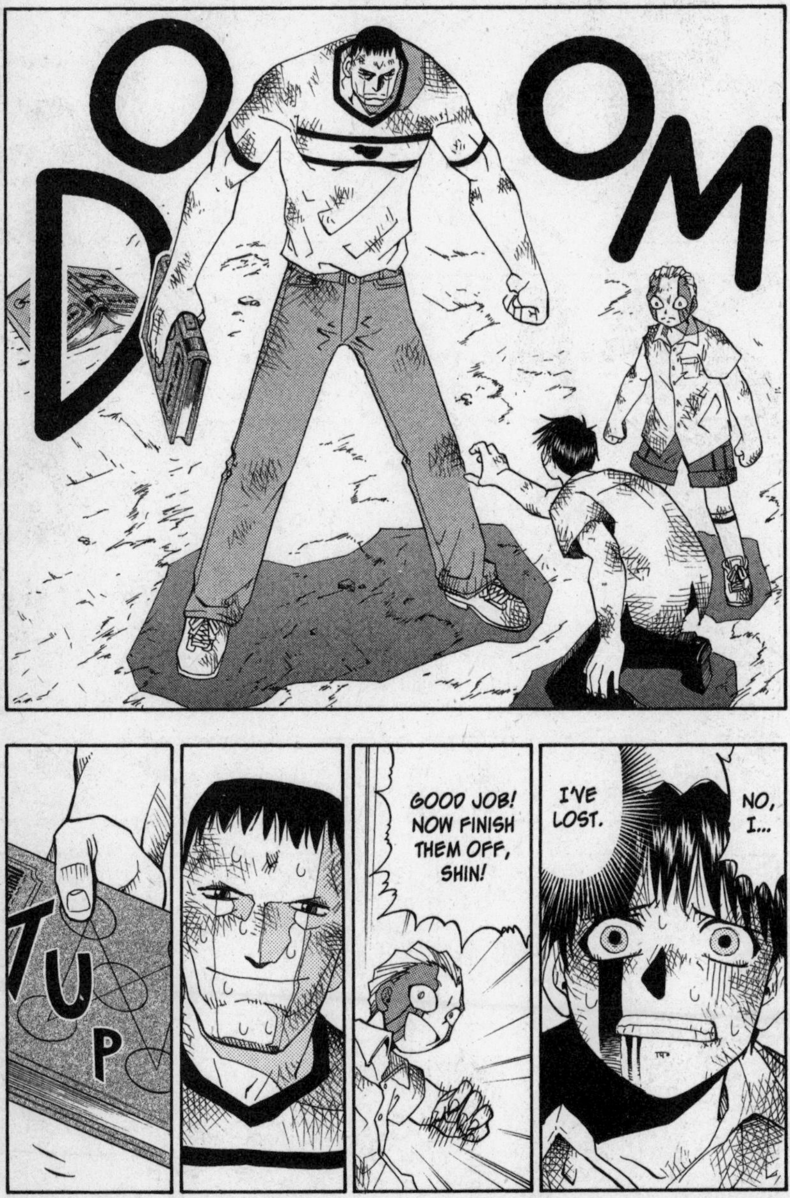
DOOM
NO, I...
I'VE LOST.
GOOD JOB! NOW FINISH THEM OFF, SHIN!
TUP

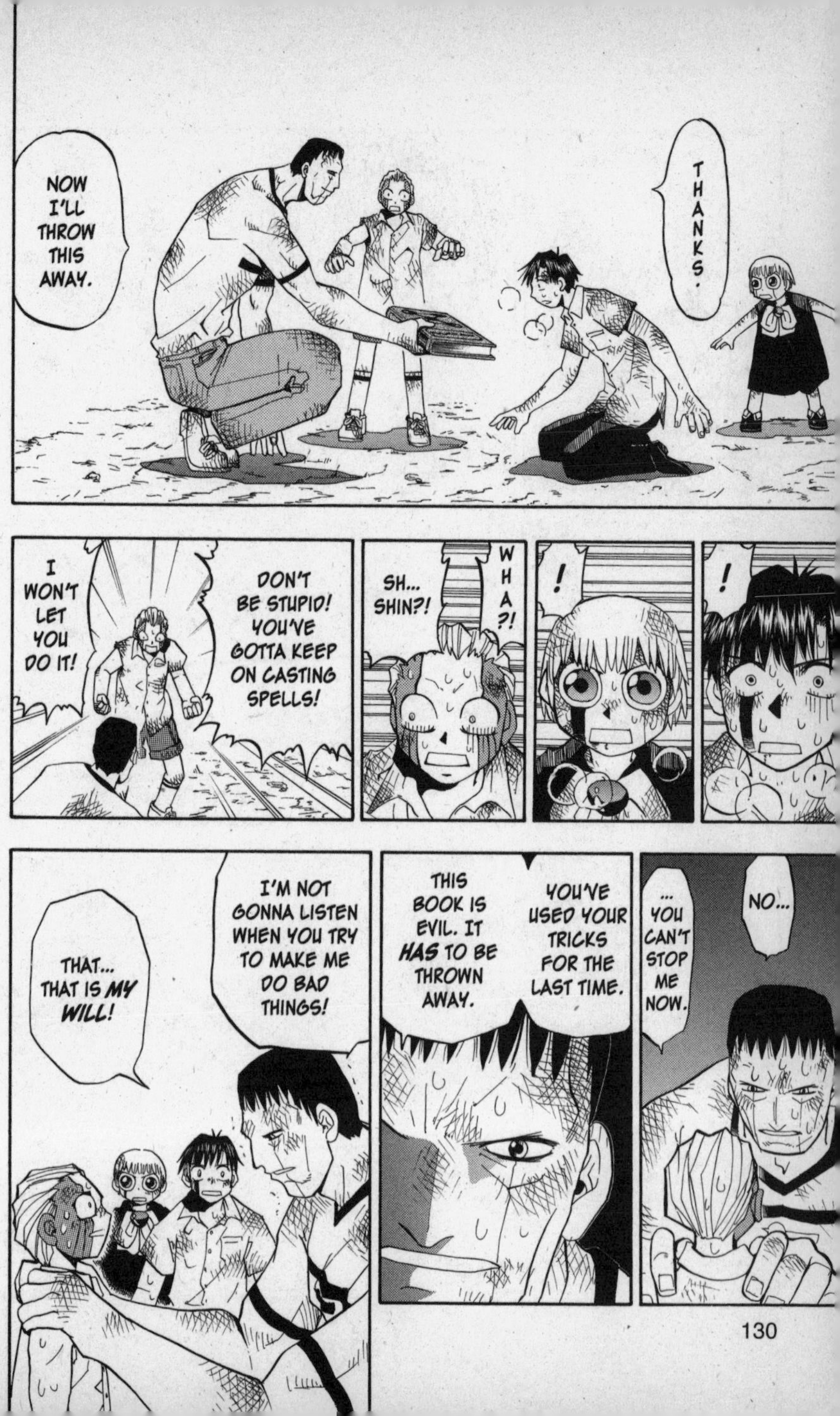
THANKS.
NOW I'LL THROW THIS AWAY.
!
!
WHA?!
SH... SHIN?!
DON'T BE STUPID! YOU'VE GOTTA KEEP ON CASTING SPELLS!
I WON'T LET YOU DO IT!
NO...
...YOU CAN'T STOP ME NOW.
YOU'VE USED YOUR TRICKS FOR THE LAST TIME.
THIS BOOK IS EVIL. IT *HAS* TO BE THROWN AWAY.
I'M NOT GONNA LISTEN WHEN YOU TRY TO MAKE ME DO BAD THINGS!
THAT... THAT IS *MY WILL*!

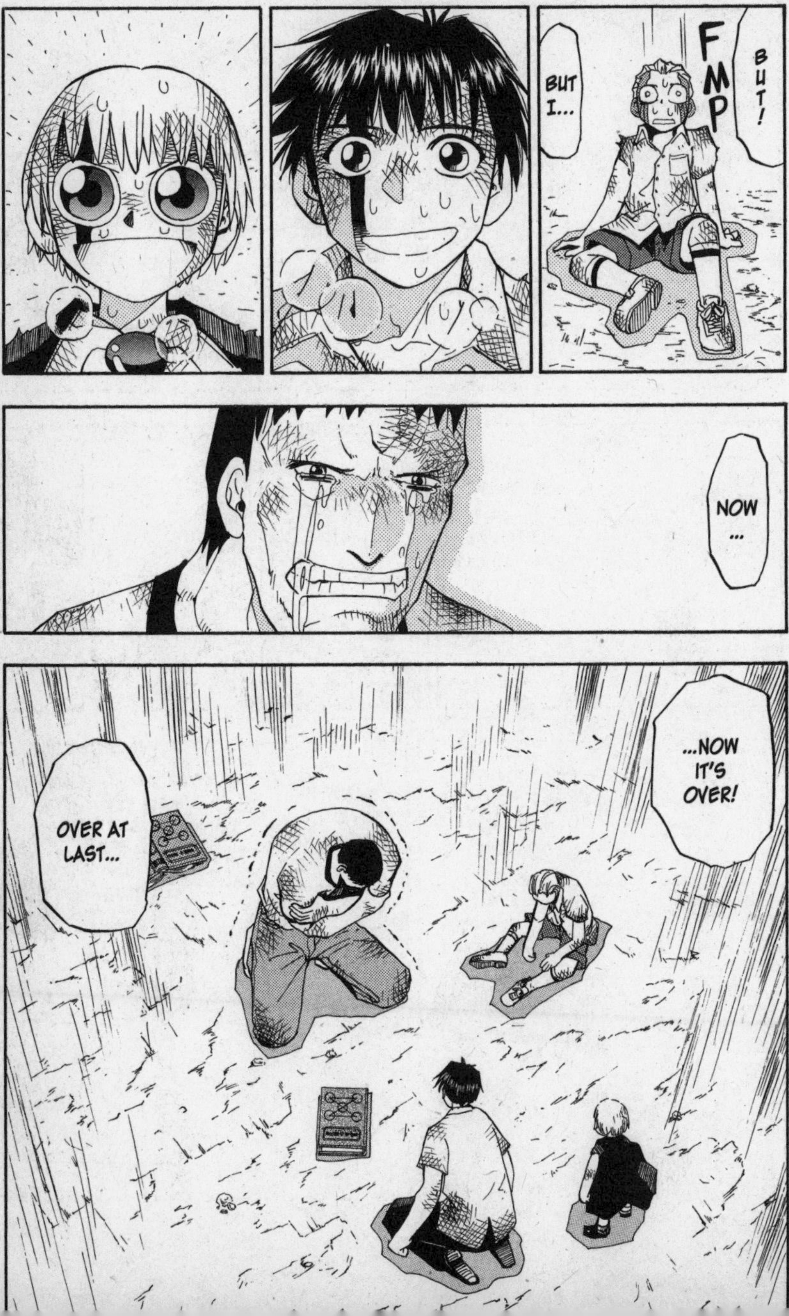
BUT!
FMP
BUT I...
NOW ...
...NOW IT'S OVER!
OVER AT LAST...

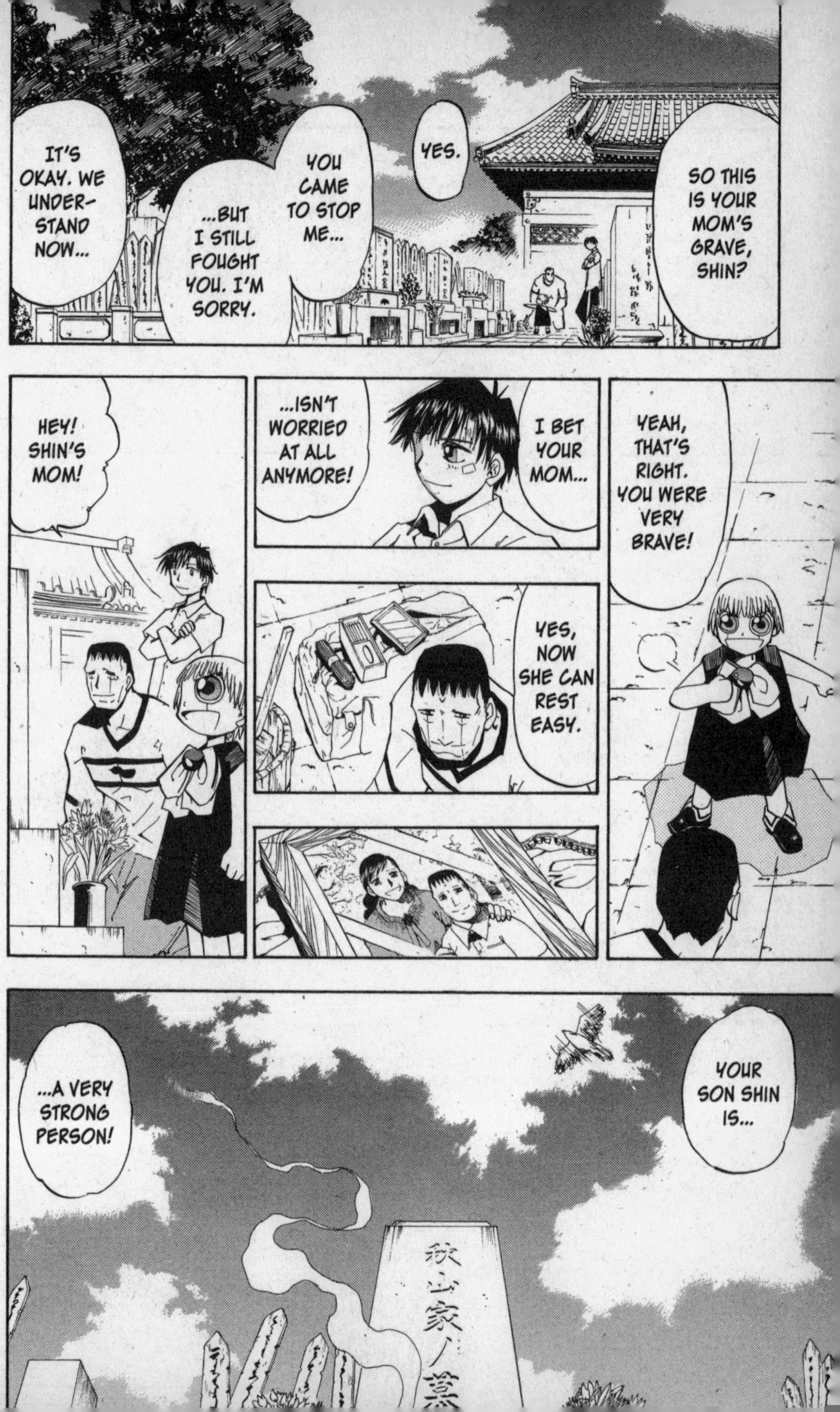
SO THIS IS YOUR MOM'S GRAVE, SHIN?
YES.
YOU CAME TO STOP ME...
...BUT I STILL FOUGHT YOU. I'M SORRY.
IT'S OKAY. WE UNDERSTAND NOW...
YEAH, THAT'S RIGHT. YOU WERE VERY BRAVE!
I BET YOUR MOM...
...ISN'T WORRIED AT ALL ANYMORE!
YES, NOW SHE CAN REST EASY.
HEY! SHIN'S MOM!
YOUR SON SHIN IS...
...A VERY STRONG PERSON!

# LEVEL 26: Kind Kiyo

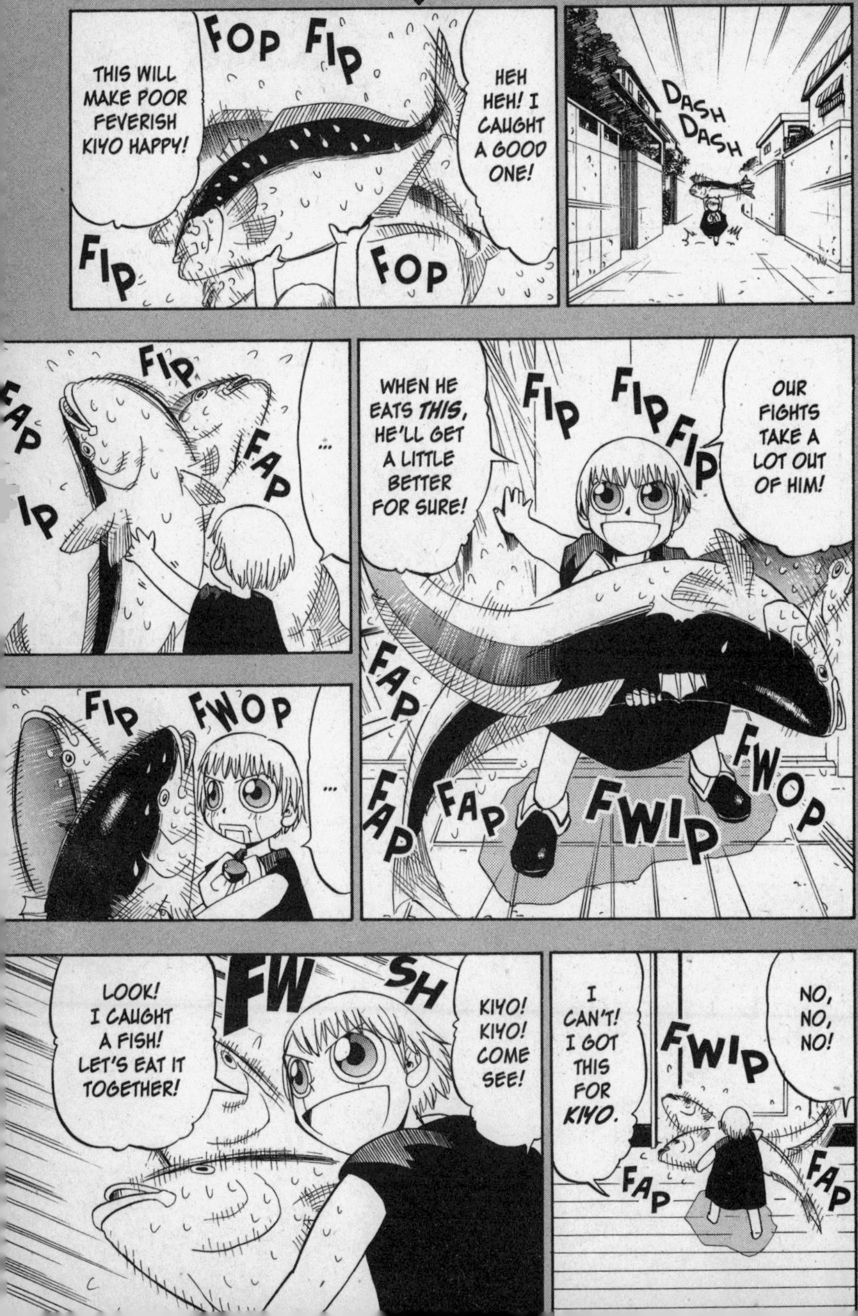
DASH DASH
HEH HEH! I CAUGHT A GOOD ONE!
FIP
FOP
THIS WILL MAKE POOR FEVERISH KIYO HAPPY!
FOP
FIP
OUR FIGHTS TAKE A LOT OUT OF HIM!
FIP FIP
FIP
WHEN HE EATS THIS, HE'LL GET A LITTLE BETTER FOR SURE!
FWOP
FWIP
FAP
FAP
FAP
...
FAP
FIP
FAP
IP
...
FWOP
FIP
NO, NO, NO!
FWIP
I CAN'T! I GOT THIS FOR KIYO.
FAP
FAP
KIYO! KIYO! COME SEE!
SH
FW
LOOK! I CAUGHT A FISH! LET'S EAT IT TOGETHER!

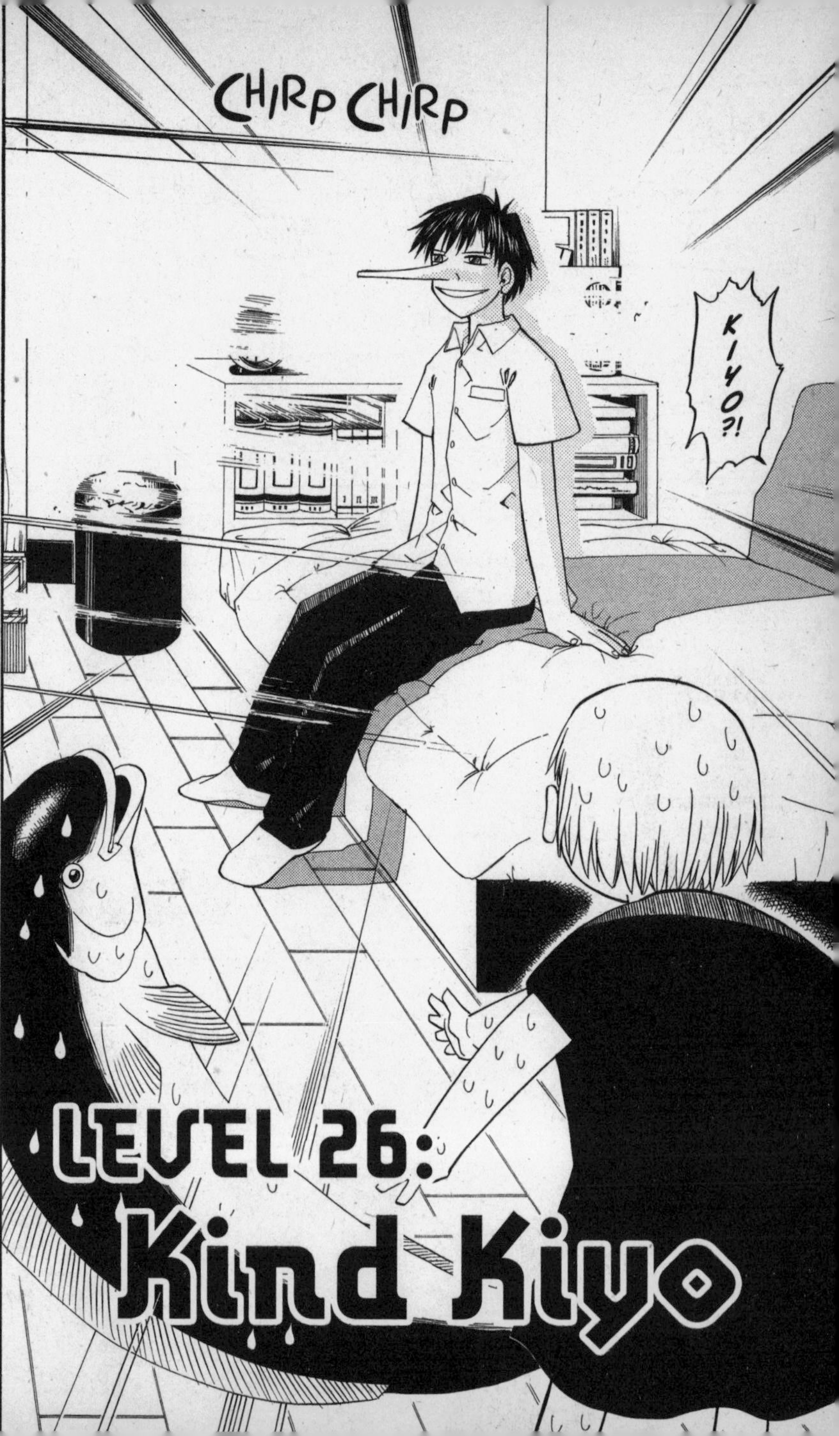
CHIRP CHIRP
KIYO?!
LEVEL 26:
Kind Kiyo

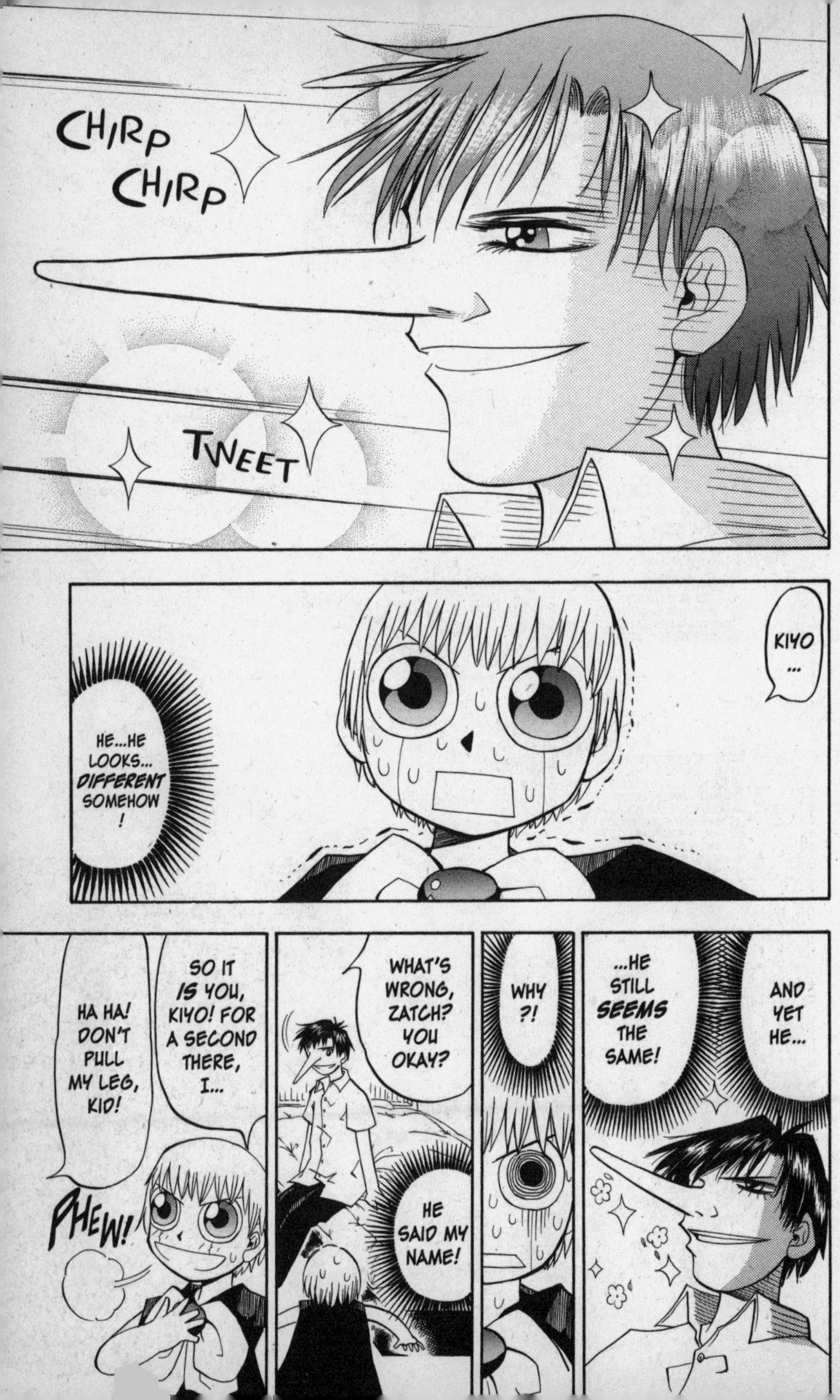
CHIRP CHIRP
TWEET
KIYO...
HE...HE LOOKS... DIFFERENT SOMEHOW!
AND YET HE...
...HE STILL SEEMS THE SAME!
WHY?!
WHAT'S WRONG, ZATCH? YOU OKAY?
HE SAID MY NAME!
SO IT IS YOU, KIYO! FOR A SECOND THERE, I...
HA HA! DON'T PULL MY LEG, KID!
PHEW!

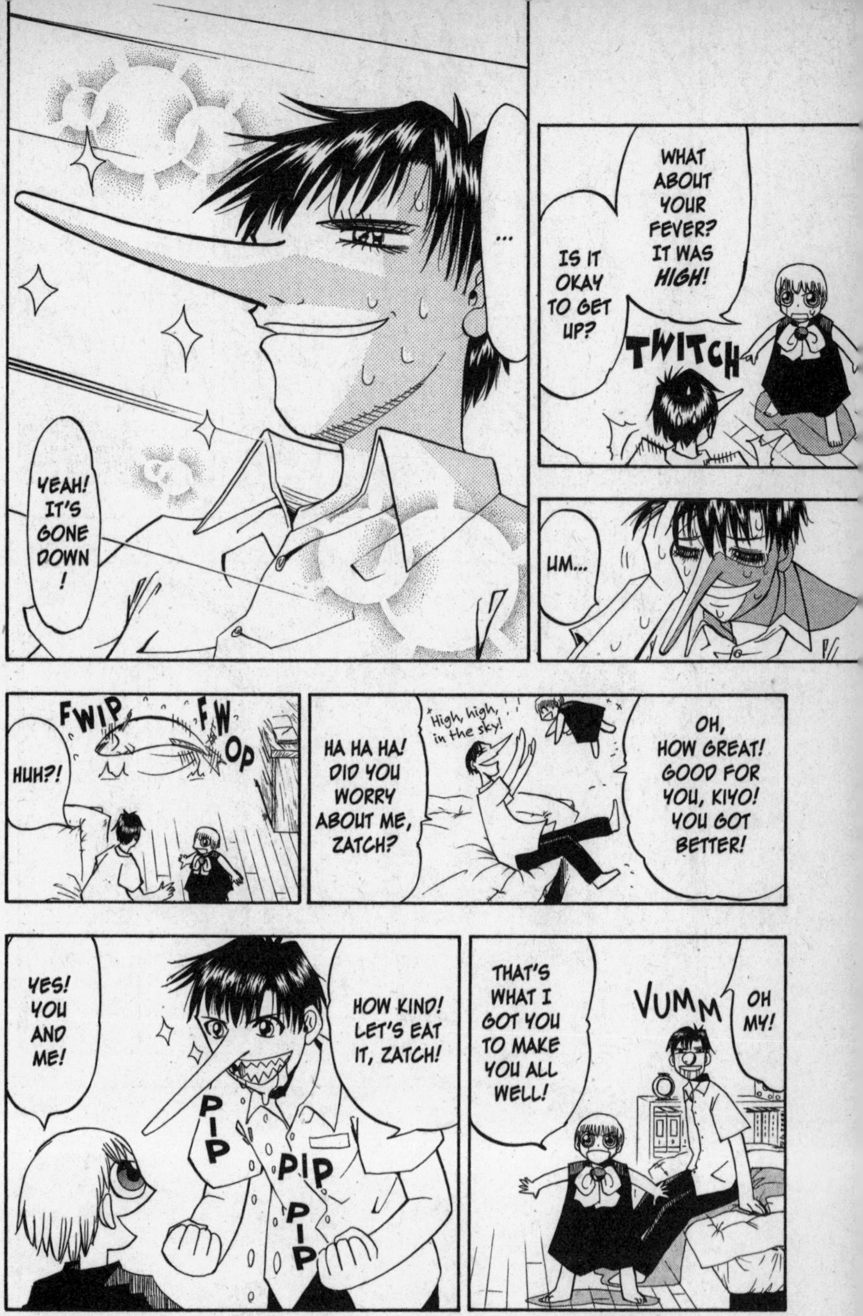
WHAT ABOUT YOUR FEVER? IT WAS HIGH!
IS IT OKAY TO GET UP?
TWITCH
UM...
...
YEAH! IT'S GONE DOWN!
OH, HOW GREAT! GOOD FOR YOU, KIYO! YOU GOT BETTER!
High, high, in the sky!
HA HA HA! DID YOU WORRY ABOUT ME, ZATCH?
FWIP
FWOP
HUH?!
OH MY!
VUMM
THAT'S WHAT I GOT YOU TO MAKE YOU ALL WELL!
HOW KIND! LET'S EAT IT, ZATCH!
YES! YOU AND ME!
PIP
PIP
PIP
PIP

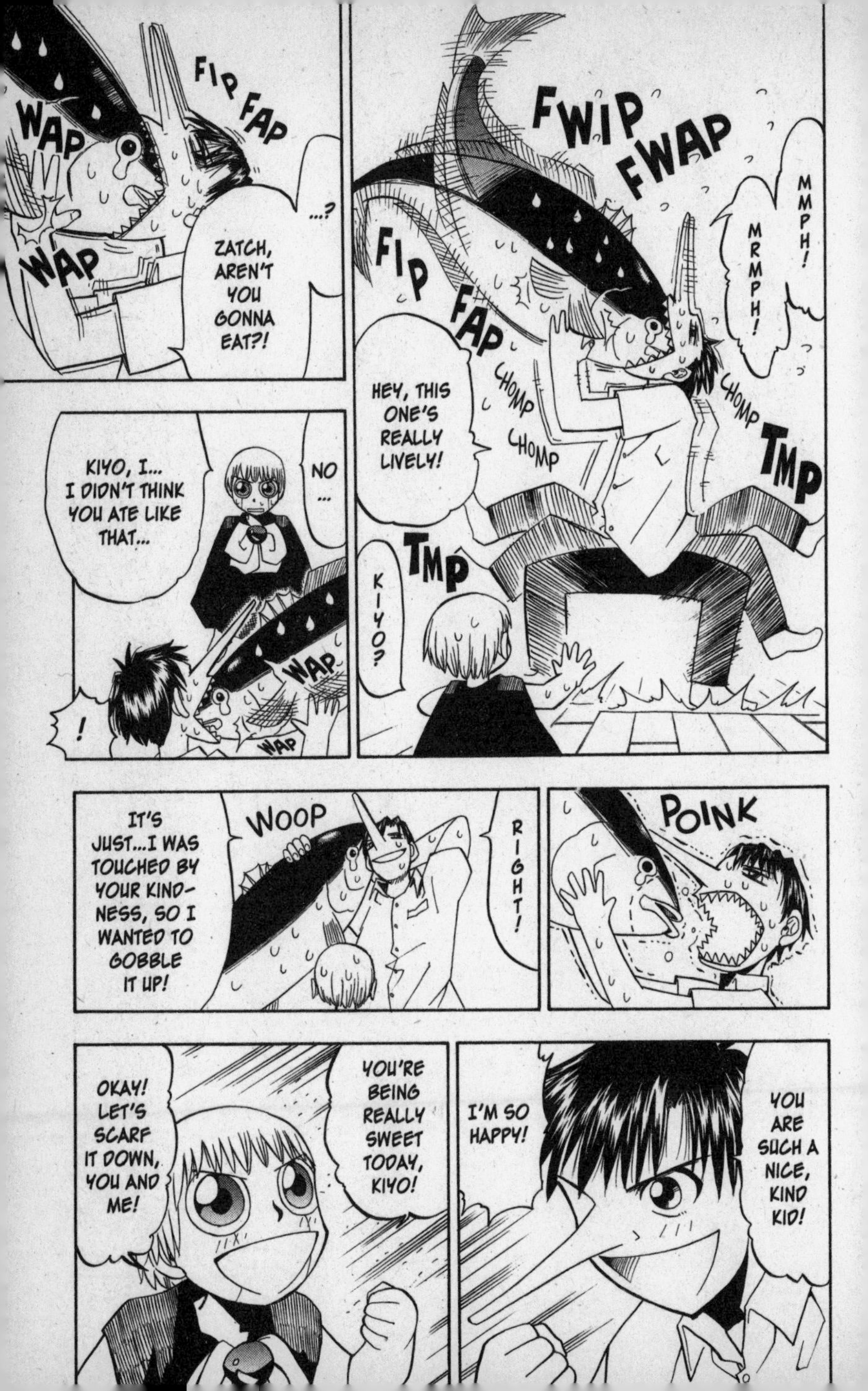
FWIP FWAP
MMPH!
MRMPH!
FIP FAP
HEY, THIS ONE'S REALLY LIVELY!
CHOMP
CHOMP
CHOMP
TMP
KIYO?
TMP
FIP FAP
WAP
...?
ZATCH, AREN'T YOU GONNA EAT?!
WAP
NO...
KIYO, I... I DIDN'T THINK YOU ATE LIKE THAT...
WAP
!
WAP
POINK
RIGHT!
WOOP
IT'S JUST...I WAS TOUCHED BY YOUR KIND-NESS, SO I WANTED TO GOBBLE IT UP!
YOU ARE SUCH A NICE, KIND KID!
I'M SO HAPPY!
YOU'RE BEING REALLY SWEET TODAY, KIYO!
OKAY! LET'S SCARF IT DOWN, YOU AND ME!

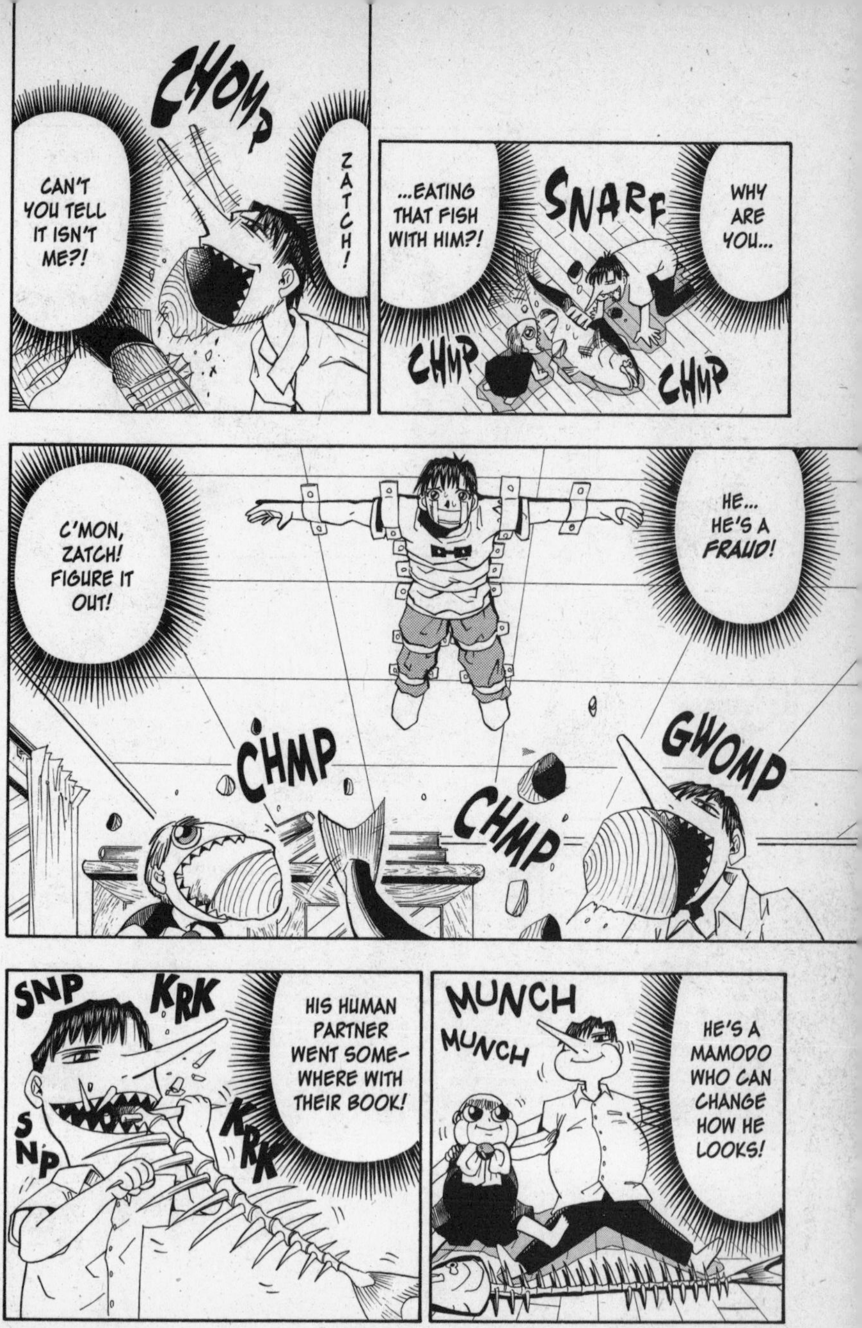
WHY ARE YOU...
SNARF
...EATING THAT FISH WITH HIM?!
CHMP
CHMP
ZATCH!
CHOMP
CAN'T YOU TELL IT ISN'T ME?!
HE... HE'S A *FRAUD*!
GWOMP
C'MON, ZATCH! FIGURE IT OUT!
CHMP
CHMP
HE'S A MAMODO WHO CAN CHANGE HOW HE LOOKS!
MUNCH
MUNCH
HIS HUMAN PARTNER WENT SOME-WHERE WITH THEIR BOOK!
KRK
SNP
KRK
SNP

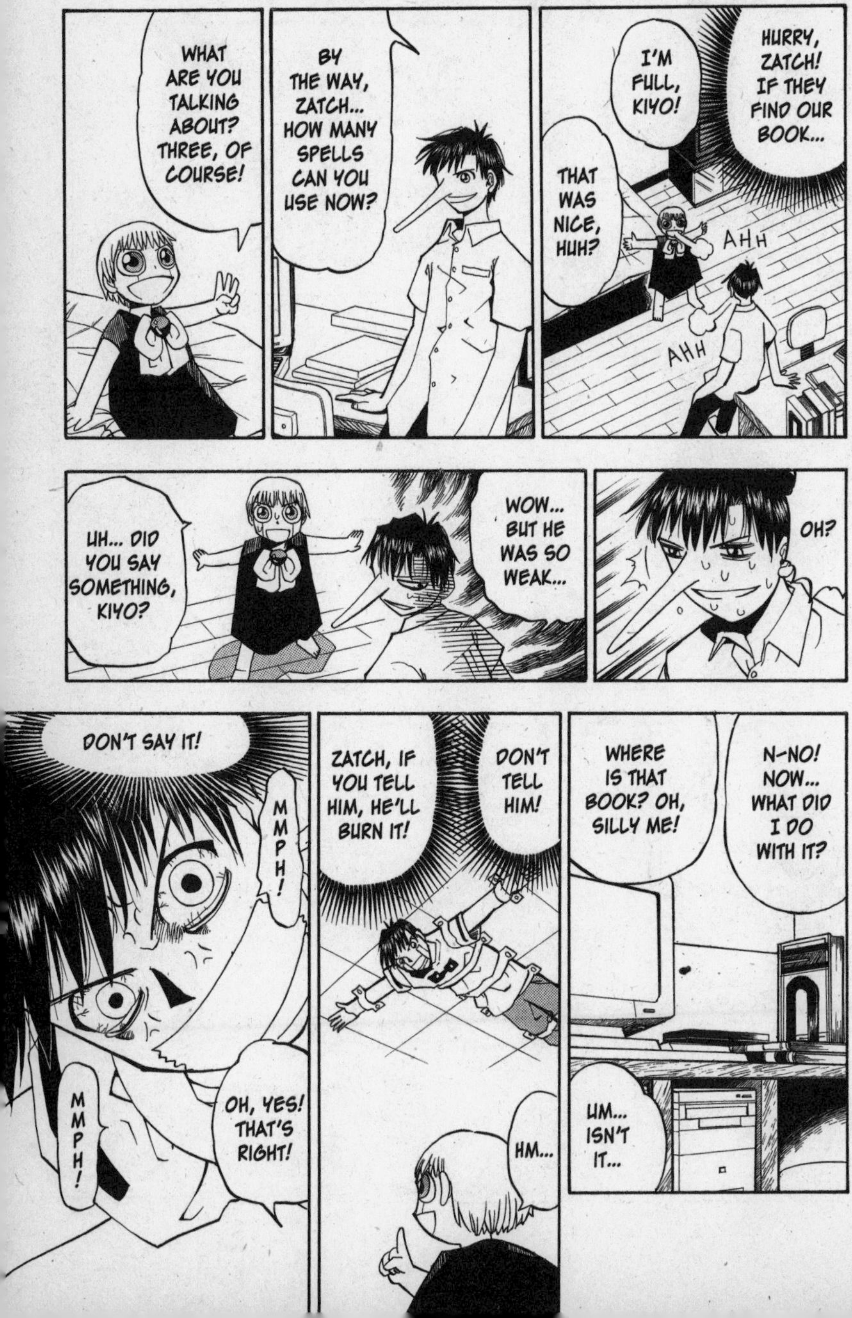
HURRY, ZATCH! IF THEY FIND OUR BOOK...
I'M FULL, KIYO!
THAT WAS NICE, HUH?
AHH
AHH
BY THE WAY, ZATCH... HOW MANY SPELLS CAN YOU USE NOW?
WHAT ARE YOU TALKING ABOUT? THREE, OF COURSE!
OH?
WOW... BUT HE WAS SO WEAK...
UH... DID YOU SAY SOMETHING, KIYO?
N-NO! NOW... WHAT DID I DO WITH IT?
WHERE IS THAT BOOK? OH, SILLY ME!
UM... ISN'T IT...
DON'T TELL HIM!
ZATCH, IF YOU TELL HIM, HE'LL BURN IT!
HM...
DON'T SAY IT!
MMPH!
OH, YES! THAT'S RIGHT!
MMPH!

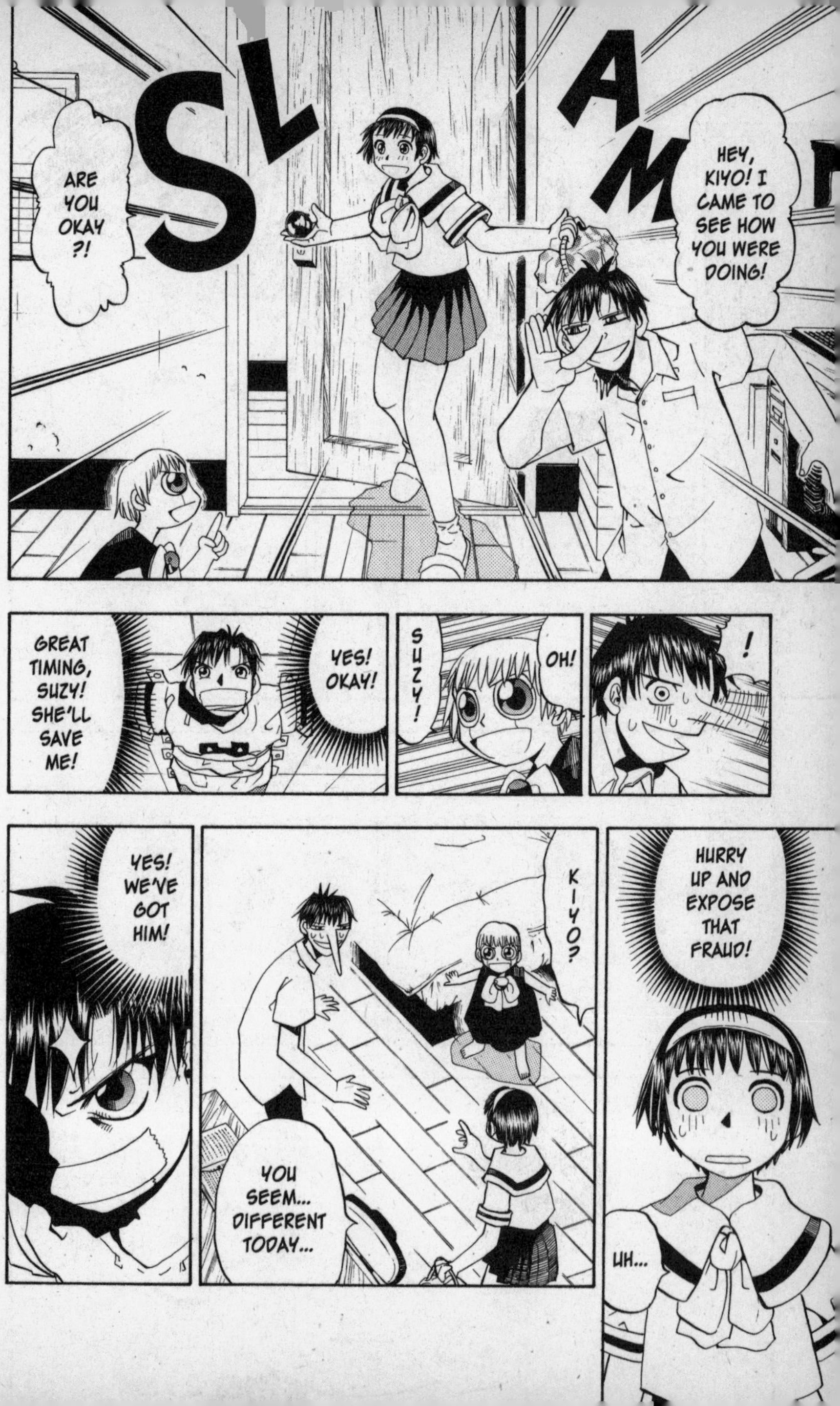
HEY, KIYO! I CAME TO SEE HOW YOU WERE DOING!
SLAM
ARE YOU OKAY?!
!
OH!
SUZY!
YES! OKAY!
GREAT TIMING, SUZY! SHE'LL SAVE ME!
HURRY UP AND EXPOSE THAT FRAUD!
UH...
KIYO?
YOU SEEM... DIFFERENT TODAY...
YES! WE'VE GOT HIM!

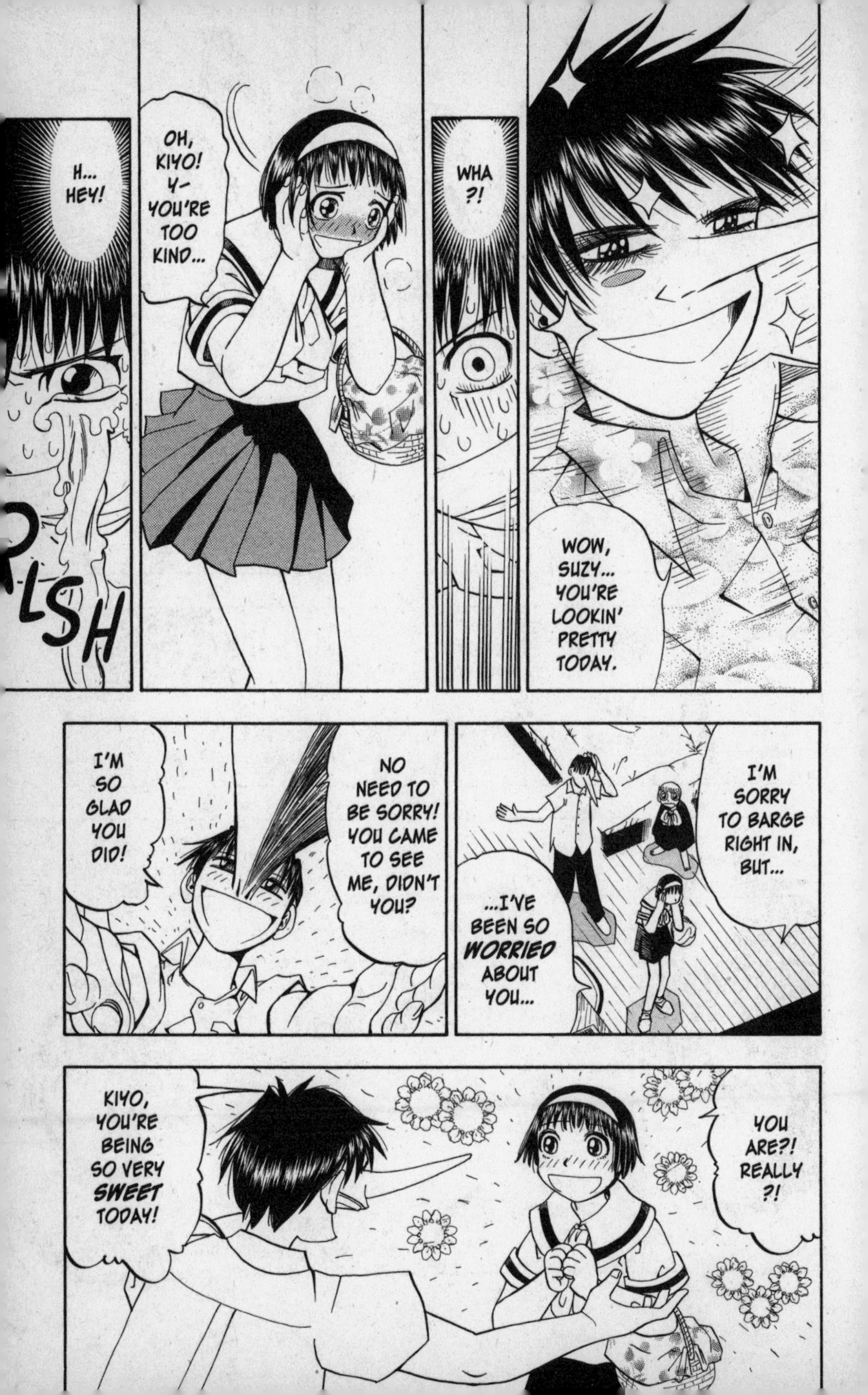
WOW, SUZY... YOU'RE LOOKIN' PRETTY TODAY.
WHA ?!
OH, KIYO! Y-YOU'RE TOO KIND...
H... HEY!
RLSH
I'M SORRY TO BARGE RIGHT IN, BUT...
...I'VE BEEN SO **WORRIED** ABOUT YOU...
NO NEED TO BE SORRY! YOU CAME TO SEE ME, DIDN'T YOU?
I'M SO GLAD YOU DID!
YOU ARE?! REALLY ?!
KIYO, YOU'RE BEING SO VERY **SWEET** TODAY!

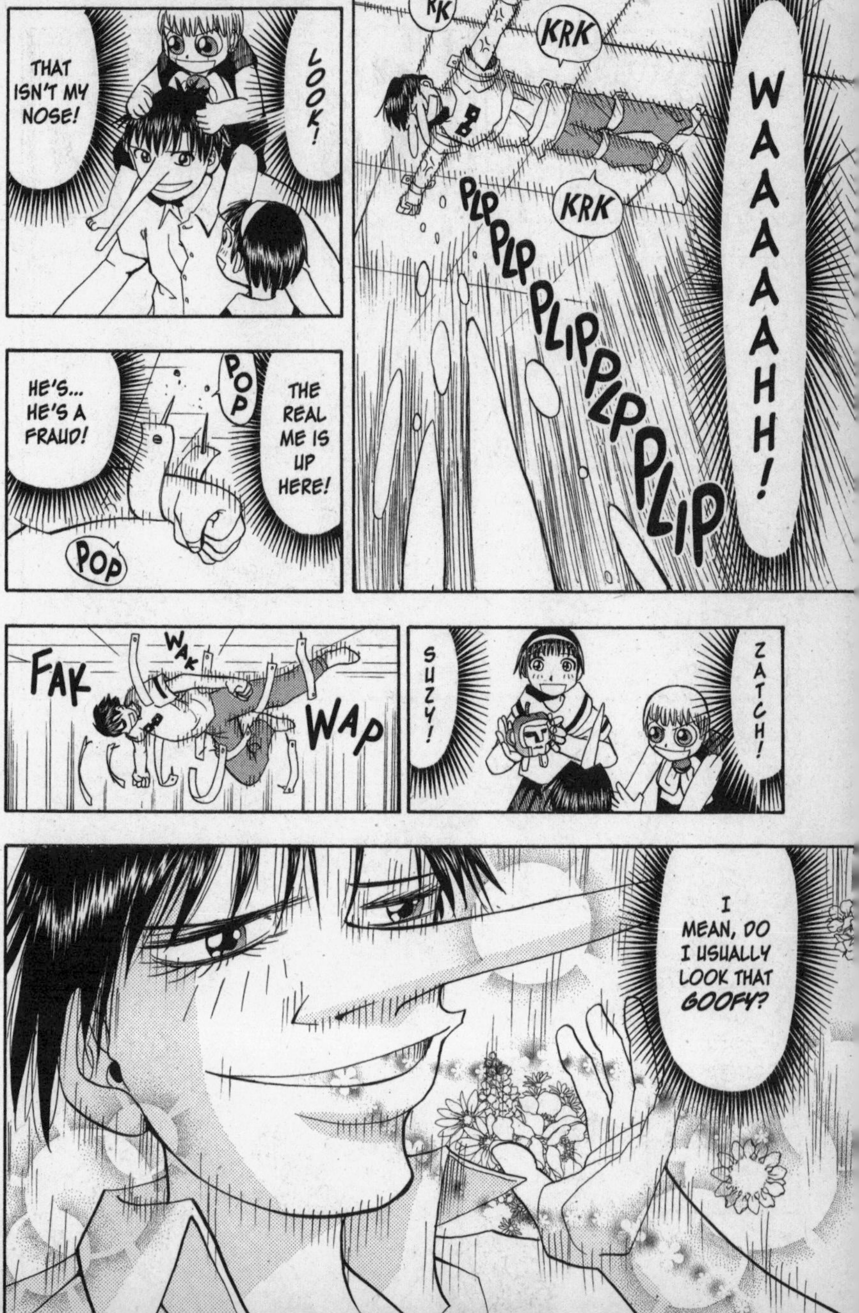
WAAAAAAHH!
KRK
KRK
KRK
PLP PLP PLIP PLP PLP PLIP
LOOK!
THAT ISN'T MY NOSE!
THE REAL ME IS UP HERE!
POP
HE'S... HE'S A FRAUD!
POP
ZATCH!
SUZY!
WAK
FAK
WAP
I MEAN, DO I USUALLY LOOK THAT GOOFY?

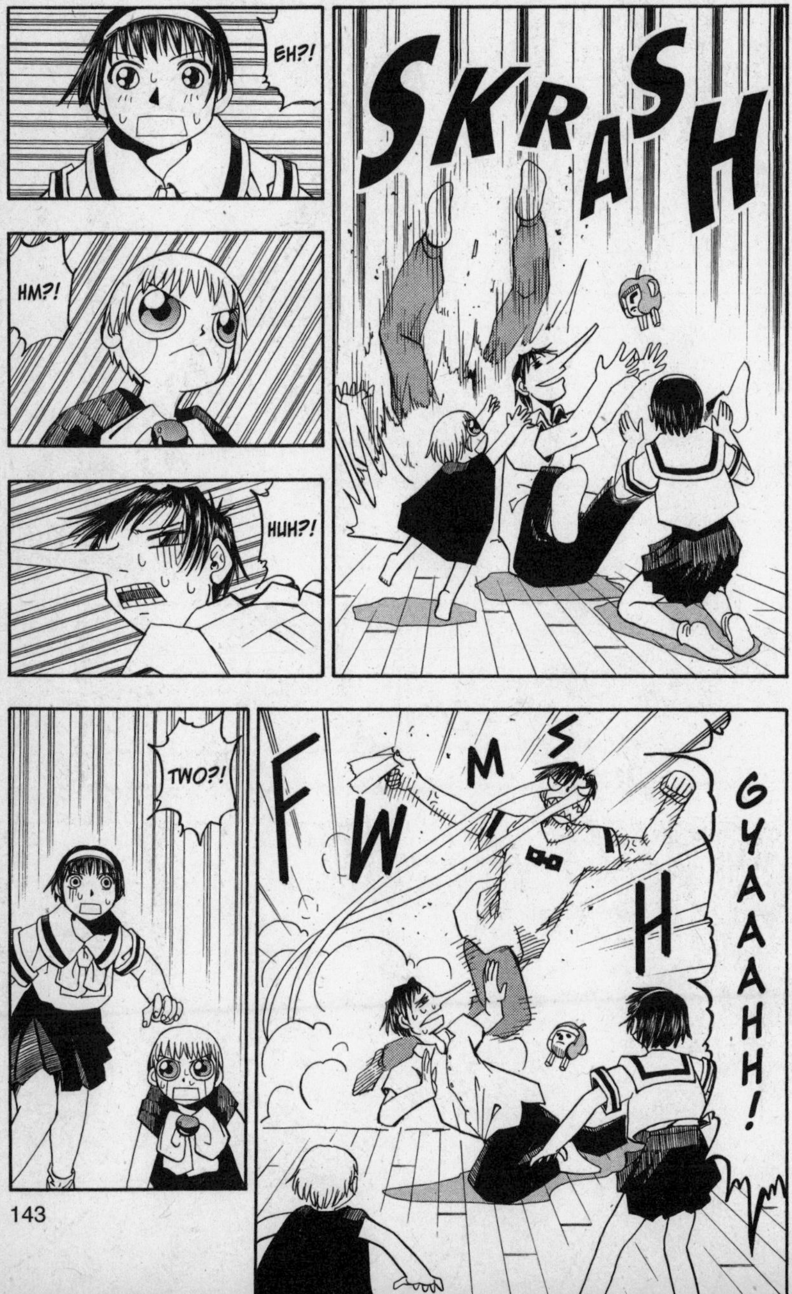
SKRASH
EH?!
HM?!
HUH?!
FWMSH
GYAAAHH!
TWO?!

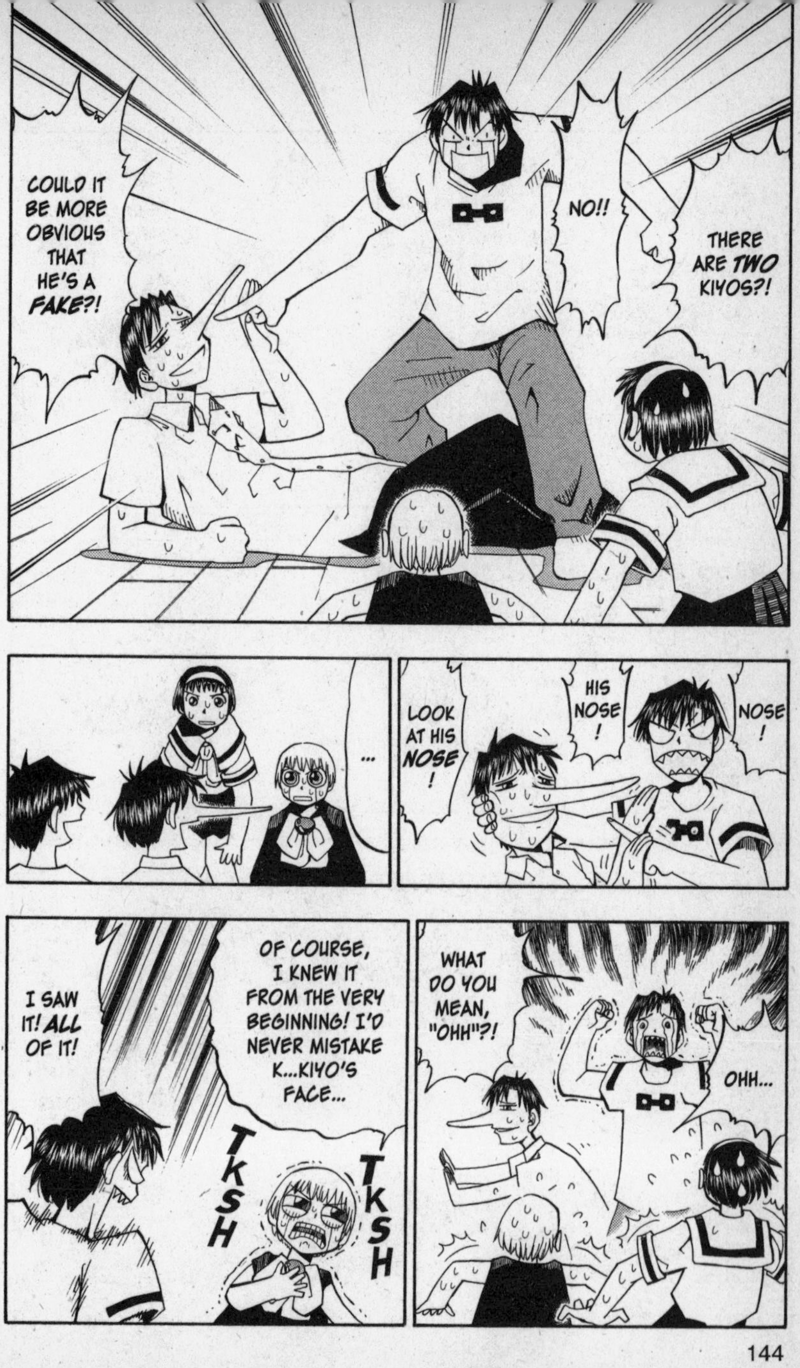
THERE ARE TWO KIYOS?!
NO!!
COULD IT BE MORE OBVIOUS THAT HE'S A FAKE?!
NOSE!
HIS NOSE!
LOOK AT HIS NOSE!
...
OHH...
WHAT DO YOU MEAN, "OHH"?!
OF COURSE, I KNEW IT FROM THE VERY BEGINNING! I'D NEVER MISTAKE K...KIYO'S FACE...
I SAW IT! ALL OF IT!
TKSH
TKSH

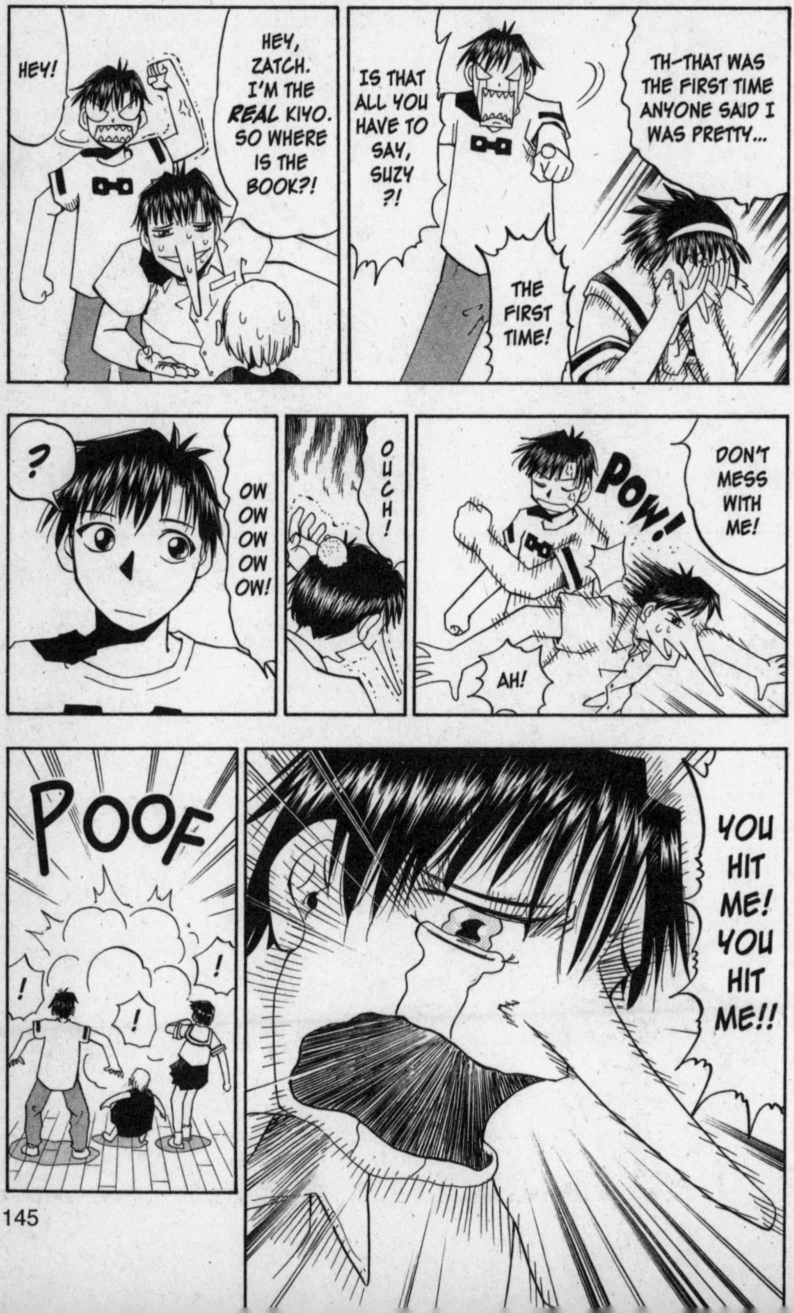
TH-THAT WAS THE FIRST TIME ANYONE SAID I WAS PRETTY...
IS THAT ALL YOU HAVE TO SAY, SUZY?!
THE FIRST TIME!
HEY, ZATCH. I'M THE *REAL* KIYO. SO WHERE IS THE BOOK?!
HEY!
DON'T MESS WITH ME!
POW!
AH!
OUCH!
OW OW OW OW OW!
?
YOU HIT ME! YOU HIT ME!!
POOF
!
!
!

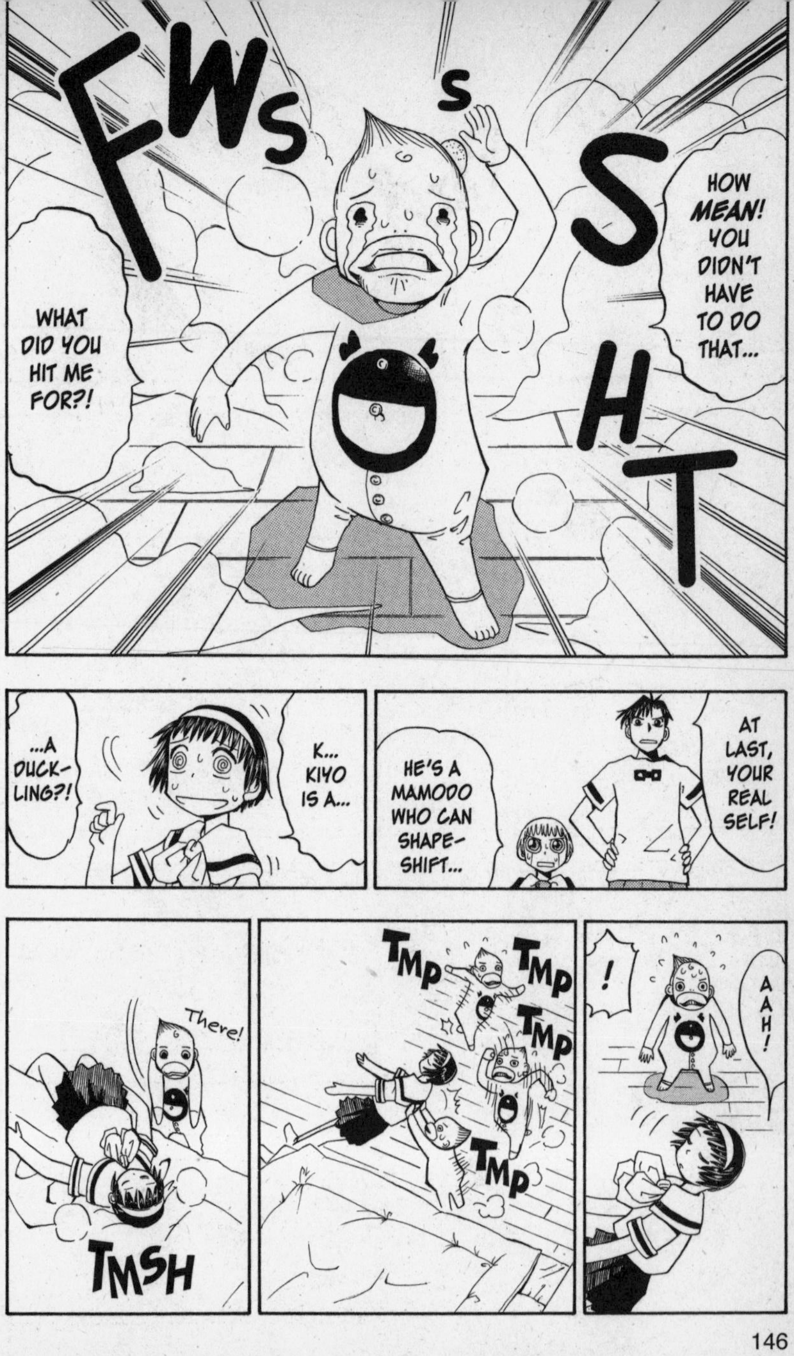
FWSSSHT
HOW MEAN! YOU DIDN'T HAVE TO DO THAT...
WHAT DID YOU HIT ME FOR?!
AT LAST, YOUR REAL SELF!
HE'S A MAMODO WHO CAN SHAPE-SHIFT...
K... KIYO IS A...
...A DUCKLING?!
AAH!
!
TMP
TMP
TMP
TMP
There!
TMSH

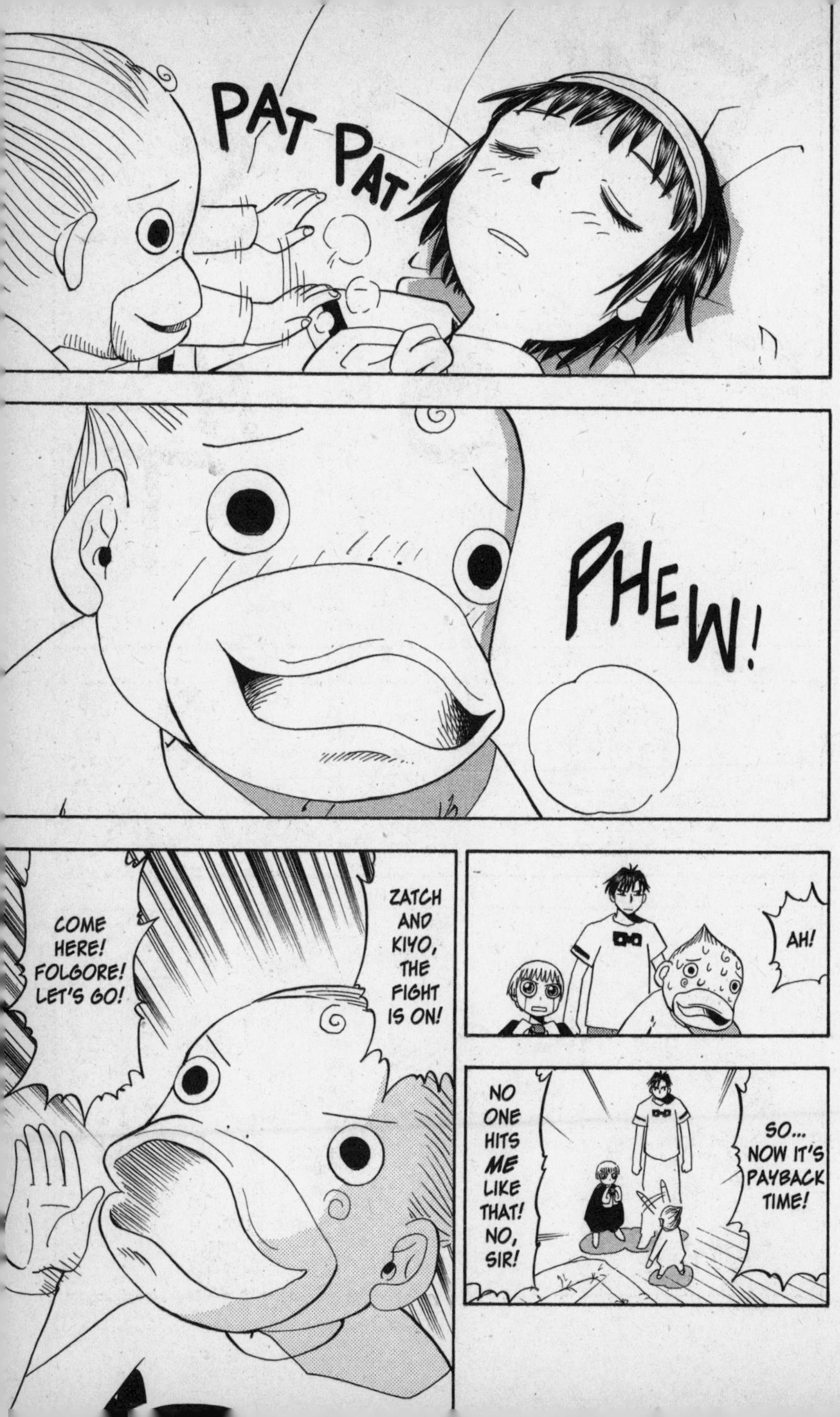
PAT PAT
PHEW!
AH!
SO... NOW IT'S PAYBACK TIME!
NO ONE HITS *ME* LIKE THAT! NO, SIR!
ZATCH AND KIYO, THE FIGHT IS ON!
COME HERE! FOLGORE! LET'S GO!

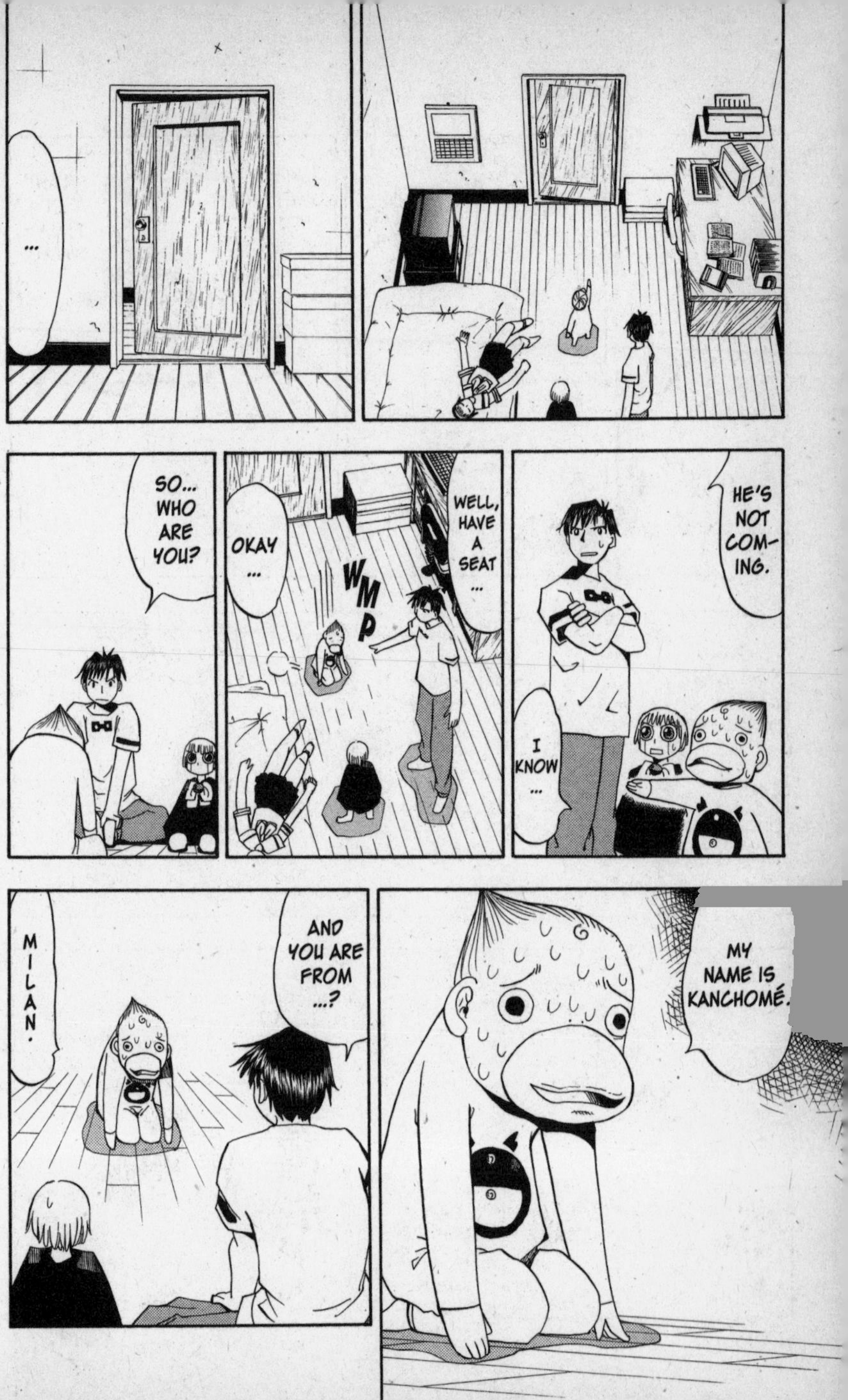
...
HE'S NOT COMING.
I KNOW ...
WELL, HAVE A SEAT ...
OKAY ...
WMP
SO... WHO ARE YOU?
MY NAME IS KANCHOMÉ.
AND YOU ARE FROM ...?
MILAN.

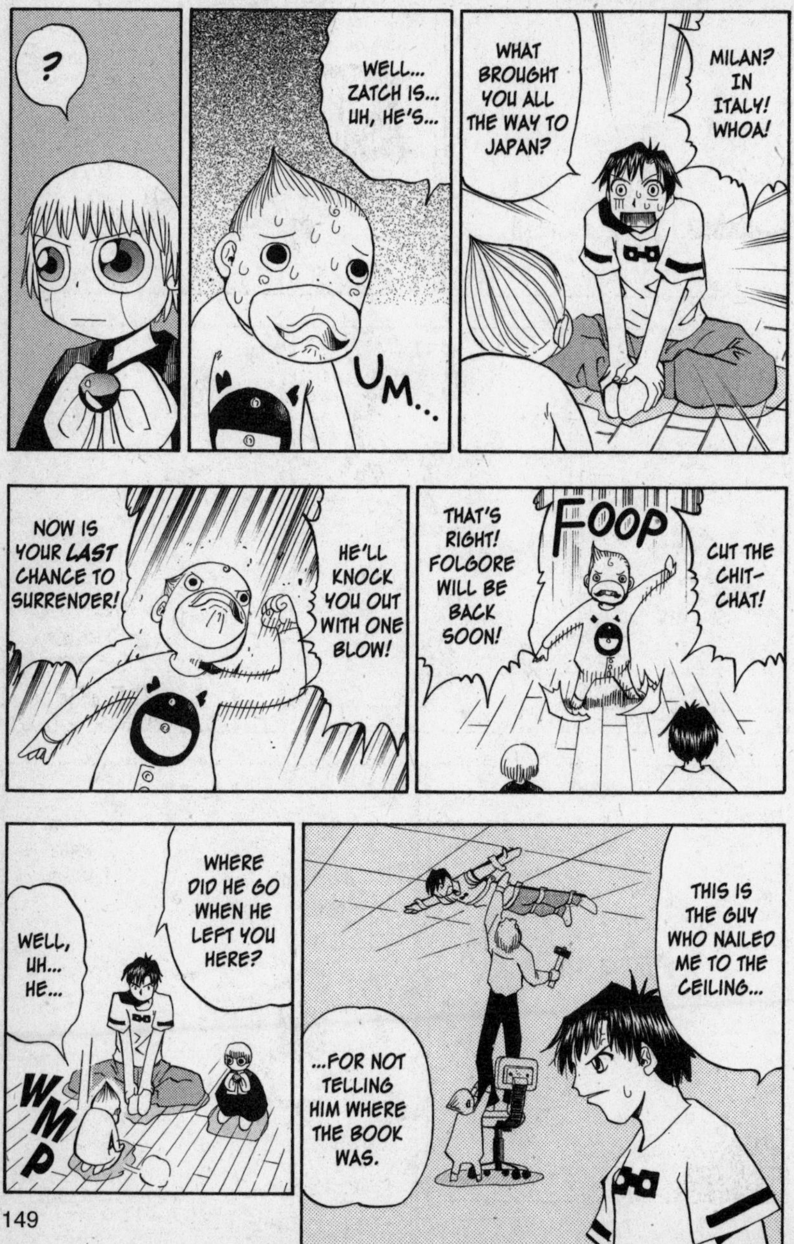
MILAN? IN ITALY! WHOA!
WHAT BROUGHT YOU ALL THE WAY TO JAPAN?
WELL... ZATCH IS... UH, HE'S...
UM...
?
CUT THE CHIT-CHAT!
FOOP
THAT'S RIGHT! FOLGORE WILL BE BACK SOON!
NOW IS YOUR LAST CHANCE TO SURRENDER!
HE'LL KNOCK YOU OUT WITH ONE BLOW!
THIS IS THE GUY WHO NAILED ME TO THE CEILING...
...FOR NOT TELLING HIM WHERE THE BOOK WAS.
WHERE DID HE GO WHEN HE LEFT YOU HERE?
WELL, UH... HE...
WMP

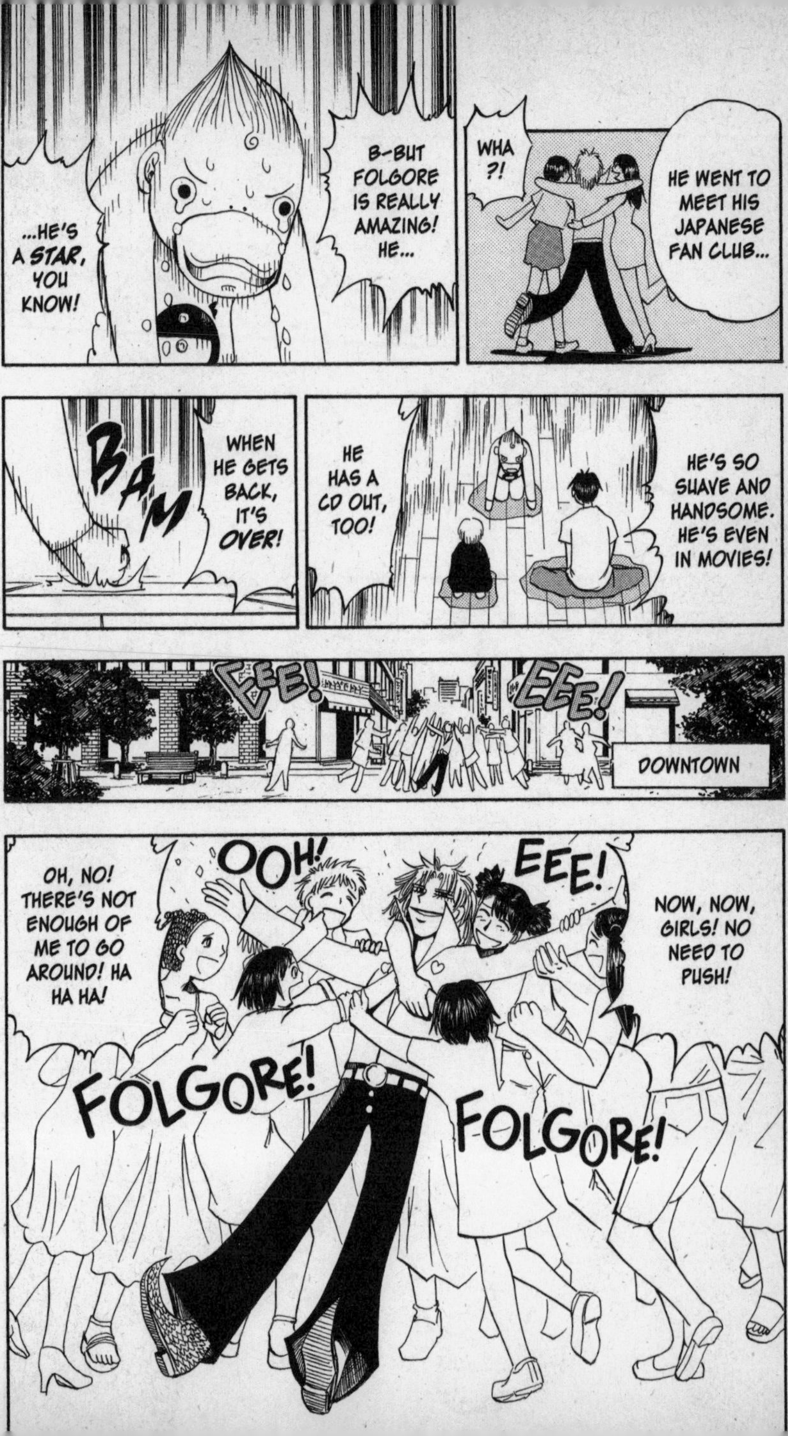
HE WENT TO MEET HIS JAPANESE FAN CLUB...
WHA ?!
B-BUT FOLGORE IS REALLY AMAZING! HE...
...HE'S A STAR, YOU KNOW!
HE'S SO SUAVE AND HANDSOME. HE'S EVEN IN MOVIES!
HE HAS A CD OUT, TOO!
WHEN HE GETS BACK, IT'S OVER!
BAM
EEE!
EEE!
DOWNTOWN
NOW, NOW, GIRLS! NO NEED TO PUSH!
EEE!
OOH!
OH, NO! THERE'S NOT ENOUGH OF ME TO GO AROUND! HA HA HA!
FOLGORE!
FOLGORE!

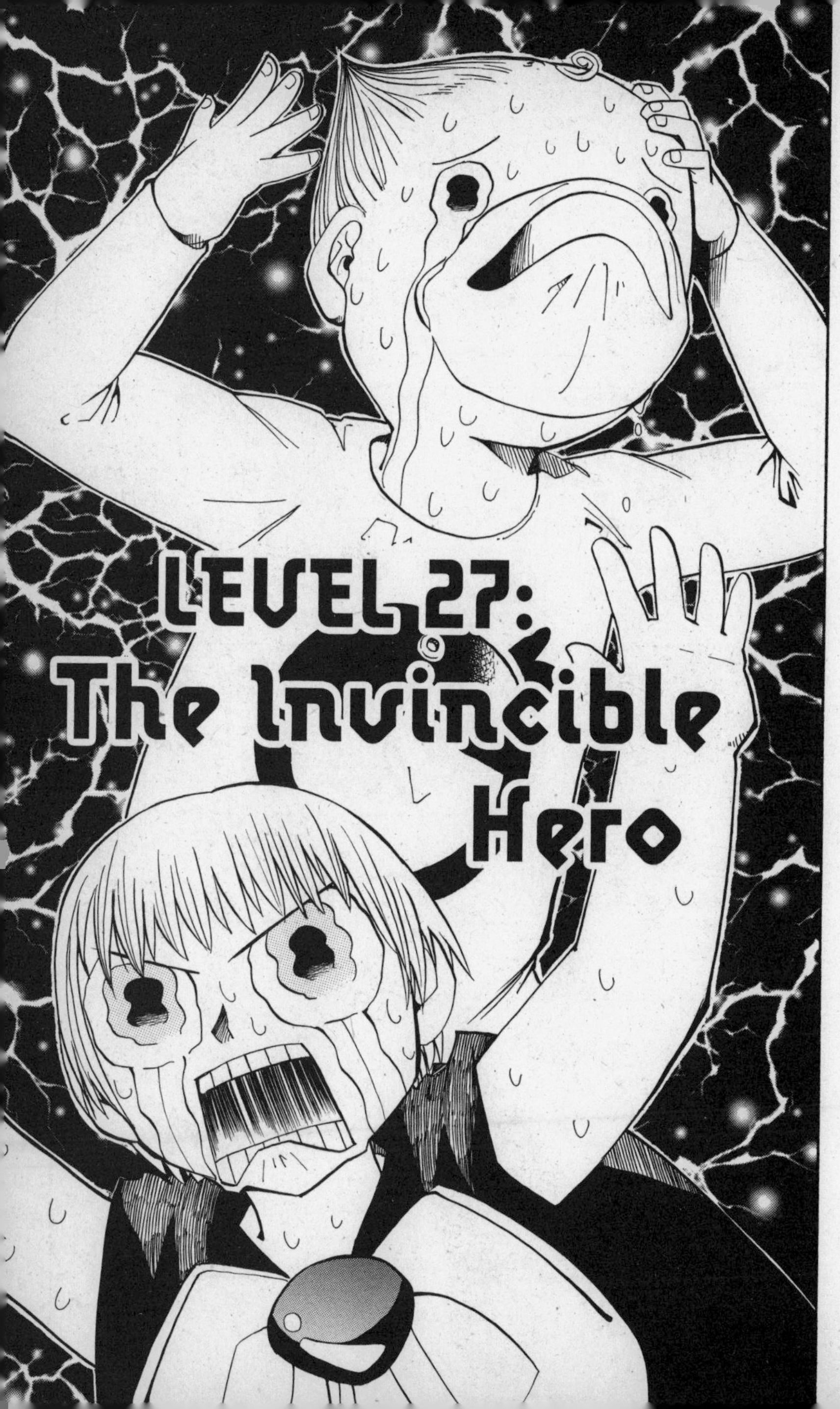
LEVEL 27:
The Invincible Hero

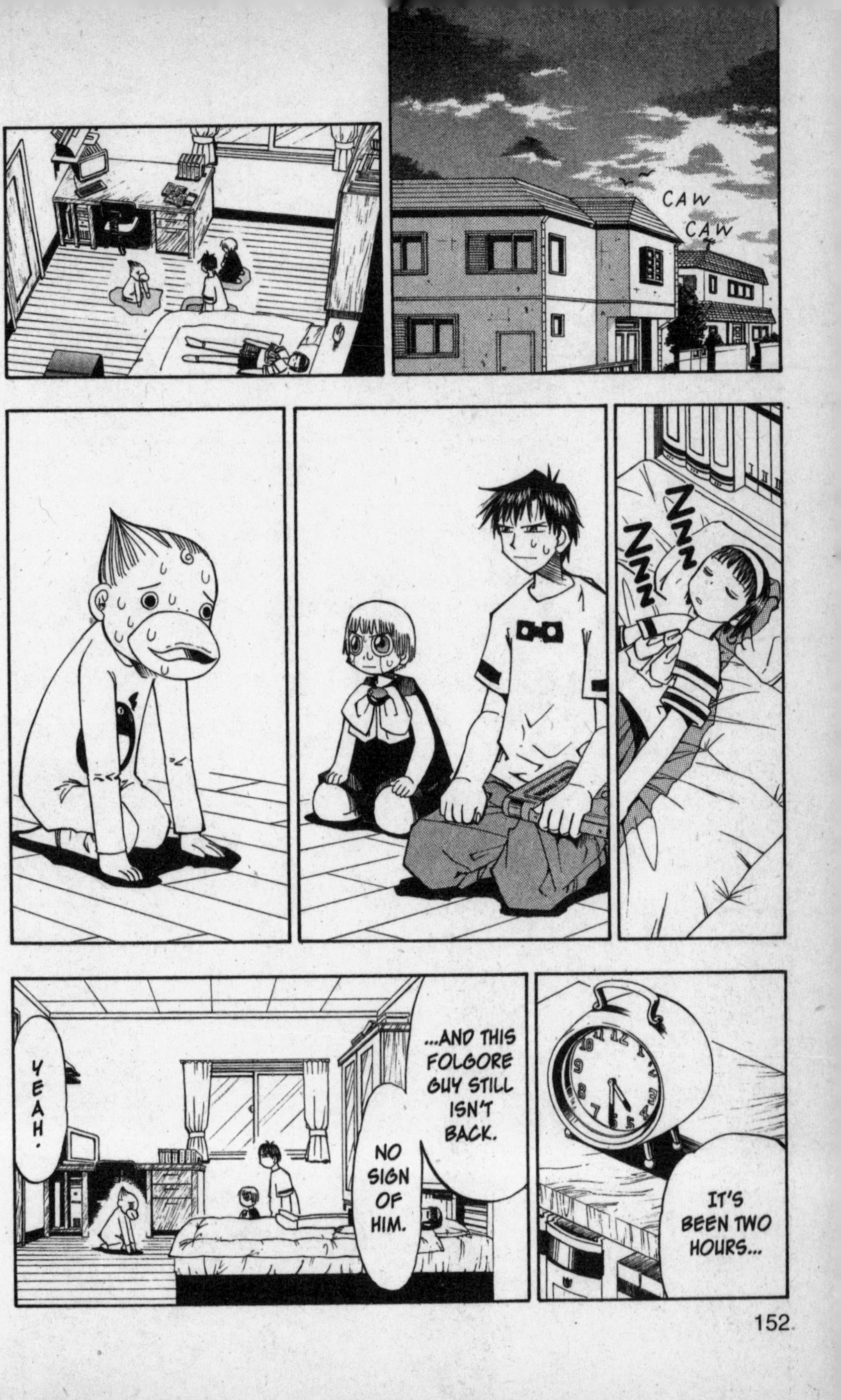
CAW
CAW
ZZZ
ZZZ
IT'S BEEN TWO HOURS...
...AND THIS FOLGORE GUY STILL ISN'T BACK.
NO SIGN OF HIM.
YEAH.

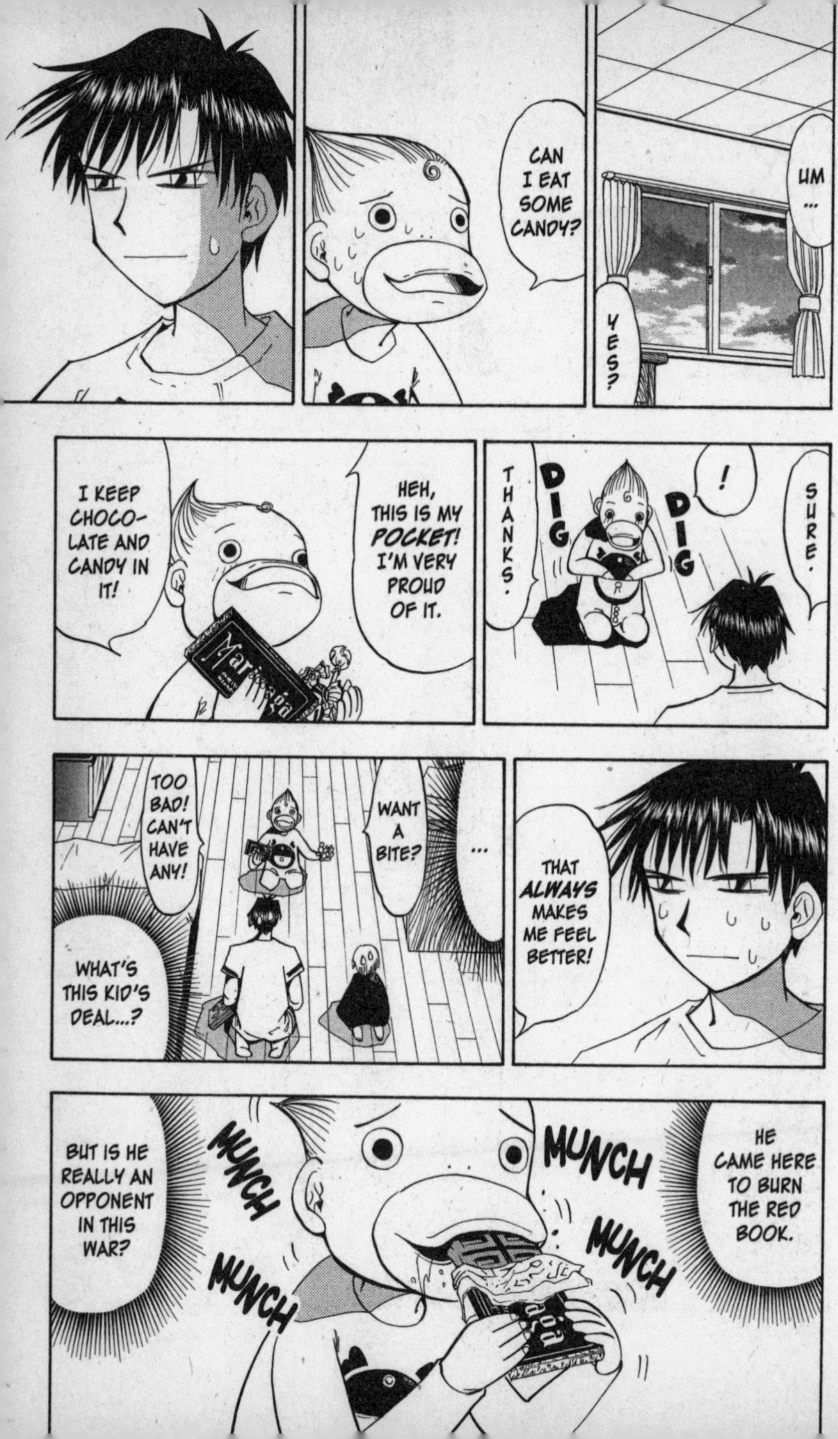
UM ...
YES?
CAN I EAT SOME CANDY?
SURE.
!
DIG
DIG
THANKS.
HEH, THIS IS MY *POCKET*! I'M VERY PROUD OF IT.
I KEEP CHOCOLATE AND CANDY IN IT!
THAT *ALWAYS* MAKES ME FEEL BETTER!
...
WANT A BITE?
TOO BAD! CAN'T HAVE ANY!
WHAT'S THIS KID'S DEAL...?
HE CAME HERE TO BURN THE RED BOOK.
MUNCH
MUNCH
MUNCH
MUNCH
BUT IS HE REALLY AN OPPONENT IN THIS WAR?

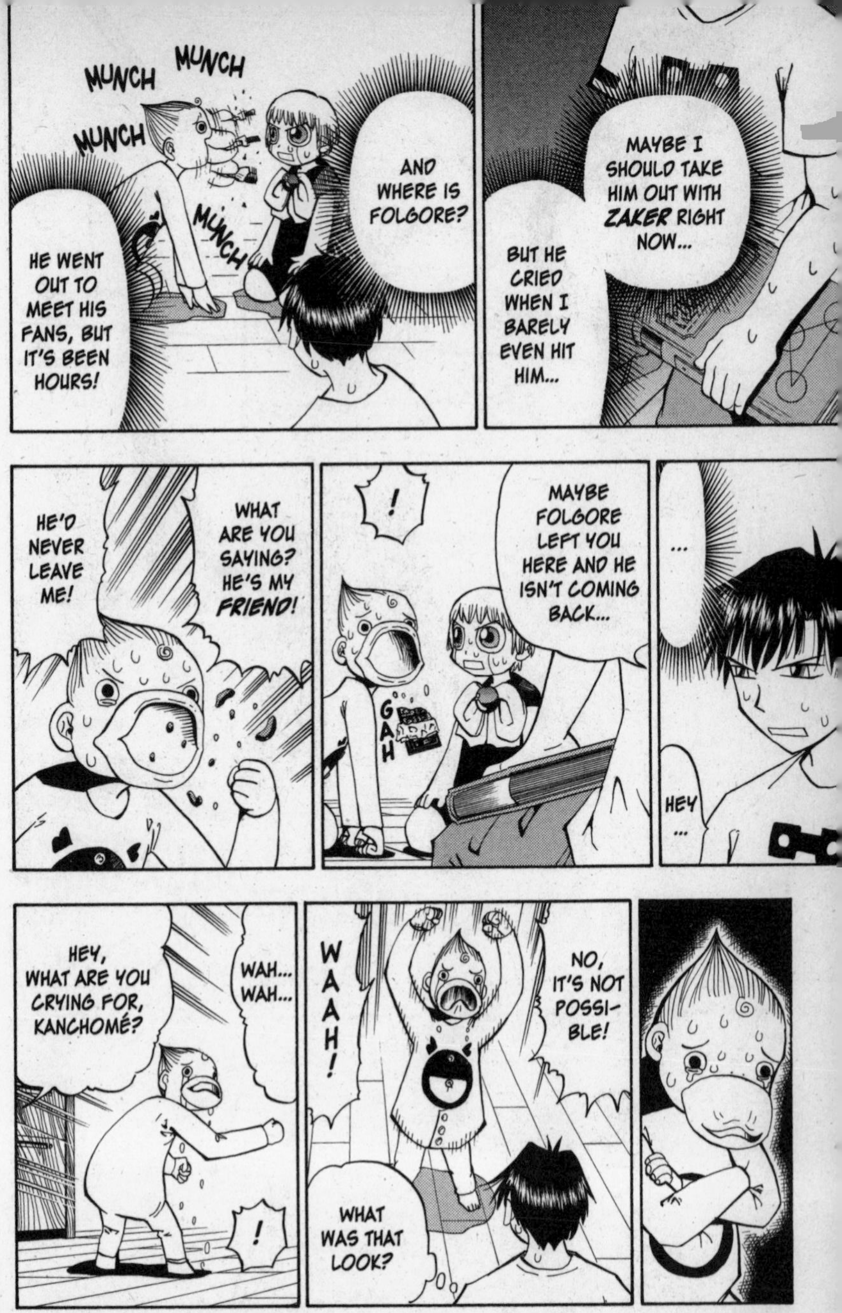
MAYBE I SHOULD TAKE HIM OUT WITH ZAKER RIGHT NOW...
BUT HE CRIED WHEN I BARELY EVEN HIT HIM...
AND WHERE IS FOLGORE?
MUNCH
MUNCH
MUNCH
MUNCH
HE WENT OUT TO MEET HIS FANS, BUT IT'S BEEN HOURS!
...
HEY...
!
MAYBE FOLGORE LEFT YOU HERE AND HE ISN'T COMING BACK...
GAH
WHAT ARE YOU SAYING? HE'S MY FRIEND!
HE'D NEVER LEAVE ME!
NO, IT'S NOT POSSI-BLE!
WAAAH!
WHAT WAS THAT LOOK?
WAH... WAH...
HEY, WHAT ARE YOU CRYING FOR, KANCHOMÉ?
!

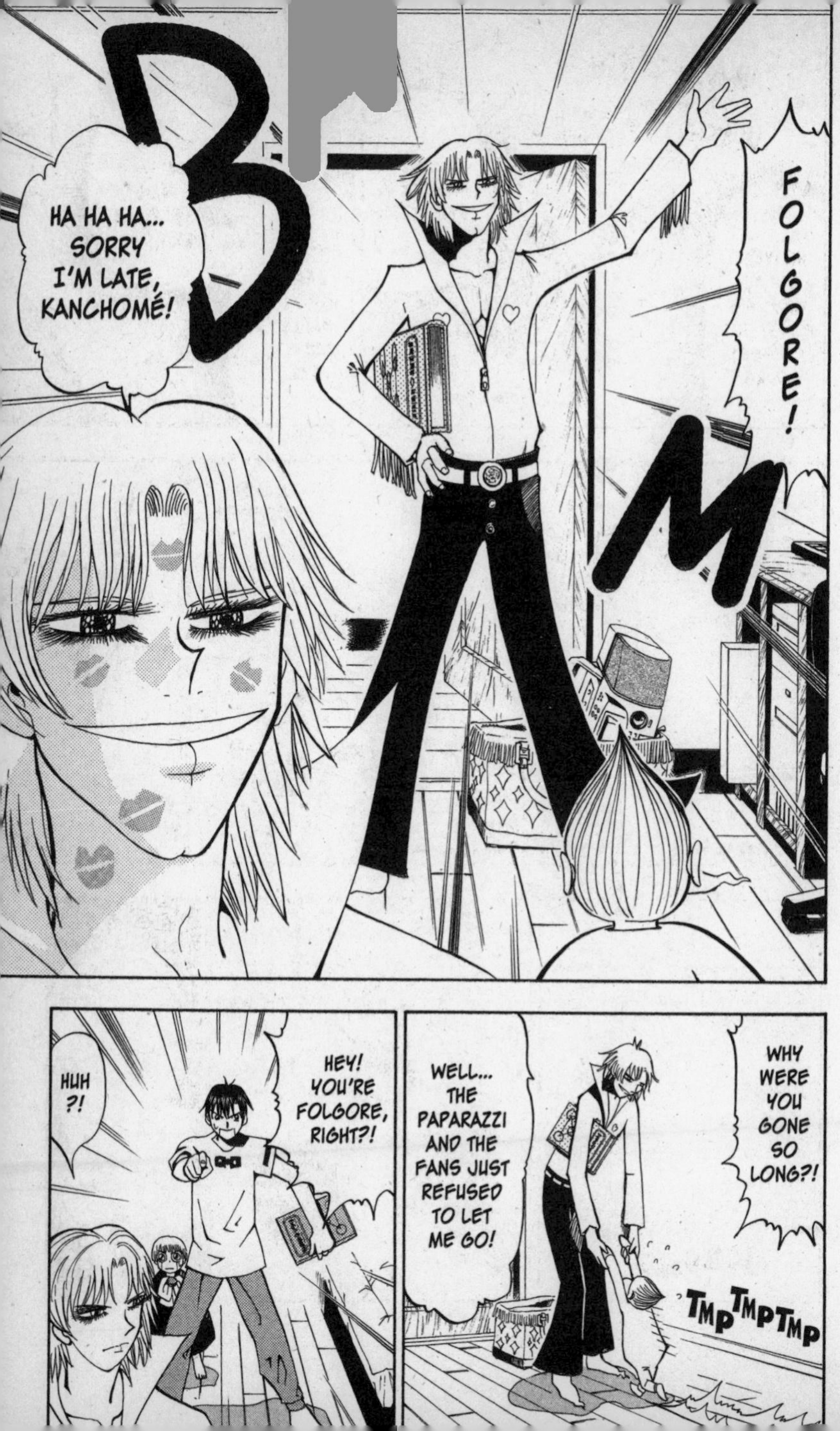
FOLGORE!
HA HA HA... SORRY I'M LATE, KANCHOMÉ!
WHY WERE YOU GONE SO LONG?!
WELL... THE PAPARAZZI AND THE FANS JUST REFUSED TO LET ME GO!
TMP TMP TMP
HEY! YOU'RE FOLGORE, RIGHT?!
HUH ?!

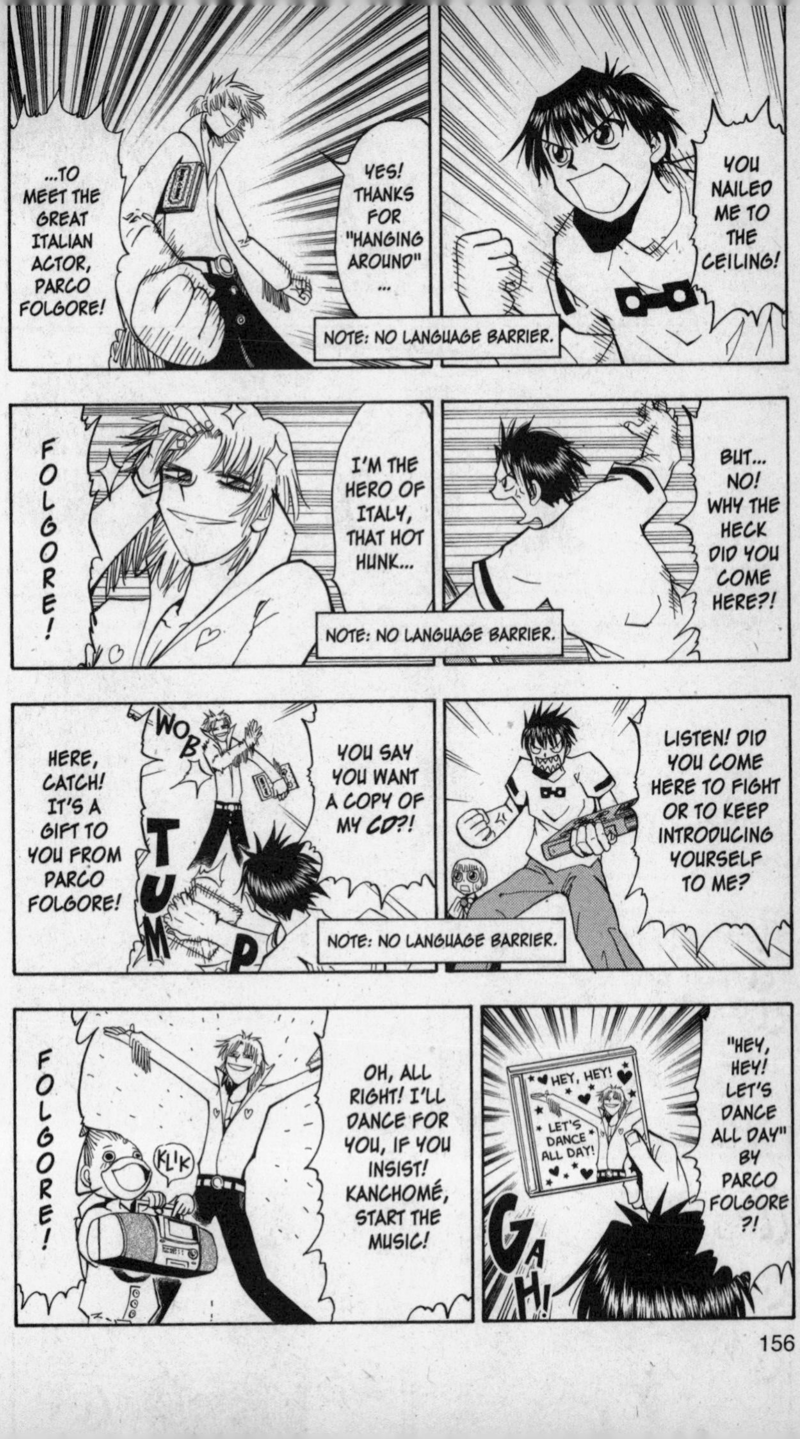

YOU NAILED ME TO THE CEILING!
YES! THANKS FOR "HANGING AROUND"...
...TO MEET THE GREAT ITALIAN ACTOR, PARCO FOLGORE!
NOTE: NO LANGUAGE BARRIER.
BUT... NO! WHY THE HECK DID YOU COME HERE?!
I'M THE HERO OF ITALY, THAT HOT HUNK...
FOLGORE!
NOTE: NO LANGUAGE BARRIER.
LISTEN! DID YOU COME HERE TO FIGHT OR TO KEEP INTRODUCING YOURSELF TO ME?
YOU SAY YOU WANT A COPY OF MY CD?!
WOB
HERE, CATCH! IT'S A GIFT TO YOU FROM PARCO FOLGORE!
TUMP
NOTE: NO LANGUAGE BARRIER.
HEY, HEY! LET'S DANCE ALL DAY!
"HEY, HEY! LET'S DANCE ALL DAY" BY PARCO FOLGORE?!
GAH!
OH, ALL RIGHT! I'LL DANCE FOR YOU, IF YOU INSIST! KANCHOMÉ, START THE MUSIC!
KLIK
FOLGORE!

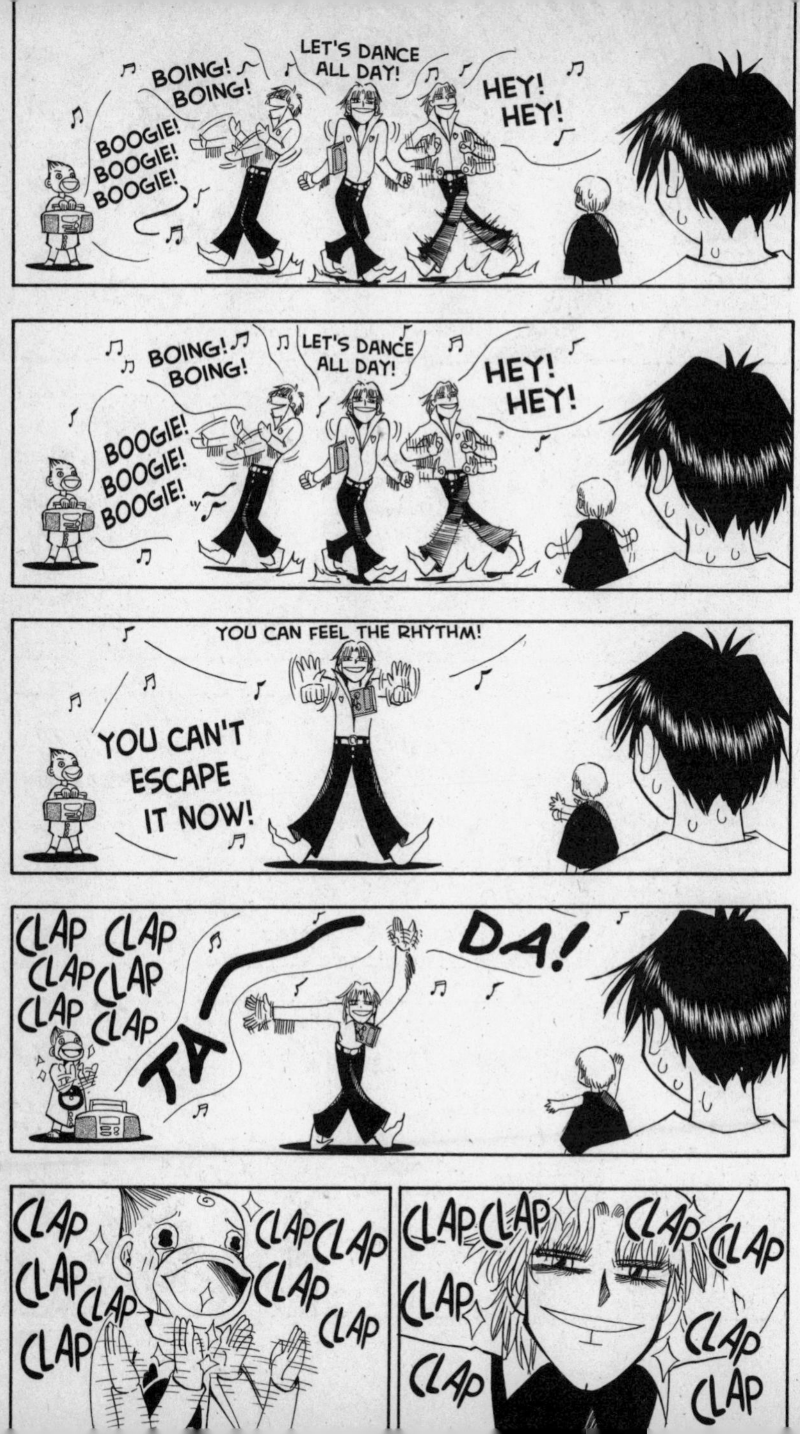
HEY! HEY!
LET'S DANCE ALL DAY!
BOING! BOING!
BOOGIE! BOOGIE! BOOGIE!
HEY! HEY!
LET'S DANCE ALL DAY!
BOING! BOING!
BOOGIE! BOOGIE! BOOGIE!
YOU CAN FEEL THE RHYTHM!
YOU CAN'T ESCAPE IT NOW!
DA!
TA
CLAP CLAP CLAP CLAP CLAP CLAP
CLAP CLAP CLAP CLAP CLAP CLAP CLAP
CLAP CLAP CLAP CLAP CLAP CLAP CLAP

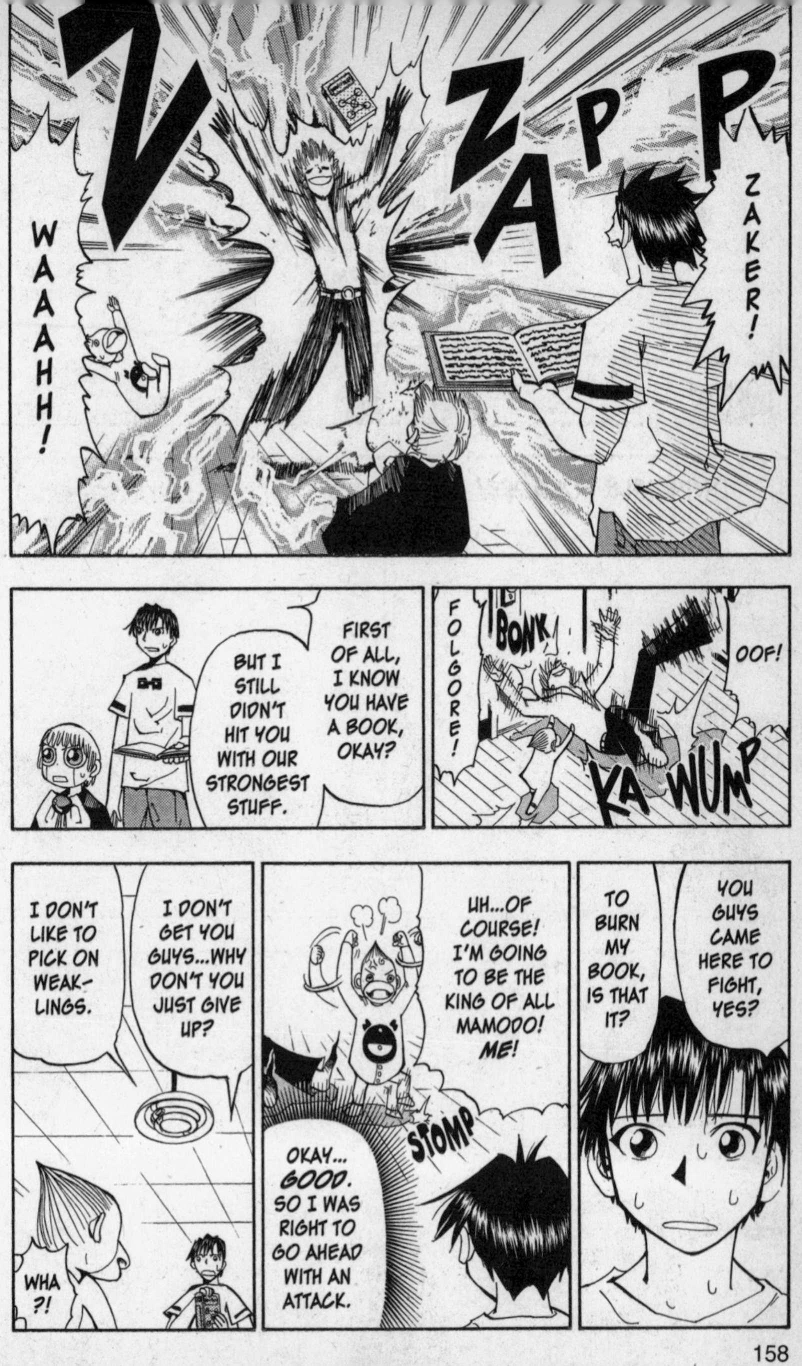
ZAKER!
ZAPP
WAAAAHH!
OOF!
BONK
FOLGORE!
KA WUMP
FIRST OF ALL, I KNOW YOU HAVE A BOOK, OKAY?
BUT I STILL DIDN'T HIT YOU WITH OUR STRONGEST STUFF.
YOU GUYS CAME HERE TO FIGHT, YES?
TO BURN MY BOOK, IS THAT IT?
UH...OF COURSE! I'M GOING TO BE THE KING OF ALL MAMODO! *ME!*
STOMP
OKAY... *GOOD.* SO I WAS RIGHT TO GO AHEAD WITH AN ATTACK.
I DON'T GET YOU GUYS...WHY DON'T YOU JUST GIVE UP?
I DON'T LIKE TO PICK ON WEAK-LINGS.
WHA ?!

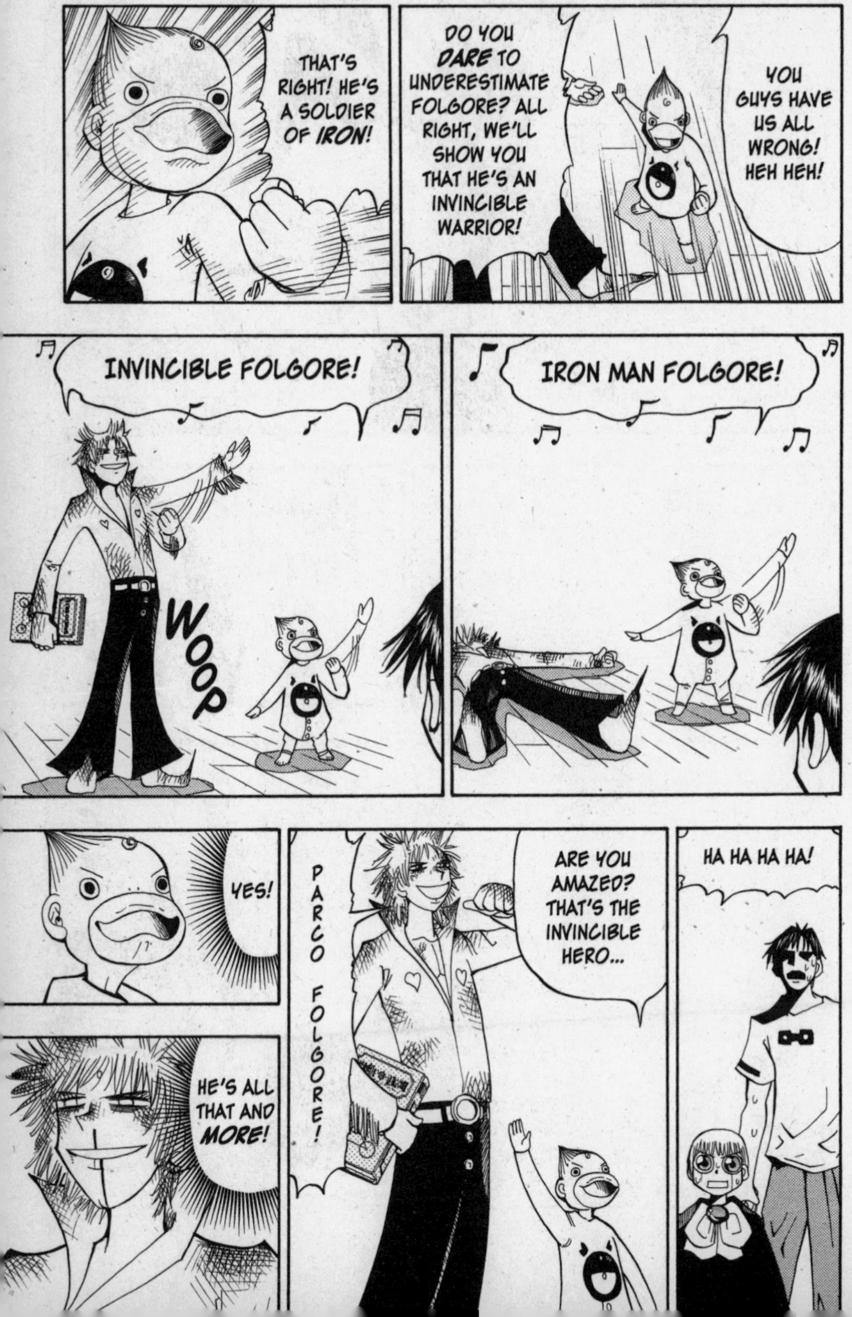
YOU GUYS HAVE US ALL WRONG! HEH HEH!
DO YOU DARE TO UNDERESTIMATE FOLGORE? ALL RIGHT, WE'LL SHOW YOU THAT HE'S AN INVINCIBLE WARRIOR!
THAT'S RIGHT! HE'S A SOLDIER OF IRON!
IRON MAN FOLGORE!
INVINCIBLE FOLGORE!
WOOP
HA HA HA HA!
ARE YOU AMAZED? THAT'S THE INVINCIBLE HERO...
PARCO FOLGORE!
YES!
HE'S ALL THAT AND MORE!

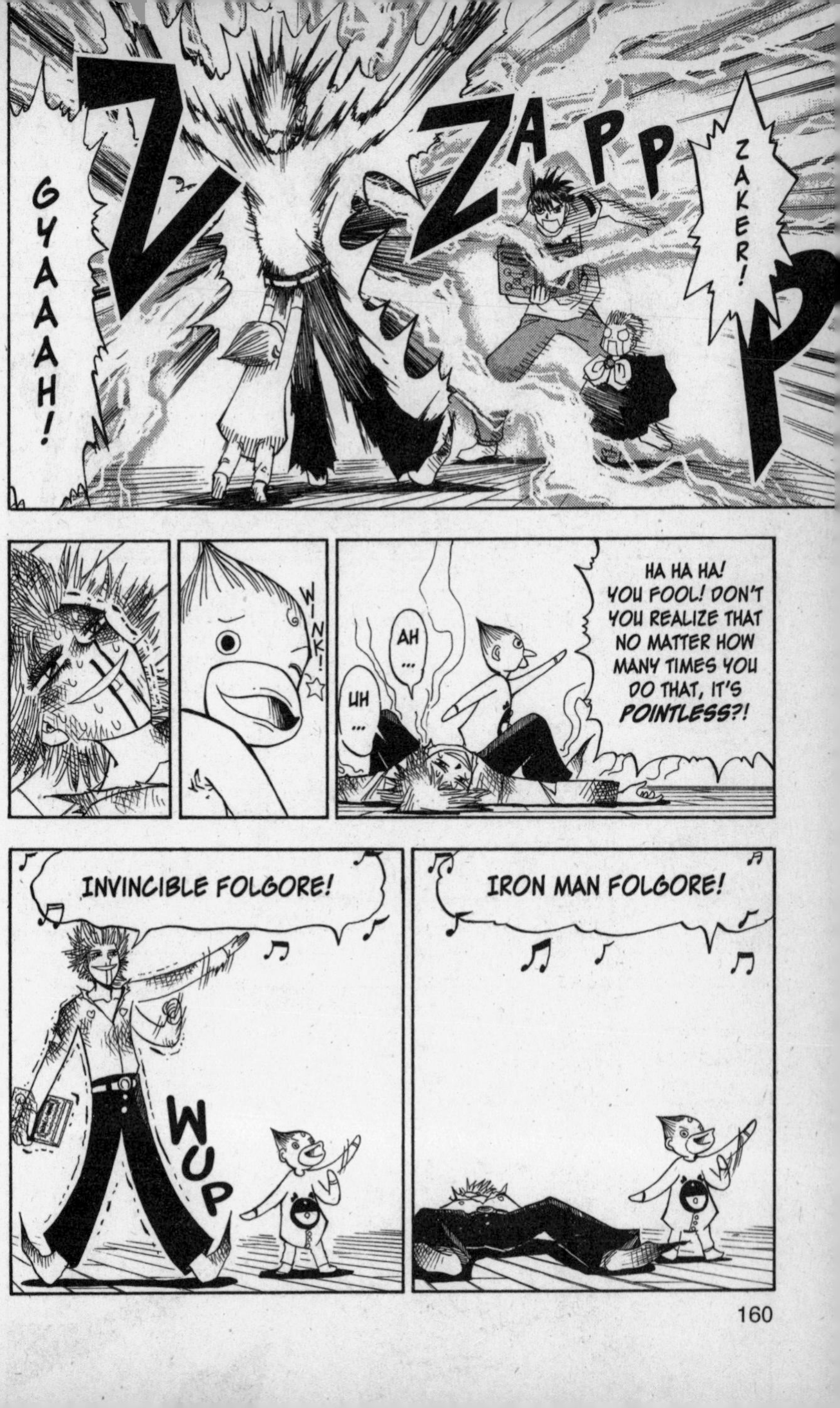
ZAKER!
ZAPP
GYAAAAH!
HA HA HA! YOU FOOL! DON'T YOU REALIZE THAT NO MATTER HOW MANY TIMES YOU DO THAT, IT'S *POINTLESS?!*
AH ...
UH ...
WINK!
IRON MAN FOLGORE!
INVINCIBLE FOLGORE!
WUP

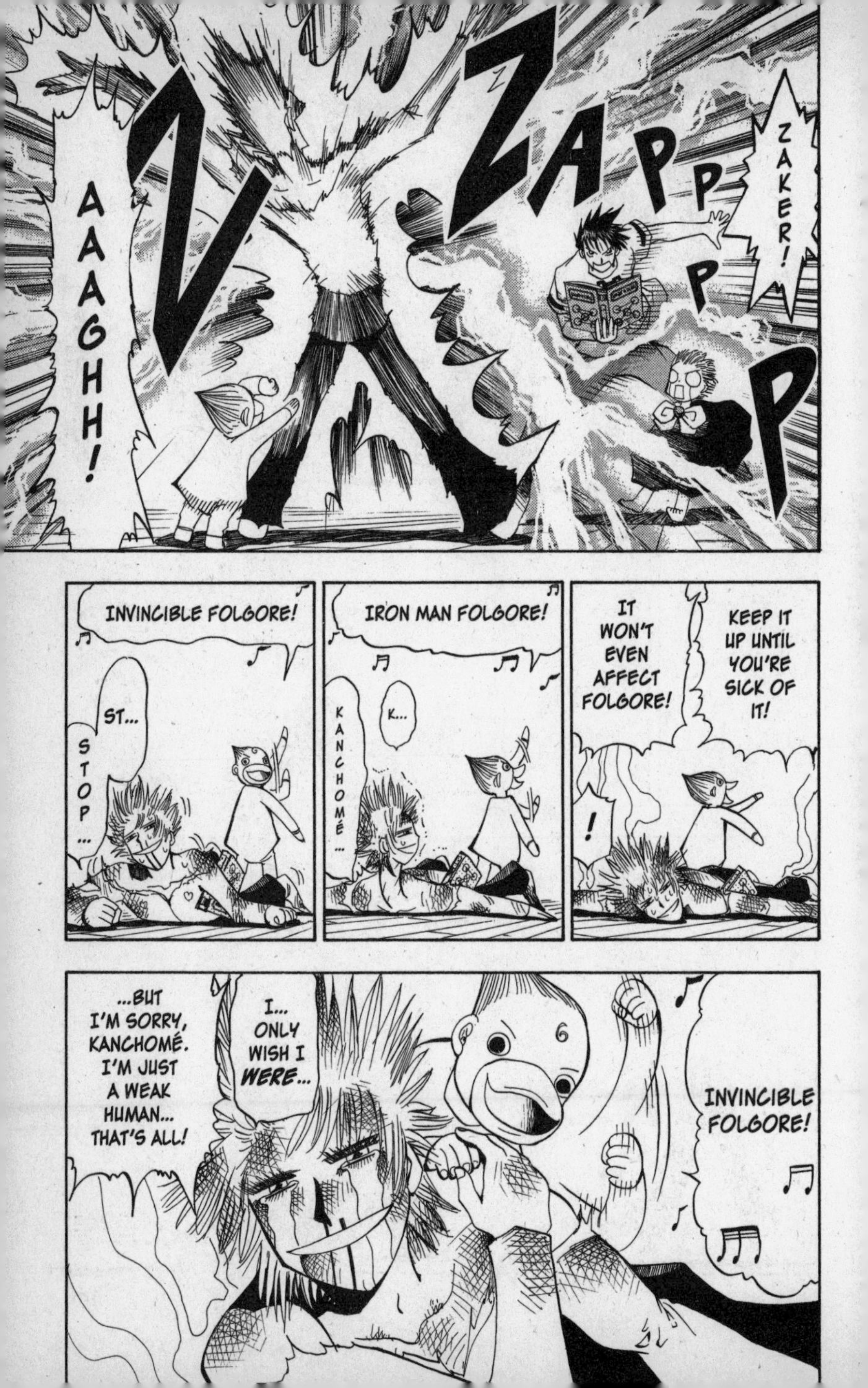
ZAKER!
ZZAPPPP
AAAGHH!
KEEP IT UP UNTIL YOU'RE SICK OF IT!
IT WON'T EVEN AFFECT FOLGORE!
!
IRON MAN FOLGORE!
K...
KANCHOMÉ...
INVINCIBLE FOLGORE!
ST...
STOP...
INVINCIBLE FOLGORE!
I... ONLY WISH I WERE...
...BUT I'M SORRY, KANCHOMÉ. I'M JUST A WEAK HUMAN... THAT'S ALL!

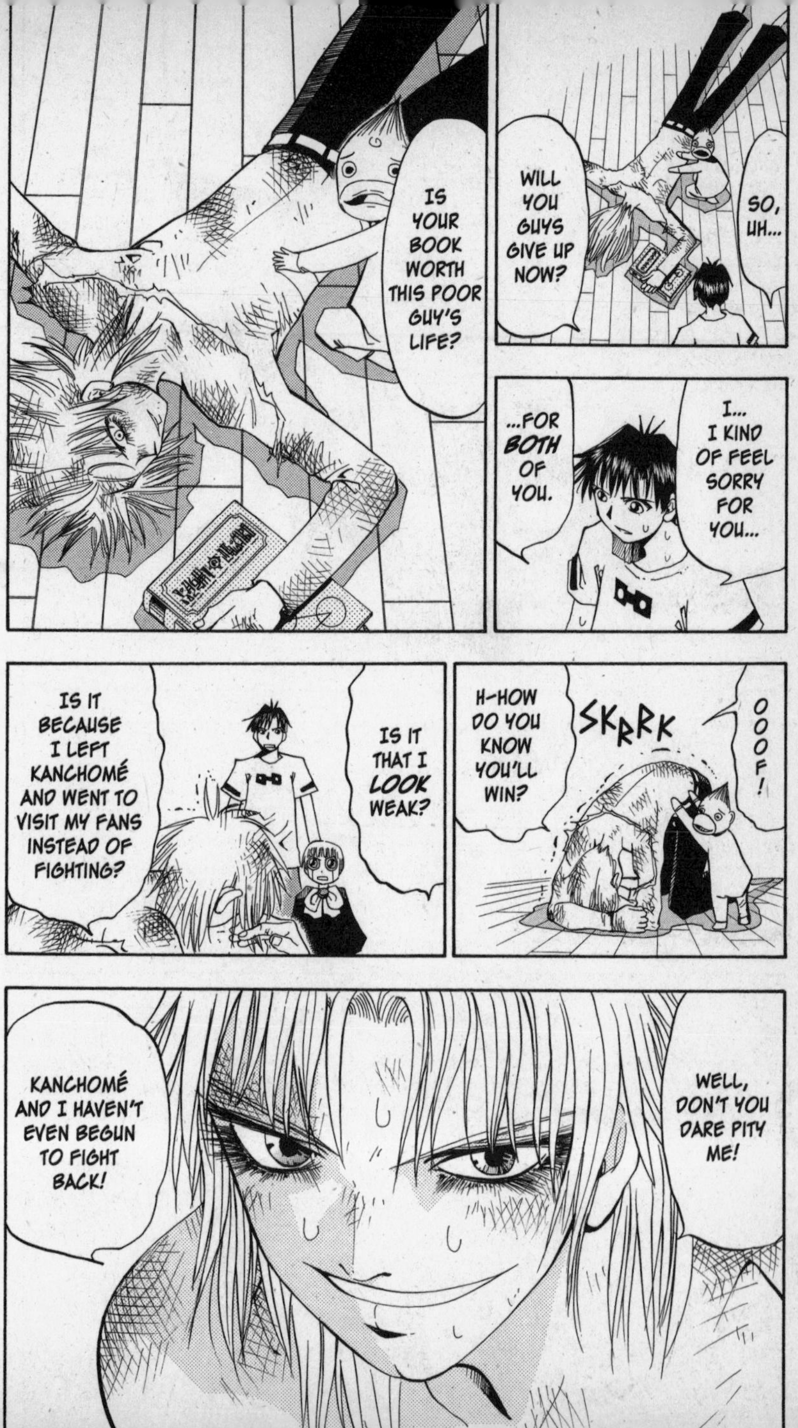
SO, UH...
WILL YOU GUYS GIVE UP NOW?
I... I KIND OF FEEL SORRY FOR YOU...
...FOR BOTH OF YOU.
IS YOUR BOOK WORTH THIS POOR GUY'S LIFE?
OOOF!
SKRRK
H-HOW DO YOU KNOW YOU'LL WIN?
IS IT THAT I LOOK WEAK?
IS IT BECAUSE I LEFT KANCHOMÉ AND WENT TO VISIT MY FANS INSTEAD OF FIGHTING?
WELL, DON'T YOU DARE PITY ME!
KANCHOMÉ AND I HAVEN'T EVEN BEGUN TO FIGHT BACK!

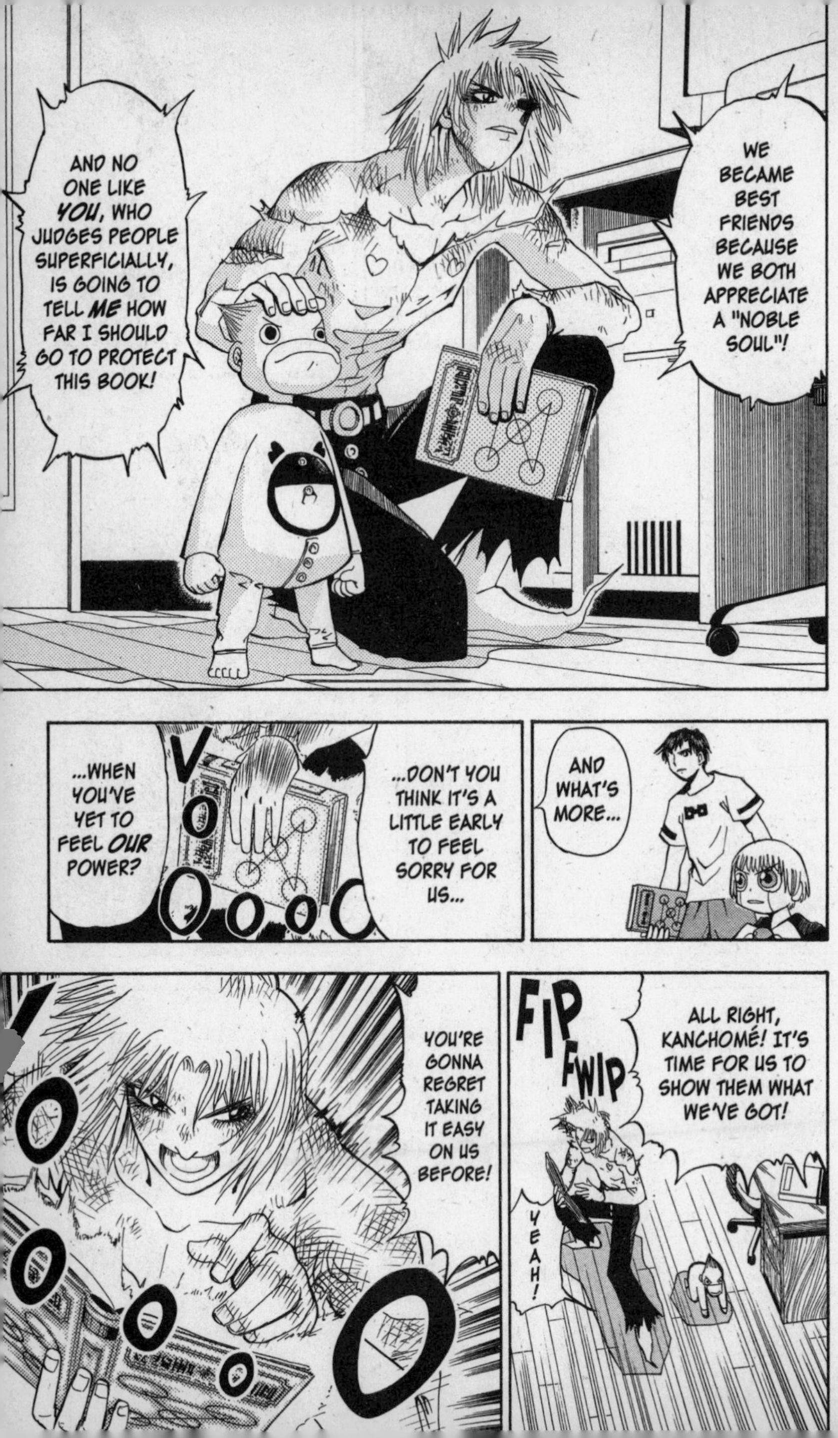
WE BECAME BEST FRIENDS BECAUSE WE BOTH APPRECIATE A "NOBLE SOUL"!
AND NO ONE LIKE *YOU*, WHO JUDGES PEOPLE SUPERFICIALLY, IS GOING TO TELL *ME* HOW FAR I SHOULD GO TO PROTECT THIS BOOK!
AND WHAT'S MORE...
...DON'T YOU THINK IT'S A LITTLE EARLY TO FEEL SORRY FOR US...
...WHEN YOU'VE YET TO FEEL *OUR* POWER?
FIP
FWIP
ALL RIGHT, KANCHOMÉ! IT'S TIME FOR US TO SHOW THEM WHAT WE'VE GOT!
YEAH!
YOU'RE GONNA REGRET TAKING IT EASY ON US BEFORE!

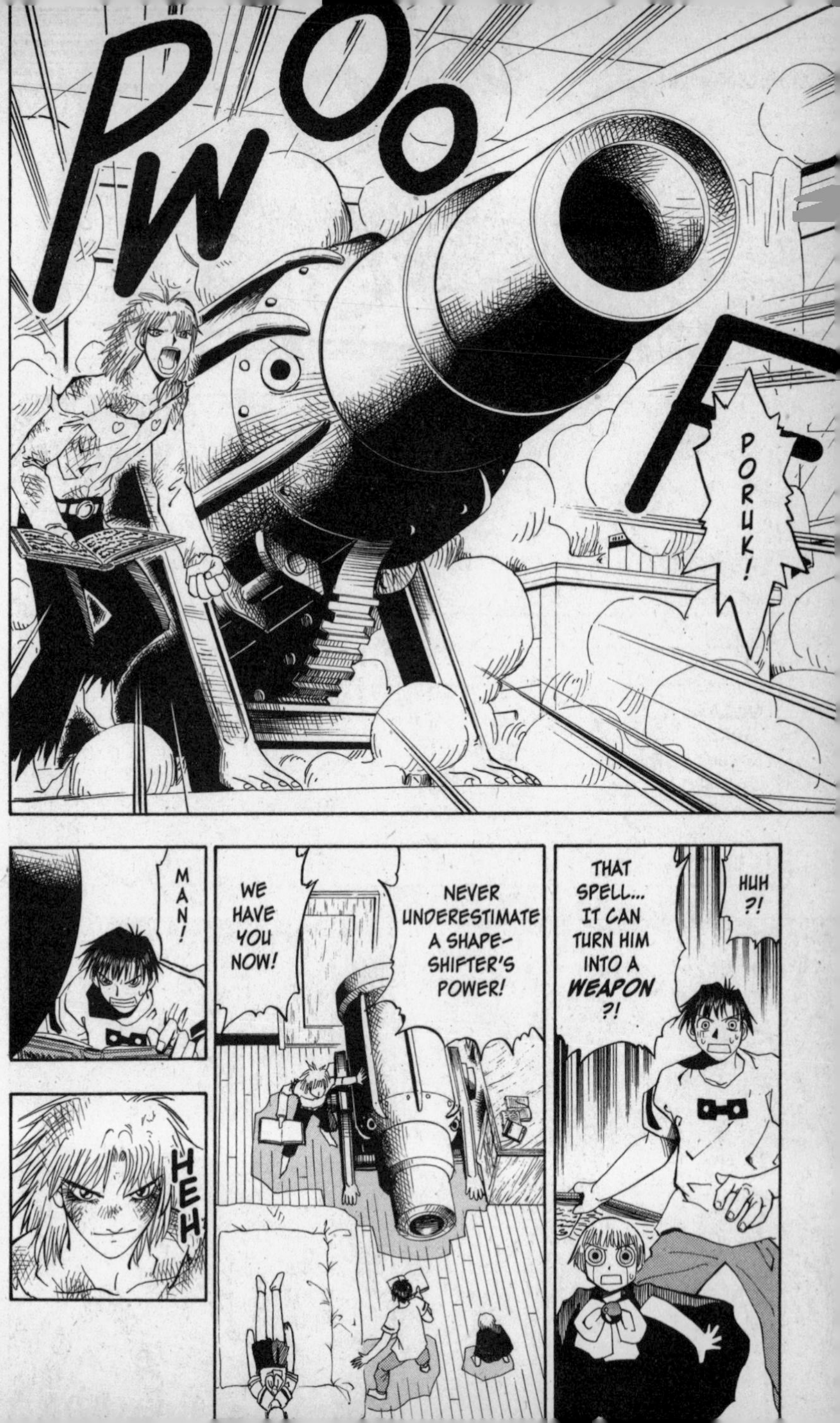
PWOOF
PORUK!
HUH ?!
THAT SPELL... IT CAN TURN HIM INTO A *WEAPON* ?!
NEVER UNDERESTIMATE A SHAPE-SHIFTER'S POWER!
WE HAVE YOU NOW!
MAN!
HEH

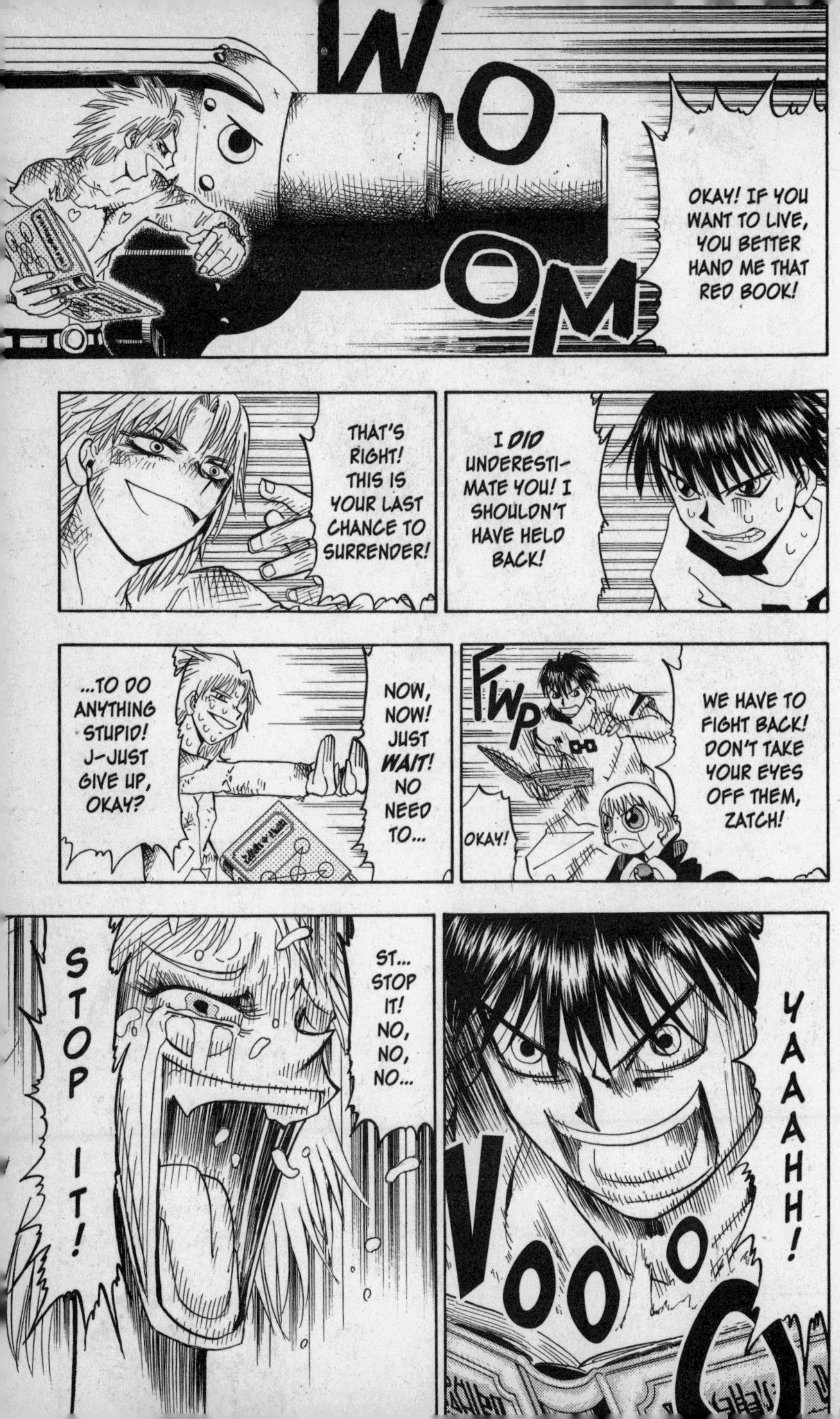
WOOM
OKAY! IF YOU WANT TO LIVE, YOU BETTER HAND ME THAT RED BOOK!
I DID UNDERESTIMATE YOU! I SHOULDN'T HAVE HELD BACK!
THAT'S RIGHT! THIS IS YOUR LAST CHANCE TO SURRENDER!
FWP
WE HAVE TO FIGHT BACK! DON'T TAKE YOUR EYES OFF THEM, ZATCH!
OKAY!
NOW, NOW! JUST WAIT! NO NEED TO...
...TO DO ANYTHING STUPID! J-JUST GIVE UP, OKAY?
YAAAAHH!
VOOOG
ST... STOP IT! NO, NO, NO...
STOP IT!

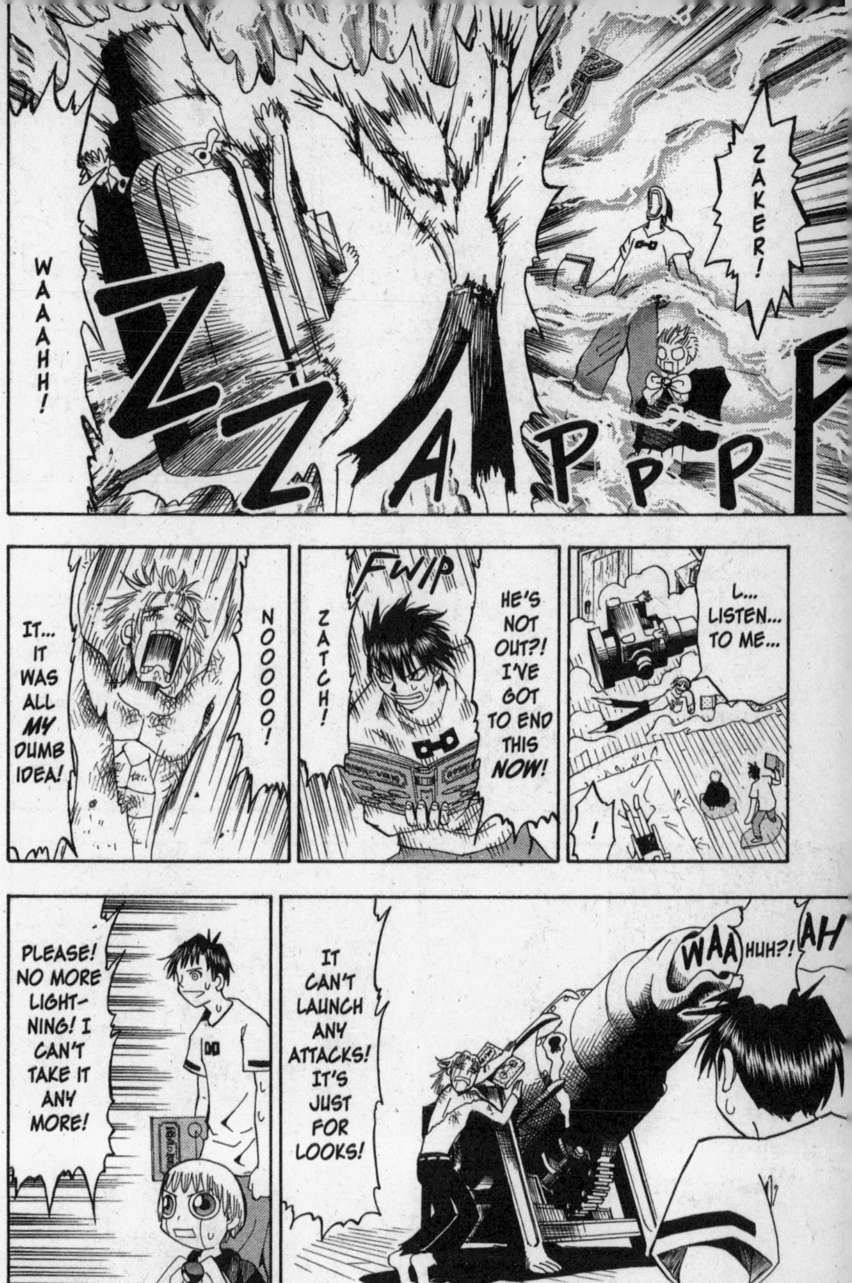
ZAKER!
ZZAPPPP
WAAAAHH!
L... LISTEN... TO ME...
!
HE'S NOT OUT?! I'VE GOT TO END THIS NOW!
FWIP
ZATCH!
NOOOOOO!
IT... IT WAS ALL MY DUMB IDEA!
AH
HUH?!
WAA
IT CAN'T LAUNCH ANY ATTACKS! IT'S JUST FOR LOOKS!
PLEASE! NO MORE LIGHT-NING! I CAN'T TAKE IT ANY MORE!

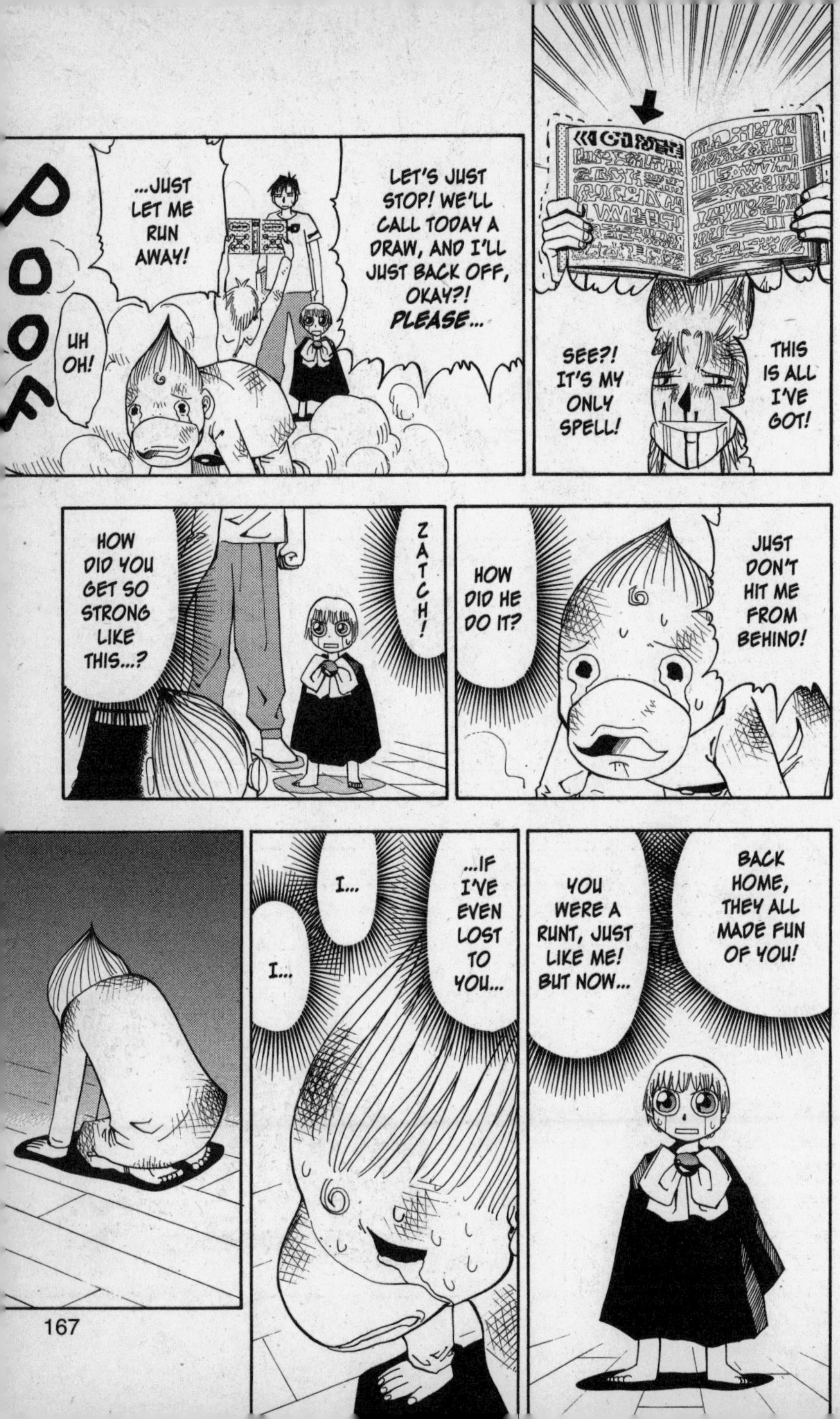
THIS IS ALL I'VE GOT!
SEE?! IT'S MY ONLY SPELL!
LET'S JUST STOP! WE'LL CALL TODAY A DRAW, AND I'LL JUST BACK OFF, OKAY?! PLEASE...
...JUST LET ME RUN AWAY!
UH OH!
POOF
JUST DON'T HIT ME FROM BEHIND!
HOW DID HE DO IT?
ZATCH!
HOW DID YOU GET SO STRONG LIKE THIS...?
BACK HOME, THEY ALL MADE FUN OF YOU!
YOU WERE A RUNT, JUST LIKE ME! BUT NOW...
...IF I'VE EVEN LOST TO YOU...
I...
I...

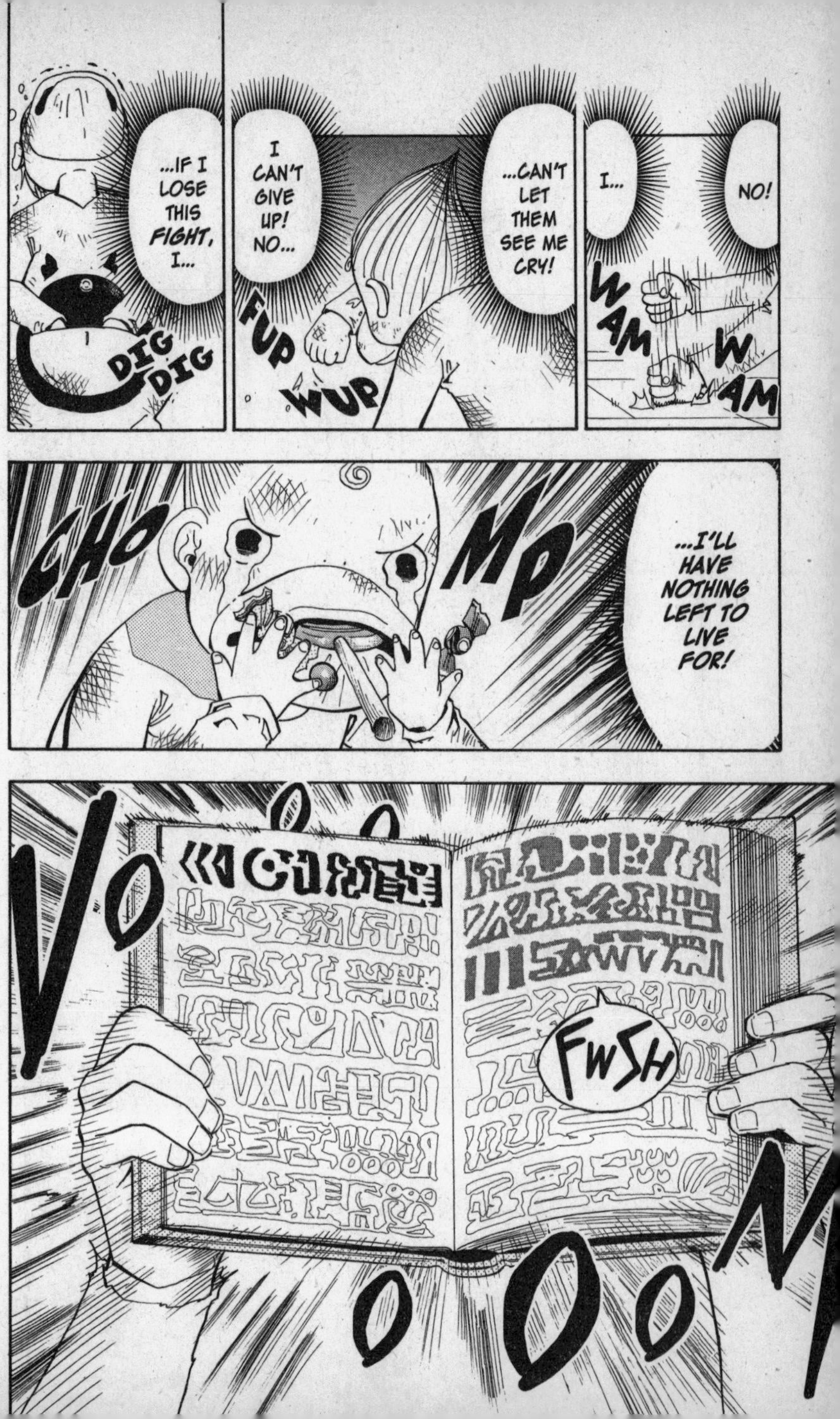
NO!
I...
WAM
WAM
...CAN'T LET THEM SEE ME CRY!
I CAN'T GIVE UP! NO...
FUP
WUP
...IF I LOSE THIS FIGHT, I...
DIG
DIG
...I'LL HAVE NOTHING LEFT TO LIVE FOR!
CHOMP
FWSH
VOOOOOOM

# LEVEL 28: A Conquerable Foe

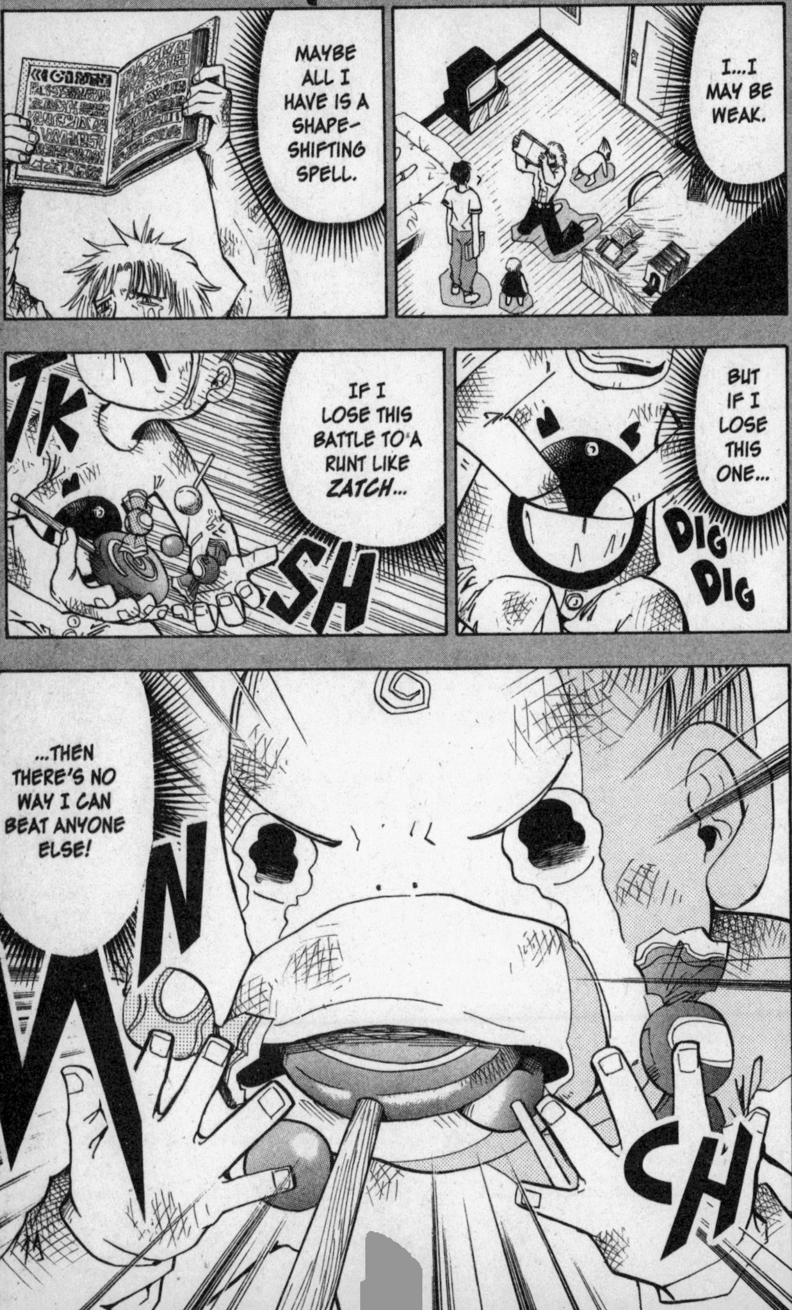
I...I MAY BE WEAK.
MAYBE ALL I HAVE IS A SHAPE-SHIFTING SPELL.
BUT IF I LOSE THIS ONE...
DIG DIG
IF I LOSE THIS BATTLE TO A RUNT LIKE ZATCH...
TK
SH
...THEN THERE'S NO WAY I CAN BEAT ANYONE ELSE!
MN
CH

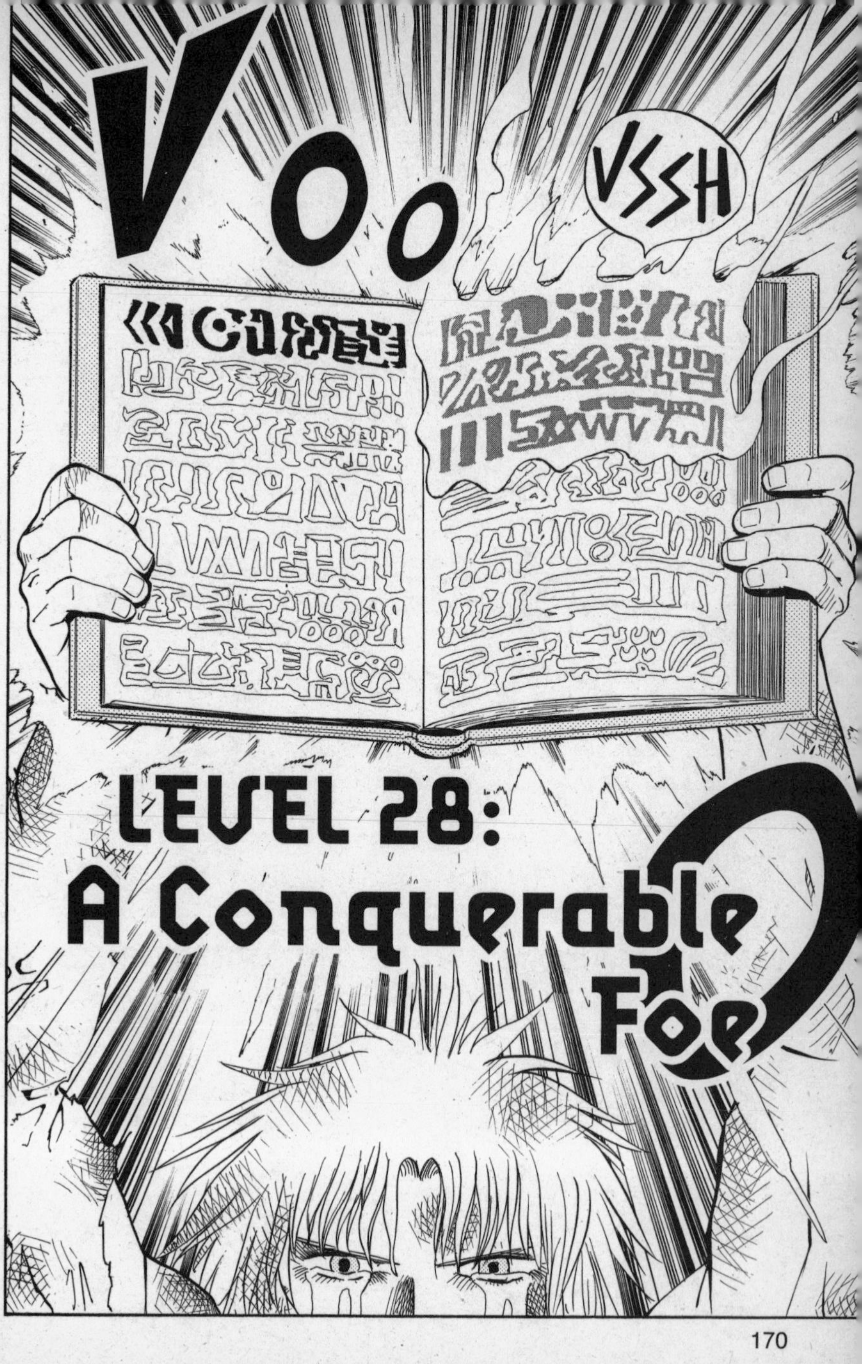
VOO
VSSH
LEVEL 28: A Conquerable Foe

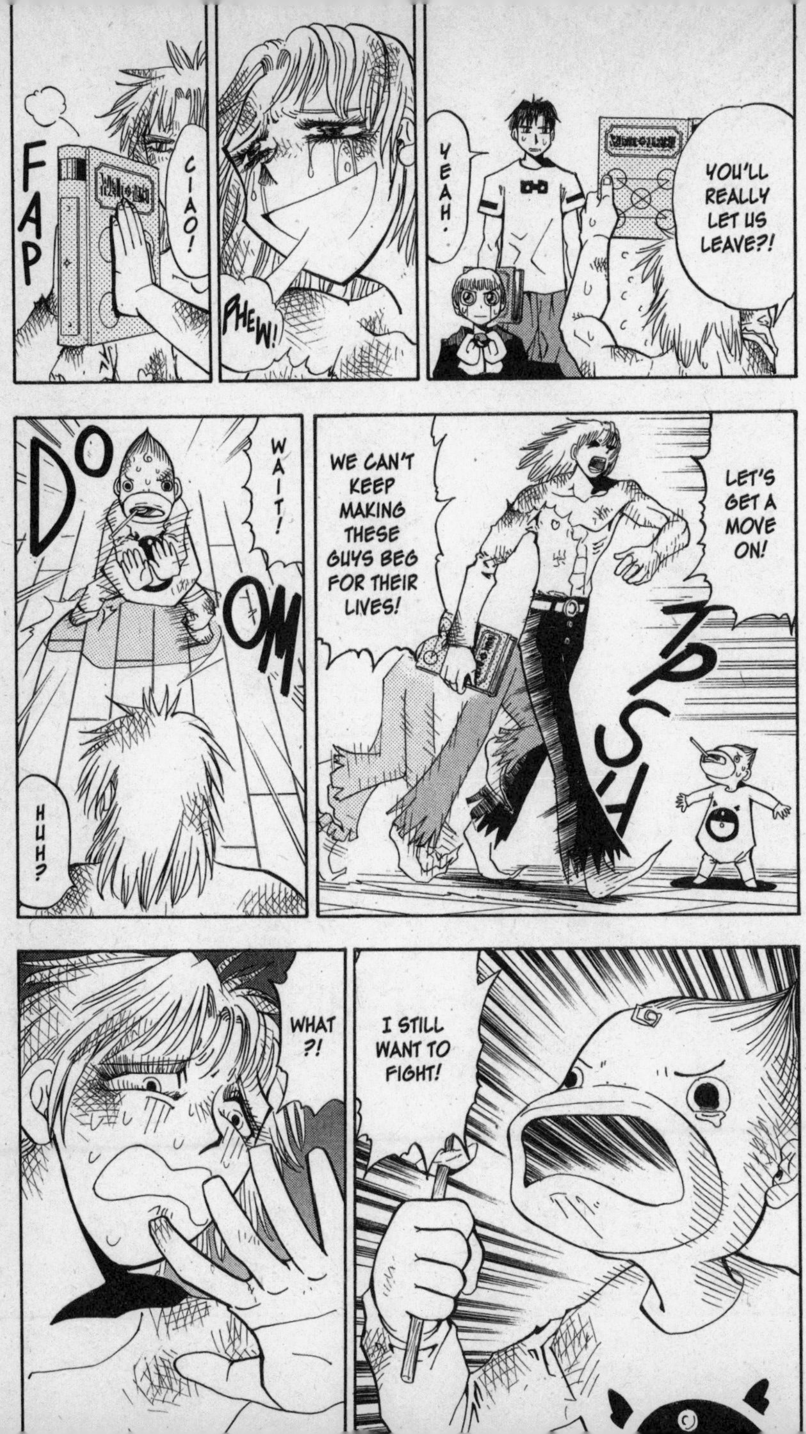
YOU'LL REALLY LET US LEAVE?!
YEAH.
PHEW!
CIAO!
FAP
LET'S GET A MOVE ON!
WE CAN'T KEEP MAKING THESE GUYS BEG FOR THEIR LIVES!
WAIT!
DOOM
HUH?
I STILL WANT TO FIGHT!
WHAT?!

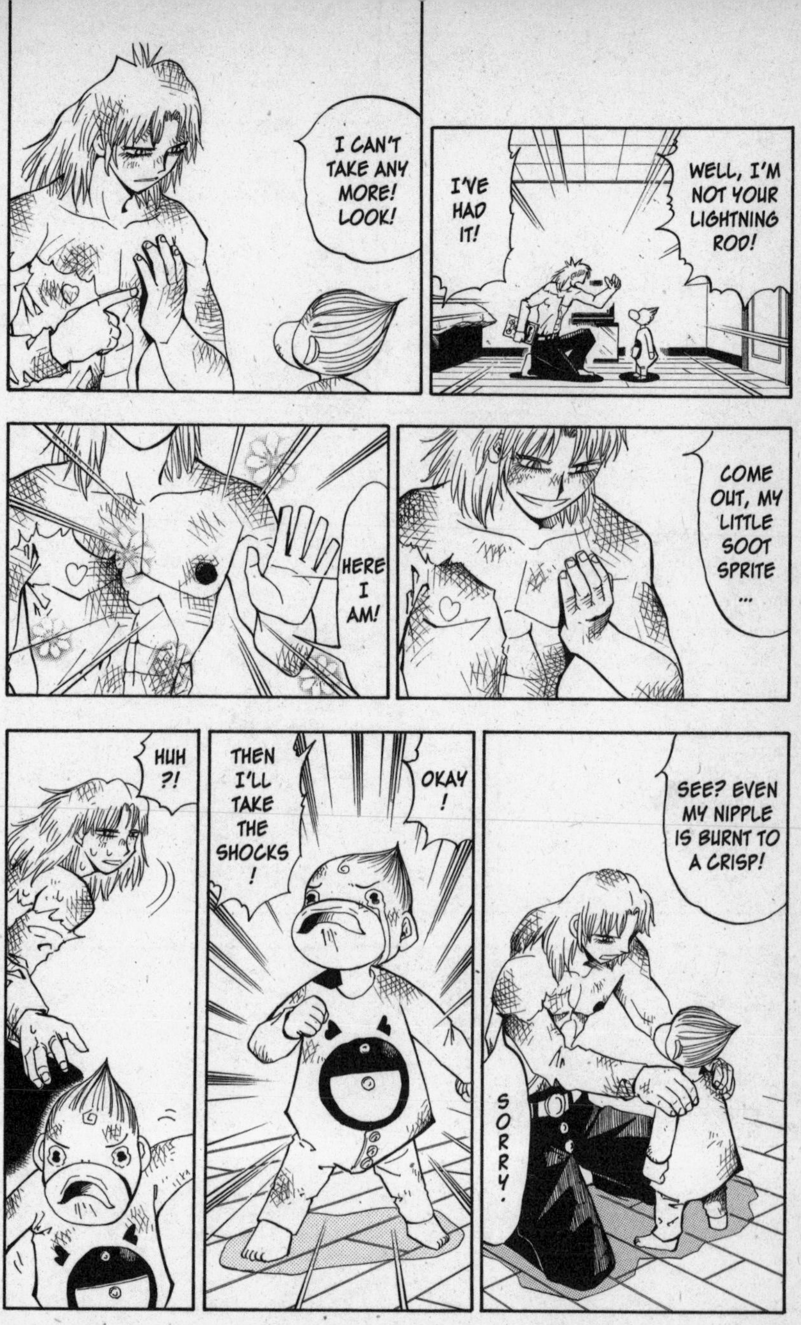
WELL, I'M NOT YOUR LIGHTNING ROD!
I'VE HAD IT!
I CAN'T TAKE ANY MORE! LOOK!
COME OUT, MY LITTLE SOOT SPRITE...
HERE I AM!
SEE? EVEN MY NIPPLE IS BURNT TO A CRISP!
SORRY.
OKAY!
THEN I'LL TAKE THE SHOCKS!
HUH?!

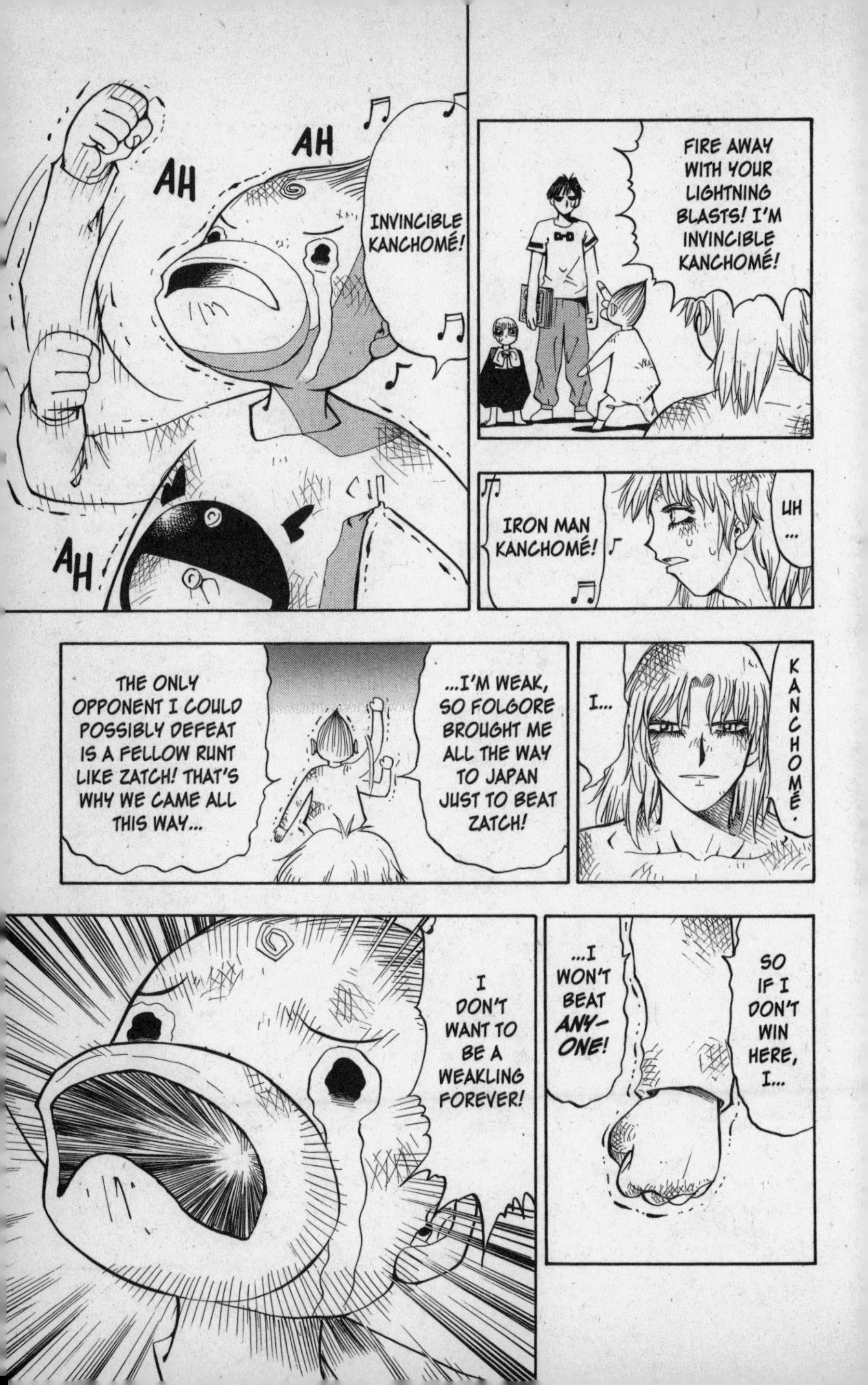
FIRE AWAY WITH YOUR LIGHTNING BLASTS! I'M INVINCIBLE KANCHOMÉ!
UH ...
IRON MAN KANCHOMÉ!
AH
INVINCIBLE KANCHOMÉ!
AH
AH
KANCHOMÉ.
I...
...I'M WEAK, SO FOLGORE BROUGHT ME ALL THE WAY TO JAPAN JUST TO BEAT ZATCH!
THE ONLY OPPONENT I COULD POSSIBLY DEFEAT IS A FELLOW RUNT LIKE ZATCH! THAT'S WHY WE CAME ALL THIS WAY...
SO IF I DON'T WIN HERE, I...
...I WON'T BEAT ANY-ONE!
I DON'T WANT TO BE A WEAKLING FOREVER!

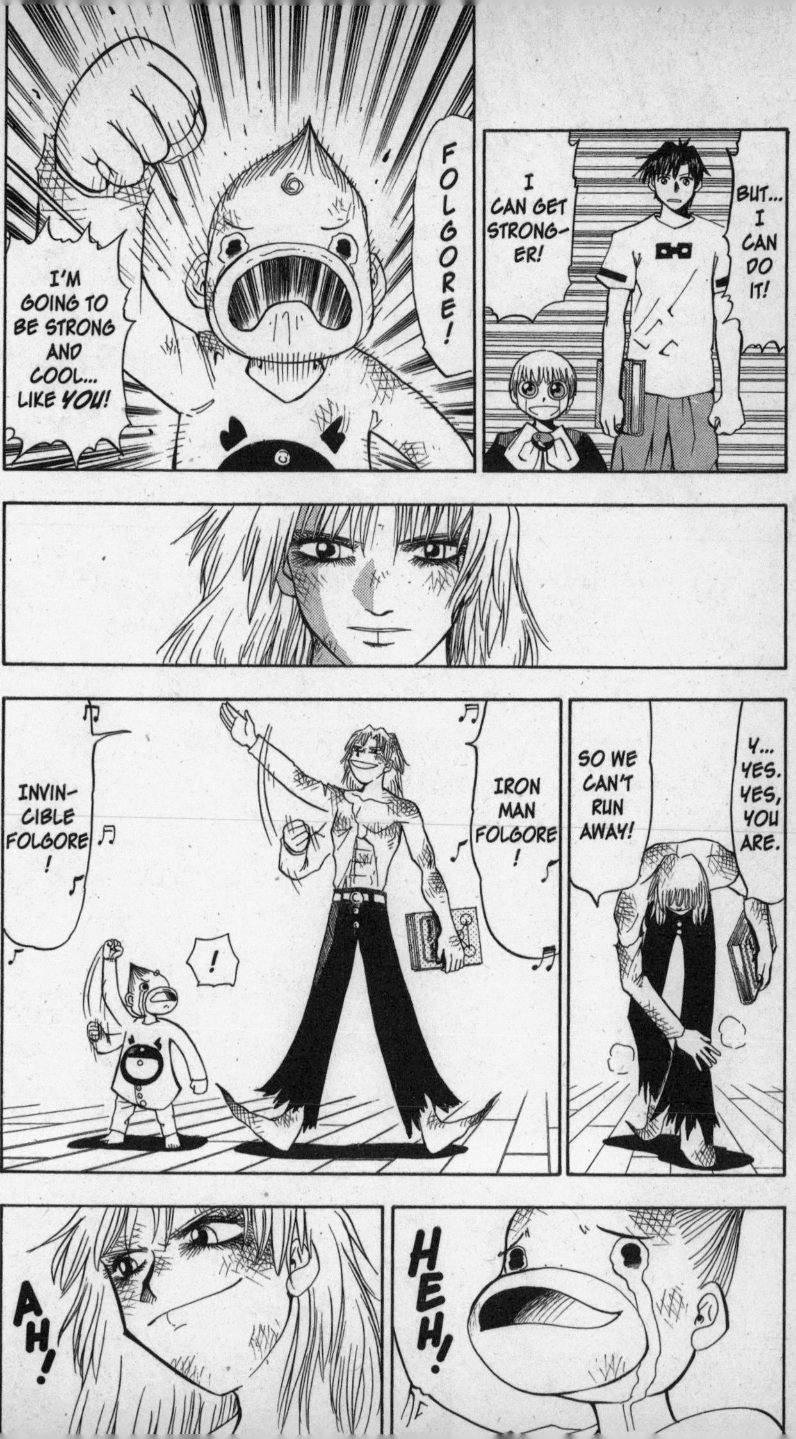
BUT... I CAN DO IT!
I CAN GET STRONGER!
FOLGORE!
I'M GOING TO BE STRONG AND COOL... LIKE YOU!
Y... YES. YES, YOU ARE.
SO WE CAN'T RUN AWAY!
IRON MAN FOLGORE!
INVINCIBLE FOLGORE!
!
HEH!
AH!

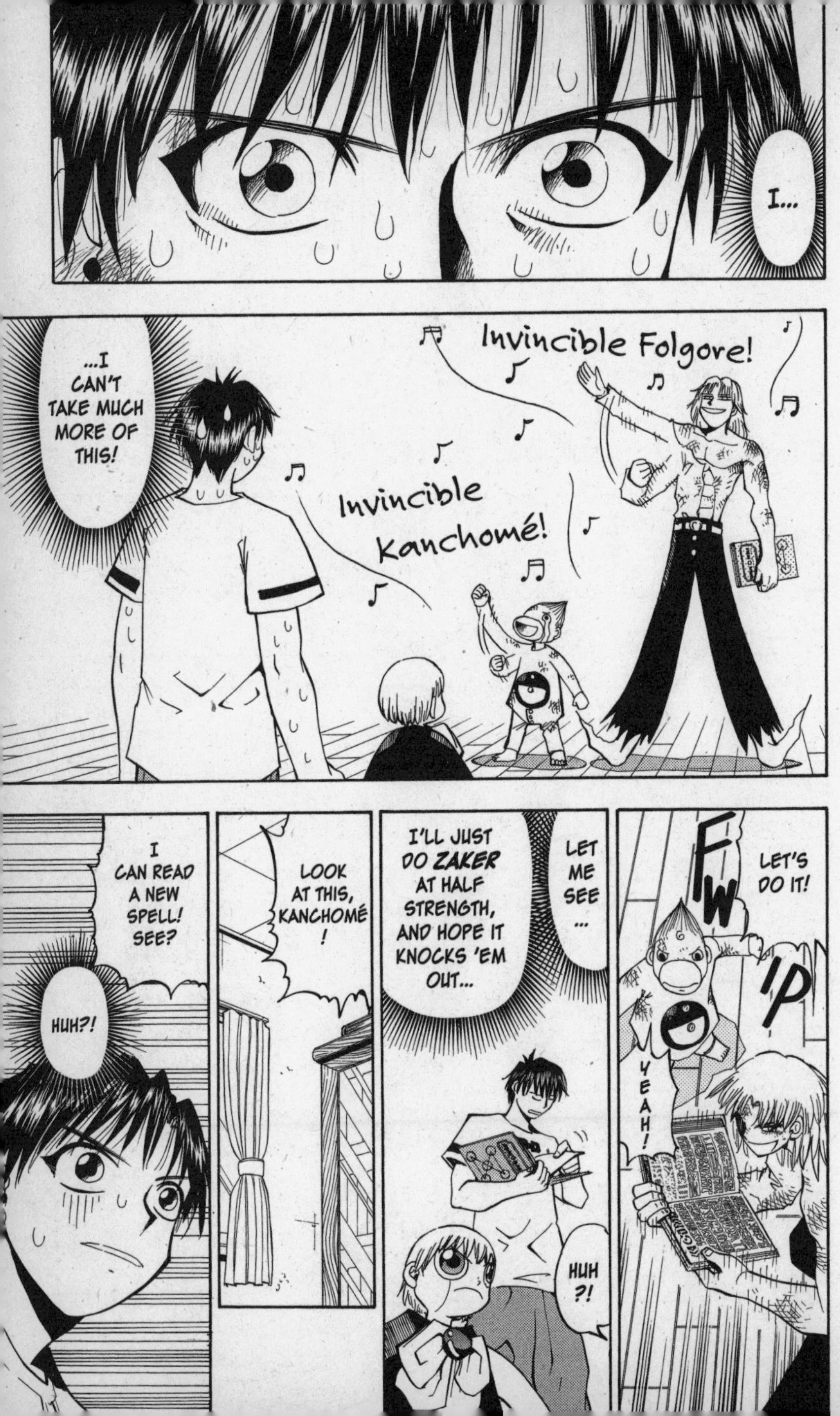
I...
Invincible Folgore!
Invincible Kanchomé!
...I CAN'T TAKE MUCH MORE OF THIS!
FWIP
LET'S DO IT!
YEAH!
LET ME SEE...
I'LL JUST DO ZAKER AT HALF STRENGTH, AND HOPE IT KNOCKS 'EM OUT...
HUH?!
LOOK AT THIS, KANCHOMÉ!
I CAN READ A NEW SPELL! SEE?
HUH?!

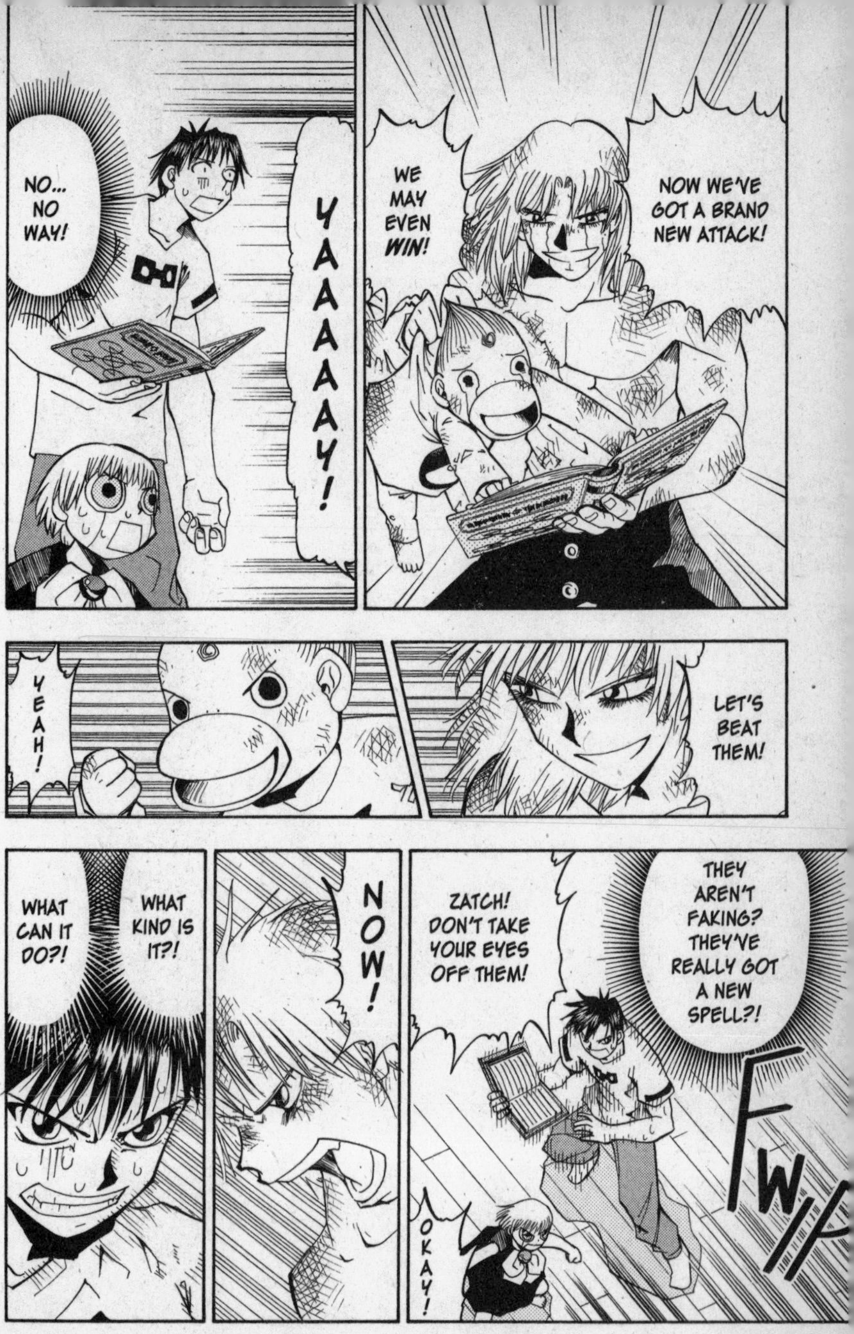
NOW WE'VE GOT A BRAND NEW ATTACK!
WE MAY EVEN WIN!
YAAAAAAY!
NO... NO WAY!
LET'S BEAT THEM!
YEAH!
THEY AREN'T FAKING? THEY'VE REALLY GOT A NEW SPELL?!
FWIP
ZATCH! DON'T TAKE YOUR EYES OFF THEM!
OKAY!
NOW!
WHAT KIND IS IT?!
WHAT CAN IT DO?!

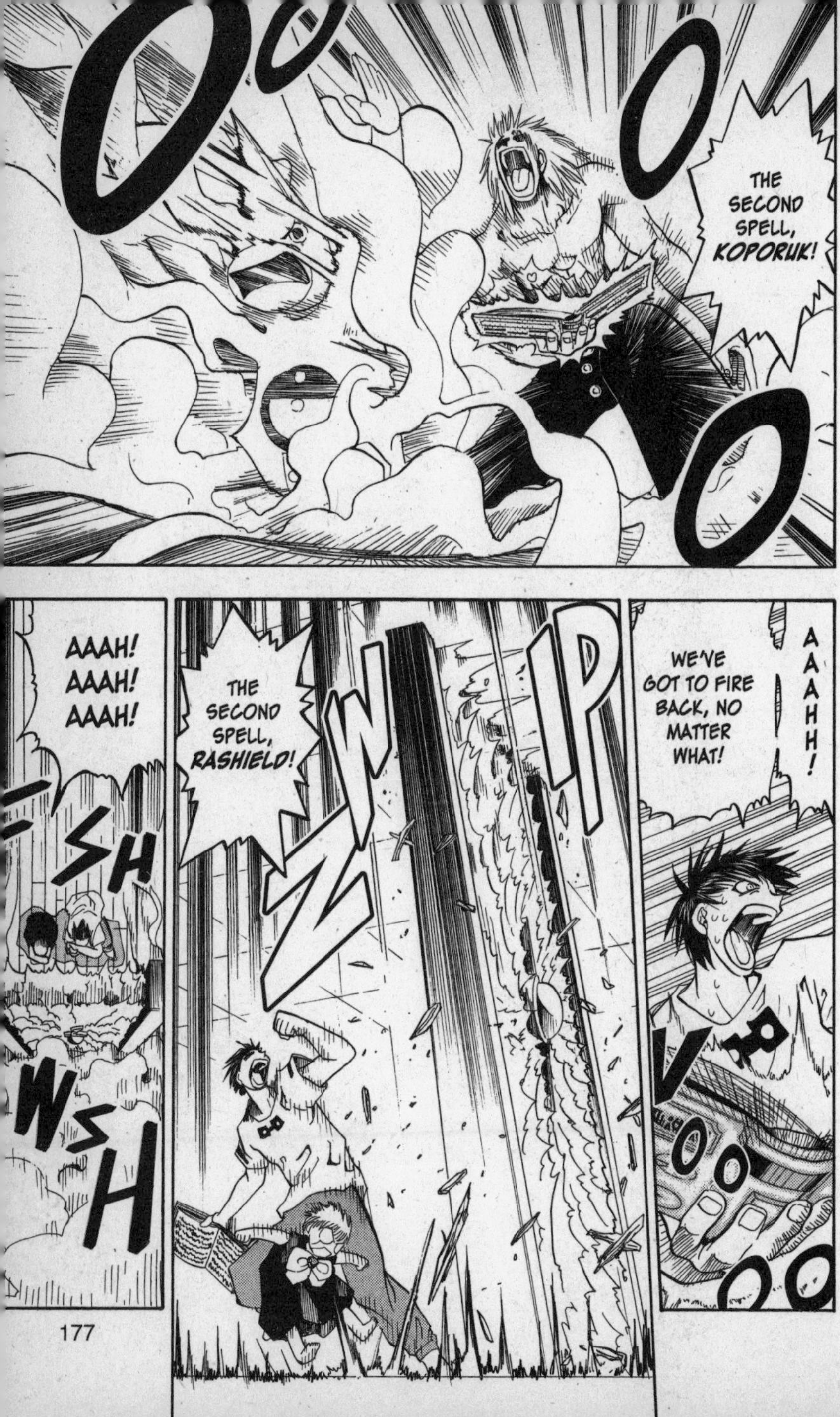
THE SECOND SPELL, KOPORUK!
AAAAHH!
WE'VE GOT TO FIRE BACK, NO MATTER WHAT!
THE SECOND SPELL, RASHIELD!
AAAH! AAAH! AAAH!

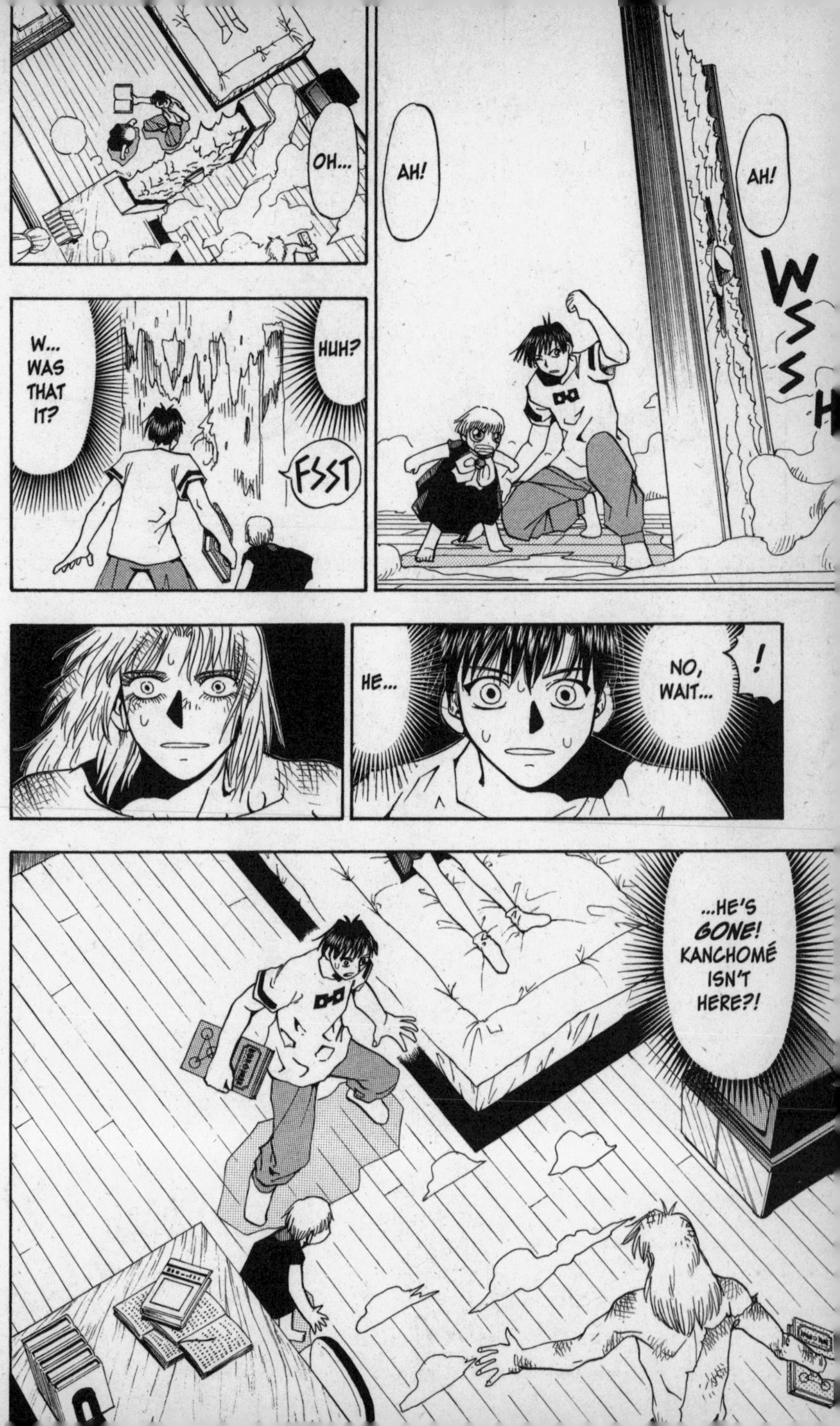
AH!
WSSH
AH!
OH...
HUH?
W... WAS THAT IT?
FSST
!
NO, WAIT...
HE...
...HE'S GONE! KANCHOMÉ ISN'T HERE?!

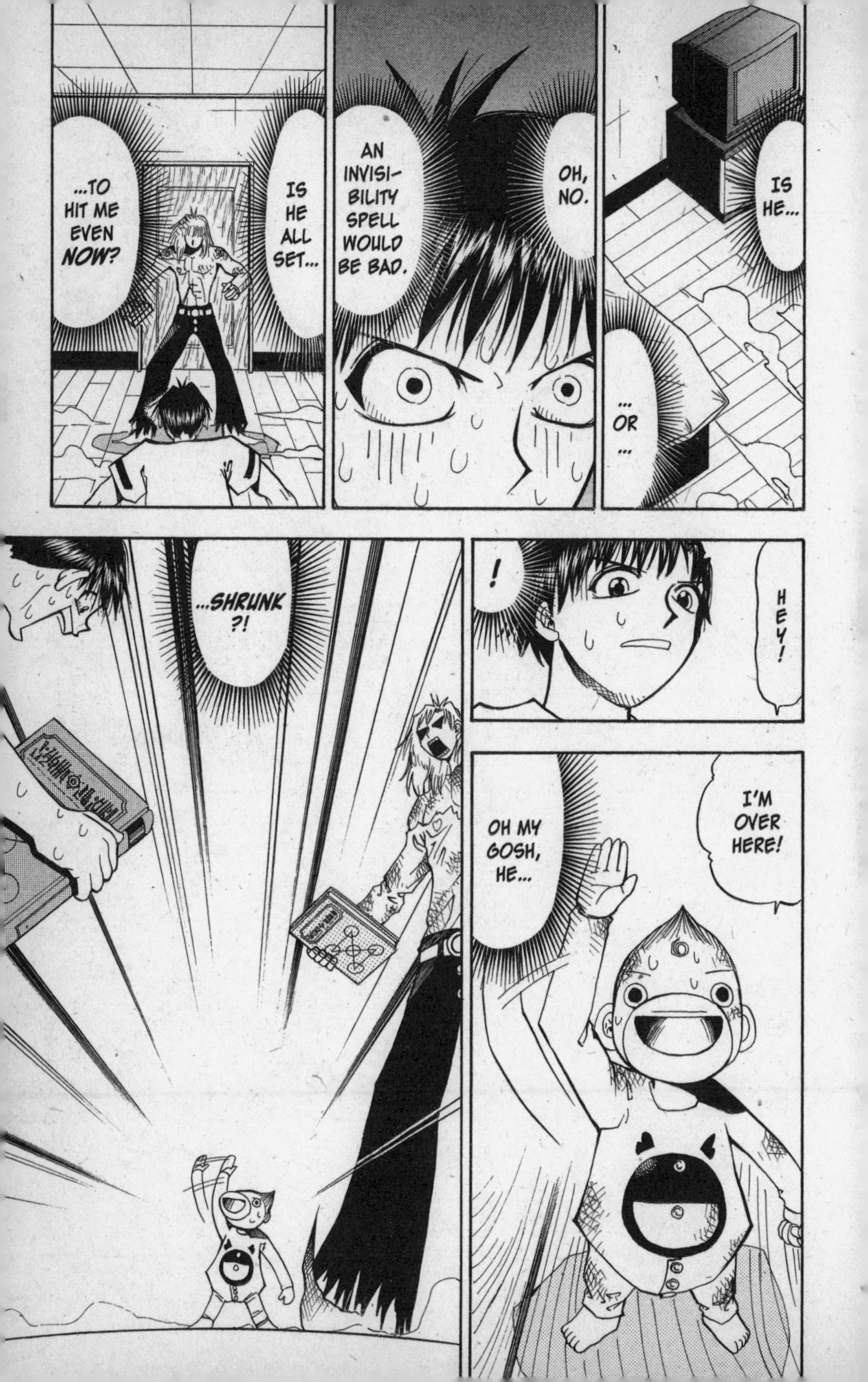
IS HE...
...OR ...
OH, NO.
AN INVISI-BILITY SPELL WOULD BE BAD.
IS HE ALL SET...
...TO HIT ME EVEN NOW?
HEY!
!
I'M OVER HERE!
OH MY GOSH, HE...
...SHRUNK ?!

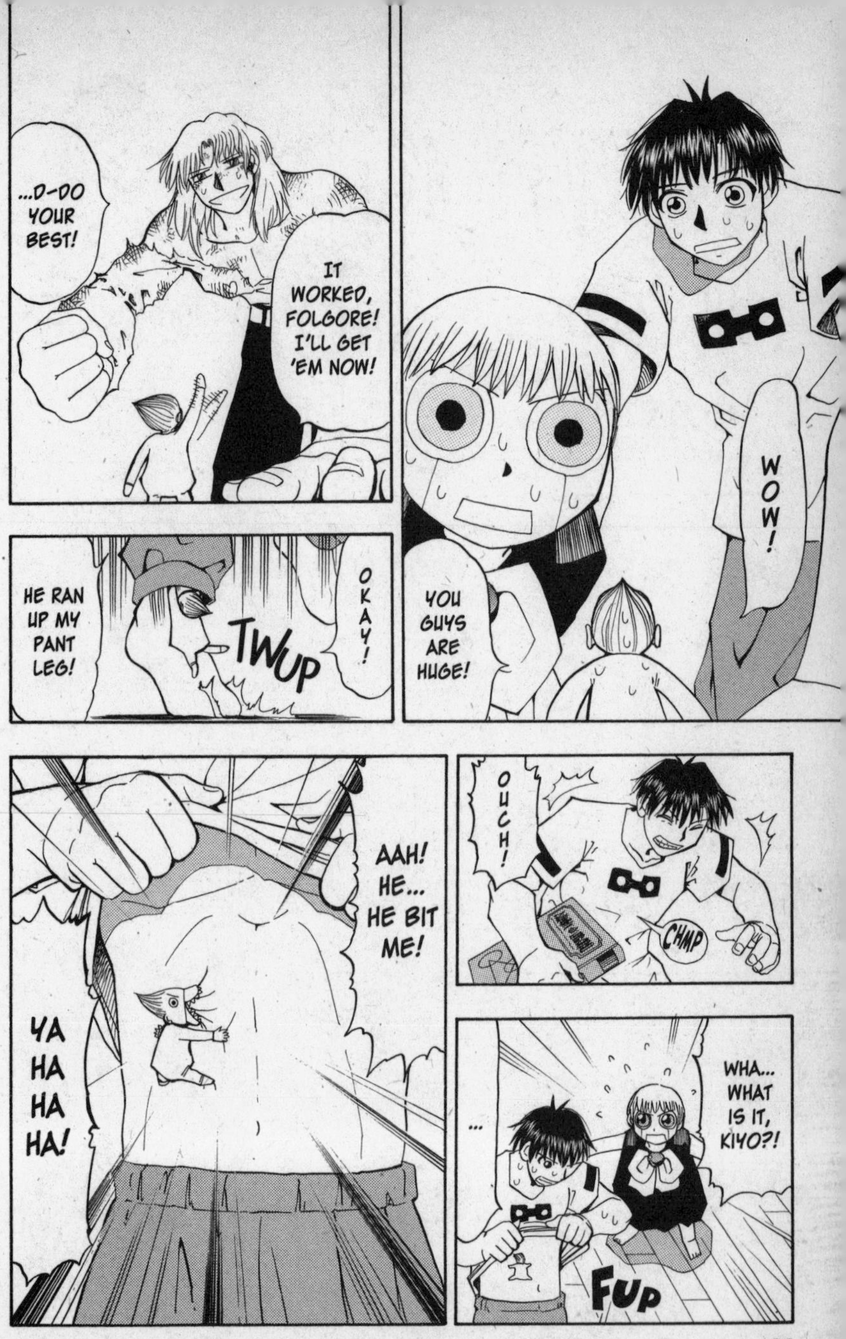
WOW!
YOU GUYS ARE HUGE!
IT WORKED, FOLGORE! I'LL GET 'EM NOW!
...D-DO YOUR BEST!
OKAY!
TWUP
HE RAN UP MY PANT LEG!
OUCH!
CHMP
WHA... WHAT IS IT, KIYO?!
...
FUP
AAH! HE... HE BIT ME!
YA HA HA HA!

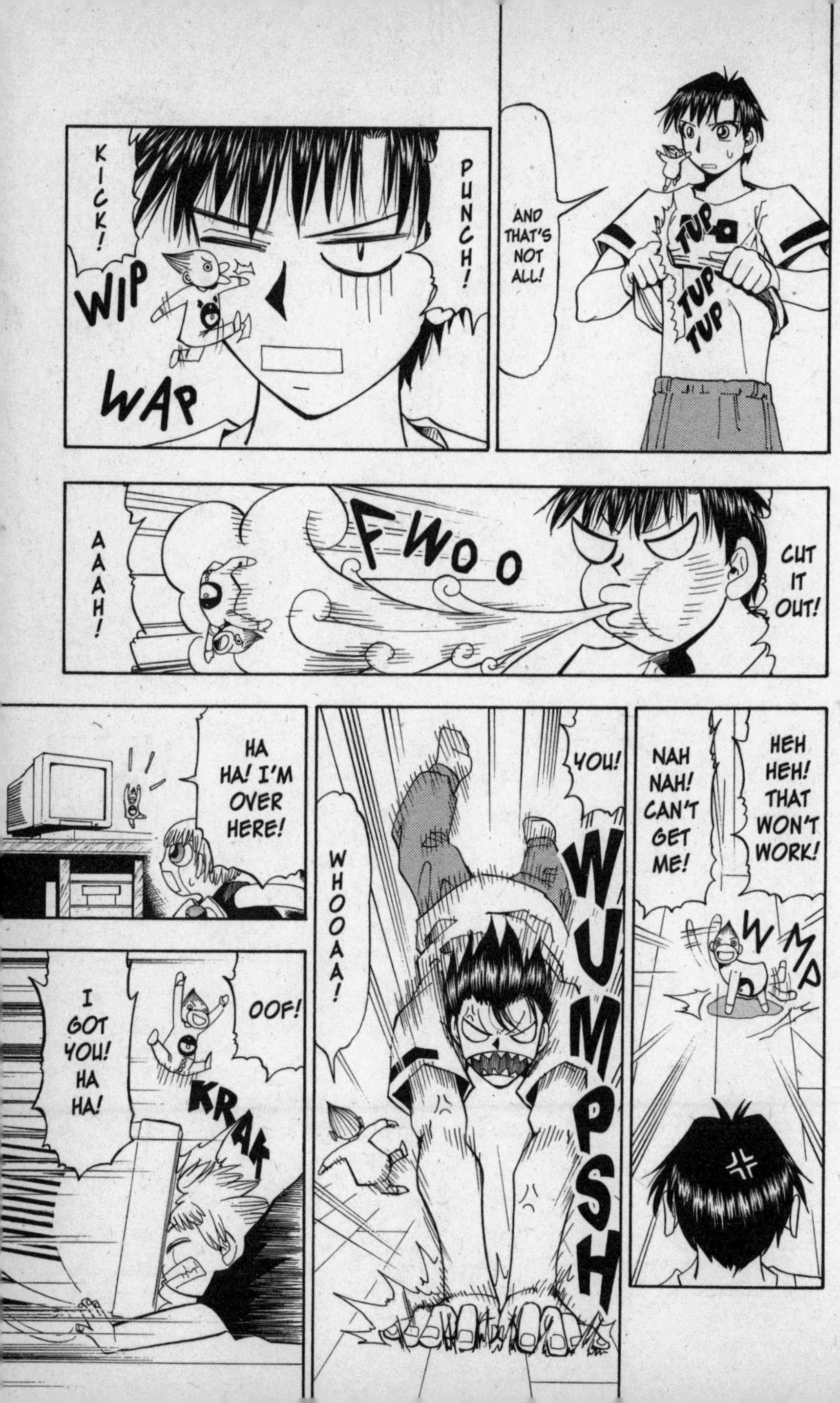
AND THAT'S NOT ALL!
TUP TUP TUP
PUNCH!
KICK!
WIP
WAP
CUT IT OUT!
FWOO
AAAH!
HEH HEH! THAT WON'T WORK!
NAH NAH! CAN'T GET ME!
WMP
YOU!
WUMPSH
WHOOAA!
HA HA! I'M OVER HERE!
OOF!
I GOT YOU! HA HA!
KRAK

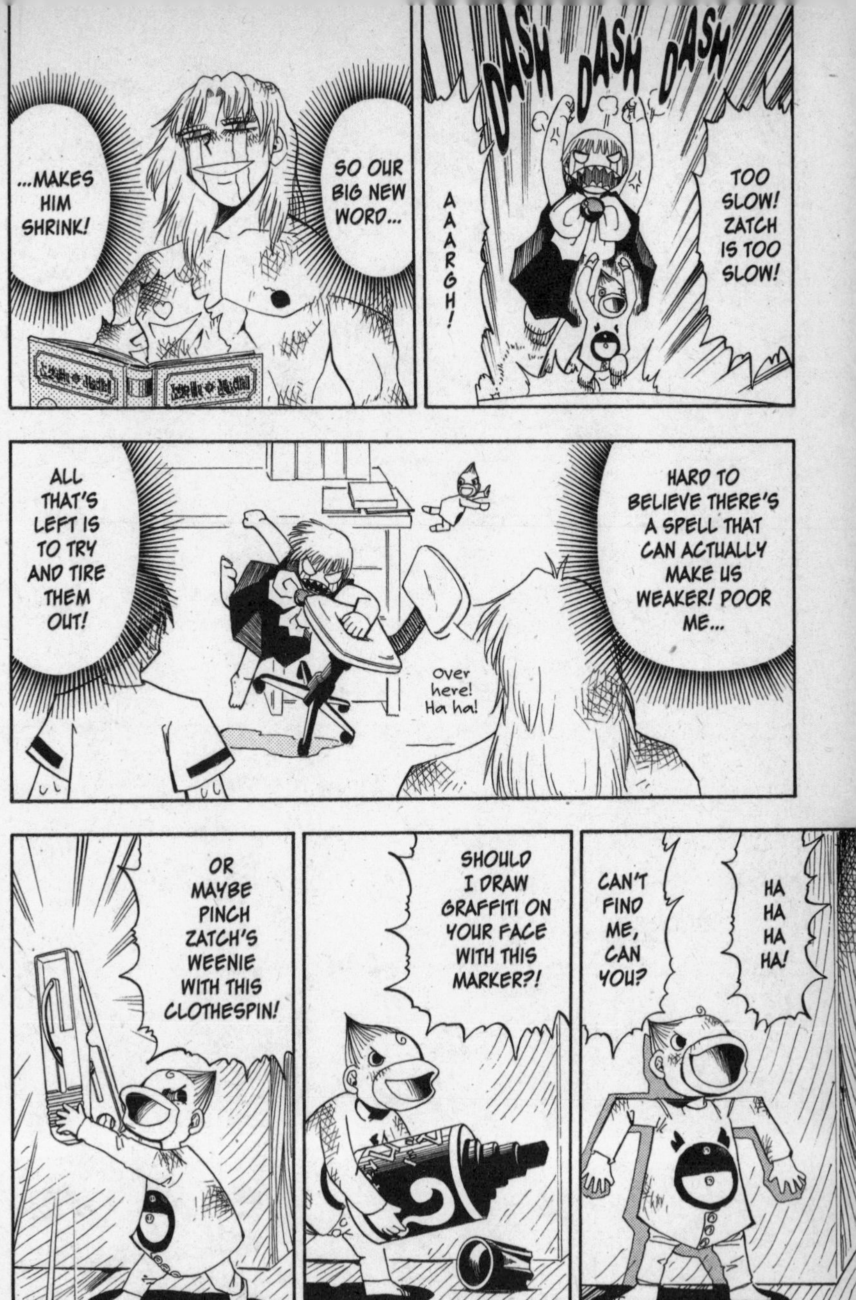
DASH DASH DASH
TOO SLOW! ZATCH IS TOO SLOW!
AAAARGH!
SO OUR BIG NEW WORD...
...MAKES HIM SHRINK!
HARD TO BELIEVE THERE'S A SPELL THAT CAN ACTUALLY MAKE US WEAKER! POOR ME...
Over here! Ha ha!
ALL THAT'S LEFT IS TO TRY AND TIRE THEM OUT!
HA HA HA HA!
CAN'T FIND ME, CAN YOU?
SHOULD I DRAW GRAFFITI ON YOUR FACE WITH THIS MARKER?!
OR MAYBE PINCH ZATCH'S WEENIE WITH THIS CLOTHESPIN!

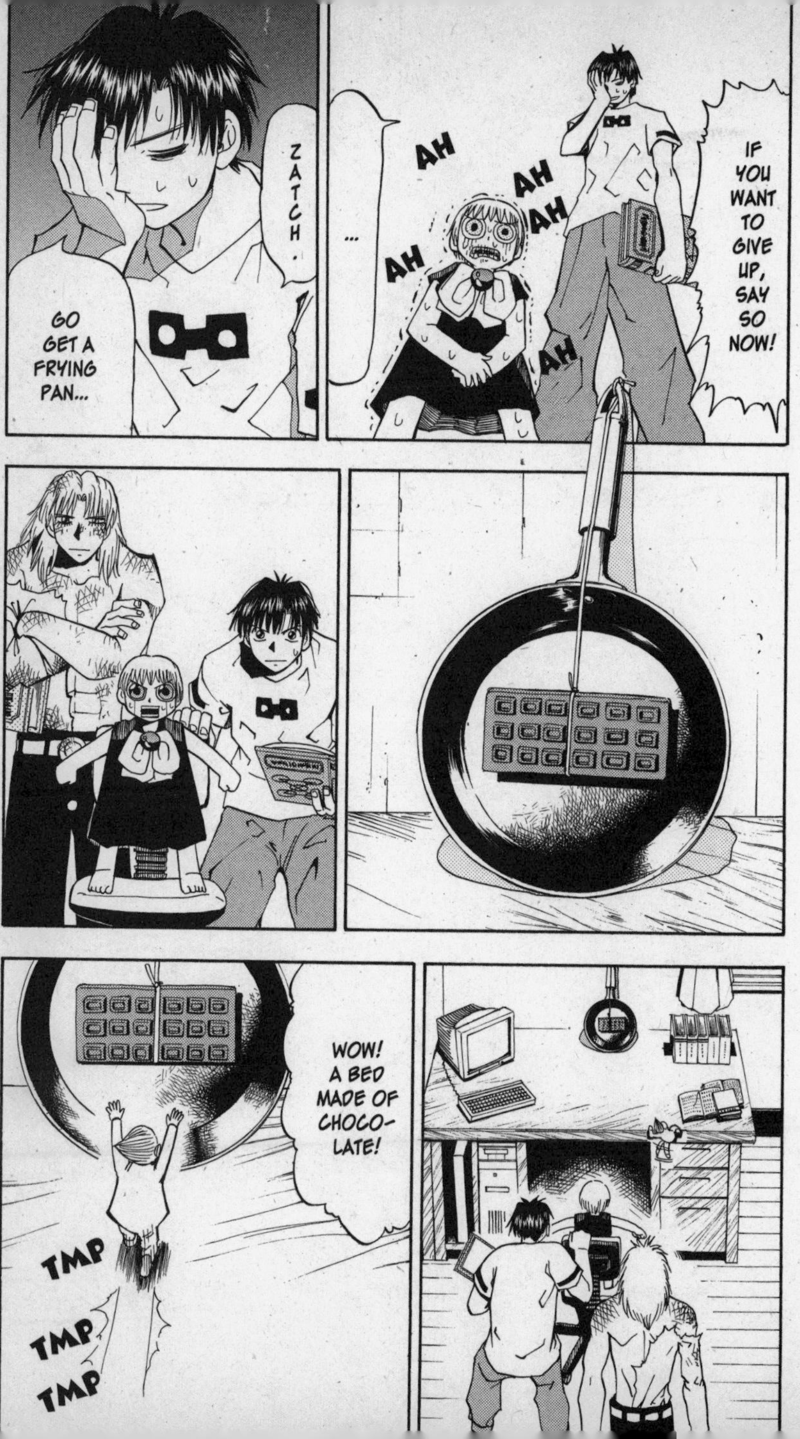
IF YOU WANT TO GIVE UP, SAY SO NOW!
AH
AH
AH
AH
AH
...
ZATCH.
GO GET A FRYING PAN...
WOW! A BED MADE OF CHOCO-LATE!
TMP
TMP
TMP

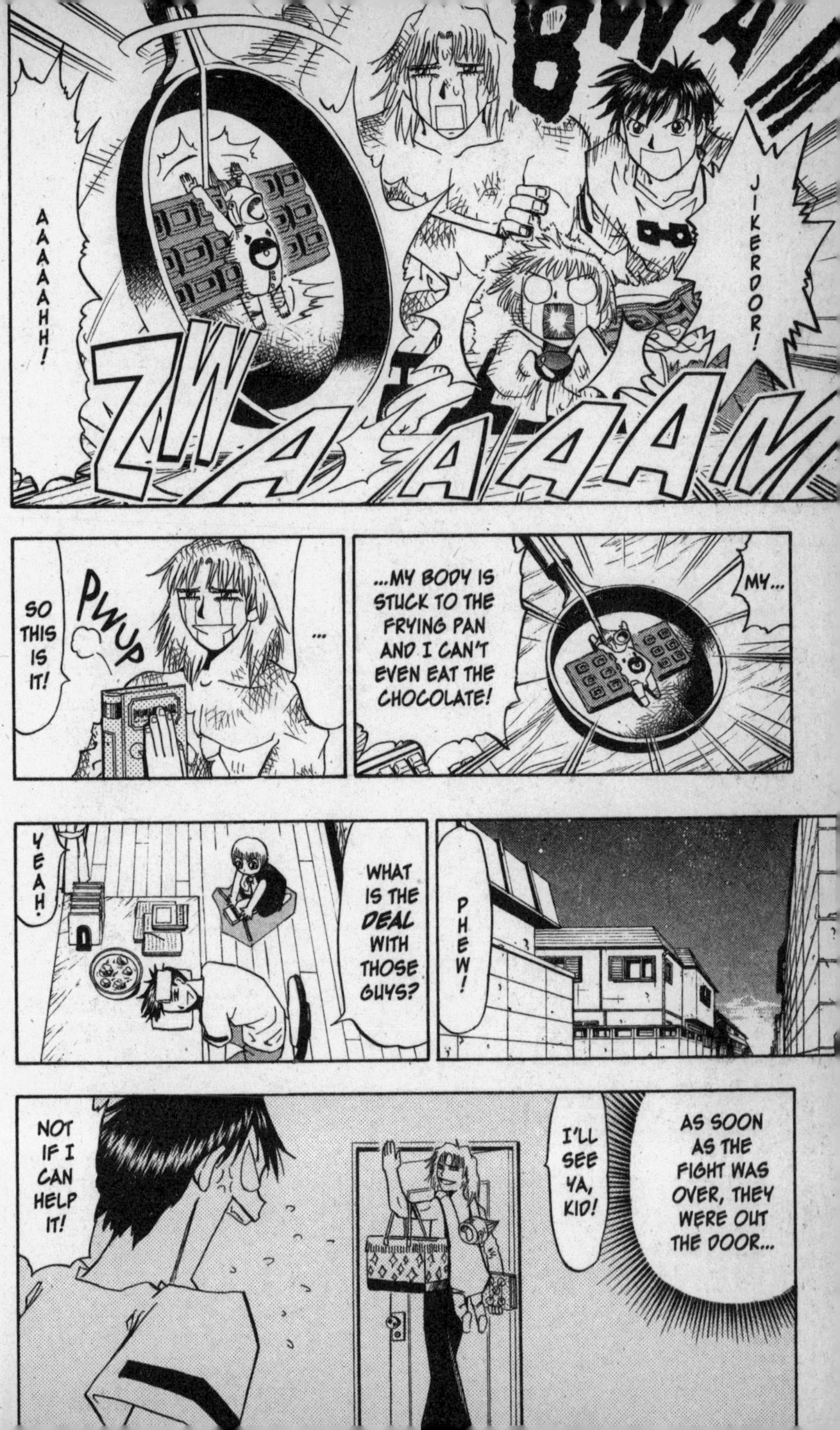
BWAM
JIKERDOR!
ZWAAAAM
AAAAAAHH!
MY...
...MY BODY IS STUCK TO THE FRYING PAN AND I CAN'T EVEN EAT THE CHOCOLATE!
...
PWUP
SO THIS IS IT!
PHEW!
WHAT IS THE DEAL WITH THOSE GUYS?
YEAH!
AS SOON AS THE FIGHT WAS OVER, THEY WERE OUT THE DOOR...
I'LL SEE YA, KID!
NOT IF I CAN HELP IT!

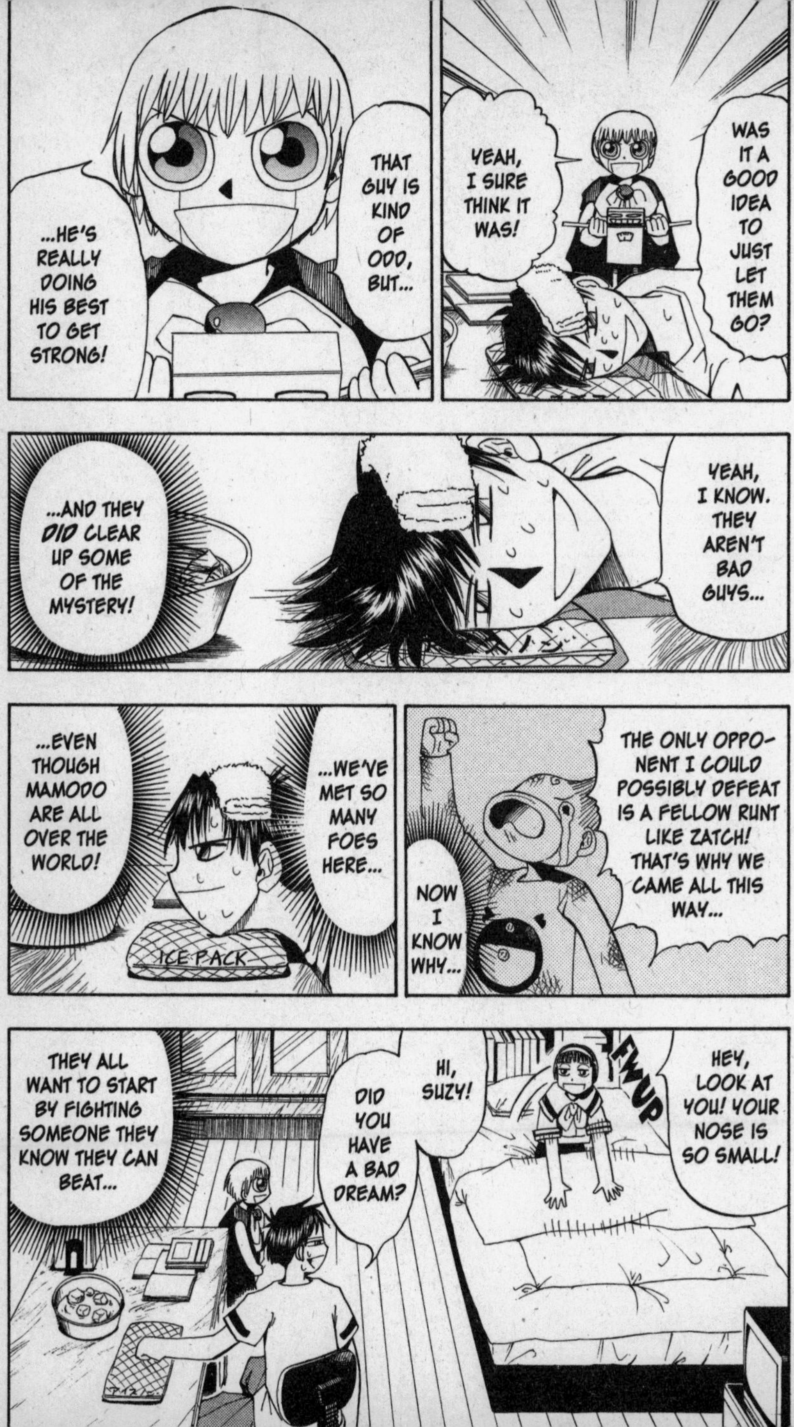
WAS IT A GOOD IDEA TO JUST LET THEM GO?
YEAH, I SURE THINK IT WAS!
THAT GUY IS KIND OF ODD, BUT...
...HE'S REALLY DOING HIS BEST TO GET STRONG!
YEAH, I KNOW. THEY AREN'T BAD GUYS...
...AND THEY *DID* CLEAR UP SOME OF THE MYSTERY!
THE ONLY OPPONENT I COULD POSSIBLY DEFEAT IS A FELLOW RUNT LIKE ZATCH! THAT'S WHY WE CAME ALL THIS WAY...
NOW I KNOW WHY...
...WE'VE MET SO MANY FOES HERE...
...EVEN THOUGH MAMODO ARE ALL OVER THE WORLD!
ICE PACK
FWUP
HEY, LOOK AT YOU! YOUR NOSE IS SO SMALL!
HI, SUZY!
DID YOU HAVE A BAD DREAM?
THEY ALL WANT TO START BY FIGHTING SOMEONE THEY KNOW THEY CAN BEAT...

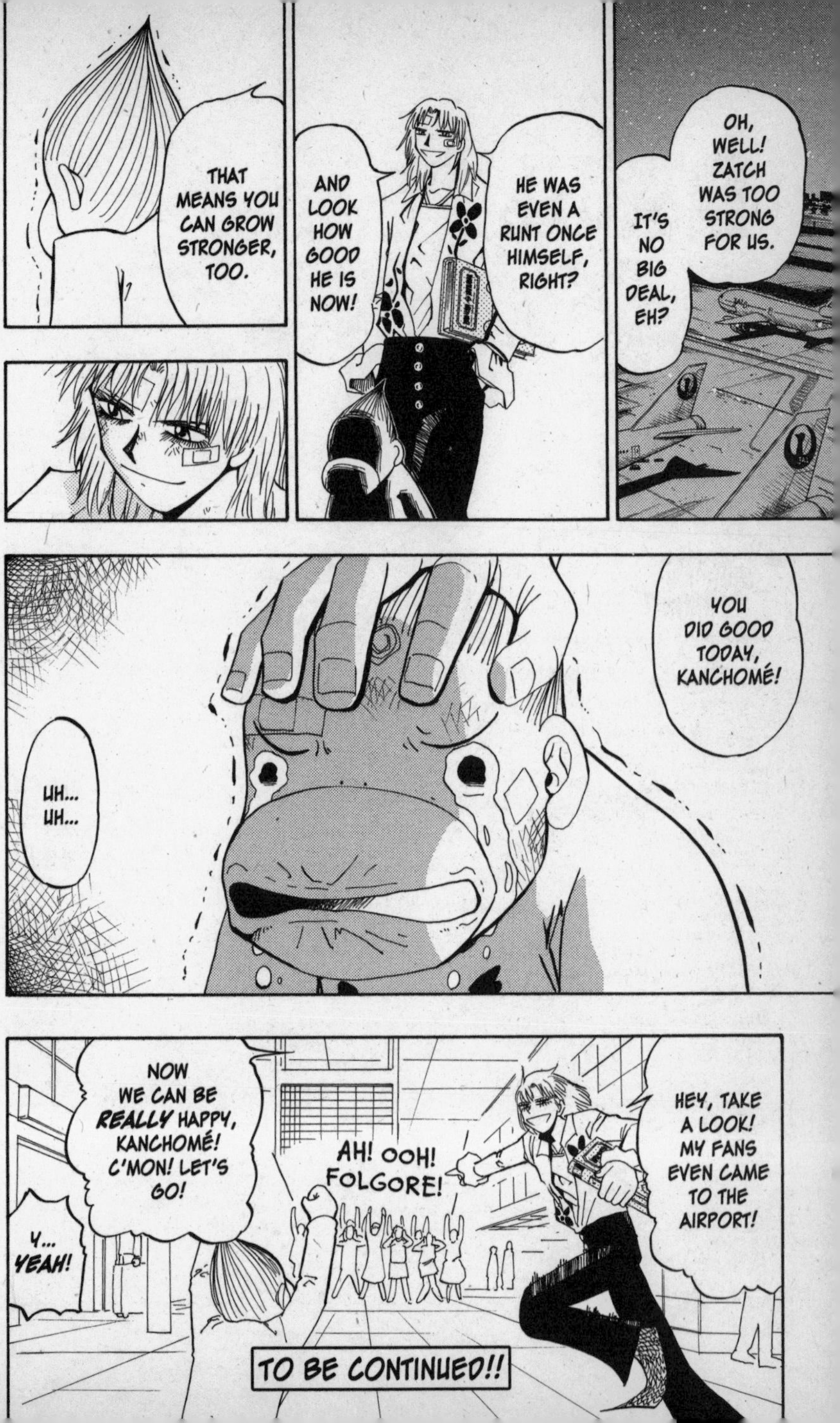
OH, WELL! ZATCH WAS TOO STRONG FOR US.
IT'S NO BIG DEAL, EH?
HE WAS EVEN A RUNT ONCE HIMSELF, RIGHT?
AND LOOK HOW GOOD HE IS NOW!
THAT MEANS YOU CAN GROW STRONGER, TOO.
YOU DID GOOD TODAY, KANCHOMÉ!
UH... UH...
HEY, TAKE A LOOK! MY FANS EVEN CAME TO THE AIRPORT!
AH! OOH! FOLGORE!
NOW WE CAN BE REALLY HAPPY, KANCHOMÉ! C'MON! LET'S GO!
Y... YEAH!
TO BE CONTINUED!!

# Bonus Pages

BY MAKOTO RAIKU

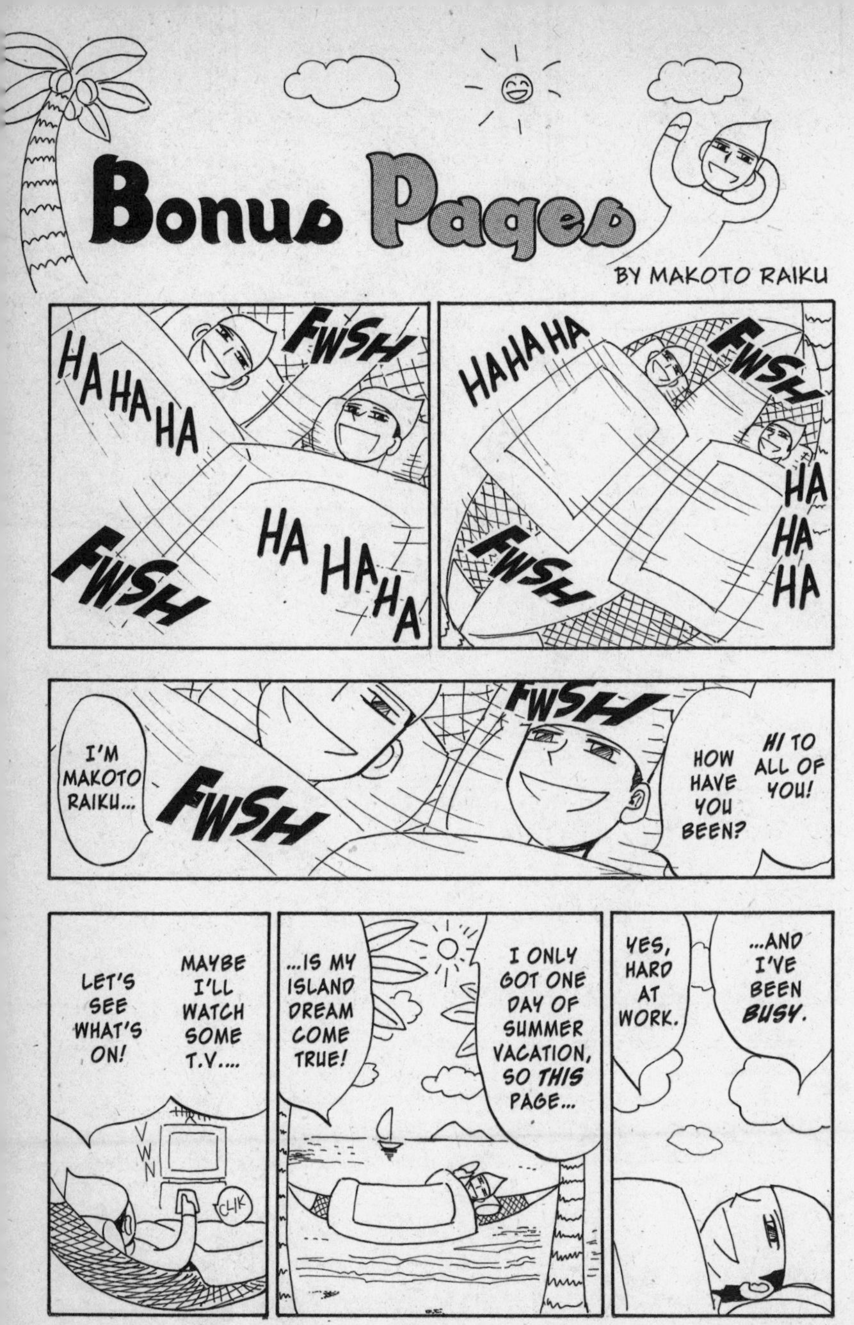

HAHAHA
FWSH
HA
HA
HA
FWSH
FWSH
HA HA HA
HA HA HA
FWSH
FWSH
HI TO ALL OF YOU!
HOW HAVE YOU BEEN?
FWSH
I'M MAKOTO RAIKU...
...AND I'VE BEEN *BUSY*.
YES, HARD AT WORK.
I ONLY GOT ONE DAY OF SUMMER VACATION, SO *THIS* PAGE...
...IS MY ISLAND DREAM COME TRUE!
MAYBE I'LL WATCH SOME T.V....
LET'S SEE WHAT'S ON!
VWN
CLIK

# THE ULTRA SHOW!

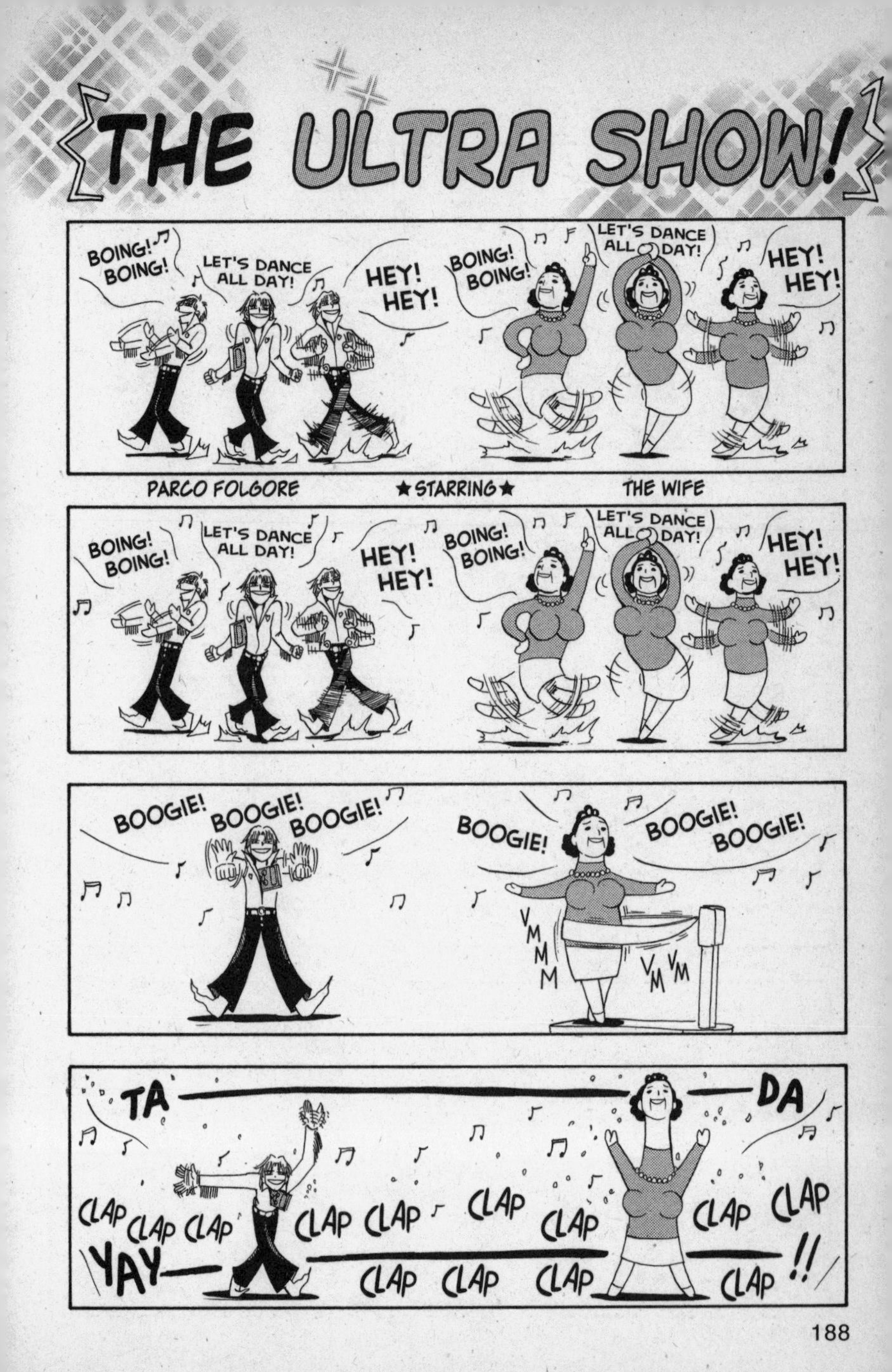

HEY! HEY!
LET'S DANCE ALL DAY!
BOING! BOING!
HEY! HEY!
LET'S DANCE ALL DAY!
BOING! BOING!
PARCO FOLGORE ★STARRING★ THE WIFE
HEY! HEY!
LET'S DANCE ALL DAY!
BOING! BOING!
HEY! HEY!
LET'S DANCE ALL DAY!
BOING! BOING!
BOOGIE! BOOGIE! BOOGIE!
VMMM
VM VM
BOOGIE! BOOGIE! BOOGIE!
TA——DA
CLAP CLAP CLAP CLAP
!!
CLAP CLAP CLAP CLAP CLAP CLAP CLAP
CLAP CLAP CLAP
YAY—

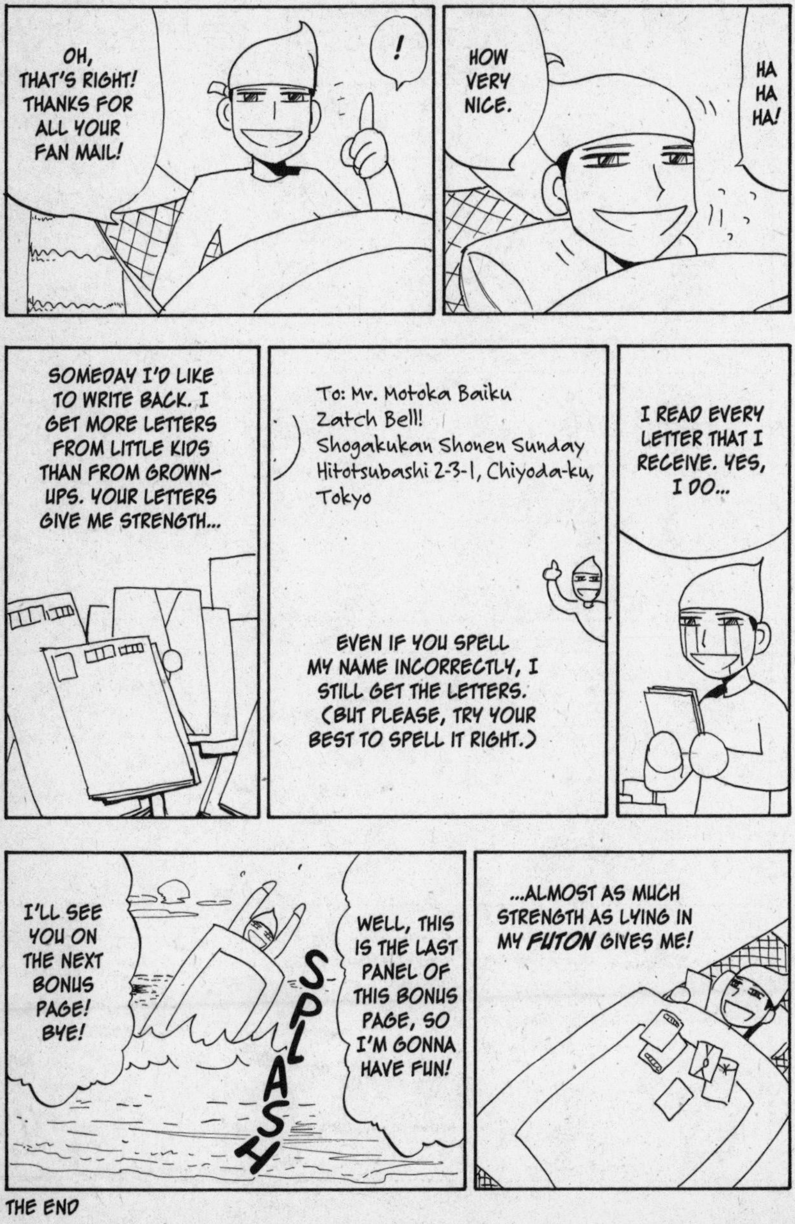
HA HA HA!
HOW VERY NICE.
!
OH, THAT'S RIGHT! THANKS FOR ALL YOUR FAN MAIL!
I READ EVERY LETTER THAT I RECEIVE. YES, I DO...
To: Mr. Motoka Baiku
Zatch Bell!
Shogakukan Shonen Sunday
Hitotsubashi 2-3-1, Chiyoda-ku, Tokyo
EVEN IF YOU SPELL MY NAME INCORRECTLY, I STILL GET THE LETTERS. (BUT PLEASE, TRY YOUR BEST TO SPELL IT RIGHT.)
SOMEDAY I'D LIKE TO WRITE BACK. I GET MORE LETTERS FROM LITTLE KIDS THAN FROM GROWN-UPS. YOUR LETTERS GIVE ME STRENGTH...
...ALMOST AS MUCH STRENGTH AS LYING IN MY *FUTON* GIVES ME!
WELL, THIS IS THE LAST PANEL OF THIS BONUS PAGE, SO I'M GONNA HAVE FUN!
SPLASH
I'LL SEE YOU ON THE NEXT BONUS PAGE! BYE!

THE END

# ZATCH & SUZY

BY MAKOTO RAIKU

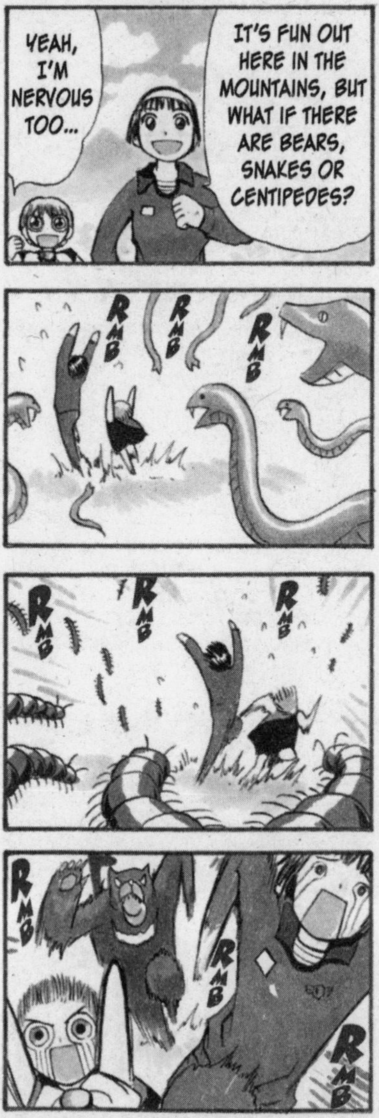
IT'S FUN OUT HERE IN THE MOUNTAINS, BUT WHAT IF THERE ARE BEARS, SNAKES OR CENTIPEDES?
YEAH, I'M NERVOUS TOO...
RMB
RMB
RMB
RMB
RMB
RMB
RMB
RMB
RMB

⏺ From the front

⏺ From the side

# MAKOTO RAIKU

I got fat.
I usually only look at the mirror while I'm facing it—
but when I saw my profile, I realized that there was no
longer a line separating my chin from my neck!
So I'm on a diet. A year from now, there will be a clear
line between my chin and neck...definitely!

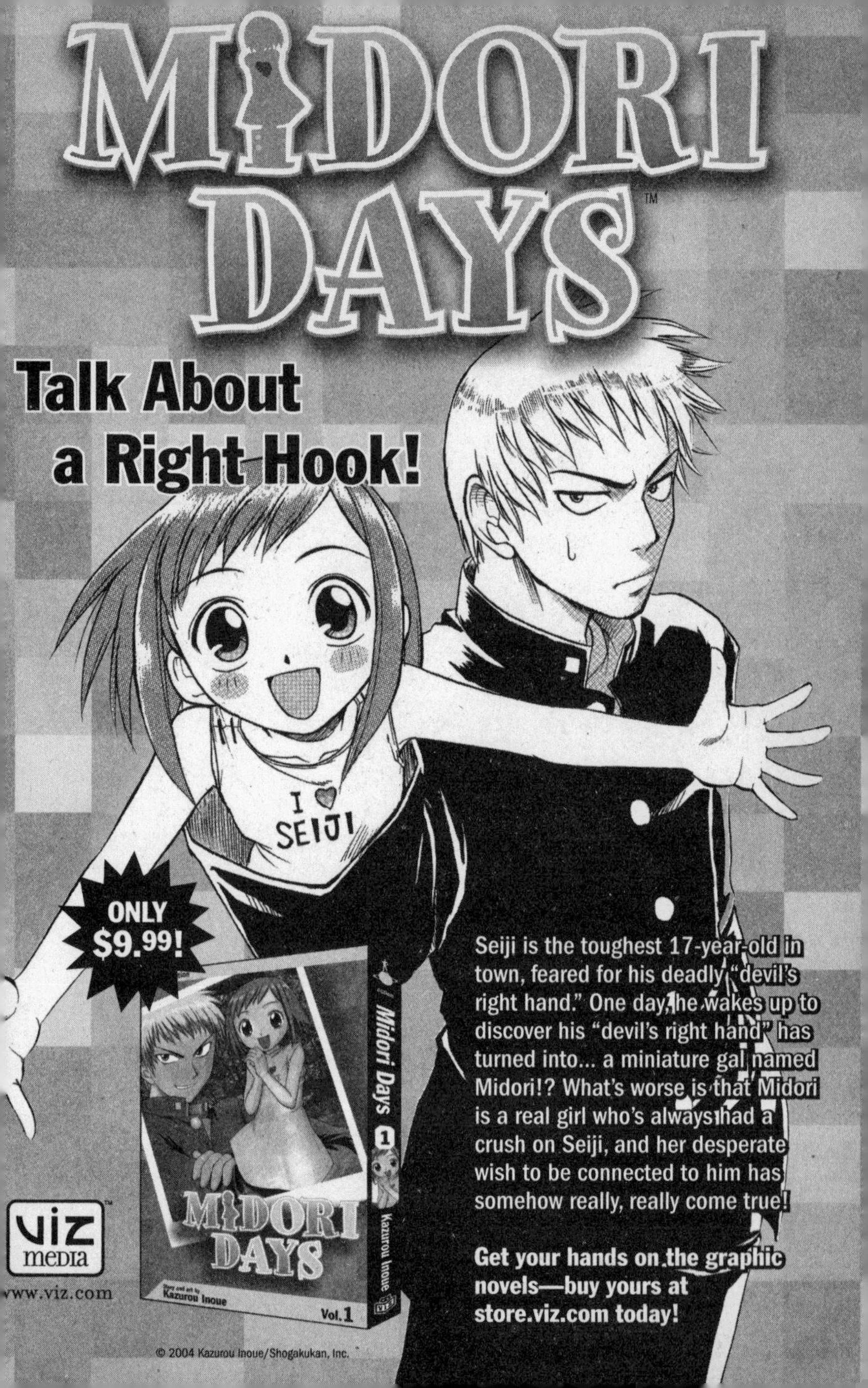
MIDORI DAYS™
Talk About a Right Hook!
I ♥ SEIJI
ONLY $9.99!
Midori Days 1 Kazurou Inoue
MIDORI DAYS
Story and art by Kazurou Inoue
Vol. 1
Seiji is the toughest 17-year-old in town, feared for his deadly "devil's right hand." One day, he wakes up to discover his "devil's right hand" has turned into... a miniature gal named Midori!? What's worse is that Midori is a real girl who's always had a crush on Seiji, and her desperate wish to be connected to him has somehow really, really come true!
Get your hands on the graphic novels—buy yours at store.viz.com today!
viz media™
www.viz.com
© 2004 Kazurou Inoue/Shogakukan, Inc.

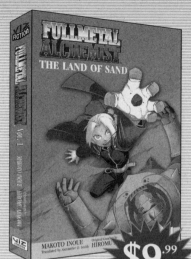

# A Novel Concept

## Introducing VIZ Media's new fiction line!

When we tell a story, we have the habit of giving you everything—the storyline *and* the visuals. But we're reinventing how you connect to your favorite series through our new line of full-length novels. Follow the characters you've come to love as they embark on new adventures. Except this time, we're just telling the story—we'll let your imagination do the rest.

## Socrates in Love
### by Kyoichi Katayama

The best selling novel of all time in Japan with over 3.2 million copies sold! Finally, U.S. readers can experience the phenomenon that became the inspiration for a blockbuster movie, a hit TV show, and the Shojo Beat manga, also available from VIZ Media.

When an average boy meets a beautiful girl, it's a classic case of young love—instant, all consuming, and enduring. But when a tragedy threatens their romance, they discover just how deep and strong love can be.

**SB FICTION** **$17.99** hardcover

# LOVE MANGA?   LET US KNOW!

☐ Please do NOT send me information about VIZ Media products, news and events, special offers, or other information.

☐ Please do NOT send me information from VIZ Media's trusted business partners.

Name: _____

Address: _____

City: _____ State: _____ Zip: _____

E-mail: _____

☐ Male   ☐ Female   Date of Birth (mm/dd/yyyy): ___ / ___ / _____   ( Under 13? Parental consent required )

## What race/ethnicity do you consider yourself? (check all that apply)

☐ White/Caucasian          ☐ Black/African American          ☐ Hispanic/Latino

☐ Asian/Pacific Islander   ☐ Native American/Alaskan Native  ☐ Other: _____

What VIZ title(s) did you purchase? (indicate title(s) purchased) _____

_____

What other VIZ titles do you own? _____

_____

## Reason for purchase: (check all that apply)
☐ Special offer            ☐ Favorite title / author / artist / genre

☐ Gift                     ☐ Recommendation              ☐ Collection

☐ Read excerpt in VIZ manga sampler    ☐ Other _____

## Where did you make your purchase? (please check one)
☐ Comic store        ☐ Bookstore        ☐ Grocery Store

☐ Convention         ☐ Newsstand        ☐ Video Game Store

☐ Online (site:_____)   ☐ Other _____

**How many manga titles have y**
(please check one from each column)

MANGA
- ☐ None
- ☐ 1 – 4
- ☐ 5 – 10
- ☐ 11+

- ☐ 5 – 10
- ☐ 11+

**How much influence do special promotions and gifts-with-purchase have on the titles you buy?**
(please circle, with 5 being great influence and 1 being none)

1 2 3 4 5

**Do you purchase every volume of your favorite series?**
☐ Yes! Gotta have 'em as my own ☐ No. Please explain: ________________

**What kind of manga storylines do you most enjoy?** (check all that apply)

- ☐ Action / Adventure
- ☐ Comedy
- ☐ Fighting
- ☐ Artistic / Alternative
- ☐ Science Fiction
- ☐ Romance (shojo)
- ☐ Sports
- ☐ Other ________________
- ☐ Horror
- ☐ Fantasy (shojo)
- ☐ Historical

**If you watch the anime or play a video or TCG game from a series, how likely are you to buy the manga?** (please circle, with 5 being very likely and 1 being unlikely)

1 2 3 4 5

**If unlikely, please explain:** ________________

**Who are your favorite authors / artists?** ________________

________________

**What titles would like you translated and sold in English?** ________________

________________

**THANK YOU! Please send the completed form to:**



VIZ media™

**NJW Research**
42 Catharine Street
Poughkeepsie, NY 12601

**Your privacy is very important to us. All information provided will be used for internal purposes only and will not be sold or otherwise divulged.**